AMERICAN WOMEN POETS
IN THE 21ST CENTURY

AMERICAN WOMEN POETS
IN THE
21ST CENTURY

WHERE LYRIC MEETS LANGUAGE

EDITED BY

Claudia Rankine

AND

Juliana Spahr

Wesleyan University Press

MIDDLETOWN CONNECTICUT

Copyright © 2002 by Wesleyan University Press
All rights reserved.
Published 2002
Printed in the United States of America

⊖   The paper used in this publication meets the requirements
of the American National Standard for Information Sciences—Permanence
of Paper for Printed Library Materials, ANSI Z39.48–1984

Library of Congress Cataloging-in-Publication Data
American women poets in the 21st century : where lyric meets language /
edited by Claudia Rankine and Juliana Spahr.
    p. cm. — (Wesleyan poetry)
Includes bibliographical references.
  ISBN 0-8195-6546-6 (alk. paper) — ISBN 0-8195-6547-4 (pbk. : alk.
paper)
  1. American poetry—Women authors. 2. Women—United States—Poetry.
3. American poetry—21st century. I. Title: American women poets in
the twenty-first century. II. Rankine, Claudia, 1963– III. Spahr,
Juliana. IV. Series.
  PS589 .A44 2002
  811'.60809287—dc21

            2002002

CONTENTS

ACKNOWLEDGMENTS

THE EDITORS thank Suzanne Tamminen for suggesting this project. Thanks also to Mary Ann Caws for help with citations. And thanks to Jil di Donato.

Rae Armantrout's "View" originally appeared in *Extremities* (Great Barrington: The Figures, 1978); "Up to Speed" in the *Chicago Review* 47(1) (2001); and "As We're Told," "The Plan," and "Manufacturing" in *Veil: New and Selected Poems* (Middletown, Conn.: Wesleyan University Press, 2001). All are reprinted by permission of the author and Wesleyan University Press. An earlier version of "Chesire Poetics" appeared in *Fence* 3(1) (2000) and is reprinted by permission of the author. Excerpts from Armantrout's work in Hank Lazer's "Lyricism of the Swerve: The Poetry of Rae Armantrout" reprinted by permission of Rae Armantrout.

Mei-mei Berssenbrugge's "From *Four Year Old Girl*" and "From *Kali*" originally appeared in *Four Year Old Girl* (San Francisco: Kelsey St. Press, 1998) and is reprinted by permission of the author and Kelsey St. Press. "From *The Retired Architect*" originally appeared in *Aufgabe* 1 (2001); reprinted by permission of the author.

Lucie Brock-Broido's "Am Moor" originally appeared in *The Master Letters* (New York: Alfred A. Knopf, 1995); "Periodic Table of Ethereal Elements" in *The Paris Review* 154 (2000); and "Myself a Kangaroo Among the Beauties" in *By Herself: Women Reclaim Poetry*, ed. Molly McQuade (St. Paul: Graywolf Press, 2000) and in *Fence* 3(1) (2000). All were reprinted by permission of the author.

Poems 640 and 338 by Emily Dickinson in Thomas Gardner's "Jorie Graham and Emily Dickinson: Singing to Use the Waiting" are reprinted by permission of the publishers and the Trustees of Amherst College from *The Poems of Emily Dickinson,* Thomas H. Johnson, ed. (Cambridge, Mass.: The Belknap Press of Harvard University Press, © 1951, 1955, 1979 by the President and Fellows of Harvard College). Excerpts from *Erosion* by Jorie Graham, © 1983, reprinted by permission of Princeton University Press. Excerpts from *The End of Beauty, Region of Unlikeness, Materialism, The Errancy,* and *Swarm* by Jorie Graham, © 1987, 1991, 1993, 1997, 2000, reprinted by permission of HarperCollins Publishers.

Jorie Graham's "Exit Wound" originally appeared as "Bouleversement" in the *Boston Review* (December 2000/January 2001); "Covenant," "Prayer," and "Gulls" originally appeared in *Conjunctions* 35 (2000); "The Complex Mechanisms of the Break" originally appeared in *The London Review of Books* 23(13) (2001); "In/Silence" originally appeared in *Countermeasures* 2 (2000); and *Philosopher's Stone* originally appeared in *The Kenyon Review.* All are reprinted by permission of the author.

Barbara Guest's "Valorous Vine," "If So, Tell Me," and "Confession of My Images" originally appeared in *If So, Tell Me* (London: Reality Street Editions, 1999). Reprinted by permission of the author. "Words" and "The Fairwell Stairway" originally appeared in *Fair Realism* (Los Angeles: Sun & Moon Press, 1995). Copyright 1995 by Barbara Guest and reprinted by permission of the publisher. "Defensive Rapture" originally appeared in *Defensive Rapture* (Los Angeles: Sun & Moon Press, 1992). Copyright 1992 by Barbara Guest and reprinted by permission of the publisher. "The Forces of the Imagination" originally appeared in *Fence* 3(1) (2000) and is reprinted by permission of the author. "The Countess from Minneapolis" and "An Emphasis Falls on Reality" originally appeared in *Selected Poems* (Los Angeles: Sun & Moon Press, 1995) and is reprinted by permission of the publisher. "The View from Kandinsky's Window" originally appeared in *Fair Realism* (Los Angeles: Sun & Moon Press, 1995) and is reprinted by permission of the publisher.

Lyn Hejinian's "from *Writing Is an Aid to Memory*" originally appeared in *Writing Is an Aid to Memory* (Los Angeles: Sun & Moon Press, 1996). Copyright 1996 by Lyn Hejinian and reprinted by permission of the publisher. An earlier version of "Some Notes toward a Poetics" appeared in *Fence* 3(1) (2000) and is reprinted by permission of the author. "from

Happily" originally appeared in *Happily* (San Francisco: Post-Apollo Press, 2000) and in *Language of Inquiry* (Berkeley: University of California Press, 2001). Reprinted by permission of Post-Apollo Press and University of California Press.

Brenda Hillman's "A Geology" originally appeared in *American Poetry Review* and in *Cascadia* (Middletown, Conn.: Wesleyan University Press, 2001) and is reprinted by permission of the author and Wesleyan University Press. An earlier version of "Twelve Writings toward a Poetics of Alchemy, Dread, Inconsistency, Betweenness, and California Geological Syntax" appeared in *Fence* 3(1) (2000) and is reprinted by permission of the author.

Susan Howe's "There Are Not Leaves Enough to Crown to Cover to Crown to Cover" originally appeared in *The Europe of Trusts* (Los Angeles: Sun & Moon Press, 1990). Copyright 1990 by Susan Howe and reprinted by permission of the publisher.

Ann Lauterbach's "Stones (Istanbul, Robert Smithson)" was originally published in *Avec Sampler* 2 (1998), and a version of "As (It) Is: Toward A Poetics of the Whole Fragment" was published electronically as "On Flaws" in *Theory & Event* by Johns Hopkins University Press in 1999. Both are reprinted by permission of the author. "In the Museum of the Word (Henri Matisse)," "Rapture of the Spoken," and "Ashes, Ashes (Robert Ryman, Susan Cryle)" originally appeared in *And For Example* (1994) and are reprinted by permission of Viking Penguin, a division of Penguin Putnam, Inc. The quotations in Christine Hume's "'Enlarging the Last Lexicon of Perception' in Ann Lauterbach's Framed Fragments" from Ann Lauterbach's "In the Museum of the Word (Henri Matisse)," "Rapture of the Spoken," "Ashes, Ashes (Robert Rymna, Susan Crile)" are from *And for Example,* copyright 1994 by Ann Lauterbach. The quotations from "A Clown, Some Colors, A Doll, Her Stories, A Song, A Moonlit Cove" are from *On a Stair* by Ann Lauterbach, copyright 1997 by Ann Lauterbach. All are used by permission of Viking Penguin, a division of Penguin Putnam, Inc.

Hank Lazer's "Lyricism of the Swerve: The Poetry of Rae Armantrout" originally appeared in a somewhat different version in *A Wild Salience:*

The Writing of Rae Armantrout, ed. Tom Beckett (Cleveland: Burning Press, 1999). Parts of this essay are reprinted by permission of Robert Drake.

Ming-Qian Ma's "Articulating the Inarticulate: Singularities and the Countermethod in Susan Howe" was originally published in *Contemporary Literature* 36(3) (1995). It is reprinted by permission of the Board of Regents at the University of Wisconsin System.

Harryette Mullen's "Wino Rhino" originally appeared in *Lipstick Eleven* 2 (2001), "Fancy Cortex" in *Booglite* 2 (1999), "Music for Homemade Instruments" and "Sleeping with the Dictionary" in *Facture* 1 (2000), "The Anthropic Principle" in *Aufgabe* 1 (2001), and "Imaging and Unimagined Reader" in *Boundary* 2 26(1) (1999) and *Fence* 3(1) (2000). All are copyrighted by Harryette Mullen and reprinted by permission of the author.

AMERICAN WOMEN POETS
IN THE 21ST CENTURY

INTRODUCTION

Juliana Spahr

WHILE THE word "lyric" is not in the title *American Women Poets in the 21st Century,* what is most provocative about the poems and the essays included here is their revisioning of the lyric tradition. This book's beginnings can be seen in the "Where Lyric Meets Language" conference that was held at Barnard College in April 1999 and presented women poets whose writing is in some way in dialogue with lyric, gender, and innovation. But, this collection is not the proceedings of that conference. Rather, it is an introduction to the work of ten contemporary women poets, many of whom attended the conference: Rae Armentrout, Mei-mei Berssenbrugge, Lucie Brock-Broido, Jorie Graham, Barbara Guest, Lyn Hejinian, Brenda Hillman, Susan Howe, Ann Lauterbach, and Harryette Mullen. Each poet offers a representative sample of work and a brief statement, and each chapter includes a critical essay about the poet. The essays are written as introductions to each poet and provide much-needed context to readers new to this work.

Lyric is not and never has been a simplistic genre, despite its seeming innocence. It is only recently, after modernism, that it has gotten its bad name for being traditional, for being romantic in the derisive sense.[1] And while much ink has been spilt on defining lyric,[2] there is no consensus on its value. Some argue that the lyric's intimate and interior space of retreat is its sin. This is essentially Adorno's argument, which leads to his famous declaration that "to write poetry after Auschwitz is barbaric" (1981, 34).[3] Some argue that because lyric is a retreat, it resists. María Rosa Menocal, for instance, writes, "When the world all around is calling for clear distinctions, loyalties to Self and hatred of others, and, most of all, belief in the public and legal discourses of single languages and single states—smooth narratives—what greater threat exists than that voice which rejects such easy orthodoxies with their readily understood rhetoric and urges, instead, the most difficult readings, those that embrace the painfully impossible in the human heart?" (1994, 89).[4]

This debate about retreat is one that the poets included here often enact and discuss. Brock-Broido, for instance, echoes Adorno but without his judgment when she writes, "My logic of Lyric does not permit me to assign a Politic to language. . . . The I is the Alpha, not 'Witness.'" And on this topic, Hillman notes simply that "lyric has its limits." She is right to admit this. The lyric has not transcended the limits of aesthetics much recently. Even this collection, which makes room within lyric for language writing's more politicized claims, focuses mainly on formal and aesthetic issues. Most of the poets and critics in this collection use the word "lyric" to refer to interiority and/or intimate speech that avoids confession, clear speech, or common sense. Many poets here speak of lyric as the genre of and about impossibility and difficulty. In short, when they talk of innovation, they often talk of lyric. Brock-Broido, for instance, aligns with lyric's difficulty when she declares, "I want a poetry which is inorganic, an artifact or artifice, riddled with truth." And so does Graham when she ends "Poetic's Stone" with:

> sensation of beauty unseen; an owlet's
> cry;
> a cry from something closer to the ground that's uttered
> twice and which I cannot name—although it
> seems bright yellow in its pitch.

Likewise, Lauterbach writes of her interest in a poetics of "a whole fragment," one where "meaning abides or arises exactly at the place where 'use' appears." This desire to articulate those moments where meaning is slipping away is lyric's great tradition.

But what is exciting about this collection is how the social and the cultural keep intruding and developing an aesthetic frame whether the poets admit it or not. In part these concerns intrude because of the collection's frame of women and their relation to innovation. Lyric has often had a troubled history of relation with women. Many blame the Petrarchian tradition with its male lover and female beloved. Yet it is not that women avoid or have avoided writing lyrics. Sappho is the obvious otherwise. Many critics also point out how women have been busy reclaiming the lyric from the centuries of mythically gendered male tradition.[5] But because this collection emphasizes innovation, the poems presented here have little resemblance to this tradition and the small space women have claimed for themselves. As Howe puts it, "I write to break out into perfect primeval Consent." Innovation is a word that is as hard to define as lyric, but for the most part here it means the use of agrammatical modernist techniques such as fragmentation, parataxis, run-ons, interruption, and disjunction, and at the same time the avoidance of linear narrative development, of meditative confessionalism, and of singular voice. Many of these writers have taken to heart Kathleen Fraser's and Rachel Blau Du Plessis's suggestion that modernist innovation is a feminist space,[6] even though much of this work does not appear conventionally feminist at first glance. There is in this collection little attention to how women, or these poets themselves, are oppressed or marginal—little attention to gender asymmetry. Few of the poets here present a poetry of uplift with positive images of revised femininity. Instead, much of this work investigates representation itself to suggest alternatives to lyric's troubled and limiting history for women. It moves away from too easily separated and too easily declarative identities.

Because of its alphabetical organization, the concerns of the poets and critics in *American Women Poets in the 21st Century* loop around and into each other. The collection begins with Rae Armentrout's up-front statement about her association with language poetry even as she quickly moves to earlier, and more lyrical, influences such as William Carlos Williams and Emily Dickinson. Armentrout's work is distinctive in this volume for how directly it documents the various power struggles between and within genders. In "A Story," a wonderfully telling revision of lyric intimacy, she replaces the lyric's lover and beloved with a "good mother" who tells the child:

> "I love you, but I don't
> like the way you lie there
> pinching your nipples
> while I'm trying to read you a story."

This poem points to the value of the lyric in exposing how our intimacies are watched by others and thus, with this stare, also restricted. In "Lyricism of the Swerve: The Poetry of Rae Armentrout," Hank Lazer calls this the "swerve" of Armentrout's poetry, a quality that he defines as "peculiarly teasing, humorous, thoughtful (and thought-provoking) engagement at those junctures, joints, and sites of adjacency." This swerve, Armentrout notes in "Cheshire Poetics," has feminist roots in what Pound called the slither of H.D. And while Lazer mentions that Armentrout's work is often seen as "less" political in comparison to her fellow language writers, his essay importantly points to "the inherently political nature of her calculated subversion of comfortable and comforting assumptions." His essay, as it places Armentrout's work in the context of lyric written by women, clearly points out how Armentrout uses lyric's intimacy and language writing's politics to suggest a feminist, engaged lyric, or what he calls "an ethics of writing."

While Armentrout can declare her allegiance to language writing simply and easily at the beginning of her essay, Mei-mei Berssenbrugge's work has always existed in between the many social formations that define contemporary poetry. She clearly has alliances with language writing; in "By Correspondence," she mentions conversations with James Sherry as an influence. And she just as clearly has alliances with Asian-American groups such as the Basement Workshop and the Morita Dance Company, which produced a performance of "Fog," and also the Hawai'i-based Bamboo Ridge. She also clearly has alliances with the arts scene, as her collaborations with Kiki Smith and her husband Richard Tuttle demonstrate. All of these alliances combine to make her work distinctly exploratory of the internal but not the confessional or the intimate. The excerpt included here from *Four Year Old Girl,* for instance, begins inside the body with detail:

> The *genotype* is her genetic constitution.
> The *phenotype* is the observable expression of the genotype as structural
>   and biochemical traits. (1)

This looking inside at the complicated ways in which human emotion becomes constructed is Berssenbrugge's innovative contribution to lyric's tendency to concentrate on interior emotion.[7] Linda Voris in "A Sensitive Empiricism: Berssenbrugge's Phenomenological Investigations" argues that Berssenbrugge's work "is compositional in method, accreting observations, contingent possibilities, and contradictions that seem to materialize by stretching ever outwards, much like Tatlin's compositions built out from the corners of the room." While Voris, who concentrates more on the form and aesthetics of Berssenbrugge's work, does not much address it, there is an interesting dialogue between feminism and the lyric in this work. In "By Correspondence," Berssenbrugge writes, "I also identify with my mother's and my grandmother's feminism, which seemed immediate to me, perhaps because of matriarchal character that is part of Chinese culture." This feminism is clearly evident within Berssenbrugge's attention to how bodies, mainly female ones, are represented in writing and art. *Four Year Old Girl,* for instance, avoids conventional representation and looks at genotype and phenotype to observe that "Between her and the displaced gene is another relation, the effect of meaning."

While this book brings together a number of women writers who define themselves as innovative, many are innovative in different ways and for different reasons. Further, many of these poets do not feel at all aligned with each other. Some of this division is merely about who breaks bread with whom. But one strong difference in this collection is between those who turn to modernist techniques for political reasons and those who do so for aesthetic reasons. Lucie Brock-Broido, for instance, begins her essay "Myself a Kangeroo among the Beauties" by stating, "My logic of Lyric does not permit me to assign a Politic to Language." Later in the essay she explicitly separates her work from language writing: "A poem which the world longs to call a Language Poem is too open for my taste" and "After I had been the recipient of a particularly thrashing review, Charles Wright, in a letter of solidarity & sympathy, wrote to me regarding LANGUAGE (?) Poetry. He wrote: 'What have we been doing all this time anyway, Barking?'" Instead Brock-Broido claims that she aspires to be "a New Elliptical."[8] In terms of the formal devices used in poems such as "Carrowmore" and "Am More"—fragments, phrases, run-ons, and ambiguity—Brock-Broido's work does not differ that much from poets who assign a politics to language (and one cannot help but hear Howe's pivotal *My Emily Dickinson* in Brock-Broido's *The Master Letters*) and are heavily influenced by language writing such as that by Norma Cole, Fraser, or Cole Swensen. Yet her work avoids the politics of empowerment of these poets. Brock-Broido's poems, for instance, draw from feminism's tendency to represent female subjects and their voices, yet her work avoids conventional uplift. As Stephen Burt notes in "'Subject, Subjugate, Inthralled': The Selves of Lucie Brock-Broido," "The selves Brock-Broido invokes are almost always victims; many are, or imagine they are, imprisoned, wounded, helpless." And as he writes of Brock-Broido's *The Master Letters*, "The poems depict divided, troubled speakers and writers who appeal, implore, or submit to others—to 'masters,' to readers—to complete them and resolve their divisions." Burt's negotiation is to see Brock-Broido's poems as "masochistic" in the feminist sense that Jessica Benjamin gave that word. When Burt places Brock-Broido's work in the context of poetry, he turns mainly to master canonical figures such as John Berryman, Robert Browning, John Donne, T. S. Eliot, Richard Howard, Stanley Kunitz, and Alexander Pope, rooting her work more in lyric's dramatic monologue than in feminist issues of representation (even those complicated by machoism).

While the works of Jori Graham and Brock-Broido travel very different paths, both reflect similar concerns. Graham also explores issues of speech and the difficult unruliness of language that has been the lyric's territory since its origins. As much as Dickinson's work has influenced Brock-Broido, so it influences Graham's work, as Thomas Gardner argues in "Jorie Graham and Emily Dickinson: Singing to Use the Waiting." Gardner locates Dickinson in Graham in "the poet's broken speech to the absent beloved," in similar approaches to silence. Graham uses innovation for individual and free expression: "I believe most signature styles are born as much out of temperament—and its rare *original* idiosyncracies—as anything else." In "Philosopher's Stone," Graham expands on this:

....the hole
filling back in on itself—as the self fills in on itself—a
collectivity–a
god making of himself many
creatures [in the cage there is food] [outside only the great
circle called freedom] [an empire which begins
with a set table] and I should like, now that the last washes of my gaze
let loose over the field, to say, if this peering,
it is the self—there—out to the outer reaches of
my hand

The emerging phenomenon of the aesthetically focused female poet who turns to more modernist/innovative forms reaches its apex in Graham's work. That this phenomenon has been limited to mainly women poets seems to suggest that Fraser's and Du Plessis's theorizing on innovation and gender still resonates. Graham's work is often the most disjunctive published by established journals and presses, yet in the overall picture of contemporary poetry, Graham celebrates, as Helen Vendler notes and as Gardner quotes in his article, "middleness."

Instead of the poem as an act of individual expression, Barbara Guest emphasizes the poem's reach in "The Forces of the Imagination": "This position of 'subjectivity' or 'openness' is what the poem desires to obtain, free to be molded by forces that shall condition the imagination of the poet." Just as Graham's work does not fit easily into conventional categories, neither does Guest's. But while Graham sees poetry as idiosyncrasy, Guest sees it as connective intimacy. How Guest is always reaching out and putting things together is the focus of Sara Lundquist's "Implacable Poet, Purple Birds: The Work of Barbara Guest." As Lundquist notes, "Guest eludes because her scope and range are so variable and large, and because she so elegantly presents so many seemingly contradictory qualities." This variable largeness is just one of many characteristics that makes Guest such an important figure in the New York School. But also, socially, Guest is a wonderfully complicated figure. As Lundquist notes, Guest was at the Barnard conference as "modernism's representative, yet [she] reached quite effortlessly across the generations to the youngest poets there." This connective intent defines Guest's "Mysteriously Defining the Mysterious: Byzantine Proposals of Poetry," which is full of names and places and travels. Lundquist's essay demonstrates the largeness of Guest's work when she describes her own experiences reading and teaching Guest. She ends her essay by describing a much marked-up copy of Guest's *Rocks on a Platter* and the way "the words consort, their mixing-it-up on the page, their intercourse, their dance, their oxymoronic tussle, their sighs and hiccups and jokes and caresses."

Like Guest, Lyn Hejinian's emphasis is on relation. Her "Some Notes toward a Poetics" begins, "Poetics is not personal. A poetics gets formed in and as a relationship with the world." As she quotes from her own teaching notebook:

> Language is one of the principal forms our curiosity takes.
> The language of poetry is a language of inquiry.
> Poetry takes as its premise that language (all language) is a medium for experiencing experience. It provides us with the consciousness of consciousness.

Here poetry is again about thinking. With Armentrout, Hejinian has been socially and aesthetically a part of language writing in the Bay Area since the 1970s. Her excerpt from *Happily* deeply explores inquiry or, as she writes, "The dilemmas in sentences form tables of discovery of things created to create the ever better dilemma which is to make sense to others." The poem is written, new sentence-style,[9] as a nonpersonal mix of confession and observation. Juxtaposition guides more than narrative. Consider, for instance, the avoidance of the linear development of narrative's progress in these lines:

> Nostalgia is another name for one's sense of loss at the thought that one has
>   sadly gone along happily overlooking something, who knows what
> Perhaps there were three things, no one of which made sense of the other two
> A sandwich, a wallet, and a giraffe
> Logic tends to force similarities but that's not what we mean by "sharing
>   existence"

This project of inquiry defines much of Hejinian's work. She is perhaps best known for *My Life* (Hejinian 1980), a formally shaped autobiography.[10] And of all the writers included here, Hejinian's work is the farthest from lyric conventions. It is rarely intimate and almost always explores larger, more communal relations in long, inquiring sentences. Craig Dworkin's "Parting with Description" concentrates mainly on Hejinian's *Writing Is an Aid to Memory* (an early work that is more lyrical than most). His essay is a wonderfully "paranoid" (his term) reading of connection in this work. As he notes, "Like many of her colleagues, she was interested in 'putting things together in such a way as to enable them to coincide' and thus 'make a way of seeing connections see writing.'"

Brenda Hillman in "Twelve Writings toward a Poetics of Alchemy, Dread, Inconsistency, Betweenness, and California Geological Syntax" writes, "It doesn't matter where you begin because you'll just have to do it again." She then locates a similar philosophy of change in mercury, chaos, and the feminine. In this essay she also describes how her writing moved from meditative realism to a feminism that has been influenced by the formal techniques of language writing. In the poem "A Geology," change is exemplified by an attention to verbs, the shifting teutonic plates of California, and drug addiction:

> There are six major faults, there are skipped
> verbs, there are more little
> thoughts in California. The piece of coast
> slides on the arrow; down is
> reverse. Subduction means the coast
> goes underneath the continent, which is
> rather light. It was my friend. I needed it.
> The break in the rock shows forward; the flash
> hurts. Granite is composed of quartz, hornblende
> and other former fire. When a drug
> is trying to quit it has to stretch. Narrow comes
> from the same place as glamour.

Lisa Sewell's "Needing Syntax to Love: Expressive Experimentalism in the Work of Brenda Hillman" also charts these changes in Hillman's style. She points to how "Hillman is both an innovator and a traditionalist who seems to question but also take for granted the expressive, communicative powers of language" and notes that Hillman's "experimental approach grows out of her life experiences." In her biographically influenced essay, Sewell argues that Hillman's disenchantment with meditative realism is the result of life experiences. This relation between form and autobiography is a provocative one in Hillman's work.

Susan Howe often turns to history, especially U.S. history, to write a poetry of lyric and recovery. Her by now famous statement "I wish I could tenderly lift from the dark side of history, voices that are anonymous, slighted—inarticulate" from "There Are Not Leaves Enough to Crown to Cover to Crown to Cover" reflects her revisionary and feminist uses of the lyric. Her essay begins with autobiography: "I was born in Boston Massachusetts on June 10th, 1937." Yet the autobiography turns to history in the next paragraph. Howe's work is singular for its attention to the uses and abuses of history. In "Articulating the Inarticulate: Singularities and the Counter-method in Susan Howe," Ming-Qian Ma points out that "to articulate the inarticulate, Howe's poetic praxis pivots on a lyric consciousness upon which impinges a double mission of rescuing and breaking free: rescuing the 'stutter' that Howe hears in American literature." This attention defines Howe's unique style as having a politics, not just an aesthetics. As she notes in "C H A I R":

Art has filled my days
Strange and familiar not
for embellishment but
object as it is in itself

As Ma notices, Howe often writes from and through a source text. Because the "inarticulate," another word for what is called innovative in this collection, often comes from history, her project is less about making new or breaking down the conventions of contemporary languages and more about giving voice to what is often overlooked by history's master narratives.

Lauterbach turns to "chance and change" in her "As (It) Is: Toward a Poetics of the Whole Fragment." Chance and change, she points out, revise the modernist fragment so that it "eschews totalizing concepts of origin, unity, closure and completion." In her poem "In the Museum of the Word (Henri Matisse)," this attention to revising the modernist fragment is phrased as such:

impermanent oracular trace so that
not any fragment will do counting my steps
from margin to margin/scenic on foot
turning a page.

Lauterbach's work has a longer history than most of the work emerging now that is poised between meditative attention and language writing. Her use of ekphrasis has meant that the subject of much of her work has been about aesthetics, and with her interest in modernism and her social association with language writing, her work has greatly expanded the concerns of ekphrasis. As Christine Hume in "'Enlarging the Last Lexicon of Perception' in Ann Lauterbach's Framed Fragments" writes, "If we recognize a defining condition of the lyric, from Sappho to C.D. Wright, as authorial control and singular heroic expression, then, Lauterbach fractures and implodes this tradition with wildly generous lyric capacities, large enough to contain competing demands of sensual and analytic intelligences."

An alphabetical accident places Mullen's work at the end of this collection, which is fortunate because her work also points to an emerging use of lyric intimacy for reasons beyond aesthetics. Mullen's work is especially attentive to how lyric can be an exploratory genre with which to negotiate the debate about whether identity is stasis or flux. Her work combines numerous influences. One can hear the identity-inflected lyric of writers such as Lucille Clifton and Jayne Cortez, the identity-resistant lyric of writers such as Myung Mi Kim, movements and poetic groupings as diverse as Black Arts, Umbra, and language writing. Mullen's work disrespects none of these influences and yet takes them all somewhere else. What emerges is a discussion of gender and race that moves between essentialism and constructivism to suggest that what is essential about identity is its flux, the "divergent universification" that she locates in Cortez's brain in "Fancy Cortex." It is this inclusiveness that Elisabeth A. Frost notes when she writes, "Mullen's poetry critiques the enforcement of difference, of 'apartheid,' both on and off the page." Mullen's work, as much of the work in this collection, provides a telling reply to those who would argue that lyric innovation should be, or just is, an inappropriate genre for examining the political, the social, or the cultural.

This collection only presents ten poets. It makes no claim to comprehensiveness. One sleepless night I made a list of the influences and alliances and friendships that I felt resonating here among these writers: Gwendolyn Brooks, Marilyn Chin, Cortez, Clifton, Cole, Du Plessis, Carolyn Forche, Fraser, Joy Harjo, Erica Hunt, Claudia Keelan, Kim, Bernadette Mayer, Tracie Morris, Thylias Moss, Cathy Song, Swensen, Ann Waldman, Rosemarie Waldrop, Susan Wheeler, C.D. Wright, and Lois-Ann Yamanaka. And in the morning I realized how incomplete this list was and made a note to begin another.

Reading these essays all together has shown me that while there is a clear difference in intent between a poem written for investigating the self and one written for investigating language or community, it is more and more the case that the techniques used might be similar. In other words, form is no longer the clear marker of intention or meaning that it was thirty years ago.

This essay is a rewrite of a much shorter introduction that I originally submitted to begin this book. In this earlier draft I wrote, "in this collection, poets who only on rare moments find themselves in the same room are here together." And also, "The divergent work included within this collection suggests that women's poetry in America is thriving not through its samenesses but through its mixture of diversity and collectivity." My feeling was that it was important not to see this book as yet another attempt to stake a boundaried territory or to suggest a new movement. I felt that the poems and essays here were gathered less with an attention to coverage and more to suggest new possibilities for dialogue, new pedagogical opportunities, and that there were significant disagreements and differences among the poets and critics collected here (even if they rarely erupt on the page except in Brock-Broido's "Myself a Kangaroo among the Beauties").

An anonymous reader's report contained this response: "Reservation: what keeps nagging at me is that the anthology coheres not because it dramatizes competing poetries (as Ms. Spahr claims in the introduction) but rather consistently makes a persuasive case for varieties of *innovative* poetries."

I think this reader is right—that this collection does not dramatize competing poetries (such a collection might feature of boxing match between Gerald Stern and Bruce Andrews). Its attention is to the contemporary poetries that are attentive to modernism's forms. Yet I would not want to suggest that innovation is a value in itself or that all these poets use innovation with the same intent. What matters is what innovation does, where it takes readers. I find value (and its cousin beauty), for instance, in what Hejinian calls "inquiry." And I would add the word "expansive" to that inquiry. I find value in lyrics that retreat from individualism and idiosyncracy by pointing to heady and unexpected yet intimate pluralisms. And lyrics that help me to place myself as part of a larger, connective culture. Lyrics that, in other words, are not at all ignorant about structures. Lyrics that, as Menocal points out, are "constantly engaged in the onerous but exhilarating struggle with the myriad institutions that surround it" (1994, 58). Lyrics that comment on community and that move lyric away from individualism to shared, connective spaces. Lyrics that reveal how our private intimacies have public obligations and ramifications, how intimacy has a social bond with shared meaning. It thus matters to me that lyric not be given up to aesthetics *only* or even aesthetics *mainly*, that its retreat not be from argument but from overly clear arguments, to use Menocal's language again, from single languages and single states and smooth narratives.

I think the anonymous reader is right that there are varieties of innovative poetries. This collection begins a dialogue between the two often falsely separated poetries of language and lyric. The unevenness of these two terms, one a social grouping and the other a genre, remains a sign of some dissonance even as critics often pit language and lyric against each other with straw-man models. Yet there is a conversation about form among these poets even as there is not one about poetry's intentions.

This collection does not even begin to attempt to represent the varieties of innovative poetries in the United States right now. With the exception of Mullen, poets who directly and variously explore racial identity are missing. Instead, the collection presents a variety of ways that modernist techniques are being used within lyric contexts. That this sort of innovation is so rarely used to address race deserves more attention. While some might say that modernist techniques are inadequate to the discussion, these techniques have often and successfully been used to investigate gender and to suggest more collective, connective models of intimacy beyond a lover and a beloved. My feeling, and that is as assertive as it gets, is that these forms have been perceived by many as elitist or privileged spaces.[11] I think that this perception is a misreading and that the work of many of the poets included here proves otherwise. But I worry that this feeling in the air, even unsubstantiated, has limited the sorts of inquiry that writing in modernist, innovative forms might explore—that it has both directed writers who identify as other than white or privileged by class away from them and suggested that these forms might be less than ideal for critique of certain subjects.

One valuable aspect of the writers associated with language writing has been their attention to the variety of critiques that modernist innovation makes possible. Yet this group of writers has, with the exception of Bruce Andrews, often avoided addressing racial politics. That Mullen is now taking these same techniques and their attention to critique to examine race makes her work so valuable. In an interview with Farah Griffin, Michael Magee, and Kristen Gallagher, Mullen says that

> one reason I wrote *Muse and Drudge* is because having written *Tree Tall Woman,* when I went around reading from that book there were a lot of black people in my audience. There would be white people and brown people and maybe other people of color as well. Suddenly, when I went around to do readings of *Trimmings* and "Spermkit," I would be the one black person in the room, reading my poetry. . . . I felt, "Well, this is interesting. This tells me something about the way that I'm writing now," although I didn't think I was any less black in those two books or any more black in *Tree Tall Woman.* But I think that the way that these things get defined in the public domain is that, yeah, people saw "Spermkit" as being not a black book but an innovative book. And this idea that you can be black or innovative, you know, is what I was really trying to struggle against. And *Muse and Drudge* was my attempt to show that I can do both at the same time. (Griffin, Magee, and Gallagher 1997)

In this anecdote, Mullen points to how she finds lyric as a place for an intimate, self-aware investigation of her own relationship to race, class, and gender, to dominant and subordinate cultures, to her role as spokesperson for "minority experience." Yet at the same time she points to how the form of the work can change the construction of a segregated social space. Similarly, in "Poetics Statement" Mullen points to the possibilities of writing in a world of expanding illiteracy (she means both the illiteracy of not being able to read and the growing nominally educated who cannot read critically). Here, while acknowledging the limitations of her work—its limited distribution and its nonstandard forms—she states that her future (ideal?) reader is "the offspring of an illiterate woman" and that she writes (echoing Stein) "for myself and others." My hope is that through Mullen's example, other writers, especially those with dominant (white and also middle- and upper-class) identities, will continue to use lyric as a place for resistance of racial separation. While contemporary lyric often avoids discussing categories of identity, Mullen's work turns lyric's establishing subjectivity into communal opportunity.[12]

Much has been made of the transition from lyric to narrative, from metaphor to allegory, from seduction to possession, from incantation to realism. Yet despite the constant intrusion of new genres and new media, lyric persists. Is it possible to have a culture without it? "The poem and you need each other" is how Guest expresses this. From reading the works presented here, I have learned much about how lyric might be an ideal genre for certain sorts of critique, and how the lyric space of intimacy has the potential to be an exemplary space for examining political intimacies, race and gender intimacies, and community intimacies in addition to its relentless attention to more personal intimacy. Berssenbrugge writes of a "collaborative space that is larger and more fertile for me than writing alone." And Mullen writes that her poetry "explores the reciprocity of language and culture" and "is informed by my interactions with readers, writers, scholars, and critics, as well as my interest in the various possibilities for poetry in written and spoken American English." Although I find comparisons between contemporary poets and old masters to be often silly, I cannot help but think of Dante's use of the colloquial in lyric in this context. What I mean is not that Mullen is the new Dante, but that the emphasis on innovation in this collection is a return to what made lyric so valuable centuries ago. Lyric is by definition innovative. When it stops being innovative it is no longer lyric. This collection points not only to how women writers are using innovation attentively, but also to how women are major contributors to innovation. Here, where the "you" and the "I" are no longer clear, there is much to be hopeful about the lyric in the beginnings of the twenty-first century.

NOTES

1. As Marjorie Perloff points out when she discusses the collection *New Definitions of Lyric: Theory, Technology, and Culture:* "For Walker, as for the other essayists, romantic lyric thus becomes a derogatory term; it connotes inwardness, subjectivity, monovocality, and transparency—all of these politically suspect in the age of multiculturalism. But in making these claims, Walker, McGuirk, and the others seem to be conflating two things: the attenuated, neo-romantic lyric of the later twentieth century, as that lyric has been promoted by such leading critics as Harold Bloom, and the actual English lyric of the Romantic period" (1998, 245–46).

2. See, for instance, Frye (1985), Genette (1992), Hollander (1985), and Johnson (1982) for the never-ending discussion of what lyric might be. An interesting recent article on this subject is Walker (1998).

3. Steve Evans, a critic of contemporary poetry, recently pointed out to me that Adorno revises this statement in *Negative Dialectics* (1990, 363). The assumption that lyric is apolitical is often perpetuated by contemporary poets who define themselves as "lyric poets." See also Li (1994).

4. Paul Allen Miller notes similarly that despite lyric being "an ambiguous voice, straddling the line between public importance and private reflection," it "is always somewhat subversive. It separates the individual from his or her communal ties and responsibilities, and examines his or her most intimate thoughts and feelings, in the process lifting a corner of that veil of socially useful repression which allows us to interact with one another in a reasonably civilized manner" (1994, 124, 127). For more on lyric's resistant possibilities, see Altieri (1991), Lazer (1997), McGuirk (1998), Schultz (1995), Wallace (1996), and the introductions to the first three issues of the journal *Apex of the M.*

5. This criticism concentrates on women's subversion within accepted forms. Women, these critics often argue, take the form and move within its box to make room for themselves. Studies of women's subversion of the sonnet have tended to look at how women do not leave the box of form nor its alliances to the court of courtly love. Instead, they move into the box in order to claim it, in order to establish what gets called lyric subjectivity, for themselves. Ann Rosalind Jones, for instance, argues that women poets of 1540–1620 act as negotiators who "accept the dominant ideology encoded into a text but particularize and transform it in the service of a different group" (1990, 4). The argument remains similar about more contemporary work. Mary B. Moore notes that "Victorian and modernist women could write the Petrarchan sonnet because its apparent focus on the heart allowed them to veil their sometimes subversive ideas about gender and eroticism, even as they claimed Petrarchan complexity, and hence subjectivity through the mode" (2000, 11). Nina Miller points out that Edna St. Vincent Millay "used traditional verse to turn her (inescapable) female sexuality to artistic authority" (1998, 39). Stacy Carson Hubbard (1992) points to an appropriative practice in Brooks's sonnets that work in a highly traditional form even as they articulate a nontraditional voice. Maureen Honey (1989) argues similarly about women poets of the Harlem Renaissance and Lynn Keller (1994) about Marilyn Hacker's sonnets.

6. See Kathleen Fraser's *Translating the Unspeakable* (2000), especially the essay "The Tradition of Marginality . . . and the Emergence of *HOW(ever),*" and Rachel Blau du Plessis's *The Pink Guitar* (1990). For the larger discussion of modernist techniques and feminism, see the work of French feminists such as Julia Kristeva, especially *Revolution in Poetic Language* (1984), and Hélène Cixous, especially *The Exile of James Joyce* (1972).

7. See Altieri's "Intimacy and Experiment in Mei-Mei Berssenbrugge's *Empathy*" (forthcoming) for a more detailed reading.

8. See Burt's (1999a, 1999b) essays on ellipticism in *American Letters and Commentary.*

9. See Silliman (1987).

10. See Samuels (1997) for a discussion of the canonical status of *My Life*.

11. See, for instance, Perelman (1994).

12. For more on lyric subjectivity see Miller (1994), and Fineman (1988). Miller notes that lyric "is the re-presentation not simply of a 'strong personality,' but of a particular mode of being a subject, in which the self exists not as part of a continuum with the community and its ideological commitments, but is folded back against itself, and only from this space of interiority does it relate to 'the world' at large" (1994, 5). Tilottama Rajan also notes that "pure lyric is a monological form, where narrative and drama alike are set in the space of difference. The latter present the self in interaction with other characters and events. But lyric, as a purely subjective form, is marked by the exclusion of the other through which we become aware of the difference of the self from itself. Lyric consciousness, in other words, comes as close as possible to approximating what Sartre calls a 'shut imaginary consciousness,' a consciousness without the dimension of being-in-the-world" (1985, 196).

WORKS CITED

Adorno, Theodor W. 1981. *Prisms,* trans. Samuel and Shierry Weber (Cambridge: MIT Press).

———. 1990. *Negative Dialectics,* trans. E. B. Ashton (New York: Continuum International Publishing Group).

Altieri, Charles. 1991. "Responsiveness to Lyric and the Critic's Responsibilities." *Contemporary Literature* 32 (1991): 580–87.

———. Forthcoming. "Intimacy and Experiment in Mei-Mei Berssenbrugge's *Empathy.*" In *We Who Love To Be Astonished: Experimental Women's Writing and Performance Poetics* (Tuscaloosa: University of Alabama Press).

Burt, Stephen. 1991a. "About Ellipticism (Round Two)." *American Letters and Commentary* 11: 72–76.

———. 1991b. "The Elliptical Poets." *American Letters and Commentary* 11: 45–55.

Cixous, Hélène. 1972. *The Exile of James Joyce,* trans. Sally A. J. Purcell (New York: D. Lewis).

Du Plessis, Rachel Blau. 1990. *The Pink Guitar* (New York: Routledge).

Fineman, Joel. 1988. *Shakespeare's Perjured Eye: The Invention of Poetic Subjectivity in the Sonnets* (Berkeley: University of California Press).

Fraser, Kathleen. 2000. *Translating the Unspeakable: Poetry and Innovative Necessity* (Tuscaloosa: University of Alabama Press).

Frye, Northrup. 1985. "Approaching the Lyric." In *Lyric Poetry: Beyond New Criticism,* ed. Chaviva Hosek and Patricia Parker (Ithaca, N.Y.: Cornell University Press), 31–37.

Genette, Gérard. 1992. *The Architext: An Introduction,* trans. Jane E. Lewin (Berkeley: University of California Press).

Griffin, Farah, Michael Magee, and Kristen Gallagher. 1997. *Combo* 1 (1997): <http://wings.buffalo.edu/epc/authors/mullen/interview-new.html>

Hejinian, Lyn. 1980. *My Life* (Los Angeles: Sun & Moon Press).

Hollander, John. 1985. *Vision and Resonance: Two Senses of Poetic Form* (New Haven: Yale University Press).

Honey, Maureen. 1989. *Shadowed Dreams: Women's Poetry of the Harlem Renaissance* (New Brunswick: Rutgers University Press), 1–41.

Hubbard, Stacy Carson. 1992. "'A Spintery Box': Race and Gender in the Sonnets of Gwendoyn Brooks." *Genre* 25 (1992): 47–64.

Johnson, W. R. 1982. *The Idea of Lyric: Lyric Modes in Ancient and Modern Poetry* (Berkeley: University of California Press).

Jones, Ann Rosalind. 1990. *The Currency of Eros: Women's Love Lyric in Europe, 1540–1620* (Bloomington: Indiana University Press).

Keller, Lynn. 1994. "Measured Feet 'in Gender Bender shoes': The Politics of Form in Marilyn Hacker's *Love, Death, and the Changing of the Seasons.*" In *Feminist Measures: Soundings in Poetry and Theory,* ed. Lynn Keller and Cristanne Miller (Ann Arbor: University of Michigan Press), 260–86.

Kristeva, Julia. 1984. *Revolution in Poetic Language,* trans. Margaret Waller (New York: Columbia University Press).

Lazer, Hank. 1997. "The Lyric Valuables: Soundings, Questions, and Examples." *Modern Language Studies* 27(2): 25–50.

Li, Victor P. H. 1984. "Narcissism and the Limits of the Self." In *Tropic Crucible: Self and Theory in Language and Literature,* ed. Ranjit Chatterjee and Colin Nicholson (Singapore: Singapore University Press), 3–23.

McGuirk, Kevin. 1998. "'All Wi Doin': Tony Harrison, Linton Kwesi Johnson, and the Cultural Work of Lyric in Postwar Britain." In *New Definitions of Lyric,* ed. Mark Jeffreys (New York: Garland), 49–76.

Menocal, María Rosa. 1994. *Shards of Love: Exile and the Origins of the Lyric* (Durham, N.C.: Duke University Press).

Miller, Nina. 1998. *Making Love Modern: The Intimate Public Worlds of New York's Literary Women* (New York: Oxford University Press).

Miller, Paul Allen. 1994. *Lyric Texts and Lyric Consciousness: The Birth of a Genre from Archaic Greece to Augustan Rome* (New York: Routledge).

Moore, Mary B. 2000. *Desiring Voices: Women Sonneteers and Petrarchism* (Carbondale: Southern Illinois University Press).

Perelman, Bob. 1994. *The Trouble with Genius: Reading Pound, Joyce, Stein, and Zukofsky* (Berkeley: University of California Press).

———. 1996. *The Marginalization of Poetry: Language Writing and Literary History* (Princeton, N.J.: Princeton University Press).

Perloff, Marjorie. 1998. "A Response." In *New Definitions of Lyric,* ed. Mark Jeffreys (New York: Garland), 245–55.

Rajan, Tilottama. 1985. "Romanticism and the Death of the Lyric Consciousness." In *Lyric Poetry: Beyond New Criticism,* ed. Chaviva Hosek and Patricia Parker (Ithaca, N.Y.: Cornell University Press).

Samuels, Lisa. 1997. "Eight Justifications for Canonizing *My Life.*" *Modern Language Studies* 27(2): 103–19.

Schultz, Susan. 1995. "'Called Null or Called Vocative': A Fate of the Contemporary Lyric." *Talisman* 14: 70–80.

Silliman, Ron. 1987. *The New Sentence* (New York: Roof Books).

Walker, Jeffrey. 1998. "The View from Halicarnassus: Aristotelianism and the Rhetoric of the Epideictic Song." In *New Definitions of Lyric,* ed. Mark Jeffreys (New York: Garland), 17–48.

Wallace, Mark. 1996. "On the Lyric as Experimental Possibility," July 1996: <http://wings.buffalo.edu/epc/authors/wallace/lyric.html>

RAE ARMANTROUT

AS WE'RE TOLD

At the start, something must be arbitrarily excluded.
The saline solution. Call it an apple. Call this a test
or a joke. From now on, apple will mean arbitrary
choice or "at random." Any fence maintains the other
side is "without form." When we're thrown out, it's onto
the lap of our parent. Later, though, Mother puts
the apple into Snow White's hand,
and then it's poison!

THE PLAN

"Who told you
you were visible?"

God said,

meaning naked
or powerless.

We had planned this meeting
in advance,

how we'd address each other,

how we'd stand
or kneel.

Thus our intentions
are different

from our bodies,
something extra,

though transparent
like a negligee.

Though a bit sketchy,

like this palm's
impression of a tree—

flashing scales,

on the point of
retraction.

But *sweet*.
You don't understand!

Like a lariat made of scalloped bricks

circling a patch
of grass

VIEW

Not the city lights. We want

—the moon—

       The Moon
none of our own doing!

UP TO SPEED

Streamline to instantaneous
voucher in/voucher out
system.

The plot winnows.

The Sphinx
wants me to guess.

Does a road
run its whole length
at once?

Does a creature
curve to meet
itself?

Whirlette!

       .

Covered or cupboard
breast? Real

housekeeping's
kinesthesiac. Cans

held high
to counterbalance "won't."

Is it
such agendas

which survive
as souls?

•

Vagueness is personal!

A wall of concrete bricks,
right here,
while sun surveys its grooves

and I try
"instantly" then "forever."

But the word is
way back,
show-boating.

Light is "with God"

(light, the traveler).

•

Are you the come-on
and the egress?

One who hobbles by
determinedly?

Not yet?

MANUFACTURING

I

A career in vestige management.

A dream job
back-engineering
shifts in salience.

I'm so far
behind the curve
on this.

So. Cal.
must connect with
so-called

to manufacture
the present.

Ubiquity's
the new in-joke

bar-code hard-on,

a catch-phrase
in every segment.

2

The eye asks if the green,

frilled geranium puckers,
clustered at angles

on each stem,
are similar enough

to stop time.

It has asked this question already.

How much present tense
can any resemblance make?

What if one catch-phrase
appears in every episode?

Does the language go rigid?

The new in-joke
is a pun
pretending to be a bridge.

POETIC STATEMENT
Cheshire Poetics

MY STATEMENT of poetics is going to be a personal narrative of sorts. I spent my twenties (during the 1970s) in the Bay Area at one of the origin points for what came to be known as "language poetry," and I am, of course, one of the people associated with that group. Most of you know that, but when you know that, what do you know? This group is as diverse as any poetic school you can think of, so I want to look farther back—at what first drew me to poetry. When I was a teenager, I was given an anthology and the poets I most loved there were William Carlos Williams and Emily Dickinson. I was drawn to poems that seemed as if they were either going to vanish or explode—in other words, to extremes, to radical poetries. But how do we define "radical"? Perhaps by how much is put at risk in the text, how far the arc of implication can reach and still *seem* apt. But so much rides, as always, on that word "seems." Is a writing radical when it risks being wrong, when it acknowledges our wrongness? I think my poetry involves an equal counterweight of assertion and doubt. It's a Cheshire poetics, one that points two ways then vanishes in the blur of what is seen and what is seeing, what can be known and what it is to know. That double bind. But where was I?

I was saying that I discovered Williams (and the other Imagists) early on and was very much moved by them. By what though? I would say now it was by their attempt to make the object speak, to put things in dialogue with mind and somehow make them hold up their end of the conversation. This is both an important project and a doomed one. The world enters the poem only through a kind of ventriloquy. Thing and idea don't really merge, as the poets themselves knew. Williams's red wheelbarrow (from *Spring and All*) is essentially separate from the "so much" that depends upon it. But there is so much poignancy in that gap! It is as if the Imagist poet wants to spin around suddenly and catch the world unaware, in dishevelment, see it as it is when we're not looking. And how can we not want that?

One of my favorite poems by Williams is "The Attic Which Is Desire." This poem does an amazing balancing act; it is simultaneously a realist depiction of an urban scene and an apotheosis of projected desire. I encountered it when I was quite young and discovering sexuality. I understood the poem's narrow, vaginal column of text, transfixed by the ejaculatory soda, as an amazing embodiment. I loved the way the poem was both about orgasm and about seeing the lights of a sign reflected in a dark window. In other words, I liked its doubleness. That's not a term usually associated with Imagism, perhaps. As Bob Perelman has pointed out, Pound praised H.D.'s writing by saying that it was "straight as the Greek" and with no "slither."[1] It took me awhile to see the gynophobia behind such rhetoric. I wanted my Imagism and my slither, too. My precision and my doubleness.

My earliest published poems were minimalist and neo-Imagist. A good example would be "View," a poem from my first book, *Extremities*. Looking back on it now, I see in "View" an exacerbated form of the doubleness that interested me in Williams's "Attic." "View" has not only two meanings, but two dissonant meanings. On the one hand, "we" (an already suspect first-person plural) want to see the moon as separate from our own activity (a bit of the world caught unawares). On the other hand, our yearning is framed by deflating clichés. To want the moon is to want the impossible. Our thrust toward the nonhuman moon can't escape the gravity of received language. The purportedly single voice of the nature lover and the words of a somewhat cynical crowd seem to collide. So this is a poetics of collisions and overlaps, of contested spaces. The border of the public and private is just such a contested space. To use dream imagery in a poem, for instance, is to expose something private, but what if a recent film inspired the dream? As I have become increasingly conscious of such contested spaces and the voices that articulate them, my poems have become somewhat longer and more complicated.

The concept of voice has long been associated with poetry. We all hear voices—on the radio, in the newspaper, in memory. As Whitman says, "I contain multitudes." As Satan says, "My name is legion." Various voices speak in my poems. I code-shift. I am many things: a white person, a working-class person with roots in the South, a woman, an academic of sorts, a '60s person who still likes rock and roll, someone who was raised on the Bible, a skeptic, etc. My voices manifest their own social unrest. In the last decade or so, academics have been raising the question of who speaks in literary works, and for whom. There is a contemporary poetry that enacts these same questions, a poetics of the crossroads.

As I looked over my poems, trying to extract a "poetics" for this talk, I noticed how often my poems parody and undermine some voice of social control. My poem "A Story" (from *Made To Seem*) might be an example of that. In "A Story" the characters of the Good Mother and the Doctor try to keep things in their proper places. They want pleasure postponed, categories upheld. The Child who pinches her nipples and the Stubborn Old Woman who thinks a name is a fiction are skeptics and dissidents. There is a way in which I am all of these characters—the doctor and the mother as well as the rebellious old woman and the child. These power struggles begin in the public sphere and are reenacted in private. The mother is charged with reproducing the social (linguistic) body within the single body of the child. (Clearly, gender has a lot to do with the power struggles in my poems. Increasingly so, perhaps.)

Would Pound have seen such confusion as a kind of distasteful "slither"? Let me appropriate an ally by invoking a Dickinson poem I love, the one commonly known as "A Narrow Fellow In The Grass." Pound called for "direct treatment of the thing,"[2] and "Narrow Fellow" certainly isn't that. Dickinson never identifies what she's seen as a snake. She first personifies it, rather comically, as a fellow. (Note the mock casualness, the mock intimacy there. Dickinson is mistress/master of sinister humor.) The snake is then Him, capitalized like God. Subsequently it appears as a comb, a rather phallic shaft, and a whiplash. It is gendered male, but then so is Dickinson—she presents herself as a boy. The gender dynamic is thus complex. There is more going on than a virginal fear of penetration. The last two lines evoke vividly the fear the snake arouses—but, like Satan in *Paradise Lost*, the snake is the real hero of the poem. Dickinson's persona, the barefoot boy, is just too cordial with "Nature's People." There's something almost Norman Rockwell-esque about this boy, reaching to "secure" whatever he sees. He deserves the unsecurable, eerie snake who "occasionally rides."[3] Dickinson, I would argue, is at least as much the snake as the boy. Her poems reveal the fissures in identity and ideology.

And now back to me. There's no good segue back from Dickinson. But, in their own way, I think, my poems enact such fissures. They are composed of conflicting voices. Formally, too, they are often disjunctive. The relation between stanza and stanza or section and section is often oblique, multiple, or partial. This isn't an accident. It's a way to explore the relation of part to whole. This relation is a vexed one. Does the part represent the whole? Is metaphor fair to the matter it represents? Does representative democracy work? I think of my poetry as inherently political (though it is not a poetry of opinion). In an optimistic mood, one might see the multiple, optional relations of parts in such work as a kind of anarchic cooperation.

Finally, poetry, at least the poetry I value, can reproduce our conflicts and fractures and yet be held together in the ghost embrace of assonance and consonance, in the echoed and echoing body of language.

Notes begin on page 49.

LYRICISM OF THE SWERVE

The Poetry of Rae Armantrout

Hank Lazer

> . . . but clarity need not be equivalent to
> readability. How readable is the world?
>
> —Rae Armantrout, "Feminist Poetics and the Meaning of Clarity"

RAE ARMANTROUT begins "Cheshire Poetics" by giving us a simple narrative that she then calls into question:

> I spent my twenties (during the 1970s) in the Bay Area at one of the origin
> points for what came to be known as "language poetry," and I am, of course,
> one of the people associated with that group. Most of you know that, but
> when you know that, what do you know?

Such doubleness, in this case assertion and critique, done with brevity and humor, characterizes Armantrout's poetry. Her poetry is of special importance because of the particular nature of her commitment to precision and to new possibilities within lyricism. These commitments mark Armantrout's poetry as unusual within the writings known as language poetry; they also mark her work as a noteworthy extension of an innovative lyric tradition from Dickinson to the present. The movement in Armantrout's poetry is idiosyncratic—what I think of as a peculiar mode of swerving that, for me, characterizes a kind of lyric poetry that Armantrout has been pursuing for quite some time. In reading her poetry with some care, yes, it is possible to differentiate her writing from various other modes of swerving such as we find, for example, in the poetry of Robert Creeley, bpNichol, and Emily Dickinson. Attuning our hearing/reading constitutes a beginning.

.

Is there a describable lyricism of swerving? For those poems for which the swerve, the turn, the sudden change in direction are integral, can we begin to articulate a precise appreciation? Is there a describable and *individualistic* lyricism of swerving?

I have heard Rae Armantrout spoken of as the most lyrical of all language poets. And, I have heard her work described as an important instance of contemporary innovative lyricism. As a poet, my own recent work (particularly *Days* and "Well Yes Then") explores such current possibilities. As a critic, I have written about new lyricisms.[4] But the terms themselves—lyric, lyrical, lyricism—at present mean so many different things. Of my particular current favorites in such modes—Larry Eigner, Robert Creeley, bpNichol, Theodore Enslin, John Taggart, Harryette Mullen, John Ashbery, Nathaniel Mackey, Lyn Hejinian, Susan Howe— none is a (precise or identical) twin to Armantrout. Initially, I offer descriptions and readings of several different kinds of contemporary lyricisms as a means of situating Armantrout's particular contribution.

Perhaps one task of critical writing (and of intensive reading) is to attend to, in George Oppen's words, "the thing and its distinction."[5] A most important recent "thing" by Armantrout is her Chax book, *writing/the plot/about/sets* (1998). Oppen's complete observation is of "the thing and its distinction/(which of course reveals actually the human/subjectivity: human meanings)," and it is with an eye toward those particularities of subjectivity that I wish to attend to Armantrout's poetry.

.

I am tempted to think toward a brief taxonomy of swerving. I begin with what for me is a touchstone for a particular kind of musical/sound swerving in an energetic passage of perpetual modulation and transformation from bpNichol's *Martyrology:*

> an infinite statement. a finite statement. a statement of infancy. a fine line
> state line. a finger of stalemate. a feeling a saint meant ointment.
>
> tremble.
>
> a region religion
> reigns in. a returning. turning return the lover. the retrospect of
> relationships always returning. the burning of the urge. the surge forward
> in animal being inside us. the catatosis van del reeba rebus suburbs of our
> imagination. last church of the lurching word worked weird in our heads.[6]

Such a category of swerving could and would be found elsewhere, for example, in many passages of Louis Zukofsky's work, most notably in "Songs of Degrees," which begins "Hear, her/Clear/Mirror,/Care/His error./In her/Care/Is clear."[7] Another category would highlight instances where the swerving occurred much more gradually, and my examples would come from extended quotation from the poetry of John Taggart or Theodore Enslin.[8] For example, Enslin's "Autumnal Rime" begins:

> Mindful mindful only of quality
> the quality of moritura of need
> of the need to die that all dying
> dying out of the need the need

```
to die the quality  the moritura
of quality  moritura in dying
need to  of need in the mores
that all is mortal  is mortally
wounded  the mind is a wound mindful
```

In Taggart's poetry, the swerving transformations take shape a bit more gradually. Perhaps if we were to imagine a topology of swerving, we would locate Enslin's musical turns somewhere between the quick, precise syllabic turns of Zukofsky's "Songs of Degrees" and Taggart's more extended modulations in "The Rothko Chapel Poem," Taggart's musical turns taking place not so much at the level of the syllable- or word-transformed but at the level of the phrase slowly modified:

```
Really only one has been moving us
only one within itself moving us
one scream within itself moving us
screams within the one move us away
away from the weddings wedding rooms
from those to this this black room
to our wandering in this black room
moving in this room means wandering
wandering's moving without meaning
no end to moving in this black room
it is like moving in a writhing sea
we are wandering in a writhing sea
seething and writhing in this room.
```

Perhaps one might make analogies to minimalist music, or one might call this swerving a kind of gradual modulation (and link it to the studies of gradual changes in time in Stein's *The Making of Americans,* completed in 1911 and first published in 1925, and in her *Lectures in America,* first presented in 1934 and first published in 1935). The particular sound-swervings of Zukofsky, Taggart, and Enslin seem to me to be fundamentally musical in nature.

Then, there are the more tentative, tenuous, miraculous, mystical turns in a Larry Eigner poem. In many of Eigner's poems, as in the beginning of "Letter to Duncan," those shifts occur not at the musical level of the syllable or word but at the level of the phrase, reenforced by the shifting but precise location of the phrase on the page:

```
            just because I forget
      to perch different ways
                  the fish
            go monotonous
```

            the
      sudden hulks of the trees
         in a glorious summer
    you don't realize
      how mature you get
          at 21

      but you look back

      wherever a summer
    continue 70 seasons

         this one
      has been so various

      was the spring hot?[9]

As in much of Creeley's poetry, the exact tension between the phrase—its seeming autonomy—and the sentence (which may attempt to subordinate and coordinate the various phrases) constitutes a drama of the poem's lineation and spatial arrangement. Thus, such poems enact an important ambivalence—one that is central as well to Armantrout's poetry: the tension, humor, play, and desire of what-goes-with-what.

Or, one might examine a quite different swerve-category called the "wacky juxtaposition," perhaps best exemplified in John Ashbery's poetry, when there is a sudden shift in tone, or register, or discourse, or subject matter. In "Grand Galop," for example, Ashbery's address to Surrey turns sharply (in tone and subject matter) in another direction:

Surrey, your lute is getting an attack of nervous paralysis
But there are, again, things to be sung of
And this is one of them, only I would not dream of intruding on
The frantic completeness, the all-purpose benevolence
Of that still-moist garden where the tooting originates:
Between intervals of clenched teeth, your venomous rondelay.

Ask a hog what is happening. Go on. Ask him.[10]

Or, one might look to a more recent example in the opening lines of "A Day at the Gate": "A loose and dispiriting/wind took over from the grinding of traffic./Clouds from the distillery/blotted out the sky. Ocarina sales plummeted."[11] Armantrout, in my opinion, does have some similarities to Ashbery's sense of humor, but her poems really are not much like his. That category of the wacky juxtaposition—particularly when it is based on a quick change of subject—moves me in the direction of John

Cage's realization "that two notations on the saMe/pIece of paper/automatically briNg/About relationship."[12] (Cage, interestingly, completes this realization by adding the conclusion that "my Composing/is actuallY unnecessary.")

Armantrout's particular and distinctive skill lies in the peculiarly teasing, humorous, thoughtful (and thought-provoking) engagement at those junctures, joints, and sites of adjacency.

Just as with the title to her Chax book—*writing/the plot/about/sets* (1998)—in which there are various possible combinations and multiplicities (or a simple list as a table of contents), so Armantrout's poems turn and tease, combine and resist combination, as in the opening lines of "about":

> What's the worst that could happen?
>
> "Schools of fish are trapped
> In these pools,"
> Say the anchors
>
> Who hang
> On nursing home walls.
>
> Reference is inimical,
> We find out now;
>
> Its Moebius strip
> Search called
>
> Vital
> To security.[13]

Her poems are, as her line break helps us to realize, how "we find out now." And her poems constitute specific embodiments of "now." Increasingly, I have come to think of poems as particular intervals of consciousness, as thinking, singing instances of now.

As we decipher what goes with what, Armantrout works the lyricism of that simultaneous gap-and-connection. From the outset of "about," there is an element of discomfort, combined with a resistance to a simple tendency for the poem to be "about" anything static—an edginess marked by one of the last lines of the poem: *"We're* the target audience." It is that quality of targeting and being targeted that "about" circles about. Does the first line of the poem refer to the confinement implicit in a poetry that must somehow be "about" something in a sustained, controlled manner? If such a critique is begun, the critique of "aboutness," of a subject or theme-based poetry/poetics, then we'd expect the schools and the schooled to be "trapped/In these pools," though *which* pools remains indefinite.

For me, the characteristic Armantrout swerve—with a mixture of play and investigativeness—occurs with the word "anchors." At first, we swim along from fish to pools to anchors, and it is a quiet aftershock as we must redecipher these anchors in light of their position of hanging "On nursing home walls," thus being transformed into TV anchors, hanging in and on the hypnotizing and consoling TV sets of the nursing home. These anchors do indeed anchor us—we are the target audience, and that CNN factoid "we" is part of the smart-bomb targeting of inclusivity and normalization. The hook is an authoritative voice that inevitably and clearly tells us (and informs us) "about" something, relaying a digested narrative "about" current events (to the trapped, mesmerized viewer).

If, as Oppen suggests, "a poem may be devoted to giving clear meaning to one word,"[14] then for me Armantrout's poem clarifies, by focusing attention on, "inimical." "Reference is inimical" and extends its dominion as modes of organization that bombard us, and as modes of organization that we impose and superimpose. "Inimical," from *inimicus:* enemy; hostile; viewing with disfavor; having the disposition or temper of an enemy; harmful; adverse; prejudicial in tendency, influence, or effects. Not that there is a place utterly *outside* reference or outside aboutness either. The strip we read and ride on twists Moebius-style; it is a continuous one-sided surface upon which we circulate and recirculate. That surface continues smoothly unless there is a sudden interruption; thus Armantrout breaks the continuity with a poet's principal resource, the line break, so that the continuous strip becomes a "strip/search," though that momentary glitch is taken into account as part of a greater habit of security and as part of a process that makes sure we "just keep moving." If we are the target audience, the target of what? Targeted to do or be or become what? In the imperial gathering of "we" in the factoid world,[15] as good Americans, as consumers of the news, soon, as in Armantrout's next poem, we'll learn that "'We're' bombing Iraq again." As with aboutness and reference, two inimicals, there is not a space outside of the collectively imposed and imposing "we."

•

A danger of the lyric: preciousness; (calculated) scarcity; a romantic exaltation of intensification. The lyric may not be enough. As a friend says of the reception of Susan Howe's poetry: so much fuss over so few words?!

•

In "sets," the final poem in *writing/the plot/about/sets,* Armantrout concludes:

Time's tic:
to pitch forward
then catch "itself"
again.

"We're" bombing Iraq again.

If I turn on the news,
someone will say, "We
mean business."

Eyes open wide
to form

an apology?
Disguised as what
might be surprise
over the raised
spoon.

That quotation-marked "we" means a certain kind of business. In our time, the rhetoric of that pronoun is no longer the kingly "we" but the "we" of fact, of data, and of persuasion of our collective deeds (and, implicitly, of our collective strength).

Is Armantrout's ending fully complicit in innocent "wonder"? Is this ending a typical or formulaic instance of lyrical closure? Or/and its mockery? That last stanza has a delicacy of sound/music—it is typically "lyrical." It is still evasive, pleasant, not overbearing in its crafted charms. I register the echoes of the long I-vowels in the sequence *eyes, wide, disguised, might, surprise,* modulating slightly into *raised,* playing off of the sequence of raspy s-z sounds in *eyeS, disguiSed, aS, surpriSe,* and *raiSed.* I hear, as well, a dialog of high and low vowel sounds (as in Plath's "Morning Song"), the high treble I and A vowels beside the low bass O sounds of *Open, apolOgy, Over,* and *spOOn.* These pretty echoing sounds incarnate the lyrical moment.

Are eyes open wide over the raised spoon an effective gesture of skepticism (by means of a feigned surprise)? Do these gestures offer a fit defense against and a reply to the inimical? Or, as the first poem, "writing," warns, "But here's the joke: syntactic space predates and dominates these words." "We" are the target audience. The smart bombs find us. We launch them all the time. "We hunker down/with short pencils/in front of the ticket booth."

A ticket to what? A ticket to the next poem called "the plot," which begins:

The secret is
you can't get to sleep
with a quiet mind;
you need to follow a sentence,
inward or downward,
as it becomes circuitous,
path-like, with tenuously credible
foliage on either side of it—
but you're still not sleeping.

Or, as Charles Bernstein has written, a pronouncement inseparable from its humor, "Poetry is like a swoon, with this difference:/it brings you to your senses."[16] For Armantrout's analytic lyrics *do* attempt to bring us to our senses. As Lyn Hejinian asks, "isn't the avant garde always pedagogical?"[17]

Let us backtrack, then. In Armantrout's first book, *Extremities* (1978), some pitfalls of lyricism are all too apparent, as in "Paradise":

Paradise
is golden.

   Sun
on wicker chair.

It is as one knew!

The joyful song
ascends (*E*, 23)

The poet risks clarity and simplicity; the poem is restricted to momentary phenomena. As in a later poem in the same volume, the poem stakes its value on the possible depth of singularity: "A single truth now occupies the mind://the smallest//distance//inexhaustible" (34). But once we know that—the Blakean infinite in a grain of sand, the depth and value of each particular—then what? We are left to assess and access the poet's moments of such integrity and realization. It may be a state about which we might say later, "Disguised as what/might be surprise/over the raised/spoon." Or, we might encounter the self-promoting medium of such proclamations, as in one of the final poems in *Extremities,* "Show":

Big Red Tomatoes—Dangling
   from Plain Sticks

To Show

Miracle
Creation of Flesh (*E*, 41)

But a mysticism of the particular is inextricable from its presentational rhetoric, and the need to capitalize already brings on a countering skepticism.

A flat mysticism of the particular is a problem, however. What's needed is a twist or turn, a kind of swerve in another direction—as Louis Zukofsky suggests, "thoughts' torsion."[18] From her earliest writing on, Armantrout brings in qualities of skepticism, self-criticism, and self-opposition to provide the kind of torsion that Zukofsky advocates. There is an element of critique (of a naïve poetry of mystical affirmation) in the capitalized display of "Show," and if we reexamine "Paradise" that poem too contains an important twist. The potential for the poem to be a flat declaration and a simple "joyful song" of a discovered paradise gets critiqued by the exclamation "It is as one knew!" As Armantrout explains,

> I intended an irony in the line "It is as one knew!" If paradise is as one knew then is it paradise or is it merely a stereotype? The exclamation makes it sound like discovery—but one can't discover what one already knew. So I think that line takes that poem out of the realm of "momentary phenomena."[19]

Exclamation marks, italics, capitalization, and quotation marks become essential print-based markers as Armantrout develops a subtly polyphonic lyricism. From early on in her writing, she gives us a typically lyrical moment, but that moment inevitably is tied to some counterbalancing skepticism, so that the moment becomes ironized or self-conflicted. She deploys a lyricism of the moment that highlights its own rhetoric of presentation. The result is a swerving within the moment itself—a two-faced or two-faceted lyrical moment, which, at its best, leaves us both engaged and on edge.

The lyric, to sustain our interest, to have complexity and beauty, and to remain compelling, requires "torsion"—that is, motion, tension, torque, and a twist. Such torsion is evident in Armantrout's "Travels":

> Among the zinnias I once thought
> I had recovered silence
>
> The power to be
> irretrievably lost
>
> Is death
> what's wrong? (*E*, 33)

It is the vertiginous swerve from the commonplace tone and diction of the first four lines in this passage (with its conventional lyrical intensifiers—*among, once, recovered, silence, power, irretrievably lost*) to the disruption and deepening of the concluding two lines that begins to characterize Armantrout's idiosyncratic lyricism. In this first book, her poetry begins to become a poetics of edges and verges, as in the concluding six lines of the title poem, "Extremities":

> the glitter of edges
> again catches the eye
>
> to approach these swords!
>
> Lines across which
> beings vanish/flare
>
> the charmed verges of presence (*E*, 7)

Armantrout's attention to edges reminds me of an earlier poetics of the edge in Williams's *Spring and All* (1923), particularly the seventh poem that begins:

> The rose is obsolete
> but each petal ends in
> an edge, the double facet
> cementing the grooved
> columns of air—The edge
> cuts without cutting

and which includes this wonderfully odd embodiment of the edge:

> What
>
> The place between the petal's
> edge and the
>
> From the petal's edge a line starts[20]

But Armantrout's is not a poetics of the edge enacted on the page (which is Williams's exuberance, his investigation—in the dawning age of the typewriter—of the line and the line break as a sculptural and visual means). Armantrout's edge-world is more one of sudden transitions and transits, sudden charges and charms. It is less affable than Williams's sense of edge, less a celebration of hard edges, more a sense of quiet pleasure, as when we see and hear "approach these swords!" as akin to "approach these words." Armantrout begins to spell out her own erotics of the edge:

> Precision. Clitoris.
> The searing crystals.
>
> Wicked. Stylish. True
>
>> stars
>> of sensation
>
> flicker all night between
> meanings. (*E*, 26–27)

Or, Armantrout's swerve (as in "Dusk," the concluding poem in *The Invention of Hunger,* 1979) can be away from the implicit and often habitual correspondence of self to nature:

> spider on the cold expanse
> of glass, three stories high
> rests intently
> and so purely alone.
>
> I'm not like that!

In *Precedence* (1985), Armantrout becomes increasingly involved in a critical relationship to the premises of the lyric, critiquing instances "When the particular/becomes romantic" (19), the lines that follow her parody of William Stafford's "Traveling through the Dark." The lyric, perhaps at all times, but certainly in our time, has a history of abuse, danger, and habit—perhaps typified by the bloated self-dramatization in Stafford's poem (and his ponderous and manipulative evocation of the scene of wonder). Armantrout, increasingly, draws tension, attention, and depth from her critique of the lyric (while, interestingly, remaining within a lyrical praxis). For example, "Round" begins by asking, "Do the children want a face drawn on everything?" (41). The lyric too often does become a neat vehicle for an act of comparison, an act of anthropomorphizing that, post-Emerson, has a habitual and reductive quality to it, adhering all too readily to the tenets established by Emerson in the language section of "Nature": "Nature is the symbol of spirit. . . . The use of natural history is to give us aid in supernatural history; the use of the outer creation, to give us language for the beings and changes of the inward creation."[21] One danger of the lyric formulaic is to rob the external world of its radical otherness by turning it into an Emersonian code book of the spirit world or into a mere vehicle for revealing the speaker's (professed) epiphanic state.

As Armantrout observes in "Another Tongue" (*P*, 34), "Coercion lets us understand what a thing means." *We* coerce those meanings into being—by our steady capitulation to given (and inadequately questioned) modes and protocols of meaning-making. And, "Early learning brackets/ the notorious product" (*P*, 37). Or, as we learn in the very first page of *writing the plot about sets:* "But here's the joke: syntactic space predates and dominates these words."

Obliquity. That kind of swerving? As mathematical, at an angle. A reticence, an ethical reticence, perhaps as with Oppen, in the pursuit of a kind of integrity, a clarity, a clarifying that bears a relationship to truthfulness, though Armantrout, unlike Oppen, does not proclaim it so. Though by now, even in Armantrout's mode of lyrical reticence, we can begin to notice how many of her sentences are, in fact, declarations. In a discussion of Bob Perelman's "China," she suggests about simple declarations, "There is a pathos in the contrast between these minimalist statements and the missing totality of the world."[22]

Armantrout's poetry is often characterized as less overtly "political" than the writings of her Bay Area language poet peers. But such a characterization fails to grasp the inherently political nature of her calculated subversion of comfortable and comforting assumptions. In "Irony and Postmodern Poetry," Armantrout responds to the critique of irony as politically paralyzing—the claim (by Fredric Jameson and others) being that an ironic perspective delights in "pointing to problems instead of imagining solutions." Armantrout's view "is that it's probably elitist as well as unrealistic to think art can point out solutions. Art is the play of resonance and dissonance. To the extent that it can foreground social dissonances, it can serve a political end by increasing people's discomfort."[23]

"Until I see a beauty/in disinterest, in digression!" (*P*, 40). But in the role of poet-juggler, be sure to decenter the juggler, for it is what is juggled not the juggler that is of import. Find that disinterest that is of interest to us.

Armantrout's lyricism may, at times, become a mobile of critiqued observations, as in "Postcards":

Man in
the eye clinic
rubbing his
eye—

too convincing. Like
memory.

My parents' neighbors' house,
backlit,
at the end of their street. (*P*, 12)

It is this teasing relationship to consecutiveness, to relatedness, that constitutes the humor and the ethics of such lyricism. Like the man in the eye/I clinic, Armantrout's poems ask us to join her in rubbing our eyes/I's so that we might disentangle our seeing and our self-construction from merely habitual and unselfconscious activity.

Or, Armantrout may offer us attention to being on edge, as in the beginning of "Single Most":

Leaves fritter.

Teased edges.

It's vacillation that pleases.

Who answers for
the 'whole being?'

This is
only the firing (*P*, 13)

Only the firing of what? What follows (after a section division, an asterisk, or a division sign): "Daffy runs across/the synapses, hooting/in mock terror." The poem's drama—of the subgenre analytic lyric—centers on the synaptic crossing, in the teased relationship at the intersection of sense-making, connectedness, relationship, and difference.

For such a poetics, the poem "Admission" tells the primal story of the analytic lyric as the story of the eye/I thinking:

The eye roves
back and forth, as
indictment catches up?

If shadows tattoo
the bare shelf,
they enter by comparison?

A child's turntable fastened
to the wall with a white cord
will not?

Unless on its
metal core
an unspeakable radiance . . .

Think in order
to recall
what the striking thing

resembles.
(So impotently
loved the world (*P*, 20)

Yes, think. But think *in order*? And *in order to recall*? And think only to-
ward resemblance? Such sense-making and ordering may be an impotent
love in light of that core of unspeakable radiance.

In "Feminist Poetics and the Meaning of Clarity," Armantrout contrasts
the poetry of Lyn Hejinian and Lorine Niedecker to Sharon Olds's po-
etry. Armantrout critiques Olds for keeping "her imagistic ducks in a
row" and writing poems that employ "a totalizing metaphor."[24] Ar-
mantrout has little patience with Olds's tendency to create "an impres-
sion of order and clarity by repressing any consciousness of dissent."
What's at issue here is what we mean (and desire) by clarity. In Ar-
mantrout's reading of Olds's poetry, "only information tailored to the
controlling code is admissible; no second thoughts or outside voices are
allowed." The issue here is not simply an evaluation of Olds's poetry. Ar-
mantrout writes toward a fundamental redefinition of clarity and read-
ability: "Whether such a poem [as Olds's] is clear depends upon what
one means by clarity" (290).

Armantrout prefers a different mode of order: in the poetry of Hejinian
and Niedecker, she locates "a polyphonic inner experience and an un-
bounded outer world" (290). Her readings allow her to identify an impor-
tant alternative version of clarity,

> but clarity need not be equivalent to readability. How readable is the world?
> There is another kind of clarity that doesn't have to do with control but
> with attention, one in which the sensorium of the world can enter as it pres-
> ents itself.
>
> Am I valorizing a long-enforced feminine passivity here? I think not.
> Writing is never passive. Hejinian's and Niedecker's poetry is subversive.

Their poems are dynamic, contrapuntal systems in which conflicting forces and voices (inner and outer) are allowed to work. (290)

The particular mode of clarity that Armantrout's poetry embodies (as she notes in "Cheshire Poetics") depends upon "an equal counterweight of assertion and doubt."[25] If such clarity is called "ironic," then we should keep in mind Armantrout's version of that concept: "Irony, in its broadest sense, marks the consciousness of dissonance."[26] While her poetry is insistently precise, it is a precision, as we have seen, determined to swerve. As Armantrout explains in "Cheshire Poetics," "I wanted my Imagism and my slither, too. My precision and my doubleness." This insistence on at least doubleness (if not on multiplicity or polyphony) lies at the heart of Armantrout's version of clarity. Her intensification—an inseparable quality of a brief, lyric poetry—leads to an idiosyncratic clarity and precision that refuse and avoid singularity.

Armantrout has assiduously avoided what George Oppen (in "Of Being Numerous") refers to as "the shipwreck / Of the singular."[27] Or, in her own succinct and deflatingly declarative mode, she evades what she refers to in "Necromance" as the "Morbid / glamour of the singular" (N, 7). In "Necromance," one sees an analogy to the sequestered clarity of the singular as "Couples lounge / in slim fenced yards / beside the roar / of a freeway" (N, 8). Armantrout's poetry shows us that any "true"—or truly "clear"—picture must honor the juxtaposition of the fenced yard and the freeway.

*

In "Feminist Poetics and the Meaning of Clarity," Armantrout directs our attention to Hejinian's essay "Strangeness," particularly Hejinian's consideration of metonymy. Hejinian's analysis of metonymy (and how it differs from metaphor) offers an especially valuable perspective on a juxtapositional poetics that provides a foundation for Armantrout's own poetry as well. As Hejinian explains,

> Metonymy moves attention from thing to thing; its principle is combination rather than selection. Compared to metaphor, which depends on code, metonym preserves context, foregrounds interrelationship. And again in comparison to metaphor, which is based on similarity and in which meanings are conserved and transferred from one thing to something like it, the metonymic world is unstable. . . . Metonymic thinking moves more rapidly and less predictably than metaphors permit—but the metonym is not metaphor's opposite. Metonymy moves restlessly, through an associative network in which the associations are compressed rather than elaborated. (147)[28]

In Armantrout's poetry, metonymic thinking points toward the simultaneously readable and unreadable nature of the world. Her unexpected swerves and juxtapositions—what Hejinian refers to as metonymy's moving attention from thing to thing—place us within a perceptual environment where connections and disconnections become the object of our attention. Hejinian cites Jakobson's observation that "a connection once created becomes an object in its own right" and claims that "a metonym is a condensation of its context" (147). The specific context of an Armantrout poem remains irreducibly multiple (or polyphonic) and stands, implicitly, as a rebuke of a more prevalent poetics (practiced by Olds and many others) that organizes perception around a monological metaphor or theme.

•

If, then, Rae's ways of swerving often mark disconcerting shifts in direction "about," a significant but not self-glorifying turn, not exactly one perception leading directly to another but one perception placing one somewhat askew in relation to the next, so that one becomes aware of being both engaged (perhaps "alerted") and a bit decentered. Then, as in *Necromance* (1991), one might, as in "The Garden," move through a garden or gallery of shifting (and humorous, though also culturally contrived) perceptions:

> Oleander: coral
> from lipstick ads in the 50's.
>
> Fruit of the tree of *such* knowledge.
>
> To "smack"
> (thin air)
> meaning kiss or hit.
>
> It appears
> in the guise of outworn usages
> because we are bad?
>
> Big masculine threat,
> insinuating and slangy. (*N*, 11)

Within such a mobile of perceptions—at once phenomenological and cultural—Armantrout runs the hazards of either a cool ironizing (as "we" are the ones able to note the crude cultural manipulations that surround us) or a flat detachment. Within such a process of swerving notation, Armantrout's distinctive humor leavens both the irony and the disinterest:

> Buoyant continuum: a lapping made of chatter about
> who controls the ranch. Possession flickers back
> and forth, filling the room like breathing. Simile
> and alibi. If human limbs *entwine,* the morning
> glory *embraces* the fence. (Can we still drain the
> energy in sex repression off landscape?) (N, 13)

So that the swerve becomes Armantrout's tweaking of the clichéd (and often italicized) phrase, the reimagining of the italicized phrase that has become a mere cultural counter: "In a dream language, the *troubled region* has returned as a showgirl with masses of fruit on her head" (N, 16). Thus the humor comes from noticing precisely how (often subliminally, though sometimes quite frontally) "we" have been targeted: "Photos of light-houses/line the walls/of banks" (N, 28). How carefully did someone plan, at a bank, to reassure us with such photos steeped in nostalgia but also of beacons that light up to warn us and save us? One might say (to oneself, or to a few others in a poem), with a barely detectable smile, "Traffic/in surplus meaning/quite heavy of late" (N, 27). In fact, the media and mediated culture we live in are increasingly about this process of aggregate self-monitoring: "Now the news is of polls which measure our reactions to duplicity" (N, 21). Thus, as she notes in "Cheshire Poetics," where she cites "A Story" (in *Made to Seem*) as a particular example, Armantrout's poems often "parody and undermine some voice of social control."

Odd, then, is it, to have a lyricism—of focus, of scope, for what else can we call a poetry of intensifying brevities, paired so insistently with a flatness of affect and a flatness of statement? Perhaps Armantrout's reticence occurs as it does so as *not* to interfere with our attention to something other than her *craft.* So many lyricisms run the opposite risk: they turn the poem into an occasion (merely?) for our attention and attunement with the poet's craft-on-display. In Armantrout's deliberate reticence, I detect (at a remove) an *ethics* of writing (perhaps akin to Oppen's quest for clarity). And yet that reticence and flatness are hardly unselfconscious productions: "Empty likeness/as the perfect tease:/her 'mysterious smile'/which he must recognize/quickly" (N, 23).

Such reticence, such a finely tuned swerving away from the too easy automatic mode of comparison, serves Armantrout best in her carefully drawn attention to the natural world:

Twigs stiffen
the fingers.

Love of nature
is a translation.

Secret nodding
in the figurative:

a corroboration
which is taken for
"companion."

A saw warbles,
somewhere,
and the yards too
are terraced. (*N*, 24)

"Nature," then, becomes one site to trace the entry into language of figuration and comparison. But we are far away from some Emersonian faith in correspondence. The two worlds, human and natural, both bleed into one another and resist any sort of mutual incorporation. Thus, the saw *warbles*, and the yards are *terraced*. Especially when the "natural" too readily suggests some human quality, Armantrout quickly reasserts the autonomy, the distance, and the strangeness of that other world:

Beauty appeals

　　　　　　like a cry

for help

　　　　　　that's distant

or inhuman

　　　　　　so foreclosed. (*N*, 26)

This insistence on the primacy of distance and autonomy remains throughout Armantrout's poetry, beginning with such early poems as "View" with its concluding exclamation, "The Moon//none of our doing!" (*E*, 25).

Armantrout, though, unlike Robinson Jeffers or W. S. Merwin, does not fetishize that autonomy, nor does she turn that distance from human modes of meaning-making into some fortune-cookie formulaic for wisdom. Instead of Jeffers's masculinist heroics of tough, existential inhumanism, Armantrout's declared affinity, with a quiet humor of recognition, may be a linguistically impersonal oddity: "The 'you'/in the heart of/molecule and ridicule" (*N*, 39). Her ethic, then, is one of clarifying notation, of proper perspective:

Perspective is a can of worms
but nausea defends us
against distraction

as a bird noise seethes
from everywhere at once
unlike the human

fugue where each note
is compensatory,
ringing "true." (*N*, 31)

Most of what "we" call "true" proves to be, upon further scrutiny, as Armantrout notes, "compensatory" and self-serving. With Armantrout, we may take pleasure in a world of perspective where nothing is required or expected to ring "true."

One particularly productive tension at work (and play) in Armantrout's poetry is between an infinite variability of relationship and an utterly finite act of willful placement (which establishes or declares or notices a certain relatedness). On the one hand: "On conditions/so numerous/nothing can begin" (*N*, 48). On the other hand: "Place things/in relation/when I want them/permanent" (*N*, 27).

In *Made to Seem* (1995), Armantrout's humor is a bit more pronounced. Why not explore how what we see/know is *made* to seem? If we are within the circle of shared analysis, then we share in the humor of unraveling the codes and constructions of order-making:

The sky darkened
then. It seemed
like the wrong end
of a weak simile.
That was what shocked us.
None of our cries
had been heard,
but his was.
When something has happened
once, you might say
it's happened, "once and
for all." That's what
symbols mean

and why they're used
to cover up envy. (*M, 36*)

Such an analytic lyric involves more than merely unmasking the plots of others. One may, midway in the deed, critique the lyrical pathway one is in the process of making:

Leaf still
fibrillating on the vine;

watch it closely
for a minute

as if listening
to a liar. (*M, 38*)

The lie may stem from the habitual associations with the too readily symbolic, organic leaf. The swerve is a humorous one, ethical as well, as one withdraws from the heartfelt verbiage of "fibrillating," that *fib*-word itself marking the space of a (possibly inadvertent) liar. In part, then, it is an ethics of self-correction, an analytic lyric marking out what is possible or plausible once the suspected contaminants are identified:

It's strange to see traffic backed up at this checkpoint—people scattering—heading for the hills or darting across the freeway toward the beach. There are words connected with this scene. "Aliens" is one. If I can avoid these words, what remains should be my experience. (*M, 45*)

Perhaps the space of attention becomes lyricized by means of an activating desire for clarity. At times, I have referred to such desire in Armantrout's poetry as involving reticence and a muted ethical imperative, so that we might see with something approaching accuracy:

Evenly spaced
on the heavenly floor,

those hairy stalks
do not object

to duplicating
one another's work.

This is creation's
diligence

in which we
stand apart. (*M*, 50)

If Armantrout's poetry explores "our place," it is a placement that stands apart from hieratic poetic impulses of self-aggrandizement. Where we are is in a world of highly particularized making:

Cellophane grass and
foil eggs.
                    The modesty

of standard presentation
does remind me of home
sickness. (*M*, 57)

It is a world in which the line break between "home" and "sickness" is all to the point. It is a world, too, of placements and turns, the swerves of the line breaks, that revivify our attention to the colloquial:

With waves
shine slides over
shine like skin's
what sections
same from same. (*M*, 58)

As in the best of Creeley's poetry, the tension between the order of the sentence and the line break puts us in an anti-Evelyn Wood mode of reading, a slowed lyrical reading that invokes an awareness of our decision-making as we place what-with-what, fashioning and refashioning the modes of order available to us in these particular word arrays. To Armantrout's credit, that perspectival pedagogy occurs with considerable (if muted) humor and tenderness:

"Well, look who missed
the fleeting moment,"

Green Giant gloats
over dazed children.

If to transpose
is to know,

we can cover our losses.

But only
If talking,

Formerly food,

Now meant
Not now

So recovery
Ran rings.

. If to traverse
is to envelop,

I am held
and sung to sleep. (*M*, 12)

Sung to and held in a word-world of precise declarations, "if to transpose/ is to know," it is time to take inventory of the particular traversings and en- velopings in Rae Armantrout's poetry. To invent along such lines would be to tell anew how such is made to seem.

·

Armantrout's poetry—in part through the idiosyncratic swerves that I have been examining—achieves an arresting mixture of clarity, audacity, sur- prise, and enigma. In a recent poem, "The Plan" (printed in this volume), each section of the poem has its own quick form of double-faceted self-en- gagement. From its audacious beginning— "'Who told you/you were visi- ble?'//God said,//meaning naked/or powerless"—the nature of the visible, the summoning into visibility, and the self-awareness of being visible ap- pear in a Genesis story set in motion by a question rather than a command. In the poem's second section, our planned meeting with the divine gets couched in the language of an assignation. Our considerations— "how we'd address each other,//how we'd stand/or kneel"—become at once rev- erential and comical. Appropriately, "our intentions/are different//from our bodies,/something extra,//though transparent/like a negligee." In a poem that begins with the shock of visibility, we soon enter the realm of transparency, where our intentions—like a filmy negligee—are, perhaps enticingly, seen through.

That is the complex site of many of Armantrout's best poems: intensi- fied vision that takes us along a moebius strip of, if not its undoing, then its endless circulation. As Bob Perelman aptly generalizes, "Rae Armantrout's poems rely tenaciously on the intelligibility of language, though the world is finally no more lucid for all that."[29] While Armantrout's language is often simple and intelligible, her vision is not susceptible to simplification. It is a poetry that is aptly and precisely enigmatic.

In "Cheshire Poetics," Armantrout asks how we define what we mean by radical poetries. She suggests, "Perhaps by how much is put at risk in the text, how far the arc of implication can reach and still *seem* apt." In "The Plan," that arc of implication—which has already involved a complex tracking of human visibility being questioned by the divine—ends in a remarkable simile:

> Like a lariat made of scalloped bricks
>
> circling a patch
> of grass

It is an arresting image—perhaps as clear a picture as is possible for the quasi-closure (deliberately without any ending punctuation) of a lyric poem—an enigmatic closure that, in keeping with Armantrout's sensibility, registers equally resonances and dissonances. The lariat—literally, *la reata* (Spanish for "the rope")—is, oddly, made of scalloped bricks. Perhaps most lyric poems are a thrown lasso—or, as most dictionaries tell it, a rope used for tethering grazing horses. Is the human story of the divine—that negligeelike filmy tale of self-dignifying encounter—not also a lasso? Or, is the divine question hurled from an invisible realm back upon the exposed, visible mortal not also a circumscribing gesture? And the poem of its telling plays out just enough rope to seem apt, and to remain taut. Armantrout's poems give us that encircled patch of grass (as she concludes in "Cheshire Poetics") "held together in the ghost embrace of assonance and consonance, in the echoed and echoing body of language."

NOTES

1. Ezra Pound, *Selected Letters, 1907–41* (New York: New Directions), 11.

2. Ezra Pound, "A Retrospect," qtd. in Hugh Kenner, *The Pound Era* (Berkeley: University of California Press, 1971), 178.

3. Emily Dickinson, poem 986. In *Final Harvest,* ed. Thomas Johnson (New York: Little Brown, 1961), 229.

4. See "The Lyric Valuables: Soundings, Questions, and Examples," *Modern Language Studies* 27(2) (Spring 1997): 25–50; and "'Vatic Scat': Jazz and the Poetry of Robert Creeley and Nathaniel Mackey," *River City: A Journal of Contemporary Culture* 17(2) (Summer 1997): 100–08.

5. Included in unpublished Oppen manuscripts, included in the George Oppen Archive, housed in The Archive for New Poetry at Mandeville Special Collections at the University of California at San Diego library, edited by Stephen Cope. This passage Cope locates as 16:19:1:2; his marking system refers to the Archive, Box, Folder, and Leaf numbers of the given page.

6. The passage is from "Scraptures: 7th Sequence" [1967], in bpNichol, *gIFTS: The Martyrology Book[s] 7&* (Toronto: Coach House, 1990).

7. See Louis Zukofsky, *ALL: The Collected Short Poems, 1923–1964* (New York: Norton, 1971), particularly "Songs of Degrees" (151–59) and "The Translation" (235–40); see also *"A"* (Berkeley: University of California Press, 1978), particularly *"A"-19* (408–34).

8. The specific examples cited come from Theodore Enslin, "Autumnal Rime," *Talisman: A Journal of Contemporary Poetry and Poetics* 12 (Spring 1994, The Theodore Enslin Issue): 37; and John Taggart, "The Rothko Chapel Poem," in *Loop* (Los Angeles: Sun & Moon Press, 1991), 150. While Enslin's earlier work is also highly musical in nature, the particular mode of gradual change that I'm highlighting is more readily visible/audible in later works such as "Scripturals" (December 4, 1993–February 7, 1994) published in *First Intensity,* issues 5, 6, 7, and 8; "Autumnal Rime," *Talisman* 12 (Spring 1994): 37–69; "Propositions for John Taggart," *tel-let* 57 (1996); and "Mad Songs," Backwoods Broadsides Chaplet Series, No. 6 (1995). Additional examples in Taggart's *Loop* include "See What Love" (17–21), "In True Night" (57–59), "Were You" (99–102), "Repetition" (113–23), "The Rothko Chapel Poem" (137–71), and "Marvin Gaye Suite" (216–24). There are many other examples in Taggart's forthcoming *Crosses* (Sun & Moon, 2002?), especially "What She Heard" and Taggart's extended discussion in "Jesus' Blood: Notes & Overlays" (a meditation on Gavin Bryars' "Jesus' Blood Never Failed Me Yet"). See also John Taggart's *Dehiscence* (Milwaukee: Membrane Press, 1983).

9. Larry Eigner, "Letter for Duncan," in *Selected Poems* (Berkeley: Oyez, 1972), 60.

10. John Ashbery, "Grand Galop," in *Self-Portrait in a Convex Mirror* (New York: Penguin, 1976), 20.

11. John Ashbery, *Can You Hear, Bird* (New York: Farrar, Straus & Giroux, 1995), 3.

12. John Cage, *Composition in Retrospect* (Cambridge, Mass.: Exact Change, 1993), 22.

13. Armantrout's Chax book is unpaginated. With twelve pages of actual text, the passages are easily located. In subsequent citations to Armantrout's various poetry, *E=Extremities; I=The Invention of Hunger; P=Precedence; N=Necromance; M=Made to Seem.*

14. Unpublished manuscript, UCSD, edited by Stephen Cope, 16:19:3:29.

15. Much of Bob Perelman's poetry is pertinent to such in inquiry into the political uses of pronouns. See particularly "Seduced by Analogy" in *To the Reader* (Berkeley: Tuumba Press, 1984) and "We" in *The First World* (Great Barrington, Mass.: The Figures, 1986).

16. Charles Bernstein, "The Klupzy Girl," in *Islets/Irritations* (New York: Jordan Davies, 1983), 47.

17. Lyn Hejinian, *My Life* (Los Angeles: Sun & Moon, 1987), 92.

18. "Mantis," in Zukofsky, *ALL,* 73.

19. Email, Rae Armantrout to Hank Lazer, September 20, 1998. I'm grateful to Rae Armantrout for her helpful critique of my initial reading of "Paradise."

20. William Carlos Williams, *The Collected Poems of William Carlos Williams, Volume 1: 1909–1939,* ed. A. Walton Litz and Christopher MacGowan (New York: New Directions, 1986), 195–96.

21. "Nature," in *Selections from Ralph Waldo Emerson,* ed. Stephen E. Whicher (Boston: Houghton Mifflin Company, 1960), 31.

22. "Irony and Postmodern Poetry," in *Moving Borders,* ed. Mary Margaret Sloan (Jersey City: Talisman, 1998), 677.

23. Ibid., 675.

24. "Feminist Poetics and the Meaning of Clarity," in *Artifice and Indeterminacy: An Anthology of New Poetics,* ed. Christopher Beach (Tuscaloosa: University of Alabama Press, 1998), 287–96. Armantrout's essay was originally published in *Sagetrieb* 11(3) (1992). All subsequent references are to page numbers in Beach.

25. Throughout this essay, I confine my attention to examples of swerving in Armantrout's poetry. There are many similar instances—particularly of assertion and doubt—to be found in her wonderful autobiographical prose book, *True* (Berkeley: Atelos, 1998). In particular, I refer the reader to the story of Rae's mother's mother (14); the story of Rae being "saved" from landing on a "harrow" (18); and her account of interactions with Denise Levertov during the People's Park demonstrations (61)—all excellent examples of the questioning and self-questioning essential to Rae's swerving.

26. "Irony and Postmodern Poetry," 674.

27. "Of Being Numerous," in George Oppen, *Collected Poems* (New York: New Directions, 1975), 151.

28. "Strangeness," in Beach, *Artifice and Indeterminacy,* 140–54. Hejinian's essay originally appeared in *Poetics Journal* 8 (1989). Subsequent page numbers refer to Beach.

29. *The Marginalization of Poetry: Language Writing and Literary History* (Princeton, N.J.: Princeton University Press, 1996), 136.

BIBLIOGRAPHY

Books by Rae Armantrout

Couverture: Selected Poems (in French). Trans. Denis Dormoy (Asnieres-sur-Oise: Les Cahiers de Royaumont, 1991).
Extremities (Berkeley: The Figures, 1978).
The Invention of Hunger (Berkeley: Tuumba, 1979).
Precedence (Providence: Burning Deck, 1985).
The Pretext (Los Angeles: Sun & Moon, 2000).
Made To Seem (Los Angeles: Sun & Moon, 1995).
Necromance (Los Angeles: Sun & Moon, 1991).
Veil: New and Selected Poems (Middleton: Wesleyan University Press, 2001).
writing the plot about sets (Tucson: Chax, 1998).

Autobiography

True (Berkeley: Atelos, 1998).

Selected Prose

"Feminist Poetics and the Meaning of Clarity." In *Artifice and Indeterminacy: An Anthology of New Poetics,* ed. Christopher Beach (Tuscaloosa: University of Alabama Press, 1998), 287–96.

"Irony and Postmodern Poetry." In *Moving Borders,* ed. Mary Margaret Sloan (Jersey City: Talisman, 1998), 674–79.

"Poetic Silence." In *Writing/Talks,* ed. Bob Perelman (Carbondale: Southern Illinois University Press, 1985), 31–47.

Selected Criticism

Beckett, Tom, and Luigi-Bob Drake, eds. *A Wild Salience: The Poetry of Rae Armantrout* (Cleveland: Burning Press, 1999). Interviews with Rae Armantrout conducted by Tom Beckett and Lyn Hejinian. Essays by Charles Alexander, David Bromige, Robert Creeley, Lydia Davis, Rachel Blau DuPlessis, Jessica Grim, Brenda Hillman, Fanny Howe, Hank Lazer, Aldon Nielsen, Bob Perelman, Kit Robinson, Ron Silliman, Ann Vickery, Bobbie West, and Susan Wheeler.

Howe, Susan. "Armantrout: Extremities." In *The L=A=N=G=U=A=G=E Book,* ed. Bruce Andrews and Charles Bernstein (Carbondale: Southern Illinois University Press, 1984), 208–11.

Leddy, Michael. "See Armantrout for an Alternate View." *Contemporary Literature* 35(4) (Winter 1994): 739–59.

Perelman, Bob. In *The Marginalization of Poetry: Language Writing and Literary History* (Princeton: Princeton University Press, 1996), 21–23, 136–40.

Peterson, Jeffrey. "The Siren Song of the Singular." *Sagetrieb* 12(3) (Winter 1993): 89–104.

Vickery, Ann. "Rae Armantrout." In *Dictionary of Literary Biography: American Poets since WW II*, Vol. 193 (1998): 10–20. Detroit: Gale Research, 1998.

———. "Finding Grace: Modernity and the Ineffable in the Poetry of Rae Armantrout and Fanny Howe." *Revista Canaria de Estudios Ingleses* 37 (1998): 143–63.

MEI-MEI BERSSENBRUGGE

FROM *FOUR YEAR OLD GIRL*

1

The "genotype" is her genetic constitution.

The "phenotype" is the observable expression of the genotype as
    structural and biochemical traits.

Genetic disease is extreme genetic change, against a background of
    normal variability.

Within the conventional unit we call subjectivity due to individual
    particulars, what is happening?

She believes she is herself, which isn't complete madness, it's belief.

The problem is not to turn the subject, the effect of the genes, into an
    entity.

Between her and the displaced gene is another relation, the effect of
    meaning.

The meaning she's conscious of is contingent, a surface of water in an
    uninhabited world, existing as our eyes and ears.

You wouldn't think of her form by thinking about water.

You can go in, if you don't encounter anything.

Though we call heavy sense impressions stress, all impression creates limitation.

I believe opaque inheritance accounts for the limits of her memory.

The mental impulse is a thought and a molecule tied together like sides of a coin.

A girl says sweetly, it's time you begin to look after me, so I may seem lovable to myself.

She's inspired to change the genotype, because the cell's memory outlives the cell.

It's a memory that builds some matter around itself, like time.

2

Feelings of helplessness drove me to fantastic and ridiculous extremes.

Nevertheless, the axis of her helplessness is not the axis I grasp when I consider it a function of inheritance.

Chromatin fails to condense during mitosis.

A fragile site recombines misaligned genes of the repeated sequence.

She seems a little unformed, gauze stretches across her face, eyelids droop.

When excited, she cries like a cat and fully exhibits the "happy puppet" syndrome.

Note short fingers and hypoplastic, painted nails.

Insofar as fate is of real order here, signifying embodiment, the perceived was present in the womb.

A gap or cause presents to any apprehension of attachment.

In her case, there's purity untainted by force or cause, like the life force.

Where, generically, function creates the mother, in this case it won't even explain this area.

She screams at her.

A species survives in the form of a girl asking sweetly.

Nevertheless, survival of the species as whole has meaning.

Each girl is transitory.

. . . .

4

Her skull is large and soft to touch.

The thoracic cavity small, limbs short, deformed and vertebrae flattened.

All the bones are undermineralized.

Bluish light surrounds her.

This theme concerns her status, since she doesn't place her inheritance in a position of subjectivity, but of an object.

Her X-ray teems with energy, but locked outside material.

One creates a mouse model of human disease by disrupting a normal mouse gene in vitro, then injecting the mutated gene into host embryos.

DNA integrated into the mouse genome is expressed and transmitted to progeny.

Like touch, one cell can initiate therapy.

The phenotype, whose main task is to transform everything into secondary, kinetic energy, pleasure, innocence, won't define every subject.

The mother's genotype makes a parallel reality to her reality, now.

She stands over her and screams.

That the exchange is unreal, not imaginary, doesn't prevent the organ from embodying itself.

By transferring functional copies of the gene to her, he can correct the mutant phenotype, lightly touching the bad mother, before.

FROM *KALI*

I

First, the beginning, presupposed as a past, goes to ground like a foundation and doubles itself.

Then, I defy inflection, in having this double outside itself.

It becomes a name, the black of an eye, a person you fear, but it's not yet in the world or fixed in time.

Black means she's unknown by people full of ignorance, since it stands for their ignorance.

Figures on a white teapot in a basin of milk come alive, white dog
   attacking a bear for spectators.

Its dark color is the density, when she substitutes her own gesture, given
   sense by my compliance.

Sense becomes a potential real space, following her like a drift of things.

Vertiginous animality tangles in pleated material of my body.

An animal mother creates a matter double for her.

Its matter is ground, blue to blackness, bare as dread reality.

. . . .

3

Now at night preserves itself as a black bird.

Form is its principle, a trace in dark of a body which couldn't be sensed.

Her being there opens out of her captivity in me, to being like swimming.

Experience of her shifts like a pronoun or originary transcendence and is
   specified through some other thing, surface of emergence (motherhood,
   environment).

"I" means a pronoun for who's speaking, so "I" cannot mean the witch.

The witch relates to "I" as an index, briefly creating the illusion, need
   doesn't exist.

Prayer, undisturbed by clamor, is not dragged in the mud, but entrusted to
   memory.

It goes to the ground and disappears.

When she threw snow at the bird on the road, it never moved.

The pronoun, whiteness, moved downward.

4

She spans a bridge over a human being.

She appears black from a distance, the way sky appears blue, but held in
your hand is colorless like larvae or an element of the voice.

Use crystals to identify this seed element introduced into my body, as if by
genetic index.

Matter becomes a matter of my expression.

A fold in matter relates to the light of memory, the way the fold catches
illumination and varies, according to the light of day.

How does a fold itself determine "thin" and superimposable depth, the
paper fold defining a "minimum" of depth on our scale, as the image
of a pleated fan casts a sense of depth in front of the image of a wall?

The cerebral cortex, gray matter, is a sheet of two-dimensional tissue,
wadded up to fit in the spherical skull.

A room transforms itself into two dimension, into consciousness,
following a line, like the proliferation of the symbol for her dark skin.

We're made to believe she is the thing per se, she is the picture.

. . . .

6

I don't care for this artificial layer any more.

Now my mother is dead and dark as the animal's eyes.

Her symbol, which has neither sound nor thought of sound, is the word
for the thing which I inwardly speak by seeing it, but can't see it and
can't say it.

Her gown glows like crystal.

The light wall lends her refinement and immateriality.

Nevertheless, her expressiveness maintains through a place that's neither
sensible nor the unity of a synthesis, like stains on patterned cloth
around her.

The selvage is sprocketed, strip of film, polka dots, her pupils, setting
point of view.

Love was not a sentiment, because in nature, this pattern had no place.

In me, nothingness utilized the pattern as a mnemonic aid, but a pattern
can change.

FROM *THE RETIRED ARCHITECT*

. . . .

3.

I tried to complete a life circumstance like a building I aspired to, loose in
space on used land.

I made a shape against sky on flat land like a cut in the weeds, but I got
bored and didn't finish.

Concrete surface needs support, and my illness made calculations
difficult; shadows fell like hinges on erasures.

This site is riddled with plastic wood paneling, plastic ducks and
discarded coach lamps.

The iconography doesn't ethically correspond to its present eroded state.

I make something, which as it changes and falls apart, offers no clues to
itself before.

Small daisies grow in the cut, preserving the shape.

Physical significance becomes an area lacking objects, a surface as limit,
like the changing surface and mass of a lake.

Nothing was completed, but there are a lot of sketches.

Actually, I designed two bungalows; the gold leaf, and one later, because I
had missed something.

The Gilding was pure decoration, irrelevant to private space.

Now, when my work expresses loss or failure, I no longer say, get rid of
that.

POETIC STATEMENT

By Correspondence

Preparatory Notes

As a statement about my poetics, I thought to offer my preparatory notes for each of the poems included in this collection.

Notes for FOUR YEAR OLD GIRL

A poem about changing my inheritance, genetic and psychological, which relates to changing my fate.

Reconstituting the self, consolidating the central mass of self, the integration and disintegration of the mass.

The emotion is the hopelessness and guilt of illness, of passing on illness and screaming.

Loving someone and keeping the self, what the self is in the face of what destroys its power. Can the poem move to constituting self in the presence of an opposing, intimate force?

Using the concept that emotions are abstract to oppose the concreteness of changing your heredity. It's not symbolic, but material. There's a tension between genetics and Buddhist formlessness.

The poem's movement is from self to other, how to reconstitute self with respect to a daughter, or move a daughter outside concrete timelessness. Using photographs of myself, my daughter, and congenitally ill children for images.

I thought about writing as a ribbon of the heart untying.

The fragment is the same as the whole. Genetics determines my form, which is how I get to spirit.

Notes for KALI

Dark came out of my left side and the dragon came out of the right side of my belly. They balanced each other. The dark side wanted to shed its outer layer.

The goal is to illuminate the source of poetry and illness, to light the witch. The complexity is one's ability to take an impossible situation and compensate for it. The image is, what a symbol is.

It's still about body and language, but at the symbolic level. The content is not transcendence, but concretion of the informed substance of language, trying to rely less on metaphor, sound, or image.

Narrative opposes transcendence.

The feeling is to keep the energy and experience of the poem as intense as my stomach turning over, seeing Count Panza's Rothkos in L.A. How a dark density is implicated by language and generates language, a dark wafer or paper in the abdomen, that is the source of my language.

You could make a poem that would be the function of the symbol, how it separates from what it originally represented, to function on its own, an internalized symbol for the dark origin that is separate from the real origin.

It's mourning, an expression of movement of the grief layers in my abdomen.

NOTES FOR *THE RETIRED ARCHITECT*

To make a structure that is not question or subject dependent.[1]

To make something, a kind of object, that as it changes or falls apart or increases in its parts offers no clue as to what its state or form of nature was at any previous time.

Different ways of applying paint so the language becomes somewhat unclear. If you do everything from one position, with consistency, then everything can be referred to that. You understand the deviation from the point to which everything refers. But if you don't have a point to which these things refer, then you get a different situation, which is unclear.

The area was defined as a vacuum situated in the center of the town, but separated from it as an unknown terrain consisting of sidings, railway sheds, warehouse allotments, and patches of ground where nature had taken over.

Communication itself that is the fluid, continuous exchange of information had been replaced by an isolated aimless, irrational emergence of unilateral utterances of the will of the building sponsors.

Might this decorative thinking then be the architectonic thinking of the future?

When we have an idea in mind, the territory delimited by the idea is blurred. It fades into something quite open.

There are reasons of course for repeated discontinuity, ignored advice, successive work ignored, misrepresented, disqualified, and often debased.

It's hard to make a good building program when status has a style.

By Correspondence

Over the course of a few weeks in March and April 2000, Berssenbrugge responded to a series of written questions about writing plays, her collaborations with visual artists and theater companies, the importance of her Chinese heritage, the apparent change in her style with *Empathy,* and her compositional method.—Linda Voris

LETTER ONE

Plays, as well as dance collaborations and artist's books were all ways to take a break from solitary writing.

My first play, *One, Two Cups,* the most literary, was directed by Frank Chin, who was seminal for Asian-American theatre and awareness. It was an imaginary dialog with his wife Kathleen Chang, a performance artist who was the only person I'd ever known who came from the same place as myself. So, in these ways, it was collaborative. In 1996, she burned herself alive as a protest for peace.

The collaborative space is larger and more fertile for me than writing alone. There are concrete problems to solve and these become an experimental ground for formal developments. I make a space out of many conversations with my collaborator from which I can then respond.

The play *Kindness* (1994) was animistic, a collaboration with the artist, my husband Richard Tuttle; the composer, Tan Dun; and Shi Zhen Chen, the great singer and director who recently brought *Peony Pavilion* to Lincoln Center from China. *Hiddenness* (1987) with Richard Tuttle and *Endocrinology* (1997) with Kiki Smith were artist's books that turned into lasting dialogues. All were subordinate to writing poems.

LETTER TWO

Friends suggested my work to Richard because of our similar temperaments. He'd been asked to participate in a series of artist-writer collaborations published by the Whitney Museum Library Fellows. He'd been looking for a poet for some time, but was unaware of the poetry published by small presses. We started with long conversations, walking, eating, going to the Metropolitan Museum, Shalako at Zuni. He went to China, etc.

He gave me sketches, which were abstract. I used them as the ground or medium for a preliminary poem that incorporated notes from our conversations. I adjusted the poem as the book developed formally. I participated in the dialog of production, a detailed and logistically difficult process, because there were so many people involved.

The breakthrough came in the layout of text. This involved placing stanzas on the page in a floating space, not within regular page margins. Opening the space of the page, even across the gutter, had the effect of making light pour out, which also happened in the paper making. The incised plane of letterpress printing and the float of the color of the hand-stamping resulted in an "illuminated" manuscript, with lights combined. There's an indigo blue cover, which I realize now is like night. It's wonderful to have real light pour out when you open a book.

LETTER THREE

Rena Rosenwasser of Kelsey Street Press asked for a collaboration for her series. When I mentioned Kiki Smith, it happened that she knew her well. Kiki came to New Mexico, where I live, her first trip there, and we started talking. I was intrigued by the pathos of implied narrative in her images and was hoping to learn from her a vital, "sentimental" narrative for my writing.

Kiki, on the other hand, had just ended a love affair and proposed to turn black organs white, inside the body. Asked about the collaborative process, Kiki says, "It was great. Mei-mei asked me questions, and I cried."

LETTER FOUR

Instead of story, Kiki gave me relatively abstract monoprints of endocrine organs. I constructed a poem from our conversations, her work, medical text books, experiences of space in the body and concepts of Western space. The design of the book came fast and casually with scissors, in a café.

She decided on a Nepalese paper that is tough and transparent like skin, showing pages underneath. The blue images, like veins or the color of blue that goes invisible when photographed. Text in strips of typing paper were cut and pasted in the same space as the images, making language the opaque, substantial element.

High standards were set for the production of the artist's book: silkscreen, lithograph, hand-set type by master craftspeople reproduced handwriting, cardboard prints, typewriter, adding the societal layer of the great tradition of U.L.A.E. books. The final book is a rather misty, transitive vessel expressing the continuum between material and immaterial (endocrine molecule, translucency), including death. Then Kelsey Street Press constructed a "facsimile" at a reasonable price. For mysterious reasons, each layer of reproduction added energy, so in many ways Kelsey Street's "cheap" edition is the more vital.

Kiki's strips of text have enabled me to break free from stanzas, ever since.

LETTER FIVE

"Fog" (in *Empathy*, 1997), which predates the artist's books, was produced as the last of a series of productions in the early '80s with the Morita Dance Company, directed by Theodora Yoshikami. This was in conjunction with Basement Workshop, a pioneering Asian-American cultural center in NYC.

Yoshikami proposed each production as a state of water. "Mizu" (water) grew out of a Japanese folktale. "Alakanak Break-up" (ice) from my years in Alaska, a kind of shamanistic compaction. "Fog," from Wittgenstein, as densities between human beings.

My voice reading text was the music, also taiko drummers, a great contrast. The text evolved parallel to choreography, out of discussion and observing rehearsals, and formally, from the pressure of deadlines and that the dancers moved. I learned to treat things (representations), which I was still taking from life, as something physical that could be cut and pasted, using red from a real bowl for red on snow, with no bowl, and so forth. The clarity comes from having been read aloud dozens of times in rehearsal, also having developed as an oral text, close to song. The published texts shed some of the original repetitions.

LETTER SIX

I can answer this more concisely, because of its not being a social process. The influences that contributed to the "more abstract" style of *Empathy* are:

1. Conversations with James Sherry, the founder of Segue Foundation, and through Segue, exposure to Language poets, when they were beginning

and the texts that influenced them, including twentieth-century French philosophy.

2. Increasing involvement with experiencing and thinking about contemporary art: performance, visual, and music, in NYC in the '70s and early '80s.
3. My collaborations with choreographers Theodora Yoshikami and Blondell Cummings and with Richard Tuttle.
4. John Ashbery's "Self-Portrait in a Convex Mirror."

To answer your question about what was continuous with early work, I kept an experiential, physical sense of landscape, personal emotion, commitment to beauty, commitment to the sentence, a Chinese sense of nature-plus-thinking, and a politically based resistance to any given form or authority.

LETTER SEVEN

I like to think about Kathleen Chang, so tomorrow I'll answer. I meant we both came from families of idealists in Beijing, who had been educated in the United States to "reform" China, but were then set adrift by Mao's revolution.

LETTER EIGHT

Having been born in Beijing is central to my work—my first memories, my first language, and my mother. Also, in general, the sense of being from somewhere else. I believe changing my language to English at the age of nine months, experiencing the relativity of language, was formative to my becoming a poet. That no thing is one thing. There's a world and language that I have and that's lost, which could be generalized. Also, innately, a tradition or template for a poetry of nature and philosophy.

Being nonwhite (and half Chinese), marginalized, is an insecure and at the same time a dynamic situation. You have to identify yourself, and there's no set point of view. It gave me access to the wonderful cosmopolitanism of the multicultural movement of the '70s, my first escape from the mainstream. On the other hand, because my mother was from an educated class where poetry was valued, I escaped the sense of marginalization about poetry itself that so many American poets seem to internalize.

I also identify with my mother's and my grandmother's feminism, which seemed immediate to me, perhaps because of matriarchal character that is part of Chinese culture.

Letter Nine

As for compositional method, I can't concentrate, so I think of an idea for a poem and just hold it in mind. I'm thinking a matrix of the idea, emotion, scene. I gather quotes from disparate selected books, cultural criticism, philosophy, Buddhism, and daily life, a few hundred notes. I cut them out and lay them out as a map of the area of the poem on a big table, plus pictures. Then over a few intense days, I write a very rough first draft, which I edit for a long time. At first I appropriated the quotes, but recently they've become more and more transformed. The whole process is very loose, to keep unconscious, and then I clarify later.

Letter Ten

In recent work, I've been reacting against the "beauty" in *Four Year Old Girl* (1998), and I've been trying for "banal narrative." No stanzas. Minor key. Emotion is direct, but deflated, so it seems indirect. The persona seems direct, but is fictional. De-emphasizing sound and structure. The title of the manuscript is *Nest. The Retired Architect* is from this group.

The poem I'm writing now is about hearing separate from hearer, as if spatial, the way compassion can be spatial. Things are going so fast, reading and even hearing seem slow and I want to think about that for a while, about the prevailing mode of the visual image and the effect on poetry. Then, I want to stop writing for as long as I can.

Notes begin on page 90.

A "SENSITIVE EMPIRICISM"

Berssenbrugge's Phenomenological Investigations

Linda Voris

> And just as there are no words for the surface, that is,
> No words to say what it really is, that it is not
> Superficial but a visible core, then there is
> No way out of the problem of pathos vs. experience.
>
> —John Ashbery, from "Self-Portrait in a Convex Mirror"

> I am committed to beauty. I am committed to the sentence.
>
> —Mei-mei Berssenbrugge

DRAMATIZING A bit to get started, one could say that Mei-mei Berssenbrugge's experimental writing begins with her book *Empathy,* published by Station Hill Press in 1989. Looking back over the course of her work beginning with *Fish Souls* and *Summits Move with the Tide,* both published in 1974, one can trace a line of recurrent properties now associated with Berssenbrugge's poetry: delicate, naturalist observation, patience and great tolerance for ambiguity, a reluctance to summarize emotion, and scenic imagination. What *has* changed is Berssenbrugge's style, her invention of a long, capacious line, and this, as they say, has made all the difference in transforming work that might have continued in an expressive, lyrical tradition into an experimental poetics.[2] Each of Berssenbrugge's books since *Empathy—Sphericity* (1993), *Endocrinology* (1997), and *Four Year Old Girl* (1998)—actively, painstakingly interrogates the very linguistic and phenomenological grounds of expressive poetry.

With her expansive, metastatic line, Berssenbrugge has developed a method to strain the boundaries established by perceptual operations and repeated in lyrical conventions. *Empathy* and subsequent collections can be said to question the premises of the poems of the earlier books by interrogating the assumptions of representational poetry, particularly with regard to how the world is positioned to convey affective states metaphorically.

With scientific vigor, Berssenbrugge's books of the last decade explore each of the Kantian principles of perception—time, space, and causality—as these pertain to and partially determine affective life and as aspects in perception of the sublime. Proceeding by means of a "sensitive empiricism," Berssenbrugge continually disrupts narrative and rhetorical representations that simplify experience by insistently tracing the myriad and minute ways in which the phenomenal world enters experience.

In place of expressive lyricism, Berssenbrugge has increasingly allowed molecular and biological models of intracellular communication to inform her interrogative structures. Recent research in biotechnology has focused on complex, intracellular communication such as that of tiny efflux pumps within bacterial cells that eject toxic substances from the cell, or the vectors that convey genes into the nuclei of cells. Like these models for intracellular signaling mechanisms, Berssenbrugge has refined methods by which spatial or temporal perceptions described in the poem operate as metadiscursive signaling mechanisms rather than as conventional metaphoric vehicles.

What this poetics is not is yet another variation on Language poetry or poetic experimentation that stages the nontransparency of language. Berssenbrugge's writing is compositional in method, accreting observations, contingent possibilities, and contradictions that seem to materialize by stretching ever outwards, much like Tatlin's compositions built out from the corners of a room. Yet, unlike so much of contemporary experimental poetry, her poetry is not significantly influenced by Stein. In place of the desire to confound and splinter reference by foregrounding the materiality of language through punning, refractive linguistic surfaces, Berssenbrugge employs a densely layered referentiality in an attempt to explore the linguistic and emotional exchanges involved in phenomenological experience. That is, her interest in the transparency or nontransparency of language is inseparably bound to her investigation of the transparency of utilitarian perceptual habits, in particular the tendency to regard space as merely the location in which events occur. The poem becomes a site in which this transparency of the world can be obstructed and examined, as can be seen in this passage from "The Carmelites":

> Apple trees bloom haphazard in the field around the nunnery.
> The atmosphere in daylight poses questions about passing light more
>   difficult than those
> the ordinary person in nature, for whom the horizon and amount of light
>   define the limits of intensity,
> has long since dissolved into a sense of spaciousness for things to take place.[3]

While avant-garde practices have often combined the demotic with a declamatory tone (Stein claimed that Picasso had the necessary courage to make "art ugly"), Berssenbrugge has had the courage in a modern/postmodern context to write a body of poetry that is beautiful and that engages aesthetic questions. While her work participates in the experimental tradition that seeks to transform poetry into a site of investigation rather than one of lyrical assertion, her poetry bears few traces of popular culture and no aural pyrotechnics. Instead, her long lines create an impersonal, meditative vista that is the verbal equivalent of valuing stillness and silence.

I

Berssenbrugge's first book, *Summits Move with the Tide,* which appeared in 1974, is a collection of short, spare lyrics evoking spirits of place or person in a wide geographical range that includes Greece, New Mexico, Nepal, and New York. Thematically, the poems convey a sense of awe for the natural world and the Romantic wish to find transcendence in nature. When the poems are not quietly ecstatic, they often express equanimity in the face of personal dissolution into the landscape. Reminiscent of the work of Latin American poets such as Mistral and Vallejo, and the Deep Image school of North American poets such as Robert Bly and James Wright influenced by them, these poems assume that heightened affinity to landscape corresponds to greater self-awareness and spirituality.

In the poem "Snow Mountains," Berssenbrugge shifts between material and spiritual realms with Imagist deftness, glimpsing movement in a mountain through a bird's flight:

> A bird flies up from the mountain
> larger than the mountain
> and down
> heart on the mountain
> wings
> two brown glaciers
> of feathers melting[4]

This compression of images (reminiscent of H.D.'s confounding of waves and grasses in "Oread") splits apart in the masterful stagings of reversible metonymic elements of her later work. So also will Berssenbrugge's early assumptions about the unity of physical and spiritual realms and the capacity of the poem to stage Baudelarian correspondences be complicated by a Lacanian scrutiny of "our first misrecognition of unity" in poems such as "The Swan" (*Empathy,* 60). Though Berssenbrugge will later revise her conception of the correspondence between landscapes and internal states in terms predicated upon the coincidences of perception, and on an analysis of desire and narrative structure, the later poetry nonetheless depends upon meticulous observation, her tremendous drive "to look again and then look" (*Empathy,* 61). The relation between the demands and limits of sensory perception and the wish for transcendence that she appears to take for granted in her early work becomes one of the critical areas of interrogation in later work. The Romantic traces we might cite in the elegiac or ecstatic responsiveness to place are destined to become Coleridge's scientific and metaphysical explorations, not Wordsworth's hymns.

To the contemporary reader, these early travel poems annotated with place and year—*Bhauda, Nepal '70*—may be off-putting in their seemingly unreflective catalog of cultural beliefs and practices, where, for example, the speaker adopts the basketweaver's voice in "Hopi Basketweaver Song." The poems from these roving residencies appear to stem from a Whitmanesque naïve belief in the capacity of immersion to bring about knowledge of the other. "I want to already know what the old know," Berssenbrugge writes, then adds, "I want to be the man and the woman/and the child and the elder" (*Summits*, 33). From this poetry in which it was possible for the speaker to assert what she wants directly, Berssenbrugge has developed a method to continually examine the grounds for knowledge, the desire for knowledge, and the means to this end. The poem "March Wind" from this early volume foretells important aspects of her future method:

> We peer with restless focus
> at a drop of pondwater or blood
> something that can only be seen
> in infinite slender sections. (*Summits*, 48)

We find this attentiveness to isolated sections next in an image of striated light in the title poem of *The Heat Bird*, where the speaker seems relieved to discover the indifferent, systemic operations that mark time beyond her personal preoccupations:

> Narrow cracks between the boards cast
> a rain of parallel bright lines across the rafters
> which seemed precise and gay in the ghost town
> They were outside its time, though with each change in sun
> they changed a little in angle and length, systematically
> They were outside the carnage of my collaborative seductions[5]

At this point in Berssenbrugge's work, however, images such as this one that depict an awareness of the sublime are drawn in contrast to the constraints of personal desire, and, as such, develop limited resonance. For the most part, the poems of *The Heat Bird* are not memorable, either as expressive lyrics or as experimental forms in the lyric. The speaker's flatly stated ambition in the opening poem— "Never mind if he calls, the places you get/through inwardness take time"—reminds us that strategies of self-protection can license narcissistic expansiveness (*Heat Bird*, 13). That is, like many of the lyrical volumes written in the 1980s, these poems chart the personal development required to lead the life that in turn makes possible these poems of close observation and self-examination. Patient efforts to withdraw and view the world with an "innocent eye" only implicate the viewer more firmly as the recipient of unique insights: "All this time/she was trying to recede until things would resemble/each other. . . ." (*Heat Bird*, 20).

The poems are most effective when they connect present landscapes, scenes from daily experience lived with village intensity in New Mexico, or descriptions of Spruce Island, with memories of the speaker's grandparents, much like the wandering dog of "Pack Rat Sieve" who crosses boundaries indiscriminately. There "sieve" refers as much to the selective method of the poem, linking seemingly arbitrary scenes, as it does to individual images of the poem, the fascination with junk and the "packrat houses/on an ore heap, sparking with foil" (*Heat Bird,* 25). But perhaps it is the very sievelike selectivity of these poems, the self-reflective tendency to gauge observations against a "longing locus," that narrows their interest and, finally, compares unfavorably to the accretive, compositional method of Berssenbrugge's recent work. Still, these poems stage some of the philosophical desires of the later work, the wish to see formal structures themselves— "This is what I am always trying to do, make/the air into its form" (*Heat Bird*, 14)—or to see the immutable flashing in the mutable:

> Only when you see completely through it can
> a mass of swifts on the far ridge like a sunspot
> or King Lumber smoke become sieved gold from a river
> You see their yellow breasts, then each yellow breast (*Heat Bird,* 14)

Ultimately, however, the intensity and critical implications of these images is derailed by hermetic narrative fragments and by recourse to logic that develops conclusions outside the terms of the poems. For now, the speaker of the poems voices a valid critique that will not be true of the later work— "I too easily give up the meaning of the picture."[6]

II

With the emergence of *Empathy* in 1989 comes a marked change in Berssenbrugge's use of space: formally, in her creation of a discursive space in long poems of long lines, and thematically, in her focus on space as a dimension of human relations mediated by language and the unconscious. Berssenbrugge is one of a generation of poets for whom Ashbery's style was influential, but not absorbing; one thinks of Ann Lauterbach encountering *Three Poems,* finding that a poem could *be that.* Likewise, for Berssenbrugge, one imagines that the encounter with *Self-Portrait in a Convex Mirror* may have illustrated the rewards of permitting the poem to accrue sufficient mass to become self-reflexive, contradictory, ruminative. With hindsight, we can say that on her own terms and in a highly individual manner, Berssenbrugge has articulated the kind of phenomenological investigation that Ashbery dreamed of in *Three Poems:*

> The facts of history have been too well rehearsed (I'm speaking needless to say not of written history but the oral kind that goes on in you without your having to do anything about it) to require further elucidation here. But the other, unrelated happenings that form a kind of sequence of fantastic reflections as they succeed each other at a pace and according to an inner necessity of their own—these, I say, have hardly ever been looked at from a vantage point other than the historian's and an arcane historian's at that. The living aspect of these obscure phenomena has never to my knowledge been examined from a point of view like the painter's: in the round, bathed in a sufficient flow of overhead light, with "all its imperfections on its head" and yet without prejudice of the exaggerations either of the anathematist or the eulogist: quietly, in short, and I hope succinctly.[7]

Empathy is a collection of poems preoccupied with the relation of affect to space. Berssenbrugge may have chosen this pairing because empathy is colloquially construed as a problem or question of space, that is, the distance between persons, or the emotional capacity of a person construed as internal space or receptivity. Now, in place of direct reports of subjective experience, Berssenbrugge is disinclined to use the self or the personal as the measure of experiential effects. Instead, she begins with impressions of the phenomenal world and carefully traces a set of views, or entryways, onto this realm, proceeding with extreme resistance to consolidating forms of emotion and perception. The saturation of the poem in elements of sensory perception implies that the developing ideas proceed from these fragments as they enter into compositional relation. Thematically, this means that one cannot think of empathy except through the imaginative acts that create space and with which space is apprehended. The spatial constellation of this aspect of human relations engages particular formal coordinates, including external and internal boundaries, the sense of limit or of expansiveness, the apprehension of movement or stasis, and the axis of concentration versus distraction.

Often in these poems there is a preliminary impulse to provide a figurative place for the scenes unfolding, an abstraction that may or may not become concrete as the poem proceeds. "Texas," for example, begins:

> I used the table as a reference and just did things from there
> in register, to play a form of feeling out to the end . . .

And in "The Star Field," the constellation of points in the night sky evokes a field that can be imaginatively scanned as surface or entered through the spatial dimensions of planes and passages:

> Placing our emotion on a field, I said, became a nucleus of space,
> defined by a rain of light and indeterminate contours of a landscape,
> like the photograph of an explosion, and gave the travel of your gaze into it,
>   or on me,
> imaginative weight of the passage along a gulf of space
> or a series of aluminum poles. (*Empathy,* 27)

The opening poems of the book recurrently describe a passageway, entrance, or courtyard delimiting a space only to indicate unlimited expanses. In "Chinese Space," for example, a poem that begins with entry into a courtyard, we learn that the architectural design of these visually busy spaces is to saturate the viewer and actively form her experiential expectations.

> First there is the gate from the street, then some flowers inside the wall,
> then the inner, roofed gate. It is a very plain wall, without expressionistic
>   means,
> such as contrasting light on paving stones inside the courtyard to the
>   calligraphed foundation stones.
> My grandfather called this the facade or Baroque experience, rendering a
>   courtyard transparent.
> The eye expecting to confront static space experiences a lavish range of
>   optical events,
> such as crickets in Ming jars, their syncopation like the right, then left, then
>   right progress
> into the house, an experience that cannot be sustained in consciousness,
>   because
> your movement itself binds passing time, more than entering directs it.
>   (*Empathy,* 29)

The saturation of visual/spatial effects described here is a property of Berssenbrugge's new style, and we can take this account of a highly crafted artifice as an analog for her method generally. "There is a craft at work/to reconcile emotion in a purely speculative ambiance," she tells us in "Duration of Water," a poem that uses the image of theater with "hundreds of painted scenes combining and recombining/in order to exaggerate situations of joy or pain on stage" (*Empathy,* 26). Simulating these choreographed effects, Berssenbrugge uses what she has called a "sentence format."[8] Berssenbrugge has explained, "Up to the middle of the *Four Year*

Old Girl, I had been committed to the sentence, an arbitrary commitment. But these sentences were arranged in stanzas. Then around the time of writing the *Four Year Old Girl* title poem and *Endocrinology* (which were written close to one another in time), I found my present format which is: Each sentence is a line. If the sentence is long, then the line runs over, as you can see."[9]

When the line is a sentence the logic of the poems depends more upon incremental, metonymic comparisons and on declarative assertions, rather than on the symbolic substitutions or equations more often associated with metaphor and simile. Berssenbrugge is fully aware that these long lines often exceed a reader's capacity, and in an interview with Laura Moriarty years ago she revealed her intentions: "[U]p until now and even with the *Heat Bird* I've really been trying to create an experience in the reader in which they are changed but they can't reiterate what happened or how it happened. So a long line helps me in doing that because you can't grasp the whole line in your mind."[10]

By elaborating and sustaining a heightened experience of space, Berssenbrugge suggests that the phenomenological world and our imaginative elaboration of it make profound and telling impressions upon us, and that these experiences, in turn, influence states of self, memory, ideation, and the unconscious in subtle ways that do not depend upon our efforts at containment. The description of the Baroque quality of the courtyard in the poem "Chinese Space," like Berssenbrugge's writing method generally, creates sufficient density to delay our entry or passage *through* the poem. She claims that the experiential demands of temporal properties—such as the summation of movement through space into an idea or an experience of duration—prevail over fleeting spatial impressions of entry and passage. We need to know more about these phenomenological events, but to do so requires that we attend to spatial dimensions of experience lest these are diminished by the "binding" forces of unity and continuity that temporality constructs.

In a sense, *Empathy* begins again and again in the multiple entrances to courtyards of the opening poems. There is a visit to Tan Tien, "a park, now," in a poem by that name, and yet another courtyard, this time in a Carmelite monastery, where "Apple trees bloom haphazard in the field around the nunnery" (*Empathy,* 14, 35). The figure of the courtyard circumscribes space, presenting entry as repetition magnified by ritual. As such, the wish for order or controlled presentation is brought to bear against the open-ended nature of composition that admits coincidence, chance, partial views, fragments, stray thoughts. The tension Berssenbrugge explores becomes apparent in the poem "The Margin," in which expanse is associated with the infinite, with indifference to human concerns, and, ultimately, with the sublime, whereas the margin is where perspective gathers and movement appears. In these poems we are immersed in sensual, spatial qualities of heft, depth, limit, shadow, distance, and passage, all the attributes we construe of objects or bounded fields:

> The way a peach-colored
> amaryllis can cut up the space of a room, depending on how he places it in the room, an environment erodes.
> An invisible plane of air is almost undetectable to touch as you walk down into the canyon,
> laden with hue. (*Empathy,* 36)

Berssenbrugge creates a scenic landscape, generally in the present tense or with minimal chronological, in which she can investigate how this sensual panorama is changed by perspective, complicated by affect, and implicated in various abstract questions. In a poem such as "Recitative," the fragmentation of continuity and duration into discrete units allows for an investigation of the formal relation of desire and linguistic structures. In this poem, the voice of someone recounting her experience on the telephone, disembodied and "insistently formal," is crossed with an account of Egypt in the third millenium B.C. where, Berssenbrugge tells us, speech acts were construed as discrete rather than continuous: "speech was spoken like an arrangement of stars,/an orderly procession of luminous beings. . . ." (*Empathy,* 34). This allusion prompts the speaker to think of language in two senses, either as the combination of discrete units or as a flow, and *this,* in turn, leads her to propose that desire is similarly double: "it seemed that love was a spiritual exercise in physical form" (*Empathy,* 34).

With the emphasis on spatial dimension, she recognizes that desire, if it is doubled by representation, might also be separated from the concept of presence, so that desire might not always be linked to expression. In the poem, this insight is accomplished by the diagonal band of light that cuts across the scene of the telephone conversation, splitting it between spaces delineated by light and shadow. "Half their conversation is in shadow, so they speak in and out of a diagonal wedge of light" (*Empathy,* 34). This attention to light creates a formal space, a stage for movement "in and out," which then makes it possible for the speaker to question whether desire need be construed as a matter of presence and absence. To the varied representations of desire, Berssenbrugge adds the imaginative pressures of odd phenomenological experiences rendered abstract, "a standard of grace in the corridor of the day." And, like the courtyards of other poems, the estuary that emerges serves as a formal figure for silence, for attention to the intervals between beats.

> For me, it seemed that love was a spiritual exercise in physical form,
>   and the diagonal was glints off an inferred line of sun lingering, as spring
> synchronized with the double space of her desire and her desire for their
>   presence
> to be hieratic, not wholly expressive, a standard of grace in the corridor of a
>   day,
> with narcissus. If it is through counting that speech is connected to time,
> then crossing an inferred estuary of this conversation is a rest in music.
>   (*Empathy,* 34)

In a way that resists paraphrase, precisely because it is fundamental to the poems, silence is instrumentally connected to the fields or apartments of space. This is evident in the still, quiet renditions of the many courtyards of *Empathy,* and also in Berssenbrugge's repeated use of the camera as analog. In the poem "The Carmelites," the camera serves as a figure for memory or desire construed as a "device," as if empathy were a matter of emotional exposure. We can understand Berssenbrugge's interest in the camera as a device that captures the very compositional elements she has under investigation—time, light, and speed. Here she asks that we hold the lens open longer until we can see the conditions for the event, silence and the immanence of the landscape, that taken together are "the interval/of the exposure" (*Empathy,* 35).

Spatial dimensions of the phenomenological realm may be thought to gesture toward the sublime because these properties are mute; space does not speak its content. The figures of the flowering apple trees, "passing light," and the "stasis of the doorway" serve as potent, luminous emblems of changing capacity—immanence or permanence—precisely because they are not emblems, but aspects of our immersion in the world that we must encounter in order to imagine transcendence or the sublime.[11] And, importantly for Berssenbrugge, these luminous spaces are cavities in which silence might collect.

> Apple trees bloom haphazard in the field around the nunnery.
> The atmosphere in daylight poses questions about passing light more
>   difficult than those
> the ordinary person in nature, for whom the horizon and amount of light
>   define the limits of intensity,
> has long since dissolved into a sense of spaciousness for things to take
>   place.
> As he or she begins to walk among the trees, each tree would be part of a
>   ceiling consisting
> of so many sunk or hollowed out compartments for the silence. For me,
> the blossoms became numerous edges of the volume of each tree, soft, or a
>   missing part

in its openness, the way an exposed nest is upturned that should be
   concealed in leaves,
or your voice that is so emotionally distant. (*Empathy,* 35)

Berssenbrugge associates this "interval/of the exposure" with the sublime
and implies that we can choose this over the expressed of the event. That
is, unlike the space of the courtyard in which we are acted upon, with the
image of the camera Berssenbrugge depicts our response to phenomeno-
logical experience, and to the sublime as an active realm in which we must
choose to see and to compose.

   Now, the sublime is the interval
   of the exposure, the way silence once signified but no longer signifies the
      limits of discourse,
   sabotaging instructive strategies of the film and the garden, in which we are
      audience or the wall.
   Not as in a Chinese garden. (*Empathy,* 35)

Emotionally, or with regard to self-exposure, the implication is that the rep-
resentation of events must not displace the constructed, partial nature of
the event itself. In the poem "Empathy," Berssenbrugge draws this danger as
a contrast between desire represented and displaced in song, and her image
for the contingent, changing aspects of desire— "a time-lapse photograph
of lightning, in proportion/to each moment you are looking" (*Empathy,*
58). Where the representation of desire and self-knowledge is at stake in
Berssenbrugge's marvelous compositional strategies, we find the force of
the book's title:

   In the same way the song must never be allowed to threaten the presentation
      of what takes place in the song,
   so that she may try to develop empathy for what she really wants to happen
      to her,
   instead of desire being the song. (*Empathy,* 58)

Claiming for Berssenbrugge an "anti-representational model of emotion,"
Charles Altieri has traced how the poems of *Empathy* imagine spaces for
intimacy that infinitely complicate the epistemes involved in lyrical repre-
sentation of emotion.

   Like Lacan, Berssenbrugge wants to challenge the essentially visual, pictorial
   ways that we now take as central to imagining closeness with other people.
   For her, the visual confines feelings to an essentially "mystical" mode in
   which we are constantly drawing inferences from particulars. In the place of
   that model she envisions a "conjectural" model of feeling. Conjecture differs
   from interpretation because it is an ongoing process of constant mobile ad-

justments, not a synthetic building of hypotheses by combining sets of signs in accord with received vocabularies for what counts as expressivity. So, with Lacan, she stresses the ways that efforts at representation and self-representation seem to elicit intimacy, but in fact block access to many dimensions of the psyches that might enable intense closeness between people. In fact the ideals of representation are as frustrating as they are seductive. The basic role of representation is to provide a stable object promising to assuage anxieties over what we actually desire and how we want to be understood. But suppose that both our desires and our intelligibility to others cannot be fully realized within such stabilities. If that is so, then we purchase self-confidence at the cost of entering self-protective illusion.[12]

But Berssenbrugge is a careful theoretician, and so she admits that the anti-synthetic impulse that underpins her "conjectural" mode has its limits, namely that we may become stranded in measured intervals, unable to extend and link perceptions together. The very methods we use to establish clarity within intervals, because these depend at least in part on comparing one set of ideas or memories with another, involve us in a series of approximations, for example, "our methods of comparing densities between human beings" (*Empathy*, 48). Therefore, midway through a book that strives for precision and clarity about the relation of affect to space, Berssenbrugge introduces a fog. This apparition is meant to convey "the power to make the space continue beyond the single perception" (*Empathy*, 50) and to suggest the ambiguity that may be necessary for belief states, memory, and intense feeling.

> Beautiful, unrepeatable, fleeting impressions can be
> framed only within the contradicting ambition of her consciousness to
>   acquire impressions and
> to retain her feeling, a way of repeating a dream. (*Empathy*, 42)

The poem "Fog" simultaneously develops two related analogies for the sense of "seeking by feeling," that of the fog and "whirling galaxies" that suspend stars and gases. The fog renders Berssenbrugge's discussion of visuality more subtle still; that is, by staging scenes in which a person is present, but not visible, she introduces the force of belief states that might otherwise be obscured, and recasts the subject of empathy yet again as a matter of "the problem of the appearance of another person" (*Empathy*, 48). Having analyzed the ways in which phenomenological properties and abstractions become objects of thought, Berssenbrugge now addresses the formless nature of the relations between two persons in which boundaries are revealed as arbitrary conventions, and suggests that these might be rendered by vibrant, idiosyncratic associations.

In any serious interaction between them, not knowing your way about
    extends to the essence of
what is between them. What can appear emotional is caused by the
    emission of energy out of her
body, which you feel, but there is also such a thing as "feeling something as
    luminous,"

thinking of him as the color of polished silver or nickel, or a scratch in these
    metals. (*Empathy*, 46)

Berssenbrugge makes evident that articulating a "complex of intervals" depends upon highly subjective, "foggy" in-between states; in practice, focus is the product of movement between intervals and is therefore complicated by amorphous narrative qualities, dream states, the pull of energy, and the stickiness of memory. Quoting Wittgenstein, she begins:

The fog of the way we feel our way into this focus, seeking by feeling, lies in
    the indefiniteness of
the concept of continuing focus, or distance and closeness. (*Empathy*, 48)

The lack of clarity or the dissolution of boundaries may be disarming, but it may also be necessary to animate our experience of spatial and interpersonal expanses in which events can be experienced as real and felt to contain relevant meaning.

Therefore, we appreciate the fog, as the power to make the space continue
    beyond the single
perception, into raw material or youth of the body, like a body of light.
    (*Empathy*, 50)

While in *Empathy* fog provides an extended analog for the wish to dissolve into darkness or the unlimited, in her next two books, *Sphericity* (1993) and *Endocrinology* (1997), Berssenbrugge suggests that flooding the body with light might test the limits of the self, thereby making it possible to apprehend aspects of being and of the sublime. The poems of these collections stage an illuminated view of the interior of the body, of the unseen, biological apparatus that operates systematically and without need of representation. This realm allows Berssenbrugge to pose a nonrepresentational epistemology at the hormonal and cellular level, a complex signaling system continually at work, unobserved and with a bent toward chaos, "a structural need to become disorganized."[13]

Written during her pregnancy, *Sphericity* examines the relation of a person's awareness of the body's interior to her perception of space and time. It is an importantly compositional and collaborative work in which each of the elements in composition—space, surfaces, light, time, frame, sequence, and scale—is evaluated for its contribution to creativity and a sense of "inner voice." The poems are exquisite studies of how two things are related by means of perceptual sequencing, scale, or the imposition of arbitrary frames to determine a third. But the speaker is skeptical of comparison and its conclusions, "[t]he illusion of meaning of the third dimension."[14] Instead, she seems intent on sustaining the moment of apprehension of compositional space just as it is about to be creatively explored or imaginatively filled, and this relational apprehension is one she joins to awareness of the physical spaces of the body.

> Two particles that make a continuum or ideal, in how the space between
>   them relates to a third event,
> as how clouds against a windowpane admit space that continues to a
>   cloud on the mountain,
> a sheath of a space of feeling in material sheaths of her body for a perceived
>   order, depend
> on your having felt the relation. (*Sphericity,* 10)

To explore the spaces around objects and the energy associated with their perception ("the oscillation of spaces/or volumes of energy"), Berssenbrugge distinguishes between "expressive energy, the content of your consciousness," which is bound up with containment, and "symbolic energy," which is a force like light or sound emitted at the boundaries of things and in the body (*Sphericity,* 17). In the poem "Size," she depicts light falling on objects as a figure for "translucency" and for the perceptual stance we might adopt if we began to think of the body as responsive, a body in exchanges with other bodies of space and light.

> Stones were chosen so impact of water on them makes acoustic harmony,
>   the way the song of a bird,
> like light, gains character from what it touches in the world, and who is
>   there to see or hear it.
> Sound refers to a depth of feeling, or exchanges for feeling. Our
>   transparency guarantees the exchange,
> so she connects frequencies during the time she listens as a science or song:
>   the transparent sound
> of water as it strikes a stone, to water in the color of a petal, in skin, and
>   innumerable points
> at the edge of a petal like sound intervals. (*Sphericity,* 15)

"You listen as you know,"[15] Stein wrote, and for Berssenbrugge as well, the pull of content makes its appeal along lines of experience, memory, and knowledge. But these change, transformed by our capacity to realize our abstractions or ideation as further compositional elements: "Emphasizing not only the ground upon which her movement builds, but matter it forms, the idea/of movement is material, also" (*Sphericity*, 25). That is, as much as possible Berssenbrugge attempts a metaphysical experiment of reversing the hierarchy in which consciousness or "state of mind" is the medium that grasps objects, or "states of being." This medium is limited by arbitrary perceptual determinants such as ordinal sequencing, graduated lines of color, size, or magnitude and might be superceded if we could only subject abstractions of our consciousness to the same generative compositional force with which we transform objects.

This we might do, Berssenbrugge suggests in the title poem, if we distinguish operationally between objects as apprehended and these images as they become representations in and of our consciousness. In "Sphericity," this distinction is accomplished through a delicate exchange of repeated images and their symbolic resonance. The horizon, "an apricot seam," "the surface of the earth," and a "one way membrane" are images that might be considered apart from their representation *as* images, as in the phrase "the image of an apricot band of light in my memory" (*Sphericity*, 28). With "sensitive empiricism," Berssenbrugge insists on distinguishing between the realm of apprehension in which objects *qua* objects appear (determined by signature features of our interest) and that of representation in which the "same" images become implicated in the content of consciousness[16]:

On the horizon,
an apricot seam is not the content of a concept of you. Knowing this light, like knowing home,
is not a content, but seeing it is a content of my consciousness. If it's an image, it
can have content, i.e., telling something to me, or if you were telling the content of your dream. (*Sphericity*, 27)

The finished poems of *Sphericity* were illustrated by the artist Richard Tuttle, and, for her part, Berssenbrugge seems to have had in mind the artist's relational use of space and color, "a new language in accidental spaces between objects" (*Sphericity*, 10). In effect, she treats narrative and descriptive elements as equivalent terms rather than representational counters. Tuttle's drawings on facing pages respond to the abstract titles of the poems with a recurrent fernlike shape also suggestive of a cog or reticulated edge that curves and seems to turn as the book progresses. Handwritten notes at the margin beneath the drawings indicate color by name and intensity as though in reference to an artist's color wheel, "Perm Yellow 15%" and "White 85%" (*Sphericity*, 18). Shapes that seem both naturalist and mechanical, together with their coded colors, correspond to the speaker's wish to use color indexically as an equivalence or correspondence that is not a representation or replacement.

> A wren in grapes reminding her of the woman, is how color belongs
>   inseparably to your consciousness of her,
> without being the consciousness. Gold on a wing bears the illusion of the
>   content of a symbolic dimension. (*Sphericity*, 12)

Here beauty emerges as an analytical activity, an integral part of the compositional process, rather than an object of aesthetic study. In Berssenbrugge's next book, *Endocrinology*, her preoccupation with the relation of language and beauty is situated within an emotional axis of the fear of having and the fear of losing. Another collaboration with an artist, this time Kiki Smith, the book is a strikingly original visual and verbal exploration of the interior landscape of the human body. Various organs, including the lungs, kidneys, and fallopian tubes, appear to float in the flat spaces of the dappled blue and tan page. The fenestration of blood vessels and star-shaped cells, pointed with nodes, isolated on the page elicit naturalist or vegetable associations. Berssenbrugge carries over her investigation of light as an agent and analog for transparency, having learned that within the body various chemical reactions actually produce light: "Shortly after phagocytosing material, leucocytes increase their oxygen consumption and chemically produce light" (*Endocrinology*, 8).

But whereas the dissolution of boundaries in previous books was useful to explore intimacy and to understand the correspondence of the self with the world, in this long poem Berssenbrugge seems troubled by the possibility that shared circulation communicates damage and preoccupied with the pressing forces of systemic entropy. "If the mother is diabetic, the fetus becomes her mother's endocrine system./This occurs in all animals whose circulations are linked" (*Endocrinology*, 9). The body, which Berssenbrugge has heretofore quietly relied upon in her phenomenological investigations, appears to have a rich and intense willfulness of its own: "Because she's in a body, it makes decisions" (*Endocrinology*, 6). Emotions are controlled in part by hormonal levels that rise and fall according to the chemical reactions that follow on the release of hormones into intracellular space.

So, the aspect of consciousness that seemed purposeful in *Sphericity*—"Her time is the center of increasing disorder, an arrow in the space" (26)—now seems afloat in interstitial fluid, suspended in intracellular space or in capillary networks. But even within this increasingly defamiliarized realm, Berssenbrugge asserts the illuminating force of concentration, this time by means of imagining a block of light traveling within the body. "She concentrates on manipulating her organs to pull the white square of light precisely into the niche" (*Endocrinology*, 16). These lighted spaces correspond to white squares cut out of the page background on which are printed the lines of the poem, isolated words ("thread," "glory"), or, in places, left conspicuously blank. In this way, Berssenbrugge and Smith have collaborated to signal visually a correspondence between linguistic signification that depends upon space and difference and the communicative spaces of the body across which chemical signaling takes place. But how these systems relate is ultimately left for the reader to decide, and the anxious tone of the poem is somewhat dissipated by the active choices one must make to chart various readings of the text.

III

The poems of Berssenbrugge's most recent book, *Four Year Old Girl* (1999), extend the study of the spatial dimension of sensory experience she began with *Empathy*. Once again, Berssenbrugge investigates the unspoken correspondence between affect and the experience of spatial modalities such as size, contrast, fit, and space emptied and occupied. Here the preoccupation with space that dominates poems in the first section of the book makes particular claims on the operations of memory, and perhaps occasions a spatial model of memory based on parallelism.[17] The unremitting focus on spatial properties allows Berssenbrugge to formulate and advance a question central to *Empathy* as well, namely, how one might allow the self *transience*, although it is to some degree composed by these spatial, sensory encounters, and so also permit a transcendental world. From outset, the first poem "Irises" proposes:

> In a world which transcends the confines of her transient being, she can reach
> and bring existences within the compass of her life, without annulling their transcendence.[18]

These poems express the desire to sustain an enlivening sense of a transient self and to preserve what Berssenbrugge calls the "implied promise" we may locate in the world despite efforts of the mind and poem to contain this abstract force. What are the forms of composition and of memory this desire requires?

The poems of the first section compose a serial study that draws a parallel between the self in its phenomenological exchanges with the world, and the transcendence of the world we may experience as a habit of living with "invisible entities" or the expansiveness associated with the sublime.

> For a still moment, we see the world as implicit promise, something human
>   that leaves the body
> at death
> and goes off on its own. The more wispy the mind, as at the edge of the
>   greenness
> of a dogwood blossom, the more fit to catch sight of such an invisible entity
>   as "parallel,"
> its distinct substance capable of having all mountains thought away and
>   still being around. (*Four,* 12)

Composed generally of four to five sections that can be imagined as freestanding screens or as panels, each joined to the next, the poems repeat and mirror the "same" images in new positions. The poems themselves are obsessed with screens—transparencies, opaqueness, frames, intervals, and spacing. Berssenbrugge presents the "interaction between an ethereal object and an organism," partly as a matter of fit—as though we are significantly primed for visual and spatial experiences because we are constitutive participants—and partly as interactions shaped by forms of representation.

The "wispy mind" emerging in these poems keeps many forms discrete and parallel: the world of appearances, the subjectively experienced world of appearances, and the forms for this experience. This parallelism of the world and the subjective observer is what makes things seem real or not, but it does not dictate the form of the experience. One retains the concept for "parallel" even after experience of a particular instance, such as the horizon line "parallel to" the mountain, fades. As a corollary, Berssenbrugge speculates that a person might be thought to fill or evacuate his or her subjective forms as if these too were stable abstractions like the concept of parallelism. "The music stops. The dancer spills across his form and moves to the edge of the floor in silence" (*Four,* 14).

Because perceptual apprehension and the sense of self are separate and parallel, we can't know the forms for experience a priori. Memory is another of these undecided and unstable visitations, "an experience that needs to be communicated." In a sentence that is exhilarating because it disjoins the "lock and key" pairing of form and content, Berssenbrugge insists on the discrete, parallel existence of each:

> No one can describe the relation between an experience
> that needs to be communicated and the form of that communication. It lies
>   next to its form

separating her, like proximity to death, the way a wild animal automatically
   lies next to its form. (*Four,* 15)

This parallelism comes about in the poems through meticulous attention to
spatial properties of perception and through the repetition of images with
variation. Nestled and shifting vehicle/tenor positions emphasize the eli-
sion possible between referential image and the image used in representa-
tion. For example, the recurrent images of irises in multiple sections of the
poem by that title are first introduced in an image for transparent overlay
and initiate a series of mimetic regressions continued by the recurrence of
the image in subsequent sections:

Her image of you, a transparency on her desire, is like a contact print of
   irises on film.
Their shallow space implies expansion within it of irises and shadows
   against a blue wall. (*Four,* 11)

Here, the compression of the irises as flowers and as an image for trans-
parency creates the space implied by the superimposition of planes. In a
later section of the poem, the iris shadows on a wall convey transparency,
now in an expanded image for the spatial perception of interval:

   The transparency of a leaf against the size it will attain
along any vector of the stem, like iris shadows on a wall, has the fluidity of
   a veil,
not opaque
size, nor relative fluidity, as of a green petal to a crimson petal, a child
   turned wrong inside her. (*Four,* 13)

The oscillation of the "same" image used differently in this and other
poems implies the shifting correspondence between objects of sight, visual
habits, and the ideational and emotional structures that follow on these
habits. The doubling of reference to the object and to its functional or per-
ceptual operations displays the flexibility and imaginative force of these
minute interactions. Through the repetition of images, Berssenburgge sug-
gests the subtle formation of these ways of seeing over time, and, simulta-
neously, imparts the capriciousness of the process. She makes this explicit
in the poem "Pollen":

Pollen condenses to mottled light on the ground. Assuming the sense of an
   activity
links to the frame of its experience, weakness in the framing process makes
   our senses vulnerable. (*Four,* 45)

Through this attention to space, Berssenburgge describes a sensory fold in
which world and person are commensurate in certain attributes—a fold

reminiscent of Merleau-Ponty's concept of "flesh," whereby he gives an account of the reciprocity between the seer and the visible. He first describes this reciprocity as though the body were "a being of two leaves, from one side a thing among things, and otherwise what sees them and touches them," and then corrects his analogy: "There are not in it two leaves or two layers; fundamentally it is neither thing seen only nor seer only, it is Visibility sometimes wandering and sometimes reassembled."[19] This entails narcissistic attention, but also responsive reception, a sense of being regarded as an object in the world: "the vision he exercises, he also undergoes from the things, such that, as many painters have said, I feel myself looked at by the things."[20] This "coiling over of the visible upon the visible" that entails the "generality of the sensible" and the "anonymity" of the self adheres to a sense of location and is generative of facticity—for Merleau-Ponty, it is what makes facts have meaning.

Likewise, for Berssenbrugge, the transcendence of the world does not imply its noncommunication. According to her, the "implicit promise" we may feel from the world comes about because something human has split off and wanders in the world. And, although representation is necessarily implicated in the transmission and comprehension of experience, Berssenbrugge insists (often through the image of proportional spacing of leaves or our odd awareness of the size that the leaves will attain) that the ineffable is not a symbol *for* or *of* something else. Instead, she struggles to make these two lines of experience parallel—the ineffable and the sensuous experience of the world—and to keep them from collapsing together. This is not an easy task because of the practice of reference.

> To formally express ethereal existence, a relation like reference picks out an
>   entity in the world,
> such as her. Tulips bloom, lighthouse of pleats. The feeling there's
>   something ineffable it's like
> to have the person, you can't learn from a sentence about her, is deep or
>   empty. It feels like expectation,
> space of rocks beyond the island, marked by graceful lamps on points of
>   land like a stage set,
> *avoiding the rocks,* your relation to time in the future or to other people,
>   like a budded tree. (Four, 23)

The trick to sustaining both the transient self and the transcendental world seems to be to regard feeling as both apparition and as a way of thinking about appearances, shifting between description (which seeks to make things appear) and enactment (which shows the work performed by these ideas). To this end, Berssenbrugge suggests that we identify precisely what the referent is in representation—meaning or the structure for meaning.

"The dream represents a meaning to me. Then, it's a structure that shelters the meaning" (*Four*, 23).

And so we return to the interplay between structure, matters of fit and location, and to sequences that trigger a cascade of events. This interplay of spatial realization (fit) and sequence makes certain requirements on what we mean by memory. To draw the operations of memory out from an internal structure into the frames of the world, we may need to regard our memories as impersonal "ineffable entities," not so dissimilar for being "ours" than the invisible entities that occupy the world.

Memory, imagined as something more like anticipation, being primed in readiness, rather than a nostalgic, internal narrative, might be useful as a means of bridging the unknown and experiences more familiar. This would be a way of picturing memory without borders and apart from the set of tropes commonly associated with memory: inclusive/exclusive, real/false, layered/singular, narrative/visual, contained/containing. The spatial focus of Berssenbrugge's book opens up further possibilities for conceptualizing memory (and forgetting) that turn on other tropes, most notably, parallelism/interpenetration, the possible and the impossible, and that inherently acknowledge memory as incorporating aspects of representation and loss. Therefore, memory cannot ever operate simply as the recovery from experiences of loss. In her fascination with bioscience, Berssenbrugge traces the gap endemic to memory to the genetic level as the difference always obtaining between genotype and phenotype:

> A child catches hold of this phylogenetic
> experience, where her own experience fails. She fills in gaps in individual
>   truth with historic truth,
> so a lack is not missing. (*Four*, 36)

I want to close this discussion with some brief observations about the title poem, "The Four Year Old Girl," about which one can safely say that nonalignment, the threat involved in the strategy of parallelism, is realized genetically. Reading the book for the first time, one discovers a startling correspondence between poems of the first section, whose ambition is to encompass the sensual experience of spatial dimension, and those of the second section, in which the "infinite expansion" seemingly promised in this enterprise is tragically foreshortened in the account of a person who suffers from symptoms associated with a genetic disorder, including the gradual loss of sight. But, the rather clinical description in "The Four Year Old Girl" is not an invitation for pity, since, in the recounting, the speaker recognizes the limitations iatrogenic to apprehension itself: "In all comprehension, there's an error, forgetting the creativity of material in its nascent form" (*Four*, 56).

But to come back to misalignment. The speaker of the poem carefully begins by noting the difference between genotype and phenotype (between genetic structural instructions and their expression) that obtains because these are not perfect subsets. There is a gap between the two that allows for parallel worlds (within the self and between mother and daughter) captured in the line, "The mother's genotype makes a parallel reality to her reality, now" (*Four*, 54), and that permits error in the ribosomal transcription process: "A fragile site recombines misaligned genes of the repeated sequence" (*Four*, 51).

This is most of section four of the poem:

4

> Her skull is large and soft to the touch. The thoracic cavity small, limbs
>   short, deformed and vertebrae flattened.
> All the bones are undermineralized.
> Bluish light surrounds her.
> This theme concerns her status, since she doesn't place her inheritance in a
>   position of subjectivity, but
>   of an object.
> Her X-ray teems with energy, but locked outside material.
> One creates a mouse model of human disease by disrupting a normal mouse
>   gene in vitro, then
>   injecting the mutated gene into host embryos.
> DNA integrated into the mouse genome is expressed and transmitted to
>   progeny.
> Like touch, one cell can initiate therapy. (*Four*, 54)

Arguably, with the X-ray image we revisit the image of irises on contact print. The poem describes human recombinant therapy, a treatment for congenital growth deficiency and other disorders of enzyme or protein deficiency, whereby synthetic proteins are produced by genes *in vitro* and then administered. Research on *in vivo* gene therapy, the direct transmission of genes into cells of the body, stimulates protein expression by using the body's own physiology. These treatments may replace defective genes with functional ones but does not yet correct the lack or error in the originary instructions, the gene itself. It is impossible to resist the analogy that genetic encoding of bases operates like language, reliant for signification on difference. Indeed, Stanley Cohen and Herb Boyer, who discovered human recombinant DNA in the 1970s, did so in part by treating nucleic sequences as palindromes, which led to their insight to recombine complementary plasmids. This is signification with real physical consequences:

Reducing a parent to the universality of signifier produces serene
    detachment in her, abstract as an
    electron micrograph of protein-deplete human metaphase DNA.
Its materiality is a teletransport of signified protoplasm across lineage or
    time, avid, muscular and
    compact, as if pervasive, attached to her, *in* a particular matriarchy of
    natural disaster, in which the
        luminosity of a fetal sonogram becomes clairvoyant. (*Four,* 57)

In this cellular model of misalignment, memory is impersonal, a language endlessly repeating nucleic sequences. As Berssenburgge comments: "She's inspired to change the genotype, because the cell's memory outlives the cell" (*Four,* 50). Referring back to the paradigm of the earlier poems, the transcendence of the world exceeds the limitations of its appearances to us. Although the stakes are higher, this poem continues the bid for a transient self in a transcendental world—subjectivity that admits the alterity of the world. These are the poem's closing lines:

The love has no quantity or value, but only lasts a length of time, different
    time, across which unfolds her
  singularity without compromising life as a whole. (*Four,* 57)

While I have focused on the operational changes memory undergoes in this collection, in this and other books Berssenbrugge's compositional method transforms the affective and perceptual elements drawn into composition. With *Four Year Old Girl,* Berssenbrugge advances her vision for engagement in both realms, the sensory world and the sublime, by articulating the method of perceptual and compositional equivalence she began in *Empathy* and *Sphericity.* That is, the minute phenomenological determinants of affect, the association of a person with color, or imaginings of the body's interior carefully traced in the earlier books here becomes a fully articulated schema of perceptual movement (including memory and belief states) in a world configured as immanent. Though it will seem a departure to some readers, *Four Year Old Girl* picks up where the last line of *Sphericity* leaves off: "Phenomenology of the space depends on the concrete value of its boundary,/not where she stops, but an opacity from which to extend her presence" (*Sphericity,* 42).

NOTES

1. Notes for "The Retired Architect" were appropriated from Jasper Johns, Donald Judd, Gerhard Mack, Chogyam Trungpa, and Richard Tuttle.

2. There are, of course, multiple entrances to Berssenbrugge's complex and demanding work. I have reviewed the course of her career with respect to the phenomenological investigations her intricate compositional strategies stage; the critical importance of her Chinese heritage, her collaborations with visual artists, her plays and her theater work, including collaborations with the Morita Dance Company, are only a few among many other significant avenues that warrant further discussion.

3. Mei-mei Berssenbrugge, *Empathy* (New York: Station Hill Press, 1989), 35. All subsequent references are to this edition and will appear in the text.

4. Berssenbrugge, *Summits Move with the Tide* (New York: The Greenfield Review Press, 1982), 19. All subsequent references are to this edition and will appear in the text.

5. Berssenbrugge, *The Heat Bird* (Providence: Burning Deck: 1983), 60. All subsequent references are to this edition and will appear in the text.

6. Given space considerations, my discussion of Berssenbrugge's early work omits the books *Random Possession* (1979) and *Packrat Sieve* (1983), some poems of which are reprinted in *The Heat Bird*. The discussion of Berssenbrugge's collections of the 1980s omits *Hiddenness* with Richard Tuttle (1987).

7. John Ashbery, *Three Poems* (New York: Penguin Books, 1986), 56.

8. Eileen Tabios, *Black Lightning: Poetry-In-Progress* (New York: Asian American Writers Workshop, 1998), 139.

9. Mei-mei Berssenbrugge, unpublished correspondence with author, April 2000.

10. Interview with Laura Moriarty, *The American Poetry Archive News,* San Francisco State University, 5(1) (Spring 1988): 6.

11. Kathleen Fraser finds this struggle to evidence the sublime in Berssenbrugge's work in earlier poems. "It is her most profound dilemma: to find a way of giving voice to that which cannot be spoken of, beneath the historical, the categorical, the identifiable. To catch the unspeakable, just as it reveals itself. . . ." Kathleen Fraser, "Overheard," *Poetics Journal* 4 (May 1984): 102.

12. Charles Altieri, "Intimacy as Lyric Ideal," in *We Who Love To Be Astonished: Experimental Women's Writing and Performance Poetics,* ed. Laura Hinton and Cynthia Hogue (Tuscaloosa: University of Alabama Press, 2001). Also, at stake for Altieri is whether Berssenbrugge's experiments with the "language of the lyric" might be considered a challenge to the binary posed between lyrical and experimental writing in current critical reception. This is a critical insight well worth repeating: "Finally, I hope that elaborating Berssenbrugge's experiments will help us oppose what I see as an imaginatively crippling binary opposition that dominates contemporary academic criticism. There any emphasis on emotion in contemporary lyric poetry is seen as trapped within the reactionary egocentricity of an enervated romanticism. Experiment then has to be positioned on the other pole. . . . Yet this binary simply does not hold for many of the most interesting contemporary poets who consider their work a radical departure from dominant contemporary styles" (n.p.).

13. Berssenbrugge, with Kiki Smith, *Endocrinology* (Berkeley: Kelsey St. Press, 1997), 7. All subsequent references are to this edition and will appear in the text.

14. Berssenbrugge, *Sphericity* (Berkeley: Kelsey St. Press, 1993), 11.

15. Gertrude Stein, "Potratraits and Repetition," in *Lectures in America* (1935; repr. Boston: Beacon Press, 1957), 169.

16. This difference is, of course, impossible to partial out from properties of language on which it depends. Leslie Scalapino sees the long line of the poems branching through the text as a line of continuous "relation" that allows Berssenbrugge to test the hypothesis that writing and seeing (the combined forces of the artistic collaboration) are different perceptual orders. "Berssenbrugge's writing is drawing relations continually, on a hypothesis that writing is other than, a different faculty from, vision. *Sphericity* subjects the comparison itself (Tuttle's seeing/perspective and Berssenbrugge's language) to comparison. The 'comparison itself' is Berssenbrugge's long line of the poems, which, as a measure/shape that extends throughout the text, is as if there were one infinite line of 'relation' that constitutes the 'event horizon' of *Sphercity*." Leslie Scalapino, *The Public World/Syntactically Impermanence* (Hanover, N.H.: Wesleyan University Press, 1999), 61. It bears noting that lines of "seeing/perspective" and "language" are instrumental in Berssenbrugge's work generally and cannot be readily distinguished. Moreover, the lines of comparison and communication established in *Sphericity* seem to also refer inward, tracing the speaker's awareness of changes to her sense of interiority: "The horizon/represented a passage in time *and* light, a one way membrane she thinks is the edge of a shadow, / like a medical procedure into her body" (*Sphericity*, 26).

17. As I hope to make evident, *Four Year Old Girl* introduces spatial models for affect and memory that Berssenbrugge borrows from the language of bioscience and biotechnology. According to Eileen Tabios (*Black Lightening*, 134), Berssenbrugge has cited the following as references for the book: *Genetics in Medicine* (M. Thompson, Roderick McInnes, Huntington Willis); *Seminar of Jacques Lacan, Book II* (ed. Jacques-Alain Miller); *Four Fundamental Concepts of Psychoanalysis* (ed. Jacques-Alain Miller); *Buddha Nature* (Thrangu Rinpoche); *Theory of Religion* (Georges Bataille).

18. Berssenbrugge, *Four Year Old Girl* (Berkeley: Kelsey St. Press, 1998), 11. All subsequent references are to this edition and will appear in the text.

19. Maurice Merleau-Ponty, *The Visible and the Invisible* (Evanston: Northwestern University Press, 1968), 137–38.

20. Ibid, 139.

BIBLIOGRAPHY

Books by Mei-mei Berssenbrugge

Endocrinology, with Kiki Smith (Berkeley: Kelsey St. Press, 1997).
Empathy (New York: Station Hill Press, 1997).
Fish Souls (New York: Greenfield Review Press, 1974).
Four Year Old Girl (Berkeley: Kelsey St. Press, 1998).
The Heat Bird (Providence: Burning Deck, 1983).

Hiddeness, with Richard Tuttle (New York: The Whitney Museum Library Fellows, 1987).
Packrat Sieve (New York: Contact II, 1983).
Random Possession (New York: I. Reed Books, 1979).
Sphericity (Berkeley: Kelsey St. Press, 1993).
Summits Move with the Tide (New York: Greenfield Review Press, 1974).

Selected Prose

"A Context of a Wave." *Conjunctions* 17 (Fall 1991): n.p.

Interviews

Interview with Laura Moriarty, *The American Poetry Archive News,* San Francisco State University, 5(1) (Spring 1988).

Selected Criticism

Altieri, Charles. 2001. "Intimacy as Lyric Ideal," in *We Who Love To Be Astonished: Experimental Women's Writing and Performance Poetics,* ed. by Laura Hinton and Cynthia Hogue (Tuscaloosa: University of Alabama Press).
Fraser, Kathleen. "Overheard," *Poetics Journal* 4 (1984): 98–105.
Scalapino, Leslie. *The Public World: Syntactically Impermanence* (Hanover, N.H.: Wesleyan University Press, 1999).
Tabios, Eileen. *Black Lightning: Poetry-In-Progress* (New York: Asian American Writers Workshop, 1998).

LUCIE BROCK-BROIDO

THE ONE THOUSAND DAYS

There is the mourning dish of salt outside
My door, a cup of quarantine, saucerless, a sign

That one inside had been taken down
By grieving, ill tongue-tied will or simple

Illness, yet trouble came.
I have found electricity in mere ambition,

If nothing else, yet to make myself sick on it,
A spectacle of marvelling & discontent.

Let me tell you how it came to this.
I was turning over the tincture of things,

I was trying to recollect the great maroon
Portière of everything that had ever happened,

When the light first stopped its transport
& the weather ceased to be interesting,

Then the dark drape closed over the altar
& a minor city's temple burnt to ground.

I was looking to become inscrutable.
I was longing to be seen through.

It was at slaughtering, it
Was at the early stain

Of autumn when the dirt-
Tinted lambs were brought down

From the high unkempt fields of Sligo, bidden,
Unbidden, they came down.

It was then that I was quit
Of speech, a thousand northbound nights of it.

Then was ambition come
Gleaming up like a fractured bone

As it breaks through the bodiced veil of skin.
I marry into it, a thistle on

The palm, salt-pelt on
The slaughtering, & trouble came.

That the name of bliss is only in
The diminishing—as far as possible—of pain.

That I had quit the quiet velvet cult of it,
Yet trouble came.

SOUL KEEPING COMPANY

The hours between washing & the well
Of burial are the soul's most troubled time.

I sat with her in keeping company
All through the afflict of the night, keeping

Soul constant, a second self. Earth is heavy
& I made no wish, save being

Merely magical. I am magical
No more. This, I well remember well.

In the sweet thereafter the impress
Of the senses will be tattooed to

The whole world ravelling in the clemency
Of an autumn of Octobers, all that bounty

Bountiful & the oaks specifically
Afire as everything dies off, inclining

To the merciful. I would have made of my body
A body to protect her, anything to keep

Her well & here—in the soul's suite
Before five tons of earth will bear

On her, stay here
Soul, in the good night of my company.

PERIODIC TABLE OF ETHEREAL ELEMENTS
—for Harry Ford

I was not ready for your form to be cold
Ever. Even in life

You did not inhabit, necessarily, a form,
But a mind of

Rarer liquid element. It had not occurred to me
You would take

Leave and it will be winter from now on, not only
Here, in the ordinary,

But there too, in the extraordinary elegance
Of calcium and finery

And loss. Keep me

Tethered here, breathtakingly awkward and alive.

If you had a psyche it was not known to me.

If you had a figure it would be heavy ivory.
If you were a man, you would be

An autumn of black carriages filled red with leaves
From sycamore trees,

Not scattering. I was not ready for such
Earthward and unease.

Goodbye to the imperium, the rinsing wind. You, cold
As God and the great

Glassed castle in which I've lived, simply
Now a house.

A girl ago, a girlhood gone like a phial of ether
Thrown on fire—just

A little jump of flame, like grief, or,

Like a penicillin that has lost its will for killing
Off, it then is gone.

AM MOOR

Am lean against.
Am the heavy hour

Hand at urge,
At the verge of one. Am the ice comb of the tonsured

Hair, am the second
Hand, halted, the velvet opera glove. Am slant. Am fen, the
    injure

Wind at withins,
Stranger where the storm forms a face if the body stands enough

In a weather this
Cripple & this rough. Am shunt. Was moon-shaped helmet left

In bog, was condition
Of a spirit shorn, childlike & herd. Was Andalusian, ambsace,

Bird. Am kept.
Was keeper of the badly marred, was furious done god, was

Patient, was bad
Luck, was nurse. Ninety badly wounded men lay baying

In the reddened reedy
Hay of Saxony, was surgeon to their flinch & hoop, was hospice

To their torso hall,
Was numinous creature to their dying

Off. Am numb.
Was shoulder & queer luck. Am among.

Was gaunt.
Was—why—for the mutton & moss. Was the rented room.

Was chamber & ambage
& tender & burn. Am esurient, was the hungry form.

Am anatomy.
Was the bleating thing.

CARROWMORE

All about Carrowmore the lambs
Were blotched blue, belonging.

They were waiting for carnage or
Snuff. This is why they are born

To begin with, to end.
Ruminants do not frighten

At anything—gorge in the soil, butcher
Noise, the mere graze of predators.

All about Carrowmore
The rain quells for three days.

I remember how cold I was, the botched
Job of travelling. And just so.

Wherever I went I came with me.
She buried her bone barrette

In the ground's woolly shaft.
A tear of her hair, an old gift

To the burnt other who went
First. My thick braid, my ornament—

My belonging I
Remember how cold I will be.

POETIC STATEMENT
Myself a Kangaroo Among the Beauties

One—Prose Fragments towards an Impure Poetry:
A Disclaimer

MY LOGIC of Lyric does not permit me to assign a Politic to Language.
To paraphrase Kenneth Rexroth: *A Bug is not an Entomologist.* Or, Dickinson: *I will never try to lift the Words which I cannot Hold.*

Two—What I Want

What I want is a poem which—when all is said & done—acts as a *palpable coffin* . . .

What I mean by coffin is not just a thing of marled stone weight, but an object which can Stay still.

Hoc est corpus: *Here* is the body.

What I want is a poem which is an act of Will: chiseled, bony, all ivory tusk.
I want a poetry which is inorganic, an artifact of artifice, riddled with truth.

Three—How Can It Be I Am No Longer I
[Michelangelo, Madrigal]

In a lyric poem, the *I* is the messenger & must be rampantly responsible.
The I is the Alpha, not "Witness." The "Thou," however, *is* negotiable, to
an extent; René Char wrote: *Every poem is married to someone* (1967, 69).

By contract, the I is responsible for all acquisition & bartering. My *I* is Acquisitive—the Great Procuress of all objects & Objective Correlatives.

As a reader, I suffer from agoraphobia—I do not wish to be left alone in the open-spaced marketplace of any page. A poem which the world longs to call a Language Poem is too open for my taste. What I want is a poem as fixed to the page as an old oak tree is set in the ground situation of its landscape, incorruptibly non-negotiable, rooted.

After I had been the recipient of a particularly thrashing review, Charles Wright, in a letter of solidarity & sympathy, wrote to me regarding LANGUAGE(?) Poetry. He wrote: "What have we been doing all this time anyway, Barking?" I aspire to be a New Elliptical.

Four—Fathoming

What I want is a form of Legibility. I am a Neo-Clarificationist. I am more & more passionate about *inclusion* (of the reader), less & less impassioned about *exclusion, mere invention, BYOB* (Bring Your Own Baggage) to the page. I've become more & more right-wing about Coherence. I'm after sinew, not gnarl. Since I am, constitutionally, an Embellisher, I've become more & more drawn to the *other* notion that *Simplicity is Clarity & Clarity is Bliss.* My motto to me is: Cut It Out.

I am quit of being "Misunderstood."
I am done with "Personae."
Already: I have Innovated already.

The *Duende* loves wounds & ledges, not cutting edges.
Dickinson: *"When I state myself, as Representative of the Verse—it does not mean—me—but a supposed person"* (1958, 412).

I *am* the Supposed Person.

Five—In Extremity's Small Room

I want a poem which is made of compression, passion, precision, symmetry, & disruption.

I want a poetry which is fetishistic, A-Moral, obsessive, erotic, a poetry of Commission, a poem of pre-meditation, beneath (not above) the law, with malice aforethought. I want a poem of omission. ["Omissions are not accidents," said Marianne Moore (1967, vii).] That which is *withheld* on the page is equal in importance to that which is Held.

Six—Trouble in Mind

In August of 1862, Dickinson wrote to Higginson: *All men say "What" to me, . . .*

Seven—Autobiography & Luciferianism

Composing, a poet has two choices: [in revealing the particulars of the Six Dramatic Situations left to consider (in the world according to I): *Bliss, Loss, Trembling, Compulsion, Desire, & Disease]*——

> *First*—To make something out of *Nothing* or
> *Second*—To make something out of *Something*.

This is where biography & Real Life enter in. I become less & less interested in Invention—less & less intent on making a poem out of Nothing, just for the sake of its own making. Slanted as it may be, I aspire to tell at least partially—a portion of a truth.

Regarding the inclusion of the Reader in the biography of the page (either through SoothSaying or TruthTelling): there are, practically, but two ways of wooing, of including the Inheritor of the page:

> First—There's the Come Hither: *This is what it was like.* (The Heaneyesque)
> & Secondly—There's the Listen: *You have never felt like this before.* (The Bidartian)

We have art in order that we not perish of [from?] the truth. If so, then art is at least a *portion* of a truth.

It is this very partiality which protects us from the whole [annihilating] truth.

Eight—Keeping Oblivion at Bay

Dickinson wrote: *"The career of flowers differs from ours only in audibleness"* (1958, 505).

Translation: The career of a thing of nature is to be Bulb, burst, bloom & die. Ours is the equivalent. Only we get to Write it All Down,

Nine—Why I Write

ED to Higginson, 25 April 1862

"*I had a terror—since September—that I could tell to none—and so I sing, as the Boy does in the Burying Ground—because I am afraid*" (Dickinson 1996, 404).

"SUBJECT, SUBJUGATE, INTHRALLED"

The Selves of Lucie Brock-Broido

Stephen Burt

SOMETIMES DESPERATE, often fanciful, Lucie Brock-Broido's poems elaborate, diverge, allude, and evade. They strive to astonish, then surprise by their reserve; their heights dizzy listeners, and their periphrases fascinate. Even when their tones connote self-abasement, apology, fresh wound, or heavy grief, their daring and wide-ranging figures give them imaginative balance. These figures rely, throughout her career so far, on *personae* and alter egos, handled in singular, sometimes baffling ways: her signature work, *The Master Letters*, offers split and partial selves that distinguish it from previous *persona* poetry and dramatic monologue. These split and partial selves link her poems' emotional trajectories to certain psychoanalysts' notions of domination and submission. Poems written since *The Master Letters* describe and critique the techniques in which that volume exulted, turning Brock-Broido's attention, and her divided selves, from the erotic to the ethical, from self-investigation to grief. Brock-Broido's two volumes, and the poems she has made public since, work together to present a self coming into the world, trying to comprehend eros, power, and mortality, placing herself in time and space, and growing up; if their backstory is more ornate, and sometimes more ambiguous, than most, a careful look into the poems can explain why.

I

Brock-Broido's earliest published poems show her drawn both to personae and to themes of hunt and prey, flight and pursuit. In "The Wind in Search of the Heat" (1982), the painter Andrew Wyeth ("Andy") dreams of predatory angels in a Pennsylvania marsh: "They are hunting ones with extra limbs,/attracted by the scent of vulnerability."[1] The even earlier "On the Poem: The Rh Variations" (1980) introduces Brock-Broido's interests in sex roles: its first two sections bear the subtitles "On the Poem about the Virgin" and "On the Poem about the Whore"—the first "will always play the Ingenue," the second "is a bride every night" ("OP," 62). The same poem test-drives some of the syntactical oddities Brock-Broido would later master: run-on sentences, symmetrically repeated words, and proliferative Empsonian ambiguities: "Nothing is not interesting./The dream is a beast. . . . That Dionysus was a woman in his sleep./He never slept. Not once" ("OP," 65). What the poem lacks is a consistent voice, a manifest self around which devices coalesce.

The first such manifestations took place in persona poems. Brock-Broido's first book, *A Hunger* (1988), flaunts its alter egos: it includes poems in the voices of basketball star Manute Bol; Edward VI of England; "Birdie Africa," a child-survivor of the Philadelphia MOVE bombing; and Jessica McClure, the Texas child trapped in a well in 1987. Some poems in *A Hunger* echo Brock-Broido's teacher Stanley Kunitz; the associative sprawls and leaps, the jagged six- and eight-line stanzas, even "&" in place of "and," suggest productive attention to John Berryman. Foregrounded in *A Hunger,* and less obvious in her later work, are concerns with time's passage, and with kinds of time: minute by minute experience, historical and geological time, and the span of one human life. The opening poem, "Domestic Mysticism," conflates adolescence with the progress of a mystical, cyclic Great Year: "In thrice 10,000 seasons, I will come back to this world /In a white cotton dress. . . . In the next millennium, I will be middle aged" (*H,* 3). Straddling domestic and mystical, visionary and "confessional" modes, the poet classes herself among damaged people, all prompted to vision by debility:

> This work of mine, the kind of work which takes no arms to do,
> Is least noble of all. It's peopled by Wizards, the Forlorn,
> The Awkward, the Blinkers, the Spoon-Fingered, Agnostic Lispers,
> Stutterers of Prayer, the Flatulent, the Closet Weepers,
> The Charlatans. I am one of those. In January, the month the owls
> Nest in, I am a witness & a small thing altogether. The Kingdom
> Of Ingratitude. Kingdom of Lies. Kingdom of *How Dare I.* (*H,* 3)

The awkwardly lengthy lines suggest the reach of Brock-Broido's conceit, the amount of material she wishes to take in, and her own vertiginous smallness in the midst of it.

More generally the "I" of *A Hunger* seems dwarfed by what she can imagine: she wants to escape into her historical figures and artistic creations. Helen Vendler's review of *A Hunger* noted Brock-Broido's tendency to present herself as a "little-small child-girl" and also noted her "oblique . . . disclosures" about anorexia (1995, 175, 171). "Ten Years Apprenticeship in Fantasy" explains coyly, "I . . . having been starving alternately for a decade" (*H*, 52). "Jessica, From the Well" explains: "Even without food I am growing/& I find this frightful that my body/will become too large to live here comfortably" (*H*, 23). Jessica's fall, like Brock-Broido's speech rhythms, seems meant as apotropaic: the rhythms and magical gestures keep away some dangerous aspect of the outer world— death, or responsibility, or social belonging, or visible maturity. These poems' dizzying temporalities suggest anorexics' purported wish to stop time, to reverse their physiological development, and to exert final control over their own bodies.[2]

The poems' uneven cadences, and their swerves into baby talk, also dramatize the speakers' vulnerability, their impossible wishes for self-mastery, and the tenuousness of their ties to other people. "Evolution," mixing up time scales again, identifies its helpless poet with "extinct creatures" and with dead royalty:

> What I want is to sleep away an epoch,
> wake up as a girl with another kind of heart.
>
> In the Vatican library, the letters
> to Anne Boleyn are pinned down to keep
> from coiling. An entire country
> changed its faith once for its king. (*H*, 8)

Not empowered to change men's hearts, as Boleyn was, the poet feels infinitely vulnerable, and hides: "I am the medieval child in the basket, rocking" (*H*, 8). Another medieval persona, the titular speaker of "Edward VI on the Seventh Day," says of his father (echoing Berryman's *Homage to Mistress Bradstreet*), "I will be him someday. . . . I am fevered I am pretty/ in a plague of white. . . . I was of my father I am King" (*H*, 20).[3] Brock-Broido's "I" and her boy-king display contradictory wishes—on the one hand, to be famous, powerful, visible; on the other, to become invisible, or to dissolve into the identity of another.

Such conflicting impulses make many of Brock-Broido's poems tell the story of fleeing selves who wish to be caught, of splintering selves who wish to be reassembled. "Jessica, From the Well," for example, wants to be *noticed* for being *unreachable:* "The earth opens for me. . . . Soon I will be famous." Fractured identities and withdrawals, uneasy locations in time and space would define the approach of her second book, *The Master Letters* (1995); all appear in "Lucie & Her Sisters." The "Lucie" of this ten-paragraph prose poem looks backward to familiar teenage escapes, up to future incarnations of herself, and far afield to her sisters, who seem to her like people she might have become. Brock-Broido imagines herself as "a locust . . . learning in the next life how to fly transparently, how to deposit my old skins on the outside of the screened-in porch in some pastoral set" (*H,* 40).

Focusing on its evasions and exhibitions, its fugitive and feinting sets and roles, I have been neglecting aspects of *A Hunger* that hold other readers' attention. Among these are the book's interests in American evangelical religion, American lower-class dialect, crime and criminal insanity. These interests pervade 1992's "Black Arcadia," the only poem Brock-Broido published in the 1990s that could not have been meant for *The Master Letters.* The eight-page poem is spoken by Betsy Reese, who poisoned six children in Arcadia, Florida, in 1967 by mixing insecticide into their lunch. (The children's father spent years on death row for the killings; he was freed only in 1988, when Reese confessed.) Reese's motives, as the poem draws them out, combine religious mania, self-obsession, and the familiar puritan conviction that the flesh is evil and departure from it a good: "Once I loved my /self like a queen . . . I wanted to be pretty for Him, clean" ("BA," 32). The poem provides a frightening, lurid coda for the motifs in *A Hunger* which William Logan disparaged as "haute couture vulgarity."[4] Its reliance on true-crime narrative would not recur in her later work.

If "Black Arcadia" looks like a farewell performance, the surprisingly awkward 1987 poem "In the Economy of Diminishing Resources" sounds now like a rehearsal for techniques central to Brock-Broido's poems of the 1990s. The poem (written, her note says, about a Harvard colloquium) contrasts its speaker's intensely personal idiolect with the anodyne jargon that professors around her use. Its jump-cuts and long lines also show Brock-Broido learning to jump from context to context, voice to voice. While a professor offers "*to drive his skepticism deep,*" Brock-Broido evokes a "wild *intersection of two personhoods*" and says "that I belong to you—*the self,/the soul*—/that I desire you like this."[5] The final poem in *A Hunger,* an intricate ladder of parallel clauses called "After the Grand Perhaps," evoked "the dazed shadow/of the self as it follows the self" (*H,* 56). Such hiding and splintered "selves" and "souls" foreshadow the selves and forms of *The Master Letters.*

"It is true that each self keeps a secret self that cannot speak when spoken to," Brock-Broido declares early in *The Master Letters* (*ML*, 6). Her book-length sequence gives its selves and secrets plenty of settings—prehistoric and present-day Ireland, medieval, Renaissance and Victorian England, antebellum Virginia and Massachusetts, contemporary Louisiana. The poems depict divided, troubled speakers and writers who appeal, implore, or submit to others—to "masters," to readers—to complete them and resolve their divisions. If, as Allen Grossman has argued, a poem is "a case of the construction of the countenance, the willing of the presence of a person," then Brock-Broido's poems present, so to speak, more than one first-person, and less than two (1992, 344). It is on these dramatically split-up selves that Brock-Broido founds her style.

To see how *The Master Letters* work, it helps to see how they use their older models. Emily Dickinson's so-called Master Letters, from which Brock-Broido derives her title, are three missives Dickinson left in the box that held her poems: two address only "Master," and one has no heading at all.[6] Brock-Broido's "Preamble" to *The Master Letters* describes Dickinson's trio as "gracious, sometimes nearly erotic, worshipful documents . . . dramas of entreaty & intimacy." The letters are certainly passionate, and equally difficult to interpret, mixing prayer, love letter, sermon, and confessional. One speaks of "A love so big it scares her, rushing among her small heart," pleading, "Master—open your life wide and take me in forever . . . nobody else will see me, but you. . . ." (Dickinson 1985, 167–68). Another exclaims: "I heard of a thing called 'Redemption'—which rested men and women. You remember I asked you for it—you gave me something else" (Ibid., 159). These ambiguous, strenuously yearning attitudes resemble those of *A Hunger*. Brock-Broido, in *The Master Letters,* sometimes quotes Dickinson's other letters, and (less often) Dickinson's verse. But the much-remarked Dickinsonisms are only some of Brock-Broido's guises, and she tends to wear several in the course of a poem.

Brock-Broido's formal cues, and her "Preamble," suggest that we read the whole sequence not as letters from or about Dickinson but more generally as epistolary poetry. The sequence began as a set of prose poems; some are laid out as letters, including references to previous correspondence, requests for advice, salutations, and sign-offs. One poem begins "*Master—/* You say I have misenveloped and sent you something else" (*ML*, 62). Others address "*My Most Courteous Lord*" (4), "*My Dear Sir—*" (30), "*Recipient Unknown*" (44), or conclude "*Your Gnome*" (10), "*Your/Faithfull Friend*" (31). It may be the special project of epistolary poems to construct a "you" on which an "I" depends, to realize persons by means of their relations to the people they address. "Sir, more than kisses, letters mingle Soules," one of John Donne's verse-epistles begins (1967, 71). Donne addressed intimate male friends and dignified ladies; Alexander Pope displayed his character in verse-letters to patrons and confidantes. Brock-Broido's preamble describes the Master her work addresses as "Editor, mentor, my aloof proportion, the father, the critic, beloved, the wizard—he was beside himself" (*ML*, viii).[7] Brock-Broido's urgent, if submerged, backstories of romance, dependence, and betrayal recall the now-obscure subgenre of Ovidian or "heroic epistles," impassioned verse-letters from historical or legendary women to men who have abandoned them.[8] Alexander Pope, for example, wrote a verse-letter from Eloise to Abelard, and another from Sappho to her male lover Phaon (1965, 253, 29). To Pope's cloistered, pleading Eloisa, readers might compare the abandoned student-lover in Brock-Broido's "His Apprentice," remembering "when you wanted me as much / As promises & fame" (*ML*, 11, 36).

Yet Brock-Broido's contemporary heroic epistles are very much odder, and more oblique, than any single impersonation makes them seem. Another convention links historical epistle to historical fiction in general; it is a convention Brock-Broido characteristically violates. Historical fiction in verse or in prose—George Eliot's *Romola*, or Pope's Eloisa—makes invisible accommodations between historically specific otherness and apparently "timeless" subjectivity. Eliot writes in the Proem to *Romola*, "The great river-courses which have shaped the lives of men have hardly changed; and those other streams, the life-currents that ebb and flow in human hearts, pulsate to the same great needs" (Eliot 1993, 3).[9] As the maker of a realist historical fiction, Eliot promises to blend the changeable with the changeless, the historically specific with human nature as the readers of 1860 (or 1999) might recognize it. In doing so she has to avoid anachronism—everything changeable or contingent in *Romola* has to smack of the 1490s, not the 1590s or the 1860s.

We can find the same goals in realist historical poetry, in poems that present themselves as speech and writing by and about the people of some other time—in Pope's heroic epistle, or in dramatic monologues by Robert Browning or Richard Howard. However obedient to their own times' conventions, historical impersonations such as these integrate their historical elements with others that lack historical marking, and thus create consistently situated characters. Pope's Eloisa adopts Augustan cadences, but her range of reference is what Pope took to be that of a medieval Catholic. Browning's Italian Duke might admire wildness in the arts, but he can't refer to Turner, or quote Shelley, or turn, halfway through the poem, into a Scottish laird with the same emotional makeup.

But the impersonations of *The Master Letters* do just those sorts of things. If historical realism involves blending, Brock-Broido's poems are more like emulsions—their elements won't merge to create one consistent historical setting or speaker. Not only is *The Master Letters*, collectively, a set of possible selves (as many collections of poems are), but the "I" in a single poem will be sometimes a medieval monk, Anne Boleyn, or an early twentieth-century rural Southern girl, and at other moments in the same poem another historical figure, or a contemporary. In "From the Proscenium" Brock-Broido is at once a Renaissance sailor, with "Tudor Disregard" in an "Elizabethan cargo hold"; an actor in a theater; and a worker "in the basement of a bad girls' School" (*ML*, 31). "Haute Couture Vulgarity" (which takes its title from Logan's harsh review) juxtaposes a "palmer's chastity," a "Nun starving for idea" and the "Imperial wizards" of the Ku Klux Klan (*ML*, 44–45). The "she" of "Desunt Non Nulla" is both a medieval sleepwalker who wakes in a garden, and a later reader of medieval books, fascinated by Latin tags. And "Everything Husk to the Will" presents itself both as a vigil in an American Jewish cemetery and as an attempt to inhabit Emily Brontë's windy Yorkshire. Willard Spiegelman complained that in *The Master Letters*, "One often wonders exactly *who* is speaking": that jangle of incompatible speakers is part of its method (1996, 167).

The psyche Brock-Broido's poems display thus exhibits more than one historical self, but seems comfortable in none. Almost the last in her sequence of personae are twins conjoined at the heart, in a poem (the last of the Master Letters to be written) called "How Can It Be I Am No Longer I."[10] She identifies with both of the twins, "where two made a monstrous/ Braid of other" (*ML*, 73). In the same vein Brock-Broido identifies with the historical personae, but finally fails to impersonate any one of them. Instead she seeks to be two or more people at once, as if no single given self, no one body or incarnation, could accommodate her desires or needs.

This doubling inheres in many poems' relation to Dickinson. But such historical projection and anachronistic removal occur throughout *The Master Letters*, not only with Dickinson's language and Dickinson's era, but with each persona, locale, and historical period. In other poets, unusual diction can provide historical and geographical locators. Brock-Broido's odd words instead point to incompatible places and times: to medieval alchemists' laboratories and nineteenth-century schools, to Dickinson and to Anne Boleyn, to Renaissance mariners and to high school plays. "The Supernatural Is Only the Natural, Disclosed" incorporates "blacksmiths," "cobblers," "a form of sorcery" and a custodian who flips a light switch (*ML*, 10). "Everybody Has a Heart, Except Some People" imagines its worried speaker in a "daguerreotype/With its ghostly subtexts," wearing "Anne Boleyn's clean cotton cap/Soiled on the day of her death," and "wed to mercurial rings//Like spooks—a vapor from another time" (*ML*, 56). By the time we have finished this half of that sonnet, Brock-Broido has projected herself into at least three periods—Anne's Tudor era, Dickinson's nineteenth century, and our own day, home of terms such as "spook" and "subtext."

Grammatical oddities work together with anachronisms to give the psyche in any given poem more than one historical, physical incarnation. The poems flaunt idiosyncratically doubled personal pronouns— "Wherever I went I came with me"; "I am an extraordinary I & not you" (*ML*, 3, 19). Brock-Broido also cherishes run-on sentences: "Parts of the mouth are not clean, unholy by growing old I am afraid" (*ML*, 7). Such two-headed sentences evoke two speakers or subjects—one of whom speaks for Brock-Broido, while the other feels what she feels. Other sentences lengthen unexpectedly in strings of dependent clauses: "When he died, he went on *like* a loaded//Trout stream—*toward* a Body larger than this one/ *Is*, wading hip-high *in* the loaded//Dark *of* boneless water, moving On" (*ML*, 59; emphasis mine). Brock-Broido brings in intransitive verbs used transitively, prepositions juxtaposed inappropriately, long strings of appositives, and ambiguities: "I was at homeward"; "How many druid doctors/ I have known & long ago when druidry//Was my first dream, debriding" (*ML*, 63). (To "debride" is to remove matter from a wound; here it also means, punningly, to restore virginity by magic.) Brock-Broido also favors the Berrymanesque form "I am X, I am Y, I am Z," where X, Y, and Z are incompatible objects or persons: "I am angel, addict, catherine wheel"; "nobody's panther, nobody's/Tinny cigarbox, nobody's violin, no/Midsummer naïf" (*ML*, 8, 32).[11] Through all these syntactic and semantic dislocations, speaker and self-spoken-of seem now one person, now a brigade of uneasy actors, "a brood of voice" (*ML*, viii).

Brock-Broido's quotations also assist her "emulsifying" strategy. Her notes reminded Spiegelman of *The Waste Land;* her integration of Dickinson's sentences, and of phrases from Wyatt and others, suggest T.S. Eliot's frequent appropriations of lines and phrases from earlier writers.[12] Following his famous essay "Tradition and the Individual Talent," Eliot's own quotations can be read as attempts to convert the lyric "I" into a hidden site—a catalyst, "a shred of platinum," as he put it—where others' work may interact (1975, 41). Writing constituted for the young Eliot "an escape from personality"—though "only those who have personality and emotions know what it means to want to escape from these things" (1975, 43). Quotational self-concealment in Eliot, "escape from personality" into personae, becomes in Brock-Broido's quotational tactics an incomplete and flaunted concealment, a serious game of hide-and-seek. The sources and historical situations serve *The Master Letters* as props, as properties—

but properties their owner cannot discard, since they constitute her, make her evident: "I possess too many things," she says, "Cannot be quit—acquiring" (*ML,* 24).[13] This is one step away from an admission that she becomes "too many" people—her historical and literary personae are what she cannot discard, since they seem to constitute her.

"Carrowmore," the first poem in the volume, introduces readers at once to Brock-Broido's historically inconsistent personae, and to her doubled pronouns and run-on sentences. The poem casts Brock-Broido as a Stone Age Irish girl, and as a modern tourist who describes the girl. Its first-person pronoun represents two people: one speaks the poem in the present while visiting Ireland, the other seems speechless and powerful, prehistoric and permanently hidden. "I remember how cold I was, the botched/Job of traveling, and just so," Brock-Broido writes, intending both a chilly passenger airplane and resurrection; she continues,

> Wherever I went I came with me.
> She buried her bone barrette
>
> In the ground's wooly shaft.
> A tear of her hair, an old gift
>
> To the burnt other who went
> First. My thick-braid, my ornament—
>
> My belonging I
> Remember how cold I will be. (*ML,* 3)

This predecessor-I, who is, or gives her hair to, a buried "burnt other," recalls the corpse in Seamus Heaney's "Punishment": a "little adulteress," "flaxen-haired,/undernourished . . . poor scapegoat" (1980, 193). She also resembles or stands for a sort of mute id—a part of the psyche that cannot be present to language without help from some other, more conscious part. The split in the subject, the I who speaks, skews not only declension but also verb tense, the marker of subjective time: at once prehistoric, present-day and posthumous, Brock-Broido seems to have remembered events that have not yet occurred.[14]

Such selves or masks, in which the I who speaks the poems seems here and there, past and present and nowhere particular, resemble Brock-Broido's Master figure, invoked as "a kind of vortex . . . beside himself" (*ML,* viii). "His Apprentice" imagines its Master both as a punitive Yorkshire "schoolmaster," and as a medieval alchemist: each role tropes the other, as both trope the wild, paradoxically assertive subordination the poem's onrushing sentences strive to recall (*ML,* 36). Bonnie Costello (1996) describes *The Master Letters* as "dominated" by the rhetorical figure called apostrophe, which "marks a poem's reflections as an address to someone or something other than the reader"—in Brock-Broido's case "to an absent, sometimes transcendental, sometimes impossible Thou." We might read Brock-Broido's transits among selves, her deliberately, showily incomplete occupation of any one self, as a series of attempts to find a voice the Master might hear, a voice to which he might respond, or a voice in which to respond to his demands. Brock-Broido's own personae are constantly, anxiously seeking some sort of response, whether they are narrating, pleading, praying, or repenting as they do so. "Dull Weather" admits, "Even my self reminds me of you" (*ML,* 29). "How Can It Be I Am No Longer I" ends in a kind of repetition that Brock-Broido has rarely used, presenting nearly the same sentence midway through the poem and again at its end: "I would not speak again" becomes, in Brock-Broido's last line, "I would not speak to you again"—as if each "I" had to make its own bow, and neither could exist without "you" (*ML,* 73).

A general situation behind these poems, then, is this: a split or "emulsified," uneasily multiplied "I" conjures up an absent Master to whom she feels she must reveal herself, who prompts the poem, and without whom she would not seem to exist. What else do the poems' situations share? What is it like to live amid these I's? And what psychological work can they do?

III

The selves Brock-Broido invokes are almost always victims; many are, or imagine they are, imprisoned, wounded, helpless. Some are martyrs—Boleyn, Thomas Wyatt, Thomas More, John Clare, Georg Trakl, victims of chemical dumping in "Toxic Gumbo," maltreated apprentices, a prehistoric human sacrifice, game animals, Strindberg's overmastered Miss Julie. Other poems invoke the costume-drama properties familiar from the fictions of S&M. "Haute Couture Vulgarity" concludes, presumably quoting Dickinson, *"All are very naughty, & I am naughtiest of all,/Ever—/His,/Penitent Friend"* (*ML,* 45).[15] (The key words here, as Brock-Broido certainly knows, have acquired connotations since Dickinson's time.) The subject-positions Brock-Broido takes, the subjects she chooses, are almost always subject in the sense of dominated, confined, punished, or ruled-over—or else nostalgic for having been so. She imagines herself compelled to speak and act, becoming a speaking subject by becoming subject to somebody, often in the same verbal space in which she flees from or remembers his dominance. "In the Attitude Desired for Exhibition" imagines Brock-Broido both as "red she/ Fox" and as that fox's taxidermist: "All afternoon I have prepared my body /For the body of none" (*ML,* 51). "A Brief History of Asylum" presents

Brock-Broido as a trepanned escapee from a nineteenth-century Virginia asylum, as a lobotomized schizophrenic, and (via lines from Robert Hayden) as a runaway slave. The poem ends:

> From
> The skull's bony porthole, rivers unbound & ran
>
> Out—mandate of docile, mandate of Sweet, no roaring
> Subaltern pain. The temples—yielding, lamblike, mild—
>
> Invalid to sorrow—right half, left half, limbic & all
> For memory or love—I am subject, subjugate, inthralled. (*ML*, 9)

Here the imagined psychosurgery replaces a kind of pain with a kind of subjugation, imagined alternately as psychic death and as a coming-to-speak.

If the queries, staged pursuits, captures, imprisonments are all strategies of submission, we may be able to understand the multiple, incomplete, transitory selves that Brock-Broido's poems project in terms drawn from the feminist psychoanalyst Jessica Benjamin, as "masochistic" attempts at "self-discovery in the space provided by" the fictive, projected Master. Many of the poems are, in Benjamin's words, attempts "to find a 'safe' open space in which to abandon the protective false self and allow the nascent hidden self to emerge" (1988, 72–73). The masochist pretends to obey, or believes he or she obeys, an exterior command, a dominant authoritative other, in showing or speaking for another self—a self that would, absent that fiction, remain unknown. This "masochistic" situation forms not so much the plot as the grounds for most of *The Master Letters*.

Such clinical or psychoanalytic models cannot do justice to Brock-Broido's verbal art—nor can they give complete accounts of any one poem.[16] They can, though, help us understand a situation the poems share. Benjamin elsewhere describes a patient who "sought some external power that would force or seduce her into giving up the deadening, reactive 'superstructure' [of her normal social responses] so that she might be known or found." The same analysand, Benjamin continues,

> described . . . her wish to be out of control and her method of dividing herself into the voice of the master and the one who had to do what the master said. . . . She closed by saying that she could not open up to anyone but that inner voice and that the analyst was in the camp of everyone who is outside. (1995, 166–67)

Benjamin's patient sounds much like the Brock-Broido of "Ten Years Apprenticeship in Fantasy," the only epistolary poem in *A Hunger*: confiding that "you're allowed, I hear, to feel healthy in erotic dreams of submission," Brock-Broido presents herself "waiting to get vulnerable again," and concludes, "I am, as ever, yours" (*H*, 53).

If that poem announces its "masochistic" ambitions, the techniques of *The Master Letters* realize them. The poems' grammatical evasions and their shifting context may be thought of as ways of inviting and then avoiding "opening[s] up" to the poetry's actual readers, none of whom can be the interior Master. At the same time these shifts and doublings dramatize the ways in which the poems' subjects respond to their absent Master, the ways in which one self refracts and discharges a felt, desired command to exhibit, for the Master, another, truer self, a hidden or farfetched or vulnerable soul. The poems' two-headed sentences, pronominal oddities, and anachronistic, shucked personae constitute dramas of self-splitting, refractions of an "I" into the components that the fiction of a Master prompts.

Benjamin's essay on transference attempts to explain how "submission to authority" can be "itself an erotic experience"; "submission to a powerful other," she concludes, "may be understood as a means, however problematic, of securing or freeing the self and, at the same time, finding recognition" (1995, 150). These are the kinds of submission the Master Letters attempt, dramatize, remember, fear, and seek. Wayne Koestenbaum aptly calls their stance "virtuoso abjection" (1998, 164). Many of the poems seem designed, in their floods of information and unresolved privacies, to give the effect of speech compelled.[17] Being Mastered, having encountered the Master she imagines, seems to Brock-Broido both a condition of speech—a prompt for poetry—and a stop to speech—a kind of suppression. In the prose block at the center of "Treason," "your Hand, concaved around my mouth, once a ravening thrill to me—now—Abstains me. The speechless throat is economical, deeper Off, the most dangerous" (*ML*, 54). "Fair Copy from a Fair World" presents an immobilized speaker who chooses to be held captive, exchanging an untenable independence for a "marriage" in which her subordination produces both muteness and the poem we are reading: "When I woke stitched in the cicatrix of our fair drab bed, I was mute. A voice bound by the long worn muslin of a mortal work. I would want to marry now, as Thomas said again, the Absences. *I didn't— be myself*" (*ML*, 35).[18] One of the chilliest poems in the book, "A Glooming Peace This Morning With It Brings," attempts to define "submission" for a "Consort," and decides that "The difference between desire & compulsion/ Is that one is wanting, one is warding off" (*ML*, 41). It can be hard (that sentence implies) for Brock-Broido to remember the difference. "Obsession, Compulsion" ends on the imploring couplet, "*Would you but guide, your—*/Punitive Divine" (*ML*, 11). And "Pompeiian" ends by asking, amid the ash of Vesuvius, "Would this/Too be a form of grovelling?" (*ML*, 46).

The poems use their historical reference points as incarnations or instances of the relations of dominance that the poems imagine: master and subject, father and daughter, pedagogue and pupil, Thomas Wyatt and Anne Boleyn, director and actor, hunter and game. The historical and contemporary personae, to quote Benjamin again, "establish fixed points on the internal map upon which the parents, the analyst [master] and the self can be imagined as movable spheres" (1995, 140). These situations of appeal and submission, of obsession or groveling, cause the "I" of the poems to split up into more than one grammatical person, and into more than one historical instance of selfhood: the compulsive subjections that the poems imagine are what allow the hidden, responsive self to coalesce and emerge—though always incompletely, and temporarily, in response to a Master who will not stick around.

Comparing his mythological personae to "a coat," W. B. Yeats promised in a famous poem to seek "more enterprise/In walking naked" (1989, 127). But Brock-Broido's poems can no more go without their coats—their reference points, their partial or disguising roles and scenarios—than they can go without nouns or verbs: what they can do is, so to speak, change their coats often, and wear them half-open, in order to make evident the bodily or hidden or alternate self that the poems feel compelled to reveal—and to hide. This doubled self, with its interior drama of approach and withdrawal, flight and pursuit, toward and away from the Master, informs most of Brock-Broido's formal choices: it governs, for example, Brock-Broido's division of every single lineated poem in her book into ferociously, teasingly unbalanced two-line stanzas. Brock-Broido explains, in a block of prose Costello rightly takes as a guide to her goals, "My voice thrown, my Other littler self on my own knee, practicing a sleight of hand, the tongue of the Inventor wagging the tongue of the Invented. It is true that each self keeps a secret self which cannot speak when spoken to" (ML, 6).

This secret "Other littler self," always about to shrink behind the historical curtains, forced to emerge by or for a Master, gets identified (just like the personae in A Hunger) with confinement, smallness, muteness. Mixing theatrical and nautical figures, "From the Proscenium" imagines Brock-Broido and her soul in a cargo hold: "How can something this Small take up such space? A Soul enters & a room fills with an odd light as if a lung took in the first Homely glint coming from the wreck of an Elizabethan cargo ship—till my heart is so Full as pure sail, I cannot breathe" (ML, 30). A reader could make her way through the whole volume by following tropes of confinement and imprisonment—in a cargo hold; underground ("Carrowmore"); in a fallout shelter ("Gratitude"); in the "locked box" in "Work" (like the one in which Dickinson left her fascicles) (ML, 3, 28, 66). In the attitude desired by the poems, this confinement reveals the already-confined soul, or secret self. After *The Master Letters* were complete, Brock-Broido told Wayne Koestenbaum: "I think of poems as autistic, in the sense that they're trapped in extremity's small room. . . . I wish—out of a fear of repetition-compulsion—that I could write from many different rooms" (1998, 146).

The saddest, most withdrawn poems in *The Master Letters,* such as "Gratitude" or "A Glooming Morning," present themselves as aftermaths: in them the encounter with the Master seems over and done with—if he is a lover, he has already left her; with him has departed the chance, and the exciting compulsion, to reveal another self. (Ironically this departure constitutes the worst punishment he can mete out.) The hidden soul cannot speak of or for itself: it can only be spoken for, in necessarily partial situations involving submission. A wholly revealed inner self, in this schema, amounts to total submission, hence silence; a wholly coherent, articulate, and articulable persona, historical realism, would signal both solitude and freedom, a distance from the Master's command so total as to constitute an unwanted and lonely self-mastery.

It is in the space between these two options—a space, created by fantasies and memories of dominance and submission—that Brock-Broido's poetics coalesce. Revealing that other self is like joining the Master; being unable to do so amounts to being profoundly alone. A poem half-dejected and half-hopeful, "To a Strange Fashion of Forsaking" asks its Master, "Warum bin ich ich, und nicht du?" ("Why am I I, and not you?") (*ML,* 19). Soon Brock-Broido explains, "I am seized with a small fever," by which she means a feverish desire to be small— "I cannot get small enough." The speaking self who wishes to shrink back into her Master's voice, who wishes to change her pronoun, portrays herself as a prisoner in Dartmoor, and as a victim of smallpox. Here the sexual dimensions are hard to miss: "I renounce Nothing. I am imprinted erotically with—One. I will need the scarf about my mouth to quiet me. I am overheated by hard riding. Dartmoor prison is a beautiful place to be punished in." Brock-Broido's punishment is being an "I," rather than being taken fully into the space the Master/second person creates, in which she would become something else: "I am an extraordinary I & not you. Is this what you may call suffering?"

When these poems start to appear in anthologies, "Work" will surely be among those chosen, in part for its verbal brilliance, in part for its relatively penetrable situation, and in part for its consonance with familiar ways of talking about women writers. But the poem is also an ideal-typical instance of Brock-Broido's central situation throughout *The Master Letters.* Here she is revealing her self, feeling compelled to reveal her self, via subjection and confinement—in this case, the posthumous confinement all writers suffer when, dead, they become their writings. The lover/poet/speaker of "Work," dying (probably of consumption), explains to her Lord/reader/paramour, "Historically, I am insatiable and cannot be beloved hard/Enough": she both seeks his love and flees it, and hides her work (as Dickinson hid hers) "in a locked box" for his daughter to find (*ML*, 65–66). The work he finds will be her revenge— "I will harm as hard /As I have sealed the ashes in their urn"—and also her sexual memorial to him: "lie/Now with me," she asks, "while I am still holy like/This—*I hid me*" (*ML*, 66). She can appeal to this Master by turning away: his attention causes her to see herself both as holy and as "little whore," and to present herself to him while concealing something of herself, something he will later, she knows, discover.

"Work" allots its speaker an unusual amount of power in deciding what to keep from the Master and when. More usually Brock-Broido remembers or anticipates—with "desire & dread, trembling & compulsion, bliss & loss"—being made to reveal herself (*ML*, 6). We readers never see all of what has been revealed, what sort of intangible or secret self the roles or exhibits conceal, because we are not the Master, and because that self would be, *in toto*, inexpressible. We know what we know in these poems of extravagant apostrophe only as eavesdroppers and only partly, through shifting incarnations and instances. "Historically insatiable," anachronistic, exhibitionist and elusive, by turns uncomfortably transparent and hermetically confined, the self of these emulsified epistles cannot be satisfied with the normal relations between writers and readers, between history and fiction, between a lyric speaker and her embodiment. Her very dissatisfaction, her wish to be compelled into something better and more revealing, gives rise to the fiction of the absent Master, and to the poems' gorgeous, masterful, and vulnerably demanding style.

IV

The last few poems of *The Master Letters* divert their attention from *eros* to *thanatos*, from Brock-Broido's own mortal body (in all its incarnations) to others' mortality; where she had been "alone in my chamber" aspiring, she becomes "steeled/For the deaths of the few loved left living" (*ML*, 60, 73). The last of the alter egos in *The Master Letters*, the German poet Georg Trakl, whom Brock-Broido reimagines in "Am Moor," does not split up his "I" but suppresses it amid needy bodies who cannot be him:

> Was keeper of the badly marred, was furious done god, was
>
> Patient, was bad
> Luck, was nurse. Ninety badly wounded men lay baying

In the reddened reedy
Hay of Saxony, was surgeon to their flinch & hoop, was hospice

To their torso hall,
Was numinous creature to their dying

Off. Am numb. (*ML*, 76)

"Carrowmore" had conflated Brock-Broido with sacrificial lambs or sheep. "Am Moor" instead makes Brock-Broido both sheep and shepherd, taking care of others who nonetheless die.[19] Severing its speaker from her pronouns, "Am Moor" is a kind of valediction to the concerns that pervade the rest of the volume. Everything sexualized, in this atypical poem, arrives in the past tense: "was the rented room," "was chamber," "was the bleating thing," "Am anatomy." A more conventional book might end (like a successful psychoanalysis) when its speaker at last acquired a unified self. "Am Moor" suggests instead a change in Brock-Broido's project. Readers might describe that change in concerns as a shift from the grammatical second person to the third; from dominance and submission to mourning and melancholy; from the erotic to the ethical; even from adolescent to adult.

After completing *The Master Letters*, Brock-Broido told Koestenbaum: "What I should do next is to become a criminal lawyer, and just for the record I'd be a prosecutor . . . which says a lot about me and my fears of punishment, my oddly moral streak" (1998, 160). If her two books make use of her "fears of punishment," the new poems display instead the moral streak. They are at once elegies and palinodes: their self-punishment is not a matter of shame and display but of asceticism, grief, and guilt, and they make their speaker "rampantly responsible" by seeming to reject the theatrical strategies she had used. "Lucie & Her Sisters" had stated flatfootedly that "I don't want to be around to watch a family dying off. I want to be the first" (*H*, 40). She did not get her wish. The penultimate Master Letter ("The Sleeping Hollow of His Face Will Be the Straight Pass of Surrendering") describes the death of Brock-Broido's father; most of her new poems seem to respond to the death of her mother.

That recent work, imbued with numb regret, seems to complete the reorientation that "Am Moor" announced—a reorientation described with some verve and some ire in Brock-Broido's recent manifesto "Myself a Kangaroo among the Beauties." "Myself a Kangaroo" stands directly at odds with *The Master Letters* in insisting that poems are not personal letters to God or to anyone but rather are representations, accountings of deeds and sights, to a third party: "In a lyric poem, the *I* is the messenger

& must be rampantly responsible."[20] The title quotes Dickinson's letters once again, but the poetry it proposes is not like the verse of *The Master Letters*. Its goals sound considerably more stringent, even determinedly somber, a dark foreground against the bright background of the metaphors Brock-Broido continues to braid. "What I want," Brock-Broido decides, "is a poem which—when all is said & done—acts as a *palpable coffin . . .* Hoc est corpus: *Here* is the body" ("MK," 192). "Hoc est corpus" is perhaps the answer to the hypothetical question, "Where are the collected works?" It is also very close to the legal term "habeas corpus," the demand that a person in jail be properly charged with a crime or released. If the old poems elaborated and evaded, the new poems will try to stabilize, protect, accuse, and commemorate; they may also judge.

"The One Thousand Days"[21] announces itself as a return to writing poetry after three years away from it, as a poem of mourning, and as a return to life, to space outside a house. It begins with "the mourning dish of salt outside/My door": the symbolically closed door, the apotropaic salt, the slow pace and spare diction all distance the poet from the urgently playful ambitions of her older poems. The new poem describes those ambitions, but in a measured past tense: "I *was* looking to become inscrutable./I *was* longing to be seen through" (emphases mine). Brock-Broido's projects of self-concealment and self-display, flaunting and flouting a personified Master, could not keep away implacable, impersonal, unmasterable physical law, which mandates not Brock-Broido's own death but the death of her loved ones. Those loved ones appear once again as sheep and lambs, "brought down//From the high unkempt fields of Sligo"; at their slaughtering "I was quit/Of speech." Yet if her older art could not prevent harm to other people, neither could Brock-Broido's abandonment of art do any good: "I had quit the quiet velvet cult of it/Yet trouble came." The *t* and *c/q* sounds create a sort of protective enclosure, from which the word "trouble" hatches and breaks free.[22]

"Soul Keeping Company"[23] describes the practice of watching over a body before its burial. It uses repetitions and homophones (*well* and *hour/her/here, body, soul/sole*) both as a sort of mournful bagpipe drone, and as a demonstration that the poet's hoped-for word-magic has failed: verbal art might fulfill other fantasies, but never the fantasy of reviving the dead. To see the corpse in the poem is to abandon one's second self, the self one gives up when one can no longer bear to make wishes, or make magical verses out of them:

> I sat with her in keeping company
> All through the afflict of the night, keeping

Soul constant, a second self. Earth is heavy
& I made no wish, save being

Merely magical. I am magical
No more. This, I well remember well.[24]

Another repetition-driven poem of mourning, "Physicism,"[25] brings back the lambs, and the poet-as-shepherd, in order to reject even the flimsy, consoling, self-conscious fiction of religious pastoral. "Before the Babylonians, the sun was called/Old Sheep, the planets Old Sheep Stars"; now no appropriately imaginative names can be bestowed, only grotesquely generic ones:

Animal, mineral, domajigger, clock.
There are blood-sheep everywhere

But no shepherds left. Only blood sisters here,
All with the color taken from sight.

They live in black & white, material
& motherless beneath the widgit-slang of sky.

Where many of Brock-Broido's poems lean on bizarre and evocative single words, this one offers "domajigger" and "widgit," blank tokens of contemporary speakers' failure to hit accurate terms. The poem's halting, apparently hobbled speech generates nine full stops in eighteen lines, most at the ends of couplets: such a pace characterized only the bleakest few poems in Brock-Broido's earlier oeuvre.

"Physicism's" unusual properties make it a kind of farewell to fiction and fantasy in general—to the figurations of religion, and to the fantasies that had informed *The Master Letters*. "Physicism" means belief in a material world alone—no Lord, hence no shepherd: "Here there is no heaven here." At a biographical level, Brock-Broido's shepherdlessness is the condition of sisters who lack a mother. And at the level where it informs Brock-Broido's style, shepherdlessness, masterlessness, is the condition of having no one to authorize a vocative, no particular "you" for the poem to address, no one to decode the colorful language for which it seems to reach, and from which it draws back, frustrated, "in black & white." The absence of a particularized second person, here as in the other new poems, makes them collectively considerations of how grief overwhelms imagination, of how language cannot keep fancy (even masochistic fancy) viable or erotic relations possible, let alone keep people alive. One more new poem, "Entry from the Encyclopedia of Harbingers,"[26] sounds as if the poet were angry at her old poems, her old fantastic alterities, for not preventing anyone's death: "the dying was done here anyway," in the present time and place of this poem, and not in the older poems' fractured, erotic elsewheres and elsewhens:

> Not by yonder blessed celestial anything I swear:
> Not the girl who, north of nowhere
>
> Coaxed her heart so relentlessly she will never wish
> Again, not in the early Netherlandish
>
> Art of melancholia, not even in the maudlin
> Petty bourgeoisie of ruin,
>
> Nor in the sullen pity-craft before the gloom of Whitsuntide.

The catalog of negatives mirrors the forms of Brock-Broido's first successful poems, the catalog of alternate selves, for example, in "Domestic Mysticism," while the examples (Renaissance, "celestial," girlish, rural English) attack the settings of *The Master Letters*. Each phrase tries to prolong itself beyond the space of a line, while the catalog form tries to conclude each entry and move to the next. And the syntactical tensions in these distended rhymed couplets follow the emotional ones. In "Entry from the Encyclopedia of Harbingers," Brock-Broido promises an end not only to belief and fantasy but to mourning: "no more whining for the curdled milk / That was mourned or blank or bleak or spilt." Each adjective's consonantal ending sounds as if it could be the last; Brock-Broido's line, though, keeps trying to go on.

In words that describe Brock-Broido's new poems well, Jahan Ramazani suggests that "modern elegists tend . . . to resist consolation," trying instead "to reopen the wounds of loss"; more like Freudian "melancholics" than like Freud's idea of healthy mourners, modern poems about grief "refuse such orthodox consolations as the rebirth of the dead in nature, in God, or in poetry itself" (Ramazani 1994, xi). Brock-Broido's new poems specifically revisit and claim to dismantle the consolatory fantasies of her older work, impressing us with the negative space they leave. Samuel Johnson famously claimed that "Where there is leisure for fiction there is little grief" (1932, 2: 115).[27] But if all our selves are partially fictions, if all poems are letters to fictional auditors, how can a grieving poet go on writing, other than by repudiating her fictions over and over? The asceticism and clarity that the new poems promise, the memorial purposes they embody and state, remain at odds with the drive towards fancy elaboration, theatrical and willful idiosyncrasy, which continues to manifest itself in every line. The first prompts self-suppression, fictionlessness, silence; the second urges that Brock-Broido go on with her voices, situations, words.

Brock-Broido's new verses claim to turn away from *The Master Letters,* but the way the verses sound and the way they work suggest that they continue her deepest project: that of splitting up the self, making its incompletely separable, conflicting parts manifest. Yeats declared, "If we cannot imagine ourselves as different from what we are and assume that second self, we cannot impose a discipline on ourselves" (1958, 317). If Brock-Broido's new work announces a new discipline, it is the sort of discipline Yeats recommends; her split and syntactically supple voices, even as she renounces them, continue to serve her poems well.

NOTES

1. Lucie Brock-Broido, "The Wind in Search of the Heat," *Southern Review* 18 (1982): 537. Subsequent citations to works by Brock-Broido will appear as follows: "BA" = "Black Arcadia"; *H* = *A Hunger;* "MK" = "Myself a Kangaroo among the Beauties"; *ML* = *The Master Letters;* "OP" = "On the Poem: The Rh Variations."

2. Richard A. Gordon (1990, 16) describes a clinical consensus attributing anorexia to "an inability to cope with developmental demands . . . particularly the need to develop a clearly defined personal identity and sense of personal competence." These ideas are usually credited to the psychologist Hilde Bruch. The historian of anorexia Jane Brumberg (1988, 28) explains that Bruch "considered the contemporary anorectic unprepared to cope with the psychological and social consequences of adulthood as well as sexuality. . . . By refusing food, the anorectic slows the processes of sexual maturation: her menses stop and her body remains childlike. The preoccupation with controlling her appetite directs the young woman inward so that she becomes increasingly estranged from the outside world" (citing Bruch, *Eating Disorders,* New York: Basic Books, 1973, 250–55). Several of Brock-Broido's personae in *A Hunger* display other kinds of increasingly inward, and eventually pathological, estrangement, notably the twins in "Elective Mutes." Brock-Broido, *A Hunger,* 45–49.

3. Compare, in *Homage to Mistress Bradstreet:* "I am a man of griefs & fits/ trying to be my friend"; "When by me in the dusk my child sits down/I am myself. . . . Father is not himself" (Berryman 1989, 141, 143).

4. Logan also called Brock-Broido "the poet laureate of *People* magazine"; both phrases are quoted in Brock-Broido's *The Master Letters,* 81. Logan's review of *A Hunger* appeared in the *Washington Post Book World,* December 25, 1988, 6.

5. Brock-Broido, "In the Economy of Diminishing Resources," 5–7.

6. The Master's identity has been an enduring puzzle for Dickinson scholars. For Dickinson's master letters, see Dickinson (1985, 141, 159, 167). On "masochism" in Dickinson's master letters, see Noble (2000, chap. 5).

7. An earlier draft of the Preamble hypothesized that "all poems are letters to God." "Eight Poems," *American Poetry Review* (September–October 1991): 45.

8. On Renaissance imitations of Ovid's "heroic epistles," see Greenhut (1988). The Renaissance poet Michael Drayton wrote heroic epistles in the voices of medieval and Renaissance women, including Lady Jane Gray (his spelling): see Drayton (1953, 2: 445–92). On subgenres in contemporary poetry in general, see Fowler (1982, chap. 7).

9. Eliot, typically, complicates her assertion by listing the aspects of Florentine life that *have* changed—political life, dialect, commerce, or scholarship: see Eliot (1993, 9).

10. Conjoined twins had appeared in *A Hunger* as well, in "Ten Years Apprenticeship in Fantasy": "In closing, let me remind you of the Siamese twins separated not long ago in Canada. They let the little one the concave half, be girl" (*H*, 53). The whole poem is relevant to *The Master Letters*, and is discussed below. One of the psychotic twins in another poem, "Elective Mutes," says of the other, "You have no idea how much I am/she" (*H*, 49).

11. Compare Berryman's "Of 1826": "I am the little man who smokes & smokes./I am the girl who should know better but. . . ." (1969, 24).

12. For example, Eliot in "Gerontion" turned the Elizabethan playwright George Chapman's "Beneath the chariot of the snowy Bear" into "Beyond the circuit of the shuddering bear." See Southam (1994, 74–77) and Eliot (1974, 41).

13. Compare, from "Lucie and Her Sisters": "I am transfixed by possessing the things of this world" (*H*, 40).

14. Bonnie Costello (1996) writes that here "The poet projects herself into the grave . . . dismantling time and dislocating identity."

15. Italics in *The Master Letters* normally quote Dickinson's letters when no note assigns another source.

16. On masochism, selfhood, and sexuality, see also Judith Butler (1993, chap. 3). For Butler, "sexuality is as much motivated by the fantasy of retrieving prohibited objects as by the desire to remain protected from the threat of punishment that such a retrieval might bring on. . . . When the threat of punishment . . . is too great, it may be that we desire someone who will keep us from ever seeing the desire for which we are punishable, and in attaching ourselves to that person, it may be that we effectively punish ourselves in advance and, indeed, generate desire in and through and for that self-punishment" (100).

17. Vendler (1975, 71) noticed that the personae in *A Hunger* found their struggles toward language "libidinally exciting."

18. "Thomas" is the poet Thomas James, whom "the Absences" quotes; it may have overtones too of the doubting Apostle. For Brock-Broido's notes on James, see *The Master Letters*, 80, and *A Hunger*, 59. James's only book is *Letter to a Stranger* (Boston: Houghton Mifflin, 1972).

19. Trakl "was left in a barn with ninety wounded men in his charge." See Brock-Broido's note, *The Master Letters*, 83.

20. Brock-Broido, "Myself a Kangaroo among the Beauties" appears in McQuade (2000, 192–95) and is also reprinted in this volume.

21. Brock-Broido's "The One Thousand Days" appears in this volume for the first time.

22. A.E. Housman combines similar consonantal effects with disyllabic rhyme in a poem that may be a source for Brock-Broido's. Housman concludes: "The

thoughts of others/Were light and fleeting/Of lovers' meeting/Or luck or fame./ Mine were of trouble/And mine were steady/So I was ready/When trouble came" (1965, 165).

23. Brock-Broido's "Soul Keeping Company" appears in this volume for the first time.

24. Compare the end of "Grimoire," a late Master Letter: "It was a magical/ And it is nothing that I want" (*ML*, 63).

25. "Physicism" is not yet published.

26. "Entry from the Encyclopedia of Harbingers" is not yet published.

27. Ramazani (1994, 31) explains how modern elegies flout Johnson's dictum.

BIBLIOGRAPHY

Books by Lucie Brock-Broido

A Hunger (New York: Knopf, 1988).
The Master Letters (New York: Knopf, 1995).

Interviews

With Wayne Kostenbaum. "A Conversation." *Parnassus* 23(1 & 2) (1998): 143–65.
With Carole Maso. *Speak Fiction & Poetry: The Best of BOMB Magazine Interviews with Writers* (New York: G&B Publications, 1998).
With Molly McQuade. *Hungry Mind Review.* January 1, 1996 <http://bookwire.bowker.com/bookinfo/article.aspx?1478>

Selected Criticism

Costello, Bonnie. 1989. *Partisan Review* 56(4): 671–78.
———. 1996. "Poetry: The Master Letters." *Boston Review* 21(1): <http://bostonreview.mit.edu/BR21.1/poetry.htm>
Kenniston, Ann. 2001. "'The Fluidity of Damaged Form': Apostrophe and Desire in Nineties Lyric." *Contemporary Literature* 42(2): 294–324.
Vendler, Helen. 1995. *Soul Says* (Cambridge: Harvard University Press).

References

Bedient, Calvin. 1997. *Parnassus* 22(1 & 2): 282–95.
Benjamin, Jessica. 1988. *The Bonds of Love* (New York: Pantheon).
———. 1995. *Like Subjects, Love Objects: Essays on Recognition and Sexual Difference* (New Haven: Yale University Press).
Berryman, John. 1969. *The Dream Songs* (New York: Farrar, Straus & Giroux).
———. 1989. *Collected Poems, 1937–1971.* Ed. Charles Thornbury (New York: Farrar Straus & Giroux).

Brumberg, Jane. 1988. *Fasting Girls* (Cambridge: Harvard University Press).

Butler, Judith. 1993. *Bodies That Matter* (New York: Routledge).

Char, René. 1967. "Aphorism no. xvi." *Reuer et Mystere* (Paris: Gallimard).

Davis, Ellen. 1993. "Lucie Brock-Broido, An Appreciation." *Emily Dickinson International Society Bulletin* 5(1) (May/June).

Dickinson, Emily. 1958. *The Letters of Emily Dickinson.* Vol. 1. Ed. Thomas H. Johnson and Theodora Ward (Cambridge: Harvard University Press).

———. 1985. *Emily Dickinson: Selected Letters.* Ed. Thomas H. Johnson (Cambridge: Harvard University Press).

———. 1996. *The Letters of Emily Dickinson.* Vol. 2. Ed. Thomas H. Johnson and Theodora Ward (Cambridge: Har vard University Press).

Donne, John. 1967. *Satires, Epigrams and Verse-Letters.* Ed. W. Milgate (Oxford: Oxford University Press).

Drayton, Michael. 1953. *The Poems of Michael Drayton.* Ed. John Buxton (Cambridge: Harvard University Press).

Eliot, George. 1993. *Romola.* Ed. Andrew Brown (Oxford: Clarendon Press/Oxford University Press).

Eliot, T. S. 1974. *Collected Poems, 1909–1962* (London: Faber & Faber).

———. 1975. "Tradition and the Individual Talent," in *Selected Prose of T. S. Eliot.* Ed. Frank Kermode (London: Faber & Faber).

Fowler, Alastair. 1982. *Kinds of Literature* (Cambridge: Harvard University Press).

Frost, Elisabeth. 1996. "Disharmonies of Desire." *Women's Review of Books* 14(2) (November): 24–25.

Gordon, Richard A. 1990. *Anorexia and Bulimia* (Oxford: Basil Blackwell).

Greenhut, Deborah. 1988. *Feminine Rhetorical Culture: Tudor Adaptations of Ovid's Heroides* (New York: Peter Lang).

Grossman, Allen, with Mark Halliday. 1992. *The Sighted Singer: Two Works on Poetry for Readers and Writers* (Baltimore: Johns Hopkins University Press).

Heaney, Seamus. 1980. *Poems, 1965–1975* (New York: Farrar, Straus & Giroux).

Housman, A. E. 1965. *The Collected Poems of A. E. Housman* (New York: Owl/Henry Holt).

Johnson, Samuel. 1932. *Lives of the Poets.* Vol. 2 (Oxford: Oxford University Press).

Koestenbaum, Wayne. 1998. "A Conversation." Interview with Lucie Brock-Broido. *Parnassus* 23(1 & 2): 143–65.

Maso, Carole. 1998. Interview with Lucie Brock-Broido. *Speak Fiction & Poetry: The Best of BOMB Magazine Interviews with Writers* (New York: G&B Publications).

McQuade, Molly, ed. 2000. *By Herself: Women Reclaim Poetry* (St. Paul, Minn.: Graywolf).

Moore, Marianne. 1967. *The Complete Poems of Marianne Moore.* New York: Macmillan.

Noble, Marianne. 2000. *The Masochistic Pleasures of Sentimental Literature* (Princeton, N.J.: Princeton University Press).

Pope, Alexander. 1965. *The Poems of Alexander Pope: A Reduced Version of the Twickenham Text.* Ed. John Butt (New Haven: Yale University Press).

Ramazani, Jahan. 1994. *Poetry of Mourning: The Modern Elegy from Hardy to Heaney* (Chicago: University of Chicago Press).

Southam, B. C. 1994. *A Student's Guide to the Selected Poems of T. S. Eliot,* 6th ed. (London: Faber & Faber).

Spiegelman, Willard. 1996. "Poetry in Review." *Yale Review* 84(2) (April): 160–83.

Volkman, Karen. 1996. Review of Lucie Brock-Broido, *The Master Letters. Harvard Review* 11 (Fall): 17–19.

Yeats, William Butler. 1958. *The Autobiography of William Butler Yeats* (New York: Doubleday Anchor).

———. 1989. *The Collected Works of W. B. Yeats, Volume I: The Poems.* Ed. Richard J. Finneran (New York: Macmillan).

JORIE GRAHAM

EXIT WOUND

The apparently sudden appearance of—
       blossoming-out afresh, out of reach—
aiming for extinction, abandonment—
       other fossils, then again no fossils—
because of having previously lived on earth,
deviating and branching into use and disuse,
what in it that is transmitted by heredity,
that cannot help the lowest plants and animals—
what is "the lowest," where ends "environment,"
"he was therefore unable to provide a unitary theory of
                                  evolution,"
to use reason to arrive at faith,
to bring the sacred into the branchings of the un-
reasonable—the blue between the branches
pulling upwards and away so that branches
                    become
branching, their tips failing at what comes to be called dis-
                       appearance,
as if by too much compromise, straining towards justice till it
                         cannot but
fail. Alongside faith [leaping] always the
               demon, the
comparative. The presence [only the mind can do
               this] of
inner feeling up against *living force,*

what exists without having been perfected or made
                              complex,
what exists without having been made,
what exists without having been,
(therefore unable to provide a unitary theory)
(of evolution)(of regret)
what exists inside the sensation of duration—
(inside duration where is the aside to go)(how
far under)(or is it into?)—and then in the aside, the off-
hand, half-formulated, half-heard but yet still
                              living breath of a
thinking, down in the deep station of feeling—
                    though still (barely) out-
lined so as to be [branching] as-
                    certainable
and seizable, so as to be dragged up: there she
                              thought,
is my thought before me. Like a planted
thing in its pot. Not quite in nature
                    yet still alive
and—most crucially—self-evident.
And that I can feed it. [Yet she was unable still
to provide a unitary theory]. It is
(she thought looking away momentarily)(so that
looking back it could be there more fully in all
its glory: her thought) however small, a
                              catastrophe,
leafing and branching, making of itself a higher
                              and a lower
part, catastrophic, down to its
shadows cast upon the floor,
branchings so still where the leaf-ends
                              sway
in the breeze the curtains have
      touched and left off.
Outside, she thought: the point of origin.

They can call it, if they wish, she thought, the
                                supreme
being (blossoming-out afresh)(feeling as if one
had previously lived elsewhere on earth)
(out of reach even of catastrophe) (there had been,
she knew, extensive extinctions) her
                    thinking this now
deep in the *duration* [wanting
so to come back up][but up into what
                    organism of
time][or is it organization of?] the *lasting* of the minutes
                                for example,
the sensation of their being somewhere clocked
                                out in a re-
sistant form, a wage for example attached to
their beginnings and endings, beginnings and endings
                        somehow capable of being
                    exactly
cut off. That not catastrophic, therefore, for
                    example.
Not the organism of catastrophe like a
shaft of light breaking down through the crowning trees
just now [*in* the just now] as she looked out.
And could she be *associated* with it, for example,
                        that instant
of looking-up and light breaking through, could she
be imbricated into the fate [the fate's non-
                    durational
nature for example][even the recess in which
these "for examples" go][always in it, all
                        levels of
                        inwardness—
the progress by the abandonment
of some aspects of creation
                to fate]
[we call this progressionism][but there is

also the correlation of parts][in order
to determine the space to which we, each,
belong][or could it be felt—or thought—
that everything happening now was strictly
connected to something that *happened* in
the past][it was the word "happened" stopped her]
the problem as always was the problem of how
something could come out of nothing.
There was no other question: inside her,
the nothing [she could just feel it] and before her,
[the plant on the table] the something, the thought
of the nothing [for example]. The Creator loomed
                    (as it always happens)
outside, a bit far away, but still filling-in for
the unexpected. She heard the kitchen clock's gears and also the noon
                                        churchbells
on the far hill. She thought of the idea
                    of happiness
—where to place that—like a string of
                    christmas lights
dropping down into a darkened well
                    or tomb [or was it
catacomb]. She saw the images flash on
                    and off
according to the swinging of the lights. *Down there*
                    she thought. She thought
of happiness, the principle part of the
                    thinking of the thing,
its highest part, still reachable from up here by the
mind, she thought, as though a pronounced
                    looking-down,
vertiginous, a squinting, yes, but as if
one species of one's self could look back
                    far enough
(although of course here it was *down*) to
see the previous existent one had been—

the mark of *design* there upon the gap
between them now (the christmas lights)
    (the swaying intermittence of)
(the hiddenness between the frequencies)
(the frequencies)—She felt as if she could
                        reconcile
this present to that one, and that the
                      thinking
wanted that so. And that it strived.

COVENANT

This in an age in which imagination
is no longer all-powerful. Where if you had
to write the whole thing down, you could.
(Imagine: to see the whole thing written down).
Everything but memory abolished.
All the necessary explanations also provided.
A very round place: everyone is doing it.
"It": a *very* round and glad place.
Feeling life come from far way, like a motor approaching.
And in its approach: that moment when it is closest, so loud, as if
not only near you, but *in* you.
And *that* being the place where the sensation of real property
begins. Come. It is going to pass, even though right
                      now
it's very loud, here, alongside, life, life, so glad to be in it,
no?, unprotected, thank you, *exactly* the way I feel.
And you? Lord how close it comes. It has a
                seeming to it
so bright it is as if it had no core.
It all given over to the outline of seem:
still approaching, blind, open, its continuing *elsewhere* unthinkable as a

                    gear-shift
                    at this speed.
Approaching as if with a big question.
No other system but this one and it growing larger.
All at once, as if all the voices now are suddenly one voice.
Ah, it is here now, *the here.* [Love, where is love, can it too
be this thing that simply grows insistently louder]
[It seems impossible it could ever pass *by*][she thought]
the eruption of presentness right here: your veins
[Meanwhile a dream floats in an unvisited field]
[There by the edge of the barn, above the two green-lichened
stones, where for an instant a butterfly color of chicory
                                        flicks, dis-
appears] How old fashioned: distance: squinting it
                                        into
view. Even further: rocks at year's lowest tide.
The always-underneath excitedly exposed to heat, light, wind, the
being-seen. Who could have known a glance could be
so plastic. Rubbery and pushing-down on all the tiny hissing overbright
                                        greens.
O sweet conversation: protozoa, air: how long have you been speaking?
The engine [of *the most*] is passing *us* now.
At peak: the mesmerization of here, this me here, this me
passing now.
So as to leave *what* behind?
We, who can now be neither wholly here nor disappear?
And to have it come so close and yet not *know* it:
how in time you do *not* move on:
how there is no "other" side:
how the instant is very wide and bright and we cannot
                                        ever
get away with it—the instant—what holds the "know"
[as if gently, friend, as if mesmerized by love of *it*] [love of
(not) making sense] (tide coming in)(then distance taking
                                the perplexion
                                of engine

whitely in)(the covenant, the listening, drawing its parameters out
just as it approaches its own unraveling)
the covenant:yes: that there be plenitude, yes,
but only as a simultaneous emptying—of the before, where it came
from—and of the after (the eager place to which it so
"eagerly" goes). Such rigorous logic, that undulating shape
                                    we make of
                                    our listening
to it: being: being on time: in time: there seeming to be no actual
                                                    being:
all of it growing for a time closer and closer—as with a freight
                                of sheer abstract
                                abundance (the motor
sound)(is all) followed by the full selfishness (of such
                    well being) of the being
(so full of innocence) actually (for the instant) here:
I love you: the sky seems nearer: you are my first
                                person:
let no one question this tirelessness of approach:
love big enough to hide the cage:
tell them yourself who you are:
no victory: ever: no *ever:* then what "happens":
you can hear the hum at its most constant: famished: the era:
                    love bestowed upon love close-up:
(quick, ask it of heaven now, whatever it was you so
                        wished to
know) the knowing: so final: yet here is the road, the
                        context, ongoingness,
and how it does go on regardless of the strangely sudden coming un-
                                        done of
its passing away.
Silence is welcomed without enthusiasm.
Listening standing now like one who removed his hat
                        out of respect for
                        the passage.
What comes in the aftermath they tell us is richly

satisfying.
No need to make a story up, for instance.
We have been free now ever since, for instance.

PRAYER

Over a dock railing, I watch the minnows, thousands, swirl
themselves, each a minuscule muscle, but also, without the
way to *create* current, making of their unison (turning, re-
                                        infolding,
entering and exiting their own unison in unison) making of
                                        themselves a
visual current, one that cannot freight or sway by
minutest fractions the water's downdrafts and upswirls, the
dockside cycles of finally-arriving boat-wakes, there where
they hit deeper resistance, water that seems to burst into
itself (it has those layers) a real current though mostly
invisible sending into the visible (minnows) arrowing
                        motion that forces change—
this is freedom. This is the force of faith. Nobody gets
what they want. Never again are you the same. The longing
is to be pure. What you get is to be changed. More and more by
each glistening minute, through which infinity threads itself,
also oblivion, of course, the aftershocks of something
at sea. Here, hands full of sand, letting it sift through
in the wind, I look in and say take this, this is
what I have saved, take this, hurry. And if I listen
now? Listen, I was not saying anything. It was only
something I did. I could not choose words. I am free to go.
I cannot of course come back. Not to this. Never.
It is a ghost posed on my lips. Here: never.

GULLS

Those neck-pointing out full bodylength and calling
outwards over the breaking waves.
Those standing in waves and letting them come and
                                    go over them.
Those gathering head-down and over some one
                                    thing.
Those still out there where motion is
primarily a pulsing from underneath
and the forward-motion so slight they lay
their stillness on its swelling and falling
and let themselves swell, fall . . .
Sometimes the whole flock rising and running just
as the last film of darkness rises
leaving behind, also rising and falling in
                        tiny upliftings,
almost a mile of white underfeathers, up-turned, white spines
                                    gliding over the wet
sand, in gusts, being blown down towards
                        the unified inrolling awayness
            of white. All things turning white through
breaking. The long red pointing of lowering sun
going down on (but also streaking in towards) whoever
might be standing at the point-of-view place
from which this watching. This watching being risen
from: as glance: along the red
blurring and swaying water-path:
to the singular redness: the glance a
being-everywhere-risen-from: everywhere
cawing, mewing, cries where a
single bird lifts heavily
just at shoreline, rip where
its wing-tips (both) lap
backwash, feet still in
the wave-drag of it, to coast

on top of its own shadow and then down to not
landing.

•

Also just under the wave a thickening where
sun breaks into two red circles upon the
                    carried frothing—
white and roiling, yes, yet unbreakably red—red pushed (slicked) under
                each wave (tucked) and, although breaking, always
                one—(as if from the back-end-of-distance red)—
and that *one* flowing to here to
slap the red it carries in glisten-sheets
up onto shore and (also as if *onto*)
my feet.

•

[Or onto my feet, then into my eyes] where red turns into "sun" again.
So then it's sun in surf-breaking water: incircling, smearing: mind not
knowing if it's still "wave," breaking on
itself, small glider, or if it's "amidst" (red turning feathery)
or rather "over" (the laciness of foambreak) or just *what*—(among
the line of also smearingly reddening terns floating out now
on the feathery backedge of foambroken
looking)—*it is*.

•

The wind swallows my words one
                    by
one. The words leaping too, over their own
                        staying.
Oceanward too, as if being taken
                    away
into splash—my clutch of
                    words
swaying and stemming from my
                    saying, no

echo. No stopping on the temporarily exposed and drying rock
                                                    out there
to rub or rest where nothing else
                    grows.
And truly swift over the sands.
As if most afraid of being re-
                    peated.
Preferring to be dissolved to
                    designation,
backglancing stirrings,
wedged-in between unsaying and
                    forgetting—
what an enterprise—spoken out by
                    me as if
to *still* some last place, place becoming even as I speak
                              unspeakable—
and so punctually—not even burnt
by their crossing through the one great
                    inwardness of
mind, not by the straining to be held (grasped) by my
                              meanings:
"We shall have early fruit
this year" one of the shades along the way
                    calls out,
and "from the beginning" (yet further on). Words: always face-down:
listening falling upon them (as if from
                    above):
listening greedy, able to put them to death,
flinging itself upon them: them open and attached
                    so hard to
                    what they carry:
the only evidence in them of having
                    been.
And yet how they want to see behind themselves—
                    as if there is something

back there, always, behind these rows I
                gnaw the open with—
feeling them rush a bit and crane to see beneath themselves—
and always with such pain, just after emerging—
twisting on their stems to see behind—as if there were a
                                                    sun
back there they need, as if it's a betrayal,
this single forward-facing: reference: dream of: ad-
                                mission: re
semblance: turning away from the page as if turning to a tryst:
the gazing-straight up at the reader there filled with ultimate
                                                    fatigue:
devoted servants: road signs: footprints: you are not alone:
slowly in the listener the prisoners emerge:
slowly in you reader they stand like madmen facing into the wind:
nowhere is there any trace of blood
spilled in the service of kings, or love, or for the sake of honor,
or for some other reason.

THE COMPLEX MECHANISM OF THE BREAK

From here, ten to fourteen rows of folding and branching.
Up close, the laving in overlappings that pool sideways as well as suck
                                                    back.
Filamentary green-trims where the temporary furthest
                coming-forward is lost.
Suctions in three or four different directions back from pinnacle-point.
Encounter of back-suck by the foremost,
                        low-breaking, upstitching really,
arrivals,
            where it seems pebblings of sandbits ruffle-up and are ruffled
                                back into the foam of
                                the breakwater browning it.
Glassy meanwhile the frontmost arrivals, their sheets filling momentarily with

sky, with clouds fully formed (in which gulls [of sand] glide) even as they all
are drawn back
into the ruffling front-thunder
into which direct backmotion
feeds—is fed—(over which real rows of low-flying pelicans)—
(backmotion into which retreat itself feeds, slides, you'd have to say
dissolves)—
(though strangely nothing of the sea dissolves).
Behind: the crystalline green risings of just-before furling,
then the furling. Between: the wild-carrot lacings and
spume of
breakages the eye hardly caught. Lifting the eyes away one sees
in the near/far distance large upwallings
in which sometimes fish calmly ride sideways
above one,
high above, while close-up, the sky unfolds, deep, here, at our
feet—
(the eyes look down to see up)—(then, squinting, out, to see
the see-through slow uprising
holding its school). The mind doesn't
want it to break—unease where the heart pushes out—the mind
wants only to keep it coming, yes, sun making the not yet-breaking crest
so gold where the
pelicans turn as they glide—flapping then gliding—
as long as possible without too much dropping—
here and there trying to stay with the just-breaking ridge,
turning towards or away from the
watching-eye
to origami trick, artichoke wing—sheen—crank—beaks dragging the
gold-fringed, gathered garment-furl through which
the fish themselves drive (thread)
the only momentarily unbreaking line. And how there is always something
else. Up close four different brown retreating furls just now (being forced
to forward-break) re-
entering themselves. Each tripping over each as they are also forced
into retreat.

What is force? My love is forced from me as in retreat
from love. My gaze is forced back into me as it retreats
from thought. Sometimes the whole unraveling activity
                              for just an instant
pools, all its opposing motions suddenly just pattern on these briefly
lakelike flats—the shore's upslant unspooling then in only two
                              dimensions—(close your eyes)—
(although it's only when you open them you hear the seven
                                        kinds of
sound: hiss-flattenings and poolings-out [sand-suctions in the
                                        flat],
the pebbled wordlike pulling down and rolling up, the small
hush of the small first-line of white, it lowering its
                        voice as it proceeds
to crash, the crash where the larger one behind is hit and hits
                              the one of yet more force
behind it now, the singleness—(the one loud
thunder-break)—the backmost individual wave,
the lowering and sudden softening of all betweens [of which
every few minutes one] out of which the first crash
yet again can rise. Also the momentary lull: which now lets in
the sound of distance in itself: where your eye might
look up, further out: to where, it seems,
nothing but steady forward progress in its perfect
time occurs: onward, onward: tiny patterns which
seen from above, must: it is imagined: perfectly: shine).

IN/SILENCE

            I try to hold my lie in mind.
            My thinking one thing while feeling another.
            My being forced. Because the truth
            is a thing one is not permitted to *say*.
            That it is reserved for silence,

a buttress in silence's flyings, its motions
always away from source; that it is re-
served for *going* too, for a deeply
artifactual spidery form, and how it can, gleaming,
yet looking still like mere open air, mere light,
catch in its syntax the necessary sacrifice.
Oh whatever that might be. How for song
I looked today long and hard at a singing bird,
small as my hand, inches from me, seeming
to puff out and hold something within, something that
                                        makes
wind ruffle his exterior more—watched
him lift and twist a beak sunlight made burnt-silver
as he tossed it back—not so much to let
anything *out* but more to carve and then to place firmly in the
                                        listening space
                                        around him
a piece of inwardness: no visible
passaging-through: no inner complication and release:
no passage from an inner place—a mechanism
of strings, bone, hollow
chamber—no native immaterial quiver time turns material,
then towards [by mechanisms ancient and invisible] expression,
and the tragic of all upward motion—
then it all lost in the going aloft with the as yet
                                        unsung—then
the betrayal (into the clear morning air)
of the source of happiness into mere (sung) happiness.
Although there is between the two, just at the break
of silentness, a hovering, almost a penitent
                        hesitation, an
intake, naked, before any dazzling release
of the unfree into the seeming free, and it seems
it goes elsewhere, and the near (the engine) overruns
into the truly free. This till the last stars be counted?
This plus the mind's insistent coming back and coming back?

Jorie Graham | 141

This up against that coming back. The death of
uncertainty. The song that falls upon the listener's *eye,*
that seeks the sleek minimum of the meaningless *made.*
Here in the morning light. In matter's massive/
                              muscular/venerable holding-in
of all this flow. Next door the roses flow.
Blood in the hand that reaches for them flows.

PHILOSOPHER'S STONE

It's like this. There are quantities. There's on-
                              goingness—
no—there's an underneath. Over it we lay
time—actually more like takes and re-
                              takes by
mind (eyes closed) then clickings of
its opening-out and the mind fills
with gazes—thousands over some visualizations—or some
places if you wish—I wish—a few or no gazes over some
(because somewhere there must be a meadow with just such
                              grasses
no gaze has touched)—(because it *is*
touch)—and other places where millions have laid down
their mental waters in this manner). Above and
below our gaze, I don't know for sure—although I
believe there must be a truth—gravity lays,
is laid, in—like a color being washed over
the whole—a tint with a direction in it—
or rather a tint that places tiny arrowings,
or the sensation of pulling of being pulled over
all of the visualization—eyes open now—over
sky, blue, stonewall, vectoring grasses, three trees,
distance, close-up—all as if
being drawn-in without it affecting *how.*

If you open and close your eyes
there should be a difference, no, in the way
the thing seen *is*—in its weight?—and then
what the thinking has begun to make—which is
not the tint of gravity, nor the *was* of the ticking,
(what's not there if we leave
altogether for example)—because there is, on it, which we've
somehow
introduced, this wash which is duration, a very
sturdy though of course not touchable fabric, and because
we can creep along it—or simply
count lengths back—because because of it there *is* a "back"—
not a *back* on the field itself but a back to the
thinking—which *does* begin now to apprehend the edges of
skeletal diminuendos of glancings as they
ascend the manifest up towards its upper reaches—soil,
timothy, stone, manyness of stone, non-mortared
build-up of it—
mistings of just-above-stone where the
two of them meet, manifest, un-manifest [and how they
could not
know who was looking at them][and that I was from
another country][down to the very movement of my lips]
[show me a word I can use][and how all that you say
is taken from you, they take it, just like
that, it becomes smoke] smoke rising here as mist off the heavy
topmost stones
of the wall, raised so carefully up from the field,
to make this edge of precarious positionings,
that make the suddenly-green silence actually hold still, hold
up—a kind of trophy
to property, to the property of gravity—a waltz
of motions (fallings, tumblings) stilled—
a thing of number without a numbering—as if every
movement

of some gathering crowd's lips were, having uttered each one

                                              their one

request, cast forth into manifestation—slightly round with
syllable, then placed—a long wall of requests so carefully placed—
each almost pitiful with fear and desire—from each request the soil

                              scraped-off

                              where it's dug-up

from the wide field it now defines, the hole
filling back in on itself—as the self fills in on itself—a

                              collectivity—a

god making of himself many
creatures [in the cage there is food][outside only the great
circle called freedom][an empire which begins
with a set table] and I should like, now that the last washes of my gaze
let loose over the field, to say, of this peering,
it is the self—there—out to the outer reaches of
my hand, holding it out before me now, putting it into where
my breath begins to whitely manifest my difference to
night air: look: it is a law: the air
draws on itself the self's soft temperature:
it looks like rain: there is a beforehand: I brought
my life from it thus far: moments are attached.
The nets of the glance draw in. Some
admixture is caught. Some not. There is
impatience but not in the self alone. The open
has its own impatience. The edges fill with it
there where a voice is raised.
Anticipation pulls one way. Regret the other.
A smile can open or close the face. Blood
is almost touchable by sun. Footsteps bent the grass

                              a bit

to get us here. Looking behind
I see the lift in the bent weeds, I see in them
what cannot be conceived of—quite—I see *it* rise, erasing
path. As where a hand
clutches a wound, tightly, staunching the blood.

Why did we take this way? Where does this *going*
go? Maybe it can bend down now and shut its hand
over a stone. To toss it hard across the field. To have it
land somewhere. Exactly. Yes. Somebody
loves you. Elsewhere a people now is being forced
from home. Looking out, as dusk comes on,
no looking up or down anymore.
Everything taken in as stone by grass.
Does one know
what one likes. What one is like. What is a feeling
in the heart. What troubles
the soul. What troubles the jonquils nearest me
as the light, the cage of this,
goes out. What is it that can now
step *out*. And is the open door through me.
Beyond us now, but close-in, nearby,
how near I cannot tell, around us, in us, near: the
sensation of beauty unseen; an owlet's
                                    cry;
a cry from something closer to the ground that's uttered
twice and which I cannot name—although it
seems bright yellow in its pitch.

POETIC STATEMENT

At the Border

I'M NOT sure a definition of "poetics" is useful, or even possible, for a poet. In the end, I believe most signature styles are born as much out of temperament—and its rare *original* idiosyncrasies—as anything else. When I read Beckett's letters, I hear the Beckett of the novels and plays in the most occasional prose—discussing his health or the weather. We might, because of our historically defensive position, which has given rise to much fascinating theory, feel obliged, especially staring into the twin inscrutable faces of barbarism and science, to formulate and defend our temperamental instincts in more programmatic terms, of which "poetics," as a feeling and as a strongly felt notion, is a site.

At any rate, as a possible working rudder, for my own use, I would say I try, in my acts of composition, to experience subjectivity and objectivity at their most frayed and fruitful and morally freighted juncture. I try to do so as "honestly" as I can—as I believe that accurate representation of this juncture *is* possible, and that character is involved in approaching that border.

Character: good faith; generosity towards the world (when it comes to letting go of some ego, for example); admission of the *sensation* of defeat into the thinking process without having to turn immediately to defensive action (irony, for example); effort; allowing and then taking responsibility for, ambition; regard for one's elders; admission of the fear of joy; joy; admission of the fear of power; power; and, finally, courage—right there at the core of the act of composition—the courage not to let up on the belief in language; right there at the core, feeling the essential self, not being afraid of the being "found out" by philosophy; not using *intelligence* to protect from that sensation of bedrock unknowing, fundamental empty-handedness.

If there is anything I love most, in the poems I love, it is the audible braiding of that bravery, that essential empty-handedness, and that willingness to be taken by surprise, all in one voice. It is what makes the "human" sound to me. Another soul speaking across the distance—or just the *difference*—to me. And by audible I also mean audible in (or by) the form. I love the sound of what is called "earnestness." I don't experience irony with much natural, instinctive force: it seems a capacity, a world view, drawn by, and driven by, a power model of reality. In ironic perception the speaker, or the perceiver, always wins out over the world. I'm more naturally drawn, in this general arena of experience, to paradox, where the forces are more equal.

Best of all, though, I like it when the world "wins" (great acts of description, actions of mind compelled by the poem more than the poet, "cries" of their *occasion*, turns where the turning is a reaction to the world's action). I love it when the occasion is truly reached by the act of imagination, where the perceiving mind, and the imagining restlessness, is, in its language, imprinted, stained by the world, made to take the force of it in (what the miracle of syntax can absorb, encode, reveal, transmit, reenact).

As for the trustworthiness—or even the possibility—of the experience of reality: I often feel like Johnson refuting Berkeley—my toe kicking the stone. The world *is* there, but the border between the self and the world is, as I see it, a differently fluid juncture according to each poem's occasion. I "choose" occasions, therefore, with a mind to keeping the problem—with all its moral, political, spiritual, and aesthetic implications—as alive to me as possible. Shifts in my "style" are a large part of that process.

Finally, I'm not sure I believe that the problem concerning the "limits" of language—or of representation—actually affects us as much as we like to think it does. After many years of assuming that such a philosophical position was utterly natural to my own thinking—and pervasive, obviously, in the thinking of my era—I've come to some private conclusions. However much language and its capacity for representation might—and probably does—have its tortured limits, we find ourselves, as the users of it, less near its border than we might like to imagine, and at no risk of reaching it, however much we all fuss (sometimes quite wonderfully and movingly) over the issue. Such worrying *does*, of course, lend instant high-seriousness to any poetic situation. And knowing of, as well as positing, such limits to language's capacity to represent is an interesting conceptual activity. In practice, though, there's nothing being said, thought, felt, intuited, imagined—or experienced—by the user of language today that seems to me to have reached its limits.

If Shakespeare, Dickinson, and Celan didn't reach that border, we probably needn't worry the issue. In fact, when poets such as these grapple with the edges of utterance, where silence seems the only possible next step for the speaker to undertake, it is not because language has failed the author, it seems to me, but because the human speaker has reached the point where the action of mind *takes place* in silence. Just because emotion—or thought—sometimes grows wordless does not imply that words fail that emotion or thought. It implies that certain textures of experience are by their nature silent. This is an issue that interests and perhaps confuses much contemporary poetry. As far as I can tell, there's really nothing whose *nature* it is to be linguistic (even if not obviously or easily so, even thoughts or feelings that trill at the farthest reaches of the sayable) that can't be ultimately rendered by powerful and accurate uses of language.

There are, of course, some things whose nature is *not* linguistic (thoughts that dwell "too deep for tears"). One of the interesting things about poetic art is that it attempts to include those in its body as well.

That capacity to "express" the ineffable, the inexpressible, the emissary of the nonverbal territories of intuition, deep paradox, conflicting bodily impulses as well as profoundly present yet nonlanguaged spiritual insights, even certain emotional crisis states—these are the wondrous haul that the nets of "deep image," "collective emotive image," haiku image-clusters, musical effects of all kinds (truths only introduced via metrical variation, for example), and the many hinge actions in poems (turns, leaps, associations, lacunae) bring onto the shore of the *made* for us. The astonishments of poetry, for me, reside most vividly in its capacity to make a reader receive utterable and unutterable realities at once.

But where the terrain *is* linguistic, and the failure linguistic, we may just need to grow more skillful. There again it is perhaps a matter of temperament. The magnificent instrument we call language certainly isn't the problem.

JORIE GRAHAM AND EMILY DICKINSON

Singing to Use the Waiting

Thomas Gardner

IN A REMARK that at first seems surprising, Jorie Graham notes at the end of her most recent book *Swarm* (2000) that Emily Dickinson's 640 is a core text for that volume, "animat[ing] the book throughout" (113).[1] In fact, Dickinson's work has been on Graham's mind throughout her career, providing one of the crucial voices—along with those of Bishop and Stevens—with which her work could be said to be in almost constant conversation.[2] But in turning to Dickinson's 640, Graham opens both a new stage in her response to the earlier poet's work and a new stage in her own thinking. Poem 640 is an address to a beloved who has been almost infinitely removed from the speaker:

> I cannot live with You
> It would be Life—

And Life is over there—
Behind the Shelf

The Sexton keeps the Key to—
Putting up
Our Life—His Porcelain—
Like a Cup—

Discarded of the Housewife—
Quaint—or Broke—[3]

If living with him, the two becoming one flesh, were life, that world has
been ruled out of bounds. It is a possibility that has been laid aside and
locked away like a discarded cup. Simply put, there seems to be a law
against it.

Graham has always been attracted to the way Dickinson is awakened
by situations such as this in which something resists or is held back. As
Dickinson puts it in 338, a poem Graham often refers to, what resists ex-
ists in silence, a world that can't be spoken for because it can be neither
identified nor located. One might, perhaps, think of that silence as a game:

I know that He exists.
Somewhere—in Silence—
He has hid his rare life
From our gross eyes.

'Tis an instant's play.
'Tis a fond Ambush—
Just to make Bliss
Earn her own surprise! (Poem 338)

But if it is a game, Dickinson suggests between clenched teeth, it is a
"piercing[ly] earnest" (Poem 338) game in which the searcher's gleeful
sense of anticipation has the potential of being met not by a fondly sprung
ambush, but by unyielding, stony silence:

But—should the play
Prove piercing earnest—
Should the glee—glaze—
In Death's—stiff—stare—

Would not the fun
Look too expensive!
Would not the jest—
Have crawled too far! (Poem 338)

Such encounters with silence, Graham writes—crawling, broken, a law forever blocking access—are Dickinson's great legacy:

> If poems are records of true risks (attempts at change) taken by the soul of the speaker, then, as much as possible, my steps are towards silence. Silence which is the absence of speech, or the ability to speak, the reason or desire. Silence which drowns us out, but also which ignores us, overrides us, silence which is doubt, madness, fear, all that which makes the language bend and slip. . . . Dickinson's poems, her dangers, are . . . authenticated by her losses. So many of them—battles with those emissaries of silence which are the ocean, the wind, the light of day . . . and the speechlessness of pain, of fear—end on great failures of human speech.[4]

To say, then, that Graham has been in conversation with Dickinson's work throughout her career, seeking to extend it, would be to say that she has engaged in similar battles with what "ignores" or "overrides us" and has courted similar "failures of human speech." In being defeated or silenced by what won't open up to her—"God, nature, a beloved, an Idea, Abstract form, Language itself as a field, Chance, Death, Consciousness, what exists in the silence. Something not invented by the writer," Graham writes[5]—the writer senses and is marked by a world that sends her to her knees. We "hear" that larger world in those places where language is gagged. We "read" its imprint as it erases or slashes through what we have written. As that happens, writer and reader are awakened to, are forced to more fully engage, what warps or penetrates straightforward speech and thought. Graham put it this way in 1994, introducing a reading of Dickinson's work but offering insight into her own goals as well:

> I suggest listening in the poems as I read them now for the use of order and its breakdown, senses and their extinguishing, imagery and its obliteration, rhyme and its increase or failure, the speaker moving from an active to a passive stance, remembering and then forgetting, narrative that breaks off into silence, beginnings that are not beginnings, endings that are not endings; attempts at letting the timeless as experienced in extreme states of being—anguish, despair, for example, or in the presence of death—penetrate the language in order to stain it; dashes as those places where the timeless makes its inroads—where what exists in the silence seeks to be let in.[6]

Such confrontations, Graham noted in introducing another reading of Dickinson in 1999, draw the reader in as well, forcing him or her to "undergo . . . different kinds of vertigo-laden sensations that undermine any stable understanding of what's in the silence in order to be able to inhabit it fully."[7]

Inhabiting more fully a world that yet remains unmasterable, both poet and reader are brought to an awakened use of language. Graham writes:

The bedrock role of poetry, ultimately, is to restore, for each generation anew, the mind to its word and the words to their world via accurate usage. Every generation of poets has that task, and it must—each time—do it essentially from scratch. Each image achieved, each moment of description where the other is seized, where it stains the language, undertakes the same vast metaphysical work: to restore the human word to the immortal thing; to insure that the relationship is, however momentarily, viable and true. . . . To make the words channels between mind and world. To make them full again.[8]

Graham's books record the different ways, in the name of making words full again, she has tried to open and inhabit Dickinson's vertiginous moment when language or mind or stable understanding fails. In this, she shares an ambition common to a number of other contemporary writers.[9] What's particularly interesting about Graham is that her way of drawing the reader into those language-enriching, "vertigo-laden sensations" has taken a significant turn recently, a turn that I will attempt to chart in this essay and that has important implications for what we look for in contemporary writing.

In Graham's work through 1993, the poet charts confrontations with "what exists in the silence," allowing it to so charge and disrupt her language that the reader is brought into an equivalent experience of vertigo in his or her engagement with the poet's speech. As we'll see, Dickinson's poems approaching the moment when "a Plank in Reason, broke,/And I dropped down, and down—" (280) are much behind this. But Graham's more recent work has turned to another aspect of Dickinson—to those poems where she writes as a lover, recording her confrontations with those forces that hold the beloved silent and apart from her and, in doing so, seeking to arouse and awaken that figure. Dickinson's 640 is a powerful example of this aspect of the earlier poet's work.

If we return to 640, then, we could say that the poet's broken speech to the absent beloved—words thrown against silence in steady despair—is in fact an attempt to be stained by, or to inhabit more fully, the larger silence that has silenced him. If the possibility of each giving himself or herself to the other in self-erasure had been declared out of bounds when they were alive, what about dying at the same moment? What about that form of union?

> I could not die—with You—
> For One must wait
> To shut the Other's Gaze down—
> You—could not—(Poem 640)

It would have been physically impossible, she sighs: in such circumstances, one figure must always wait or lag behind to attend to the other, and in any case, she pointedly remarks, the beloved had once before been unable to wait. Neither could they rise and be united at the moment of judgment, for the lover's face "Would put out Jesus'—" (Poem 640) displaying glory so overwhelming that the promises of grace would be of no interest to her, thus forcing them apart again:

> They'd judge Us—How—
> For You—served Heaven—You know,
> Or sought to—
> I could not—
>
> Because You saturated Sight—
> And I had not more Eyes
> For sordid excellence
> As Paradise (Poem 640)

Her voice continues rising as she engages the absent lover and the powerful forces arrayed against them: "were You lost," she writes, and I somehow welcomed into the ranks of the saved, "I would be" as lost and abandoned as you; and "were You—saved" and the two of us separated, that isolated self would be as deep a torment as hell could hold.

It's that flaring passion, pressing more and more forcefully against silence—its wall or law—that Dickinson refers to in the poem's last stanza when she writes, in the present tense:

> So We must meet apart—
> You there—I—here—
> With just the Door ajar
> That Oceans are—and Prayer—
> And that White Sustenance—
> Despair—(Poem 640)

If there is to be no merging of the two bodies, no erasure of self in union, then we are left with the "meet[ing] apart," you there and I here, that occurs through the "Door ajar" of this poem—an extraordinary sort of speech so overwhelmed by the "oceans" of difference opened up by the lover's absence that it has become "Prayer." By prayer we can take Dickinson to mean speech intimate with what refuses to speak back, speech sustaining itself—being made alive by—the despairing acknowledgment of a world there but finally out of reach, an ocean of a world encountered through the door ajar of language. That is what Graham means by the great failures of speech in Dickinson: this poem, offering itself as door, ocean, and prayer. It displays language, as Graham puts it in another context, in which the lover can hear "words cutting into an element . . . crushing in its power and weight," a struggle through which we the beloved might join her in awakening to "the unsaid . . . its indifference, beauty, intractability."[10] Graham's new work, poised at the edge of a new century and following this portion of Dickinson's lead, seeks to do something similar in attempting to awaken the numb, exhausted users of language it addresses. It's an ambitious, formally daring project.

I'd like to approach *Swarm* by first describing, at some length, Graham's earlier responses to Dickinson.[11] *Erosion* (1983) argues quite straightforwardly that the moment when language bends and slips exists and that it adds something important to our approach to the world. Behind the book, one can sense such a poem as Dickinson's "A narrow Fellow in the Grass" in which taking "notice" of a snake momentarily visible at the speaker's feet produces not the familiar "transport/Of cordiality" experienced in other natural encounters but a sense of alienation and a shocked inability to respond: "Zero at the Bone" (986). One also hear echoes of Dickinson's "A Bird came down the Walk—" in which an attempt to describe and domesticate is broken off by a bird's sudden removal of itself to a realm "Too silver for a seam." The poems in *Erosion* suggest that through such suddenly speechless moments, "we know there is a wall/beyond which we can't go" (79) and further, that "on the erosion-line," where our too-easily-relied-on expectations of cordiality and access begin to crumble, we begin to grow. And we grow because we are forced to acknowledge a world in some ways fundamentally outside of us: "we are defined by what we will not take/into ourselves" (79).

Erosion's poems turn on a series of oppositions in which, as in the Dickinson poems I've just referred to, a more straightforward and confident approach to the world is broken off by an acknowledgment of the limits of that approach. For the most part, the poet looks outside of herself for examples. "Wanting a Child" points to "the waste/of time" when a river, which "has been everywhere, imagine, dividing, discerning,/cutting deep into the parent rock" is "yoked,/trussed" by the incoming tide: "pulsing upward, inland, into the river's rapid/argument, pushing/with its insistent tragic waves . . ./. . . so that erosion/is its very face" (29). "Salmon" turns from a couple making love—the poet noting "the thin black seam/they seemed to be trying to work away/between them"—to the "space of time" afterwards, when the task has been put aside and "they made a distance/one from the other/and slept" (40–41). "At Luca Signorelli's Resurrection of the Body" contrasts the painter's desire to understand the body, to arrive at a stable version of the human, with his acknowledgment that such a sense of stability is always, always receding:

> In his studio
> Luca Signorelli
> in the name of God

                    and Science
                and the believable
                    broke into the body

                studying arrival.
                    But the wall
                of the flesh
                    opens endlessly,
                its vanishing point so deep
                    and receding

                we have yet to find it (75)

Imagine, the poet writes, when Signorelli's own son "died violently" and
he began to study *that* body: "with beauty and care/and technique/and
judgment, cut into/shadow, cut/into bone and sinew." Imagine the mo-
ment, she continues, when, after days of "that deep/caress, cutting,/un-
fastening," the analytical mind came to a halt, no end to its tormenting
questions in sight, and "climb[ed] into/the open flesh and/mend[ed] it-
self" (75–77).

Most of the poems in *Erosion* work out versions of this pattern, con-
vinced that as the mind or scalpel or river halts, some sort of healing or
fuller vision begins. "I Watched a Snake" takes up Dickinson's poem di-
rectly and argues that the snake's movement— "I'd watch/its path of body
in the grass go/suddenly invisible/only to reappear a little/further on"—
can be read as "a mending/of the visible/by the invisible." The snake's dis-
appearance or apparent defeat—Graham compares it to death or "going
back under"—links it to what overcomes it or erases it: "fastens [it]/to
sturdier stuff" (34). Like a wall that cannot be broken through or a body
that cannot be fully known, that sturdier stuff silences what would possess
it; it enforces a "Zero at the Bone." At the same time, Graham argues, such
a defeat mends the mind by bringing it into contact with a previously invis-
ible world outside of its desperate-to-describe reach. It's a defeat, Graham
would say, in which we are made more whole, moving from the "quick in-
telligence that only knows" to "another, thicker, kind of sight" (4, 5).

What's most notable about Graham's next volume, *The End of Beauty*
(1987), is that she begins there the long process of trying to inhabit, for
herself, that place where the quick intelligence is turned back and forced
alive by a world that holds itself apart from her. "Vertigo" describes this
confrontation in the third person, the poet picturing herself standing at the
edge of a cliff and looking out and down to where "a real world flowed in
its parts, green, green." She reads that sudden drop as the sheer reach of
the mind, giddy in its bright ambitions:

She thought of where the mind opened out
into the sheer drop of its intelligence,
the updrafting pastures of the vertical in which a bird now rose,
blue body the blue wind was knifing upward
faster than it could naturally rise,
up into the downdraft until it was frozen until she could see them at last
the stages of flight, broken down, broken free,
each wingflap folding, each splay of the feather-sets flattening
for entry. . . . *Parts* she thought, *free* parts, watching the laws
at work, *through which desire must course*
seeking an ending, seeking a shape. (66)

Momentarily caught and held in the play of updraft and downdraft, the bird rising before her seems to have "broken free" of the world, the mind able to break it down into its constitutive parts, hungry to name or completely know its shape. But then, as in Dickinson, something shifts and, "all of an instant" the bird breaks free of the mind's ambitions, becoming "a blue/enchantment of properties no longer/knowable." Yoked or trussed, the mind is swept with a vertiginous series of questions about its drive to know and name:

What is it to understand, she let fly,
leaning outward from the edge now that the others had gone down.
How close can the two worlds get, the movement from one to the other
being death?

. . . .

How is it one soul wants to be owned
by a single other
in its entirety?—

. . . .

What was it that was *not her listening?*
She leaned out. What is it pulls at one, she wondered,
what? That it has no shape but point of view?
That it cannot move to hold us?
Oh it has vibrancy, she thought, this emptiness, this intake just
                                    prior to
the start of a story, the mind trying to fasten
and fasten, the mind feeling it like a sickness this wanting
to snag, to catch hold, begin, the mind crawling out to the edge of the cliff

and feeling the body as if for the first time—how it cannot
follow, cannot love. (67)

This is the space Graham and Dickinson are fascinated by: the world's
emptiness or silence or difference made vibrant and momentarily readable
by the mind's frantic, broken-off questions.[12] How close can the two
worlds come? What sort of entrance do we seek in self-erasure? How does
point of view pull shapelessness into form? What is lost in the process?
Those questions bring her to an awareness of her body—the body that has
always known it can't follow the mind's airy ambitions. Unable to catch
hold, sick and dizzy with its desperate (and now seen as impossible)
needs, the mind, in such a situation, is thrown back on the body and an-
other way of knowing.[13] The body knows that the distance from the edge
of the cliff to the real is unbridgeable, knows that there is a law blocking
union, but in knowing that feels the world down there brought vibrantly
into play. Those questions, that sense of vertigo, another poem puts it,
"made me hear how clean the sky . . . was of/anything I might have
trapped it with" (69).

One of the primary ways the poet allows such questions to "undermine
. . . stable understanding" is through a series of poems, many of them la-
beled self-portraits, in which she tries to imagine the inner lives of paired
figures in some of the great stories in the Western tradition. In most of the
stories, one figure reaches for or looks at or tries to touch the world he or
she loves: Orpheus "seeking [Eurydice's] edges, seeking to make her pal-
pable again" (15); Apollo wanting "to possess [Daphne], to nail [her] era-
sures" (30); Mary Magdalene desperate to touch the risen Christ, "her
longings all stitchwork towards his immaculate rent" (42). And most of
the stories pivot on the moment when that longing to possess is brought
up short: Eurydice returning to "the possible which each momentary out-
line blurs into again" (15); Daphne becoming "part of the view not one of
the actors . . ./. . . untouched, untransformed" (34); Christ saying "Don't
touch me," "want[ing] her to believe,/. . . want[ing] her to look away"
(42). The stories differ enough to lead the poet in various ways as she ex-
plores the confrontation, but as Graham attempts to keep both voices
alive (one seeking, one pulling free), what begins to emerge is a different
way of speaking. Graham describes this in "Vertigo" as the body coming
alive or into play as the mind is forced to acknowledge its limits. As
Daphne forces Apollo to acknowledge that there is a world that "would
not be the end towards which he was ceaselessly tending" (32), as she
transforms his desires into "vertigo-laden sensations," she opens a gap
that the mind can no longer assume it can traverse. As Orpheus is brought
up short and the end of the story is withheld, Eurydice, or constantly

changing process, begins to speak. We hear in these poems: "the body of talk between the start and beauty/. . . sucked alive by delay . . ./. . . the unsaid billowing round" (83, 85). Trussing the mind, acknowledging the law that keeps us apart, is crucial in bringing about a new use of language: "Siren,/reader,/it is here, only here,/in this gap/between us,/that the body of who we are/to have been/emerges" (43). Such speech, the final poem in the book argues, seeking and failing "to keep the thing clear," gives the silent or faceless world something to mark and allows it momentarily to become visible or hearable: "What would she be/without us/willing to sit and clarify and try to nail/it shut? We give her that glitzy fluttering, her body, by the one deep-driven/nail of point-of-view,/don't we?" (95–96).

In *Region of Unlikeness* (1991), Graham pushes this investigation forward in an important way. Rather than playing out the tension between mind and world as framed in our culture's stories, she plays out that tension as it is framed in her own stories—her memories. And perhaps even more significantly, in many of the poems she plays out the tension in the act of writing or remembering, sketching powerful equivalents to Dickinson's displays of the mind's movements and reversals. Some of the memories are narrated in the present tense, as if being lived out again in the writing: "She lies there. A corridor of light filled with dust/flows down from the booth to the screen" (3); or "I'm in the bathroom holding the baby down,/washing it off" (29). In other poems, the poet sorts through a memory while quite deliberately calling attention to the words she speaks or the paper in front of her or her struggle to reach the reader: "Has to do with the story about the girl who didn't die/in the gas chamber, who came back out asking/for her mother. . . ./. . . Can you help me in this?/Are you there in your stillness?" (12); "We rose from the table having paid our bill./. . . I look into the air/for your face—" (24); "He turns in his sleep./You want to get out of here./The stalls going up in the street below now for market./Don't wake up. Keep this in black and white" (37); "It was one day near the very end of childhood, Rome,/. . . Should I tell you who they are, there on the torn/page—should we count them (nine)—and then the girl who was me" (41).

What's going on here is that she's playing Eurydice to her own Orpheus—opening up a gap in the expected straightforward passageways between now and then and exploring the "body of talk between the start and beauty/. . . sucked alive by delay." The idea is the same: that when the process stalls, you face something new and wordless. Graham's term in this volume for that live space where the mind's vertigo-laden sensations are sorted through and explored is *waiting*—as in this passage where the poet remembers staring at her face in a mirror, unable to move forward after being betrayed by a father's lie:

When Psyche met the god he came down to her

   through the opening which is *waiting,*
the *not living* you can keep alive in you,
   the god in the house. We painted that alive,
mother with her hands
   fixing the outline clear—eyeholes, mouthhole—
forcing the expression on.
   Until it was the only thing in the end of the day that seemed

believable,
   and the issue of candor coming awake, there,
one face behind the other peering in,
   and the issue of
freedom. . . . (44–45)

The poems in *Region* seek to paint the unsettling issues discovered in memory alive, allowing them to awaken. As they do so, wandering in an exploratory way through the door ajar between now and then, here and there, something previously silent ("*not living*") is felt and given "expression." These issues and questions are discovered in both the scenes remembered and in the act of writing, so that one investigation spurs on the other—is in fact the same as the other. So, for example, a memory of being in a movie theater and the house lights coming on because of an emergency while the movie continued to play captures an experience of waiting—the forward progress of the movie's story was reduced to "just a roiling up of graynesses,/vague stutterings of/light with motion in them, bits of moving zeros"—and provides the impetus to meditate on similar issues raised in the writing, for example, her reluctance to sort through and choose when she knows, at some level, that writing (like the whited-out movie) is little more than "a grave of possible shapes called *likeness*" (5).

What happens in the space of waiting, then, is that the mind is stopped but still thinks, but in a more exploratory, intuitive, or bodily way. As one poem puts it, waiting is "(Where the hurry is stopped) (and held) (but not extinguished) (no)" (125). Dickinson suggests that the voice (and the mind) comes powerfully alive in this space. For her, the space of waiting is a gap "Capacious as the Sea—/Between Eternity and Time—/Your Consciousness—and Me—" (644). She proposes to "sing to use the Waiting" (850), perhaps growing "Fitter to see Him" (968) as her ability to sing and see develops in that space where such drives are "held" but "not extinguished." Graham's teasing out the issues raised by her own memories has quite similar goals.

Let me give an example. "From the New World," as we've already seen, focuses on the poet's reaction to a terrible story recounted during the trial of the man accused of being the Nazi prison guard Ivan the Terrible. A young girl came out of the gas chamber alive, asking for her mother, and Ivan ordered a man going in to rape her. Trying to touch this remembered story, the poet finds herself "unmoored," the poem stalling, and turns to the reader who now must also wait:

> God knows I too want the poem to continue,
>
> want the silky swerve into shapeliness
>   and then the click shut
> and then the issue of sincerity . . . (12)

She explores the unmoored space and the clicking shut of form by moving to her own life and memories of her grandmother's last years: the moment when her grandmother failed to recognize her and the poet fled to a bathroom, sensing her stable world unraveling around her ("Reader,/they were all in there, I didn't look up,/they were all in there, the coiling and uncoiling/billions/. . . Then the click like a lock being tried"); and an experience some years later when her grandmother had been placed in a nursing home and spent her time "sitting with her purse in her hands all day every/day, asking can I go now,/. . . the eyes unfastening, nervous . . ./. . . old whoever clicking and unclicking the clasp the/silver knobs" (13–15).

This feeling of the world coming unfastened followed by the frantic clicks of the mind trying to find purchase ties these two scenes back to both the gas chamber and the poet's stalled confrontation with the story. But the scenes don't explain the story and get it moving again; the poet keeps turning to the reader and asking, "Where would you go now? *Where.*" What happens instead is that she enters deeply into her own inability to handle the story, to settle it into an adequate likeness. Likeness itself, what she's attempting to do as she shifts from the young girl to her grandmother, becomes as charged and uncertain and desperate as the young girl's asking for her mother or the grandmother asking for home.[14] In failing to move the story forward, in painting the issues of storytelling alive, then, the poet finds herself overwhelmed by an experience of silence:

> *Like* what, I wonder, to make the bodies come on, to make
>   room,
>
> *like what*, I whisper,
>
> *like* which is the last new world, *like, like,* which is the thin
>
> young body (before it's made to go back in) whispering *please.* (16)

At the same time, these poems also fear that the space of waiting may simply become a place where, riddled with uncertainty, live expression disappears—in the language of this book, no face or expression will move forward:

> flecks of
> information,
>   fabric through which no face will push,
> proof,
>   a storm of single instances (105)

This fear, I would suggest, eventually pushes Graham's use of Dickinson in a new direction, but at this stage it merely flickers in the background. These poems hope for the opposite: that the language of waiting might become responsive to the silence pressing against it; that the poet might grow "Fitter to see Him," as in this encounter with the shroud bearing the impression of Christ's face:

> —When they held it up to us
> we saw nothing, we saw the delay, we saw
>
> the minutes on it, spots here and there,
>   we tried to see something, little by little we could almost see,
> almost nothing was visible,
>   already something other than nothing
> was visible in the *almost*. (74)

With *Materialism* (1993), Graham moves even more firmly into the present-tense act of writing, completing a sort of trilogy of works that, following Dickinson, explore ways of awakening language to what it is unable to master. The gap these poems paint alive is that between the mind (or eye) and the world. The poems are primarily attempts to bridge the space between here and there by description, tracking the way the eye seeks to know and make order[15]:

> *First* this. *Then* this . . . Oh, glance—gnawing the
>   overgrowth,
> criss-crossing the open for broken spots, leaks—
> what is there? what is
> the object? (8)

As in *The End of Beauty* and *Region of Unlikeness*, such attempts lead to a kind of vertigo, the mind or eye not able to take in all that yawns open before it and, becoming aware of its limits, yielding to other ways of knowing: "I can feel the mind at its hinge,/insane for foothold./. . . The mind feeling sure there is a beneath—a hard place—/behind the spangly news report" (51–52). Feeling the mind's flailing, dramatizing its brought-up-short attempts to caress and possess the world, fills the waiting—the idea being that as the mind is forced *down* from its above-the-world illusion of invulnerability and abstract accuracy, the world is lured *up* from its complexity into a bit of visibility. "Manifest Destiny" offers a striking image for such a manner of writing; think of language as a bullet, now in a museum case, that a soldier had bitten down on during an amputation in an attempt to hold back a scream, the poem suggests. Testifying to the struggle to master the scream and to the scream's overwhelming resistance, the bullet records a "claw[ing] for foothold," "the toothed light [biting] down hard on the sinewy scream" (99). The scream, as in Elizabeth Bishop, seems alive forever, its face showing through the "fabric" recording the struggle.[16] The bullet, like a snake moving and disappearing, issues a challenge to the writer:

> How can the scream rise up out of its grave of matter?
> How can the light drop down out of its grave of thought?
>
> How can they cross over and the difference between them swell with existence? (100)

An early poem in the book, "Steering Wheel," helps us see the manner in which Graham paints alive the descriptive mind's clawing for foothold. Backing out of a driveway, glancing in her rearview mirror, the speaker's eye is caught by a "veil of leaves" sucked up by an updraft. Quickly trying to graph the red swirl of leaves—noting their relationship to three pine trees behind them, contrasting their movement to the "rising strings" of music on the radio, "crisp with distinctions, of the earlier order"—she finds herself brought up short, unable to cross the space between eye and world: "Oh but I haven't gotten it right./You couldn't say that it was matter./I couldn't say that it was sadness" (5). And in that failure, still looking backwards, she remembers a phrase of George Oppen's:

> "we have to regain the moral pleasure
> of experiencing the distance between subject and object,"
> —me now slowly backing up
> the dusty driveway into the law
> composed of updraft, downdraft, weight of these dried
> mid-winter leaves,
> light figured-in too, I'm sure, the weight of light,
> and angle of vision, dust, gravity, solitude,
> and the part of the law which is the world's waiting,
> and the part of the law which is my waiting,
> and then the part which is my impatience—now; *now?*—(5–6)

What Graham does in *Materialism*, and this is also drawn from Bishop, is look backwards at things—hold herself backwards to the normally straightforward business of looking and placing ourselves.[17] In doing so, she experiences "the distance between subject and object," thought of here as a law against which the eye presses: the law holding eye and world separate (both waiting); the law played out in the separate paths taken by world (updraft, downdraft, dust, gravity) and observer (angle of vision, solitude, impatience to name and move on). Experiencing or fully inhabiting this drama, being broken by its pressures, the poet hopes to meet the world.

By watching herself observe—watching herself attempt to possess and colonize, but also explore and sort through—the poet tries to fill the waiting, allowing the pressure of the silent ocean of material things to be brought to bear against her words. The self-scrutiny is quite deliberate, as here, nearing the conclusion of a description of pausing before a tree filled with starlings in a snowstorm:

> The storm: I close my eyes and,
> standing in it, try to make it *mine*. An inside
> thing. Once I was. . . . once, once.
> It settles, in my head, the wavering white
> sleep, the instances—they stick, accrue,
> grip up, connect, they do not melt,
> I will not let them melt, they build, cloud and cloud,
> I feel myself weak, I feel the thinking muscle up—
> outside, the talk-talk of the birds
>
> . . . .
>
> but inside, no more exploding, no more smoldering, no more,
> inside, a splinter colony, new world, possession
> gripping down to form,
> wilderness brought deep into my clearing (85)

Let me give an extended example—a variation on Dickinson's "A Bird came down the Walk" entitled "Subjectivity." The poet encounters an unmoving Monarch butterfly on a cold morning and brings it into her house, its black and yellow colors offering an image of the way the mind's gaze seeks to take possession:

> yellow of cries forced through that mind's design,
>   like a clean verdict,
>   like a structure of tenses and persons for the gusting

> heaven-yellow
> minutes . . .
> or the gaze's stringy grid of nerves
> spreading out onto
>
> whatever bright new world the eyes would seize upon—(26)

As we might anticipate, the butterfly will not be held by the eye—a neighbor will in time explain that the butterfly is simply reacting to the cold; placed in the sun, it "ris[es] up of a sudden out of its envelope of glances—/a bit of fact in the light and then just light" (31)—but before the mind lets go, the poet plays out the distance between grid and new world, eyes and heaven. And she does so in an interesting way. She uses her body to feel out what the mind is engaged in doing, puts herself into the position of the thing seen—matter, the butterfly, heaven's yellow—in order to feel more deeply what such knowing is all about. That would be like permitting Eurydice to speak in *The End of Beauty*. It opens a space between "the start and the beauty" where a different "body of talk" can begin, allowing that space to "swell with existence."

Moving from a past tense description of the butterfly to a present tense exploration, the poet sits in a chair and watches a beam of sunlight slowly move across a slatwood floor: "making a meaning like a wide sharp thought—/an unrobed thing we can see the inside of" (26). Eventually, waiting long enough, the light touches her foot, instep, calf, and then face. As she waits, she feels something of what making form is all about, allowing that drive to take on visibility and body. As the light finally touches her face, it:

> forc[es] me to close my eyes,
> the whole of the rest feeling broken off,
>
> it all being my face, my being inside the beam of sun,
>
> and the sensation of how it falls unevenly,
>
> how the wholeness I felt in the shadow is lifted,
> broken, this tip *lit,* this other *dark*—and stratified,
> analysed, chosen-round, formed—(29)

If that is what her mind is after, such a forceful and inadequate taking on of wholeness, then her own eyes, as she returns to her own encounter with the butterfly, seem much less godlike as they are drawn out of their untouched confidence:

> these thin almost icy beams I can feel my open eyes release,
> widening as they sweep down
> out of the retina

       to take the body in—
   aerial, tunneling, wanting to be spent in what cannot
       feel them as they smear, coat,
   wrap, diagram—(31)

Through such dramas, words gain "materiality," becoming more and more aware that there is always "a tiny draft/just underneath them" and that they must "displace something to/*be*" (16).

The Errancy (1997) marks the beginning of a turn in Graham's work that I've suggested can be thought of as a shift from exploring Dickinson's dramatization of herself as a brought-up-short thinker and describer to a meditation on her dramatization of herself as a balked lover. *The Errancy* focuses on thought itself—not just memory or description but the whole attempt, grand but impossible, to "in a net . . . seek to hold the wind." Thinking, in this book, has exhausted itself: "aren't we tired aren't we/ going to close the elaborate folder/which holds the papers in their cocoon of possibility" (6); "The reader is tired./I am so very tired" (50). This is a cultural exhaustion, and one notices in this volume Graham beginning to turn her eye away from herself and outwards, towards culture itself— *Swarm*'s exhausted lover.

A series of poems spoken by guardian angels who worry over, from a distance, different aspects of our work as thinkers serves to set the context for the book. The angel who understands our drive to perfect the world— "little dream, invisible city, invisible hill"—notes how far away the dream is today: "Life buzzing beneath me/though my feeling says the hive is gone, queen gone" (2, 3). Another worries over our overdeveloped drive to strip away what only resembles or approaches the truth: "how clean/ did they want to become,/shedding each possibility with gusts of self-ex-posure,/. . . letting each thought, each resting-place, get swept away—" (15). A third knows the drive to reduce the world to something private and manageable: "the heart trying to make time and place seem small,/ sliding its slim tears into the deep wallet of each new event on the list/then checking it off—oh the satisfaction—each check a small kiss,/. . . this list you hold/in your exhausted hand" (20, 22). What about our desires, once we've exhausted ourselves, to simply give up on thinking and feeling? An-other angel understands those feelings: "You know how in a landscape you see distances?/We can blur that. We can dissolve it/altogether. You know the *previous age*?/How it lacks shape until it's cut away by/love? We gust that lingering, moody, raw affection/out, we peck and fret until it's/gone" (46). And so on: the world the angels describe is exhausted, jaded, knowing—an Apollo who knows now he'll never hold Daphne, but has nowhere else to turn.

What would it take to awaken the mind in such a difficult context? One poem powerfully compares awakened thought to a song just barely kept in circulation:

> like the slenderness of the tune
> overheard by the prisoner
> as someone singing passes by
> then stops to look at something and forgets
> to keep the song alive—the prisoner so still—
> something like madness flapping in him now
> as he holds still, so still, almost not breathing, that the song
> be made to start again—(86)

The poem goes on to argue that, as Dickinson shows, it is through an acknowledgment of the "bad fit [between itself and the world] that the mind [is forced] to awaken" (87), but the book as a whole is still searching for a strategy to bring such an awareness across. One strategy is to look for models of awakened, misfitting thought and call our attention to them ("look up!" is a constant refrain) so that the "madness flapping in [us]" at the cliff's-edge drop-off of reason might find another way to move forward. "The Scanning" compares our situation to driving on an interstate, fiddling with the radio— "the bands of our listening scan/the bands of static,/seeking a resting point" (7)—and finally pulling off, plan exhausted, no clear way to move forward. We can think of thought in that way:

> What shall we move with
> now that the eye must shut? What shall we sift with
> now that the mind must blur? What shall we undress the veilings of
> dusk with,
> what shall we harvest the nothingness with,
> now that the hands must be tucked back in their pockets (8)

An answer is discovered after the car is parked and the poet walks out along a riverbed, eventually disturbing a flock of geese who, in a way, open a door ajar from within the death of reason, sketch a new Jacob's ladder potentially re-involving heaven and earth:

> and the birds lift up—
> and from the undulant swagger-stabs of peck and wingflap,
> collisions and wobbly runs—out of the manyness—
> a molting of the singular,
> a frenzied search (unflapping, heavy) for cadence, and then
> cadence found, a diagram appearing on the air, at arctic heights,
> an armoring

the light puts on—stagger of current-flap become unacrobatic industry,
                                                no tremble in it,
no echo—below, the freeway lustrous with accurate intention—
above us now, the sky lustrous with the skeleton of the dream of
                                                reason—look up!—
Jacob dreamer—the winged volumetrics chiseling out a skull
for the dream—(10)

We find a second version of that call to look up and a new possibility for thought in two late poems in the book discussing Magritte's painting of the coat into which Pascal had sewn the "irrefutable proof of the existence of God." In Magritte's painting, reproduced on the cover of *The Errancy,* the coat is ripped and floats against the outline of a city, the night sky shining through it:

> The coat, which is itself a ramification, a city,
> floats vulnerably above another city, ours,
> the *city on the hill* (only with the hill gone),
> floats in illustration
> of what was once believed, and thus was visible—
> (all things believed are visible)—
> floats a Jacob's ladder with hovering empty arms, an open throat,
> a place where a heart may beat if it wishes
>
> . . . .
>
> It floats before us asking to be worn (65, 69)

Thought that finds and loses cadence—staggering, unacrobatic; thought whose ideal city is torn and vulnerable. These poems implore the exhausted reader to look up and slip that coat on. Wake up, Jacob, and move forward again, they coax. One torn example, of course, is the poet's own thought process: "I have put on my doubting, my wager" (69), she writes, challenging us to follow. Many of the poems are quite inventive in the ways they try to help the reader visualize how the mind might move. "Untitled Two," for example, describes thought as "a masonry of shades" who gather in a parking lot—the ghosts of "excellence, and skill, all throbbing in the parking lot" (25) like a group of powerless toughs. Thinking begins when:

> the walled-up day hives-open once again.
> And they foam-out along its veins. Syllable by syllable.
> I give them liberty. They gnarl, they sweep over the hubs,
> into the panes, they fill the seats.

. . . .

> swirling black zero we wait in,
> through which no god appears,
> and yet through which nothing can disappear,
> a maximum delay, a sense of blurred desire in it,
> a slumbering, a catch-all mirror for the passers-by,
> silky frontier in which it is all saved—(25–26)

When a group of girls "on break" hurries through the parking lot— "their voices swirling up—impregnable—. . ./. . . scales of belief,/quick blurtings-out like a bright red jug/raised high into the waves of light" (26)—one at first fears for them, and then realizes how ineffectual the shades of thought are, save for just one moment when one girl makes a "hard remark" and silence overtakes the chattering crowd for a second. Thought leans forward, almost able to penetrate the world, and then settles back again:

> a silence—like a wing raised up,
> but only one—a hum all round, heads facing forwards
> in the cars, heads pointing forwards in the cars,
> anti-freeze fingering daylight near some tailpipes, *here* and *here*,
> a brutish click, sound of black-water lobbying,
> and then one girl, like a stairway appearing in the exhausted light,
> remembers the *reason* with a fast sharp gasp,
> and laughter rises, bending, from the chalice of five memories,
> as they move past us towards the railing of the lot (26, 27)

In a similar way, we are urged to visualize thought as the "raw vertigo" of a couple making love:

> we are looking for it everywhere—
> we look on my breast, we try the nipple,
> we look in the gaiety of your fingertips, the curriculum
> of caresses
> twisting and windy in the architecture of
> my neck, my
> open mouth—we look in your mouth—
> we look, quick, into the-day-before-yesterday—we look
> away—(54)

Or, more calmly, we're challenged to imagine it as walking beside a river at night:

> Cicadas churn. My wholeness now just something *alongside*—
> a stammering, an unattachedness—hands in pockets—a walking straight
> ahead into the black,
> and walking fast—as if to seed the patiently prolonging emptiness (96)

But in all of these poems, the nagging question of how to get the reader, the culture, to look up and respond remains.

That is where *Swarm* comes in. Instead of trying to think or describe or remember, in each case opening themselves to the vertiginous questions alive in such acts, these new poems, following Dickinson's 640, explore the law against us as it is made visible in the speech of a lover to a beloved. If in previous books the speaker explored how the Orpheus or Apollo (completed form) in her would speak if it acknowledged the resistant claims voiced by Eurydice or Daphne (the body or process), in *Swarm*, as in Dickinson's 640, Eurydice speaks first, approaching and attempting to awaken her absent (blinded, maimed, exhausted) lover. If thought is exhausted and won't look up and respond to new ways of moving, then in *Swarm* process itself speaks, its voice directed outward, toward the beloved. In the book's first poem, Graham quotes a phrase from a Dickinson letter— "to all except anguish the mind soon adjusts"—and it is clearly the nonadjusted mind that speaks in *Swarm*. Accordingly, many of the poems are composed of fragments—single words, phrases—that at times draw together into moments of stunning and awakened beauty and at others will "not heal into meaning" (68). This is a bold but risky strategy; in contrast to previous books in which a forward-moving style of speaking, although constantly being halted or turned aside in new directions, was always within reach, *Swarm* begins with that exhausted voice altogether silent.

The title poem offers a fairly straightforward illustration of this new approach. Speaking to a distant beloved, the poet describes and recreates an overseas phone call she had made to him from Italy:

I wanted you to listen to the bells,
holding the phone out the one small window
to where I thought
the ringing was—

Vespers scavenging the evening air,
headset fisted against the huge dissolving

. . . .

I had you try to listen, bending down into the mouthpiece to whisper, hard,

can you hear them (two petals fall and then the   is wholly
changed) (yes) (and then another yes like a vertebrate enchaining)
yes yes yes yes (57)

She describes that moment as the coming together of the two— "We were somebody"—and the temporary reassembling of the "huge dissolving" into order:

> like a piece of the whole blueness broken off and thrown down,
> a roughness inserted,
>
> yes,
> the infinite variety of *having once been,*
> of being, of *coming to life,* right there in the thin air, a debris re-
> assembling, a blue transparent bit of paper flapping in also-blue air,
>
> boundaries being squeezed out of the blue, out of the inside of the blue,
> human eyes
> held shut,
>
> and then the whisking-open (57–58)

This *yes,* of course, is as tattered and charged a response to the silence as any of the others we've examined, but what's new is that "she" has drawn it out of "him," helped him listen. By calling him to Dickinson's "Door ajar /That Oceans are—and Prayer—/ And that White Sustenance—/Despair— ," she has made it possible for them to "meet apart," charged by the great space within which they move toward each other:

> why should you fear?—
> me holding my arm out into the crisp December air—
> beige cord and then the plastic parenthetical opening wherein I
>
> have you—you without eyes or arms or body now—listen to
>
> *the long ocean between us*
>
> —the plastic cooling now—this tiny geometric swarm of
> openings sending to you
>
> no parts of me you've touched, no places where you've
>
> gone—(58, italics mine)

Although, because of the distance, he is "without eyes or arms or body," she attempts to draw him beyond this state, offering up the space between them and revealing there a new sort of body, one not touched or entered before.

As in Dickinson's 640, much of what the speaker of these poems does is press herself in protest against the laws that seem to deny her the possibility of connection. And as with Dickinson, the protest is often directed at some version of God who has set such a world in place: "I knock on the front/ whispering open up, forgive us,/can you grow any more silent?" (22). Borrowing the agonized phrasing of Dickinson's second Master letter— "A love so big it scares her, rushing among her small heart"[18]—the narrator charges:

> But, master, I've gone a far way down your path,
> employing sounds from my throat like stones from my pockets,
> emptying them onto your lips, into your
> ear warm from sunlight.
> Not in time. My suit denied.
> What is lateness my small heart asks. (30–31)

One of the things that small heart does is demand explanation, as in an early poem about Persephone in which the narrator's voice breaks off and turns to a silent auditor, pleading in vain: "Explain the six missing seeds./ Explain muzzled," and later "Explain two are/Explain not one" (8, 10). A number of poems seem almost to listen to Dickinson's lament in 640 and hurl fragments of it up against a blank wall: "Explain *and were you lost*/ Explain *and were you saved*" (50); "Explain door ajar,/. . . Explain saturated./Explain and I had no more eyes" (55); or simply "Door ajar" (53), "Meet me" (105). This seems to be drawn from Dickinson's equally striking demand for explanation in poem 193, a work looking forward to the end of time when "Christ will *explain* each separate anguish/In the fair schoolroom of the sky—," concluding fiercely, with a protest much like Graham's speaker's, that only then, "[Shall I] forget the drop of Anguish/ That scalds me now—that scalds me now!" (193).[19]

These protests seem designed to rouse the volume's absent lover or sleeping king. Early poems speak to the lover of his (or their) situation, helping him acknowledge his blindness. For example, "Underneath (Upland)," one of a sequence of poems spoken as from "underneath" some law or pressure keeping the lovers apart, uses phrases from David Jones's description of the Welsh landscape as a "Sleeping Lord" to shed light on the king's maimed body, which it stands in for[20]:

> light swinging in the right hand of this me the follower
>
> trying to overhear the low secret though not too hard
>
> . . . .
>
> while the creatures are felled,

gracing the high slopes with cries and outstretched arms

felled, among the stout-fibered living wood (17)

"Underneath (Sibylline)" pushes him to admit fully the failure of the mind's straight paths:

Open your hiding places.

Burn all the letters.

Look in the ashes with both hands.

Finger in there for any bits intact.

Wrist-deep

in the fine grains, so cold,

feel further round for fragments,

for any last unburnt

piece of

the crashing of mind (25)

Later poems in the volume draw him, in his brokenness, toward her body—that is, toward process or suffering or shattered, door-ajar responsiveness. Together, they suggest, lover and beloved, or mind and body, might take action and risk belief. I'll sketch just a bit of this, often reading the narrator through the voices of others. Quite directly, Calypso veils Odysseus and pulls him toward her and away from his story, insisting that he join her "In anguish here under the veil./Going broken before some altar" (43). An early set of fragments, "Mastery scarcity desiccation noon" (6), tracing the decline of straightforward mastery and then its blinding reversal, is fleshed out in these terms: "Noon: we push until/like a third party/matter rages between us" (51–52). Christ's appearance to Thomas in John 20— "Reach your fingers here./Reach your hand here./Blessed are those who have not seen/yet have/believed" (54)—draws from the narrator an acknowledgment of her situation— "The repeated vacancy /of touch/begging for real work" (53)—and then, turning toward her sleeping lover, this movement forward: "Touching you in sleep/along the lips I start to wake./Inundation" (53). From Dickinson's description in 625 of "Fleshless Lovers" reunited, after "long Parting," before the throne of God with "No Lifetime—on Them," the narrator sings to the culture the attraction of just the opposite—bodies and a lifetime of struggle restored. That torment, the poem assures the lover, is the source of human meaning and feeling and all true responsiveness:

> Make the sore not heal into meaning.
>
> Make the shallow waters not take seaward the mind.
>
> Let them wash it back continually onto the shore.
>
> Let them slap it back down onto the edges of this world.
>
> . . . .
>
> Refuse rescue.
>
> Overhear love. (68–69)

Through the voice of the chorus in *The Orestia,* she reminds Orestes: "The one who acts must suffer" (72).[21] In the voice of Eurydice, she calls Orpheus to the realization that it is "as if we were a gap/in the page, a crack near the center,/without reality, though being spelled out—/Cover me up, be king" (74). And perhaps most forcefully, the narrator insists first to her lover and then to God that the wall or law keeping each from truly losing himself or herself in the other is the source of the vividness of their engagement:

> what does the wall contain we now must press
>   (together)
>
> against
>
> if you use it to enter me more
>
> vividly
>
> . . . .
>
> You who cannot be traversed
>
> we brave the middle kingdom of mere blossom
>
> we numb the intelligence
>
> we push against your law without regret
>
> we enter my body harder because of the wall (97, 98)

By entering that body, he—the mind, let's say—enters what Graham calls "the mother tongue," a new way of speaking. Dickinson wrote: "So We must meet apart—/You there—I—here—/With just the Door ajar," and Graham has sought, throughout her career, to imagine anew that invitation:

this is the mother tongue

there is in my mouth a ladder

climb down

presence of world

impassable gap

pass

I am beside myself

you are inside me as history
We exist Meet me (105)

With her most recent book, something close to "the mother tongue" itself speaks, acknowledging as always an "impassable gap" but testifying as well to the "presence of the world."

NOTES

1. I will refer to the following Graham texts in this essay: *Erosion* (Princeton: Princeton University Press, 1983); *The End of Beauty* (New York: Ecco Press, 1987); *Region of Unlikeness* (New York: Ecco Press, 1991); *Materialism* (Hopewell, N.J.: Ecco Press, 1993); *The Errancy* (Hopewell, N.J.: Ecco Press, 1997); *Swarm* (New York: Ecco Press, 2000).

2. In *The Breaking of Style* (Cambridge: Harvard University Press, 1995), Helen Vendler notes in passing Graham's "descent from Dickinson at her most metaphysical and Moore at her most expansive" (93). For Graham's response to Bishop, see "An Interview with Jorie Graham" (229–32) in Thomas Gardner, *Regions of Unlikeness: Explaining Contemporary Poetry* (Lincoln: University of Nebraska Press, 1999).

3. *The Poems of Emily Dickinson*, ed. Thomas Johnson (Boston: Little Brown, 1960). I will be quoting from this edition throughout since it is the one Graham would have used.

4. Jorie Graham, "Some Notes on Silence," in *19 New Poets of the Golden Gate*, ed. Philip Dow (New York: Harcourt, Brace, Jovanovich, 1984), 409, 411.

5. Jorie Graham, "Introduction" to *The Best American Poetry, 1990*, ed. Jorie Graham and David Lehman (New York: Collier Books, 1990), xxvii.

6. Jorie Graham, reading at the Folger Library, December 13, 1994.

7. Jorie Graham, reading at Harvard University, August 13, 1999.

8. Graham, "Introduction," xxviii.

9. For a discussion of the way a number of contemporary writers work with the moment when language or the mind fails, see Gardner, *Regions of Unlikeness*. For a fascinating collection of responses to Dickinson by contemporary writers, see "Titanic Operas: A Poets' Corner of Responses to Dickinson's Legacy," ed. Martha Nell Smith and Laura Elyn Lauth, in *Dickinson Electronic Archives*, <http://jefferson.village.virginia.edu/dickinson/titanic/index.html>

10. Graham, "Introduction," xvi.

11. Some of the comments that follow rework readings of Graham's early work in Gardner, *Regions of Unlikeness* (166–213).

12. In *The Breaking of Style*, Helen Vendler writes that "a poetry of middleness, of suspension, is Graham's chief intellectual and emotional preoccupation in *The End of Beauty*" (80). She discusses "the moment of suspension" in Graham in broader terms in *Soul Says: On Recent Poetry* (Cambridge: Harvard University Press, 1995), 224–27.

13. In *The Given and the Made*, Helen Vendler notes that this opposition is at work even in Graham's earliest writing: "How to give bodily perception its due in thought is a question already vexing Graham's verse" (96).

14. In *Soul Says*, Helen Vendler describes the poet moving in this poem "towards the overwhelming metaphysical question: . . . What is Being *like*? In what words, in what symbols, can it be made intelligible?" (230).

15. Helen Vendler writes in *The Given and the Made* that in this volume Graham "attempt[s] to describe the material world with only minimal resort to the usual conceptual and philosophical resources of lyric . . . and to make that description a vehicle for her personal struggle into comprehension and expression" (129). Willard Spiegelman offers a strong essay-length discussion of the way Graham enacts description and its limits as part of a quest to know and see in "Jorie Graham's 'New Way of Looking," *Salmagundi* 120 (Fall 1998): 244–75.

16. I have in mind Bishop's story "In the Village" and the mother's scream "alive forever" in the narrator's Nova Scotian village. See my discussion of this story in Gardner, *Regions of Unlikeness*, 63–64. In "Some Notes on Silence," Graham writes of Bishop that "the scream is in fact the voice of the silence—its foray into, possession of, speech—silence made audible," 410.

17. See, for example, Bishop's "The Man-Moth" who "always seats himself facing the wrong way" and my discussion of this poem in Gardner, *Regions of Unlikeness*, 34–35.

18. *The Master Letters of Emily Dickinson*, ed. R.W. Franklin (Amherst: Amherst College Press, 1986), 22.

19. See also Letter 892 where Dickinson remarks "'So loved her that he died for her,' says the explaining Jesus." In *The Letters of Emily Dickinson*, ed. Thomas H. Johnson (Cambridge: Harvard University Press, 1958).

20. In her notes to *Swarm*, Graham writes that "David Jones's work—especially in *Anathemata* [1952] and *In Parenthesis* [1937]—provided inspiration for this work in a very general sense." "Underneath (Upland)," however, draws from

another sequence: *The Sleeping Lord and Other Fragments* (1974). For one source of Graham's phrases, see the selection from "The Sleeping Lord" in *Introducing David Jones*, ed. John Matthias (London: Faber and Faber, 1980), 222–26. For example, compare Graham's last three lines quoted here with Jones's account of the ravaging of Wales by the mythic boar Trwyth while the maimed Arthur sleeps, attended by a light-bearer: "Not by long-hafted whetted steel axe-blades/are these fallen/that graced the high slope/that green-filigreed/the green hollow/but by the riving tusks/of the great hog/are they felled./It is the Boar Trwyth/that has pierced through/the stout-fibred living wood/that bears the sacral bough of gold." For a reading of this poem see Thomas Dilworth, *The Shape of Meaning in the Poetry of David Jones* (Toronto: University of Toronto Press, 1988), 330–43.

21. In a note on the poem "Fuse" in *Swarm,* Graham refers the reader to Robert Fagles's translation of the *Orestia* as well as to his introduction to that work. The trilogy and Fagles's reading are central to understanding *Swarm*'s work with its maimed or blinded or dismembered king, whose death (or sleep), in Fagles's words, "releases vital energies" (10)—a "bloody wedding" (18) freeing the swarming furies who must be embraced in order for regeneration to occur. For Fagles, Orestes—who avenges his father's death by killing his mother, suffers the onslaught of the equally-vengeful furies, but is then led by Athena's powers of persuasion and compassion toward restoration—is the key figure. He writes that Orestes "must suffer for 'the race of man,'" through madness being granted "the power to suffer into truth" (63). Further: "Through the Furies the language of Aeschylus suffers into truth. . . . Without them Orestes would never strive for restoration. . . . They are the Process, like the Great Mother as Nietzsche saw her, 'eternally creating, eternally driving into life, in this rushing, whirling flux eternally seizing satisfaction'" (89). See *The Orestia,* trans. Robert Fagles (New York: Bantam Books, 1982), in particular "The Serpent and the Eagle: A Reading of the *Orestia*" (1–99).

BIBLIOGRAPHY

Books by Jorie Graham

The Best American Poetry, 1990, ed. Jorie Graham and David Lehman (Old Tappan, N.J.: Macmillan Publishing Company, 1990).

The Dream of the Unified Field: Selected Poems, 1974–1994 (Hopewell, N.J.: Ecco Press, 1995).

Earth Took of Earth: 100 Great Poems of the English Language, ed. Jorie Graham (Hopewell, N.J.: Ecco Press, 1996).

The End of Beauty (New York: Ecco Press, 1987).

Erosion (Princeton: Princeton University Press, 1983).

The Errancy (Hopewell, N.J.: Ecco Press, 1997).

Hybrids of Plants and of Ghosts (Princeton: Princeton University Press, 1980).

Materialism (Hopewell, N.J.: Ecco Press, 1993).

Region of Unlikeness (New York: Ecco Press, 1991).
Swarm (New York: Ecco Press, 2000).

Selected Prose

"Introduction." *Best American Poetry, 1990* (Old Tappan, N.J.: Macmillan Publishing Company, 1990), xv–xxxi.
"Introduction." *Earth Took of Earth: 100 Great Poems of the English Language* (Hopewell, N.J.: Ecco Press, 1996), ix–xviii.
"Pleasure." In *Singular Voices: American Poetry Today*, ed. Stephen Berg (New York: Avon Books, 1985), 89–94.
A Poetry Reading: Presidential Lecture 1991 (Iowa City: University of Iowa, 1991), 1–20.
"Some Notes on Silence." In *19 New American Poets of the Golden Gate*, ed. Philip Dow (New York: Harcourt, Brace, Jovanovich, 1984), 409–15.

Interviews

Gardner, Thomas. "An Interview with Jorie Graham." *Denver Quarterly* 26(4) (1992): 79–104. Repr. in *Regions of Unlikeness: Explaining Contemporary Poetry* (Lincoln: University of Nebraska, 1999).
Graham, Jorie. "A Conversation about *Materialism*." *Seneca Review* 24(2) (1994): 5–19.
Meek, Jay. "An Interview with Jorie Graham." *North Dakota Quarterly* 54(2) (1986): 162–68.

Selected Criticism

Altieri, Charles. "Jorie Graham and Ann Lauterbach: Towards a Contemporary Poetry of Eloquence." *Cream City Review* 12 (Summer 1988): 45–72.
Bedient, Calvin. "Like a Chafing of the Visible." *Salmagundi* 120 (Fall 1998): 220–43.
———. "Kristeva and Poetry as Shattered Signification." *Critical Inquiry* 16(4) (Summer 1990): 807–29.
Costello, Bonnie. "Jorie Graham: Art and Erosion." *Contemporary Literature* 33(2) (Summer 1992): 373–95.
Gardner, Thomas. "Accurate Failures: The Recent Work of Jorie Graham." *Hollins Critic* 24(4) (October 1987): 1–10.
———. "Jorie Graham's Incandescence." In *Regions of Unlikeness: Explaining Contemporary Poetry* (Lincoln: University of Nebraska Press, 1999), 158–213.
———. "An Open, Habitable Space: Poetry 1991." *Contemporary Literature* 33(4) (Winter 1992): 712–35.
Henry, Brian. "Exquisite Disjunction, Exquisite Arrangements: Jorie Graham's 'Strangeness of Strategy.'" *Antioch Review* 56(3) (Summer 1998): 281–93.
Jarman, Mark. "The Grammar of Glamour: The Poetry of Jorie Graham." *New England Review—Middlebury Series* 14(4) (Fall 1992): 251–61.

Longenbach, James. "Jorie Graham's Big Hunger." In *Modern Poetry after Modernism* (New York: Oxford University Press, 1997), 158–76.

Molesworth, Charles. "Jorie Graham: Living in the World." *Salmagundi* 120 (Fall 1998): 276–83.

Paretti, Marie. "'What Clicks beneath This Talk': The Failure of Language in the Poetry of Jorie Graham." In *Speaking the Unspoken: Silence, Language, and Form in Contemporary Poetry*. Dissertation, University of Wisconsin-Madison, 1997.

Ramke, Bin. "Critical Mass: Jorie Graham and James Tate." *Denver Quarterly* 33(3) (Fall 1998): 100–07.

Selinger, Eric Murphy. "In Each Other's Arms, Or No, Not Really." *Parnassus* (Spring 1999): 156–84.

Shifrer, Anne. "Iconoclasm in the Poetry of Jorie Graham." *Colby Quarterly* 31(2) (June 1995): 142–53.

Spiegelman, Willard. "Jorie Graham's 'New Way of Looking.'" *Salmagundi* 120 (Fall 1998): 244–75.

Vendler, Helen. "Fin-de-Siècle Poetry: Jorie Graham." In *Soul Says: On Recent Poetry* (Cambridge: Harvard University Press, 1995), 244–56.

———. "Jorie Graham: The Moment of Excess." In *The Breaking of Style: Hopkins, Heaney, Graham* (Cambridge: Harvard University Press, 1995), 71–95.

———. "Jorie Graham: The Nameless and the Material." In *The Given and the Made: Strategies of Poetic Redefinition* (Cambridge: Harvard University Press, 1995), 91–130.

———. "Mapping the Air: Adrienne Rich and Jorie Graham." In *Soul Says: On Recent Poetry* (Cambridge: Harvard University Press, 1995), 212–34.

———. "Married to Hurry and Grim Song: Jorie Graham's *The End of Beauty*." In *Soul Says: On Recent Poetry* (Cambridge: Harvard University Press, 1995), 235–43.

BARBARA GUEST

VALOROUS VINE

Lifts a spare shadow
              encircling vine,
does not tarnish   bauble
    from overseas   and out of silver mine,
drop in clamor and volume.

          Along the footpath
    returned to mourning a lost stem,

    gauzy the stem-like saving, or ruled
    over stone to develop muscular difficulty.

          In the wind
    and overhead, held back lightning. Did
not surrender or refuse visibility and pliancy obtained.

          Or confuse VIOLETRY with stone
    or dissipate the land   land unshackled,
          budding in another country
    while dark here.

ii

It can be seen she encouraged the separation of flower from the page, that
she wished an absence to be encouraged. She drew from herself a technique
that offered life to the flower, but demanded the flower remain absent. The

flower, as a subject, is not permitted to shadow the page. Its perfume is strong and that perfume may overwhelm the sensibility that strengthens the page and desires to initiate the absence of the flower. It may be that absence is the plot of the poem. A scent remains of the poem. It is the flower's apparition that desires to remain on the page, even to haunt the room in which the poem was created.

IF SO, TELL ME

    I give you the unhinged sleeve
dropped the seam   it went onto our back
was fodderless.

    Wilted, say, by the gravel road
who ran a mile with legs apart
      neck hanging and groupless.

Bird shadow crossing the room   leave the outdoors!
Earns a pittance of food on the ledge   mother
of ten eggs   the real bird   feeds on ices
     the shadow is ten eggs.

Do you wonder if a run on sand is better than inside
does this strike you as shallow   does it tease aloud
  the action
   is part of a wing.

The building was added   it grew from an arm   protruded out of
a thigh   the upper terrace is fighting   is divided.

    To think of you turned inside
your garment rent you are appointed   apart from the rites
      lessened, as in a daring scheme.

You are beheaded
much cast out that rolls on the ground, toss out thread
of what worked
        to use or unlearn. If so, tell me.

CONFESSION OF MY IMAGES

The sliding window

        left agape, and
the neck does not swell

an octave with ardor

    is destabilized.

Of query and cultivation, of vases not known,
even as the known voice so is the alarm—.

            .

        Eros freed of the wooden seat

the crowd similarly, as

    an elbow

fits into the ancient arm

                touch
        of sweet vest
creating furor.

        to create sweet furor.

the page
                    floats on knobbled water,

debris in the atrium,   "to visit Leopardi in Naples"

supportive
                    to breathe the same idiom.

DEFENSIVE RAPTURE

Width of a cube spans defensive rapture
cube from blocks of liquid theme
phantom of lily stark
in running rooms.

adoration of hut performs a clear function
illusive column extending dust
protective screen the red
objects pavilion.

deep layered in tradition moonlight
folkloric pleads the rakish
sooted idiom
supernatural diadem.

stilled grain of equinox
turbulence the domicile
host robed arm white
crackled motives.

sensitive timbre with complex
astral sign open tent hermetic
toss of sand swan reeds
torrents of unevenness.

surround a lusted fabric
hut sequence modal shy
as verdigris hallow force
massive intimacy.

slant fuse the wived
mosaic chamber astrakhan
amorous welding
the sober descant.

turns in the mind bathes
the rapture bone a guardian
ploy indolent lighted
strew of doubt.

commends internal habitude
bush the roof
day stare gliding
double measures.

qualms the weights of night
medusæ raft clothed sky
radiant strike the oars
skim cirrus.

evolve a fable husk
aged silkiness the roan
planet mowed like ears
beaded grip.

suppose the hooded grass
numb moat alum trench a solemn
glaze the sexual estuary
floats an edge.

AN EMPHASIS FALLS ON REALITY

Cloud fields change into furniture.
furniture metamorphizes into fields
an emphasis falls on reality.

"It snowed toward morning" a barcarole
the words stretched severely

silhouettes they arrived in trenchant cut
the face of lilies . . .

I was envious of fair realism.

I desired sunrise to revise itself
as apparition, majestic in evocativeness,
two fountains traced nearby on a lawn . . .

you recall treatments
of 'being' and 'nothingness'
illuminations apt
to appear from variable directions—
they are orderly as motors
floating on the waterway,

so silence is pictorial
when silence is real.
The wall is more real than shadow
or that letter composed of calligraphy

each vowel replaces a wall
a costume taken from space
donated by walls . . .

These metaphors may be apprehended after
they have brought their dogs and cats
born on roads near willows,

willows are not real trees
they entangle us in looseness,
the natural world spins in green.

A column chosen from distance
mounts into the sky while the font
is classical,

they will destroy the disturbed font
as it enters modernity and is rare . . .

The necessary idealizing of you reality
is part of the search, the journey
where two figures embrace

This house was drawn for them
it looks like a real house
perhaps they will move in today
into ephemeral dusk and
move out of that into night
selective night with trees,

The darkened copies of all trees.

THE FAREWELL STAIRWAY

(*after* Balla)

The women without hesitancy began to descend
leaving flowers—

Ceres harried—bragged of cultivated grain—

      I saw Hecate. the gray-wrapped woman.
      in lumpy dark.

      farewell eyes revolve—
      the frontier oscillating—

            pleated moments.
            Hades at the bottom—

they laughed like twins their arms around each other
the women descending—

      birds dropping south out of wind.

I thought there were many. goodbyes twisted
upwards from the neck—

      tiny Arachne donating a web—

a common cloudy scene. no furniture.
a polished stairwell—

      women magnetized. moving. chatting.

            responding to the pull—
      the vortex—

·

curves rapidly oscillating—

       undulating to rapid pencil lines.
       or water—

       the look of stewed water.
       sensuously.

              and gnarled Charon—

·

their clothes—volumes—

       folded over. blowing.
       dresses approach the wide penciling—

Hecate was present
and that other woman looking backward—

       tearful. holding onto the rail.

I saw it futurally—

stoppered cotton slowly expanding. released.
sliding from the bottle—

·

I was outside the vortex. close to the wall.
       Hecate managed me—

             at the curve. the magic.
             floated up—spiraled—

·

they were fully dressed. their volume.
the modish descent—

antiqueness—

·

a roman *scala*.

in the neighborhood of the *stazione*.

gli addii—gli adii—
velocity—

whipped the waves.

the vortex centered. reverent.

·

you who are outside. over there.
can't feel the pull. it makes you wonder—

the oscillation. the whirling. urgent.
indicating air revolving in a circuit—

without interruption. free movement
in *cielo puro*—spider-less—

scatters everything.

something overheard—beyond Lethe.
whispered—and the corollary—

·

diminuendo on the stair.
the slowed *salutando*—
flagrant barking from the shore—

keeping a stylish grip on themselves. serapes.

                    futurally extended.

                  ·

            south dusk and fire balls—

the same at Nauplia. mythic potency—

            winding down the tower—

                  farewell. farewells.

WORDS

The simple contact with a wooden spoon and the word
recovered itself, began to spread as grass, forced
as it lay sprawling to consider the monument where
patience looked at grief, where warfare ceased
eyes curled outside themes to search the paper
now gleaming and potent, wise and resilient, word
entered its continent eager to find another as
capable as a thorn. The nearest possession would
house them both, they being then two might glide
into this house and presently create a rather larger
mansion filled with spoons and condiments, gracious
as a newly laid table where related objects might gather
to enjoy the interplay of gravity upon facetious hints,

the chocolate dish presuming an endowment, the ladle
of galactic rhythm primed as a relish dish, curved
knives, finger bowls, morsel carriages words might
choose and savor before swallowing so much was the
sumptuousness and substance of a rented house where words
placed dressing gowns as rosemary entered their scent
percipient as elder branches in the night where words
gathered, warped, then straightened, marking new wands.

POETIC STATEMENT
The Forces of the Imagination

THE FORCES of the imagination from which strength is drawn have a dis-
ruptive and capricious power. If the imagination is indulged too freely, it
may run wild and destroy or be destructive to the artist. Baudelaire be-
lieved that a passionate addiction to art was like a cancer that consumed
everything else.

If not used imagination may shrivel up. Even in old age Goethe feared
the wild tricks of a lively imagination. We can shape the intellect to secure
the dominance of reason, but imagination can still prevail.

Plato also suspected the imagination. He thought man could be trans-
formed by the imagination and suggested laws that would prohibit the
miming of extravagant evil characters. He advised changing from dramatic
to narrative language if writing became too overwrought. It is the fear of
what begins as fiction ending as reality.

Plato said that

> were a man who was clever enough to be able to assume all kinds of forms
> and to represent everything in the world to come in person to our commu-
> nity and want to show off his compositions, we'd treat him as an object of
> reverence and awe, and as a source of pleasure, and we'd prostrate ourselves
> before him; but we'd tell him that not only is there no one like him in our
> community, it is also not permitted for anyone like him to live among us, and
> we'd send him elsewhere, once we had anointed his head with myrrh and
> given him a chaplet of wool.[1]

These words express fear of the possibility of a destructive risk that lurks in poetry. Baudelaire continually reminds us that the magic of art is inseparable from its risks. And this risk is also a necessary component of poetry as it performs its balancing act between reality and the imaginative force at work within the poem. The poet enters the poem with a hood over the poet's eyes. The poet arrives from a distance, from a real world and an acrobat. Have you ever wondered why the painter is prone to painting acrobats, and not only in the famous painting of Picasso. It is because in all the arts the practitioner, the poet, the artist, even the musician with a new set of rules maintains a balancing act between reality or rules, and the imagination. And there is where the risk lies, in that balancing act, so filled with fervor and terror as the little word is placed on its spool of light. Hegel's language is radical. He believes that art exists in absolute freedom and is allowed to attach itself freely to any form it chooses that will help it exercise the imagination. We can view the poem as existing for a time in pure space, exercising imagination, no matter how mundane the exercise may appear, how untidy the bag of words it carries with it. The poem is enjoying a spatial freedom before it settles into images and rhythm and order of its new habitat on the page.

In this state of suspension the art that is created is infinitely susceptible to new shapes because no shape can be regarded as final. No form is safe when the poet is in a state of perpetual self-transformation, or where, as Hegel suggests, the artist is in a condition of infinite plasticity. This position of "subjectivity" or "openness" is what the poem desires to obtain, free to be molded by forces that shall condition the imagination of the poet. In the sixteenth century Ariosto complained that chivalry was being destroyed by the introduction of firearms. This is what Orlando Furioso is about, and I borrowed the title in my own mock epic, *Rocks on a Platter*. In Orlando Furioso we are given a setting of pure fantasy, and fantasy is written all over the poem. The reader can have no doubt of its unreality.

It is the innovation of Ariosto we admire, an alarming innovation that bespeaks the power of innovation when we are told the poem may have aided in the destruction of the codes of chivalry.

The idea of "infinite plasticity" is a noble one. It causes the poet to breathe more freely. One thinks of Prometheus Unbound. And it is the blood of "boundlessness" that enters the poem.

When I was a young poet I was immensely influenced by painters with whom I circulated. Their ideas of painting took up my young life. I envied their freedom. I began to use some of their methods. Often titles arrived after the poem was finished, as O'Hara illustrates so humorously in his poem, *Sardines*.

Painters also gave me a sense of being unconfined to a page. I became experimental without using that word. I wrote *Parachutes, My Love Could Carry Us Higher,* without considering whether my parachutes went up or down.

IMPLACABLE POET, PURPLE BIRDS
The Work of Barbara Guest

Sara Lundquist

BARBARA GUEST (b. 1920) published her first book of poems, *The Location of Things,* under the aegis of the Tibor de Nagy Art Gallery in 1960. No fewer than three collections of poetry bear 1999 as their publication date: *Rocks on a Platter: Notes on Literature* (Wesleyan), *If So, Tell Me* (Reality Street Editions), and *The Confetti Trees* (Sun & Moon Press). In the past forty years, she has produced fifteen other works including major poetry books, chapbooks, collaborations with visual artists, her *Selected Poems* (1995), as well as uncounted uncollected poems appearing in an array of literary and little magazines and in major and minor anthologies. I believe the uncollected poems will be discovered to outnumber those she has gathered (as were those of her fellow New York School progenitor, Frank O'Hara) when they are one day combined with the type- and manuscript poems held by the Yale's Beinecke Library.

Guest shows every sign of striding with her singular vigor and integrity into the new millennium of poetry, as one who has anticipated both the barely visible edges and the very heart of what that poetry might be. Her work seems to be "future's conduit," to borrow one of her own rich and felicitous phrases. Surely this is because she is and has been a writer "whose each new poem seems to exist in that very difficult to define *now* . . . someone who is actively creating [poetry's] present tense and terms," said Charles Bernstein at the New York Public Library's Celeste Baros Forum on the occasion of Guest's being awarded the Frost Medal by the Poetry Society of America in April 1999. Bernstein stressed Guest's always unassimilated achievement and remarked how wonderfully she always puts her readers in the position of being unprepared for her. "We don't know her," Rachel Blau DuPlessis mourned (1995, 23), working to claim

Notes begin on page 216.

Guest for the impressive pantheon of recovered twentieth-century American women poets, and yet this not-knowing is, I believe, part of knowing her, essential to the experience of reading her poetry, and discerning both her intent and her deep intuition. She is an elusivist, if I might coin a noun for her, which is not to say that she is either an escapist or an elitist, both of which have been used to describe Guest.[2] She won't be understood biographically, and always and everywhere deflects attention from herself to her poems, indeed from *the* poet to *the* poem. She is a proudly anomalous figure in mid- and late-twentieth-century American poetry; the words she wrote of her friend, the painter Helen Frankenthaler, apply to herself, as far back as her beginnings as a writer in New York City during the 1950s: "Frankenthaler has been active throughout her career as a painter in bringing us up to date. . . . [H]er position was separate from that of her colleagues who had located themselves as 'second generation abstract-expressionists.' In that gallery she was an anomaly. Not that she wasn't absorbing the same atmospheres, going to the same parties, sharing the same jokes, but her eye was focused differently" ("Helen Frankenthaler," 58). Guest both was and was not a "New York School Poet"; she both is and is not a feminist writer; she simultaneously joins and quits the confessionalists by declaring that "All poetry is confessional"; she both practices and questions "experimental poetics"; she both anticipated and surpasses the Language poets. Looking out from whatever venue, her eye is focused differently.

The one allegiance she does claim is too large to be called a school or camp and is pertinently *not* concerned solely with poetry or limited to the United States. It is with modernism itself—not postmodernism, which she considers a "cheap idea . . . like some sort of advertising cliché. . . . [Y]ou're either modern or you're not" (Hillringhouse interview, 26). In an interview for the *Colorado Review,* she claimed: "I grew up in the febrility of modernism. I love constructivism and cubism, all those isms . . . the white on white painting and the emptiness of a canvas. The ideas of space in modernism." To these, Anna Rabinowitz adds "more isms": "abstract expressionism and minimalism" (3). Elsewhere Guest adds surrealism, that "atmosphere brightened by Apollinaire, Éluard, Valéry and the old master, Mallarmé" ("Under the Shadow of Surrealism," 16), which meant "freedom, especially for a woman" (qtd. in DuPlessis 2000, 6), and imagism, that poetic discipline agitated by the very act of seeing. In Guest's hands, modernism indeed remains alive to the point of febrility, so responsive is she to its rich explored and unexplored veins of experimentalism. Her lifelong task of discovering "the location of things" is being accomplished in part via her acute investigations of "the ideas of space in modernism."

Like many artists whose achievement is hard to assimilate, label, or categorize, Guest eludes because her scope and range are so variable and large, and because she so elegantly presents so many seemingly contradictory qualities. She is surely one of our great poets of paradox, a mischievous and serene defector from commonly held beliefs and linguistic habits, which accounts in part for her readers' often expressed sense of perpetual freshness and challenge. Yet, her paradoxes never strain over their innate tensions; they provide (often very beautiful) access to deep, mature knowledge and feeling. This she accomplishes on the level of the phrase, in the arrangement of her lines, in the structure and conceit of whole poems, in the arch of her entire *oeuvre*. It grows increasingly difficult to adequately describe the work of her constant and constantly transforming career without the use of paradox: it is "grand, simultaneously quiet," "a focused but limitless task" (Hillman 1996, 208, 207); it is "precise, yet airy and sensual"; "her method is private and mute. The finished poem is, however, completely articulate" (Going 1991, 14). She is known both for her elegance and her unsettling disjunctions; one poem is luxuriously dense, the next minimal and irradiated by white spaces, profuse "leavings out." Musically, she encompasses Mozart and Schoenberg, attracted variously to harmony and dissonance. She is determined in her indeterminacy; in the poems we find "the sensible forms indefiniteness takes" (Welish 1990, 214). She is playfully open, cheerfully digressive, permeable to inspiration from others; yet she is an "Implacable Poet," who unswervingly knows her own path. She is self-declared both a modernist and a medievalist, a classicist— "clues, fragments of the mythologies of another time" (Einzig 1996, 7)—yet one of "Byron's Signatories" who is Keatsian in her negative capability. She writes poetry of Stevensian sinuosity and gaudiness, and yet aspires toward the abstemious Agnes Martin. She embraces beauty, and yet has been embraced by the Language poets, who often regard beauty as a "suspect term."[3] She is an egoless poet of the self, a traveler who yearns toward home. She is a biographer (the author of *Herself Defined: the Poet H.D. and Her World*) who in the long poem "Biography" interrogates the relevance to poetry of biography; she is a feminist who longs for a poetry that can "find its way to a settlement where a commodity like silk is respected" ("Mysteriously Defining the Mysterious," 13), and who, with a light heart, claims and redeems the debased title of "Poetess."

Consider these juxtapositional and enjambic surprises, these cool liberties (chosen unsystematically, but chronologically from *Selected Poems*, 1995): "My three/yellow notes, my three yellow stanzas,/my three preciseness/of head and body and tail joined" (15); "Describe that nude, audacious line/most lofty, practiced street" (18); "Why not make a perspective of ancient alleé/so that it can promenade?" (33); "It was quite a day. I brought home/an unopened poem. It should grow/in the kitchen near the stove" (37); "pushed forward by your idiom/like a giantess opening a window sash" (40); "in every breath she drew like a swimmer who draws the ocean/or a worm who draws the earth or I who draw/your heaviness as you draw" (63); "I admire you/in your Byron green suiting clipping away/at a language" (74); "Poetess riddled/her asterisk/genial" (78); "a general razing of the remnants of the late nineteenth century that in their generous furry way were suffocating the capitol" (86); "You made the autumn ginger cookies//Sniggered like mules, kind of a dumb show" (107); "I entice this novice poem with a mineral, *Beryl*" (134); "the bittersweet grapple//initiates//a mysterious mesh" (157); "cricket music for the robing" (195). The mysterious mesh and bittersweet grapple of these lines are paradox's characteristic mesh and grapple, at once an intimate fitting together, and a daring mutual clutch on an enemy opposite. How tactile, how supple the words "mesh" and "grapple" feel; they lend muscle and certainty to the faith that much truth can be carried by figuration. He "believes in a coexistence of separates," Guest wrote of the painter Robert Goodnough ("Robert Goodnough," 18); no less does she, and not just coexistence but the spark and sizzle of their interpenetration.

In these exciting pieces of poetry, Guest also displays her ample vocabulary, her intimations of the unsaid, her range of diction, her tonal variety, her ready linguistic comedy, her conviction that vitality and passion are absolute to poetry's definition, its *raison d'etre*: "I have little regard," she wrote, "for poems of mine which have become votives of obsolete reactions. These poems appear to have no conscience, and worse, are passionless" ("A Reason for Poetics," 154). Guest seems willing to discard even her own poems unless they require and sustain new reading and active engagement, not learned or remembered response, but fresh ravishment upon each reading. This unsettling sense of never quite "having" the poem in the sense of comfortably making it a touchstone or cultural artifact that will submit to analysis (or to teaching) has been my experience in reading Guest, votive-minded as I tend to be. She somehow makes obsolete the notion that poetry is "memorable language"; her tropes, her adjective-noun combinations, her audacious tonal shifts don't lodge in memory, there to grow stale, or revered and respectable. They are stubbornly loyal instead to the page and to the voice, springing to life in the act of reading, which itself becomes an act of making. These are "action" poems, not only because they, like "action paintings" in Harold Rosenberg's discussion, treat the canvas "as an arena in which to act . . . not a picture but an event" (1965, 25), but also because that "arena in which to act" and that "event" (as opposed to artifact) can and must be the reader's location and experience as well. "Art," Guest wrote in her tribute to the Abstract Expressionists who so beguiled and influenced her, "becomes more instantaneous, willful, en-thusiastic freed by action" ("Under the Shadow of Surrealism," 16).

Each of the quotations I have chosen is also mysteriously and intrinsi-cally metapoetic. One can hardly quote from Guest and not strike a rich vein of metapoesis, that is, the comments of the poem on its own processes and procedures, its music and form, its idiom, its fortunes in the world, its relationship to its creator and its readers. Despite her elusivist stance, her poems are generously and deliciously self-reflexive; each invariably "-teaches" the terms according to which they can best be understood and en-joyed. This idea that a poem, whatever else it may be about, must also "chronicle . . . the creative act that produces it" (John Ashbery), plotting its own self-creating voyage, was a key tenet of New York School poetics and one at which Guest has always excelled. This is also, no doubt, one of the qualities that has of late so attracted the Language poets to Guest's work. Yet everything metapoetical, analyzable in terms of literary theory, is also partial to the sensuous physical world, cherishing the homely and the do-mestic. The phrases quoted above may be appreciated for their gorgeous immediacy, their respect for "fair realism" and for the sheer otherness of things in the world (head, body, tail, fur, the ocean, worms, nudity, the street, the kitchen, the stove, a window sash, ginger cookies, autumn, mules, the mineral beryl, crickets, and always and everywhere *color*), while, simultaneously, wonderfully and paradoxically serving as meta-phors for the creative act.

Readers have noted the exquisite paratactical style, characterized by "fragmentation, hesitations, interruption, secret singing, the nonlinear"; Robert Long writes of Guest's attention to "the surface of a poem—of lan-guage's transparencies as well as its inscrutabilities." For her formal exper-imentation and her interest in the play of language for its own sake, Guest has been named as one of "Gertrude's granddaughters" in the company of Kathleen Fraser, Rachel DuPlessis, Rae Armantrout, and Rosmarie Wal-drop (DeKoven 1986, 13–14). Hillringhouse notes that "it seems to be a poetry which creates a field of play for language. There's a lot of special-ized language, special words, foreign terms, exotic words—'lacuna, apse, verdigris, scala, guignol'" (Hillringhouse interview, 26). Guest herself writes of Byzantine complications and convolutions necessary to language, and was fond of Mallarmé's "enduring phrase": "Not the thing, but its ef-fect." Few readers, however, have mentioned that she is one of our most sensitive and valuable nature poets, who employs imagism in order to ren-der the human meaning in weather, nature, and landscape, and in order to respect in language the nonlinguistic world, the thing *as well as* its effect. "I see that I'm still interested in weather," Guest said with wry, disarming simplicity when, in an audio interview, Bernstein asked her to discuss "the discontinuities and the continuities" between one of her most well-known early poems ("Parachutes, My Love, Could Carry Us Higher") and a more recent one ("Niege Fondant").

The following section from "Colonial Hours," from *The Blue Stairs* (1968), illustrates Guest's gift for happiness, her meteorologic poetics, her achievement in melding experimental poetics with imagism, linguistic play with representation. The poem must here also stand in for her numerous travel poems—she is possessed of a "vast travelling sensibility," and has written from and about many countries and continents. In the bio for her third book, *The Blue Stairs,* she described herself as "an incessant traveler [whose] range is from Turkey villas to Omsk, the coasts of Florida and California, hurricanes and a museum's 'blue stairs.'" Travel in her poems is, of course, everywhere a species of poetics—no subject in Guest is not also a style, a manner of performance, a verbal process; as Brenda Hillman puts it, citing the poem "Sand": "the poem 'cross-references' sand to itself" (1996, 213). Her travel poems concern "exile and loss and homelessness, houses under the threat of hurricane, lovingly realized rooms and studios, agonized leave-takings, grateful returns" (Lundquist 2000, 164), performing the emotional aura and shape of these concerns via structure and style. Here, the name of the tropical, probably Caribbean "land in wake of Prospero," is not revealed, yet a certain genius of time and place becomes apparent, made up of random radiant particulars:

> The year of the hurricane
> (we are speaking)
>   bay roadway
>   the drenching
> leaves flattened to echo
> dry velvet before
>   hush
>
>
> . . . .
>
>
> Tender magnificence
>
> Land in wake of Prospero
>
> with splayed tendrils
>   washed
>
>
> . . . . .

        sun granaries
legacies the sea strokes up
        dried as weed cemetery
or blue ballooning stingarees
        thrown
Night temples of palms
        the rain blows *tropique*
as ceiling fans

        you go in your orphan feet
        crossing the tiles (*The Blue Stairs*, 13–14)

Guest's poem is exposed to the elements: hurricane, roadway, "drenching/ leaves flattened," rain, the sea, "weed cemetery," screaming "luxurious birds," and those vivid, curious "blue ballooning stingarees." (I suspect that the word and the creature "stingaree" constitute the irresistible heart of this poem, its genesis.) She deploys myriad verbs and verbal adjectives— "speaking," "drenching," "flattened," "quarrelsome," "splayed," "washed," "shudder," "chants," "strokes up," "thrown," "blows," "crossing," "whisper," "sprang," "released," "to be fed," "cherished," "reconnoiter," "sing," "blink," "reach"—all of which add up to a world, and a poem, of amazing vivacity. Poetry more visually stimulating or more attuned to the exhilarating and unsettling vicissitudes of nature could hardly be imagined; it can be usefully contrasted with a good many formal midcentury tourist and travel poems, solemnly and staidly intent on displaying the author's (superior) erudition and taste as s/he inspects a famous monument or landmark.[4]

This poem concludes with beneficent exposure to "reality," to weather. The note struck is one of luck, joy, sexual gusto, and magnification of self and language:

        You are a lucky person who hears
            the wild the luxurious birds
        their scream is like yours
            when you fear the cold

        they sing in the heat draughts
            they slip from the fountain
        joy in their male coloring is yours
            and the neck reach

        the colonial language
        of tern sibilancy

Today you sit on the cropped grass
today looking at the map
   you blink

   Magnified world
   my education
   my craft

My fruit my oranges (*The Blue Stairs,* 15)

Four possessions (the reality of which the poem seems to extol) magnify the world, lift it out of its pettiness, its adherence to straight and narrow pathways : "*my* education/*my* craft//*My* fruit/*my* oranges" (my[!] emphasis). The combination of the palpable and tasteable fruit with more abstract attainments spans possibility. These are four things the world can and does offer for the possessing. "My craft" loops in poetry itself (as always, metapoetic layering), as the speaker's chosen mode of skillful, careful, and ingenious making. It suggests that we can hold a poem and hold an education, and claim them as our own as tangibly as we can hold an orange.

In the following poem, #32 from *The Countess from Minneapolis* (1976), a similar melding of natural imagery and metapoesis prevails—indeed the fortunes of art and spirituality amid the direst of weather conditions and the loneliest of geographies is a key theme of this book. Here, the protagonist expresses momentary confidence that locale (both because of and in spite of its essential strangeness) can be congenial to the self that expresses itself through language. She catches a poem acting as if it were at once the Minnesota sun and the Minnesota moon, traversing the Mississippi river in a boxcar over a bridge:

   There was a poem with
A moon in it travelling across the bridge in one
Of those fragile trains carrying very small loads
Like moons that one could never locate anywhere else.
The Mississippi was bright under the bridge like a
Sun, because the poem called itself the Sun also;
Two boxcars on the bridge crossing the river. (*The Countess from
   Minneapolis,* 89)

Guest has claimed, qualifying (but not denying) her connection to the Language poets: "The Language people are big on Marx, and I'm not a Marxist, and on French philosophy, and I'm not a philosopher" (qtd. in Lehman 1998, 372). She wrote of Jean Arp's poems and sculptures as having a "navel which is attached to the world" ("Barbara Guest on Jean Arp," n.p.); in just such a way do Guest's poems finesse the vexed twentieth-century philosophical and literary question of words and their attachment to or detachment from reality. In their very structure and music, the poems are about *both*: the playful, sophisticated self-referentiality of language, *and* its primitive umbilical bond to the real. Both of these to Guest are lucky and beautiful, not to be chosen between, not to be lamented, always rich compost for art's negotiations and paradoxes: "The fiction of the poet," she wrote, "is part of the restless twentieth century perception that reality is a variable, and is open-ended in form and matter" ("Poetry the True Fiction," 99). No wonder she remains "interested in" weather, so real, so restless, so variable, so much like poetry. These astute musings, always sumptuously presented, come most concentratedly to fruition in the book titled *Fair Realism* (1989), generally considered Guest's masterwork, especially in the much admired poem "An Emphasis Falls on Reality."

In the poem she confesses most poignantly and honestly from her assured position as one of postwar poetry's most successful, joyous, and daring experimentalists— "I was envious of fair realism" (*Fair Realism*, 26)— and proceeds in a series of inspired imagistic fragments to touch (wistfully, festively, insinuatingly) upon the never-settled questions of artistic representation. How do willow trees and waterways and "cloud fields" and "fountains traced nearby on a lawn" transform when they enter art? In what way are they already art? In what sense can silence be "pictorial"? And does that add to or detract from its "realness"? Is a shadow more or less real than a wall? Is a calligraphic letter as real as a wall? Is night ever not "selective" once it enters human consciousness? How does it come to be that we can say, with some aesthetic and psychological verity: "willows are not real trees/they entangle us in looseness,/the natural world spins in green" (27). How does the natural and social world come to us already constructed, every tree a copy of all trees? What part does desire play in the revision of sunrises?

I find that I have paraphrased this poem of calm periods, ellipses, and commas all in question marks, indicating my own agitation at its unfathomableness, its inscrutability, its poise, and its refusal to *be* paraphrased— would all the history of philosophical discourse on the "problem" of representation manage to paraphrase this one poem? I think I know that Guest has reached that calm of resolved paradox, where a "higher truth" is momentarily clear, and the ending of the poem moves me very much with its residual sadness (conveyed by a tactful, wistful "perhaps"), and with its two poignantly embracing "figures." This couple must be the archetypal human lovers for and about whom all poetry is said to be composed, but also, true to the poet's metapoetic bent, two "figures of speech" standing in for all the rhetorical resources of language. It is for them she has made her "house," this poem:

The necessary idealizing of you reality
is part of the search, the journey
where two figures embrace

This house was drawn for them
it looks like a real house
perhaps they will move in today

into ephemeral dusk and
move out of that into night
selective night with trees,

The darkened copies of all trees.

To me, Barbara Guest's house *does* look like a real house, both tangible and abstract, both solemn and celebratory, philosophical and playful, solid and ephemeral.[5] Perhaps I will move in today. In this as in so many of her poems, Guest creates a poetic house of immense attractions; we want to "move in" and to "move out" of it, to share that altered sense of the night and its dark beauties that art alone can confer—Guest here is in rapt colloquy with Stevens, taking the part of the mysterious Ramon Fernandez, similarly awed by "arranging, deepening, enchanting night," and uttering her own "ghostlier demarcations, keener sounds." The price of admission to the house is high, but in the end gratefully paid: we must proceed slowly and abandon our needy wish that she say without obliquity and *in propria persona* what it "means." As Anna Rabinowitz stated, "The poem's meaning came to center on *how* it said, not *what* it said—its *howness* being its *isness*" (2001, 98). "What" in Guest's rare verbal world cannot be made apparent to the casual visitor. "Howness," however, intertwining "Isness" *is* lavishly, immensely proffered.

Readers tend to seek the poet's "proper person" in her essays, in interviews, and in readings, somehow expecting prose or talk to deliver more straightforwardly or autobiographically what the poetry has seemingly cloaked, tracking its own mysterious routes of perception and insight. Instead, in all of these venues, as is her wont, Guest instinctively turns elusivist and allusionist, deflecting attention away from herself and her life, and back to *ars poetica* itself, which feels quite different urgencies. Asked to explain or discuss a poem, she will read another poem, or declare that the answer is one of poetry's secrets that she may not divulge. At the Kerouac School of Disembodied Poetics during the 1998 summer program, she joked: "So I am going to read this poem, and we're going to discuss it— Mei-mei [Berssenbrugge]'s going to tell you what it means" ("A Talk on 'Startling Maneuvers'," 8). At the conference titled "Where Lyric Tradition

Meets Language Poetry" held at Barnard College (April 1999), Guest sat in the exact middle of a panel of distinguished women poets asked to prepare a statement of their poetics. She was at once a stabilizing anchor and an "incandescent center" (Bernstein 1999, 1). One was struck with her otherworldliness and her sensible maturity, her resistance to aggrandizement, her humor, her occasional puzzlement, her patience. She was modernism's representative, yet reached quite effortlessly across the generations to the youngest poets there. She declared herself "unprepared" to speak and did not consult any notes, yet her "statement of poetics" was characteristically allusive (blending many historical eras), suggestive rather than substantive, without autobiographical reference of any kind, keen to turn from statements about poetry back to poetry.

Consider the exquisite remove of the poet, the utter egolessness in these passages from "A Reason For Poetics" and "Mysteriously Defining the Mysterious," two of her very poetic, very elusive, very Guestian prose essays.[6] The poet as Guest portrays her is always at the service of the poem, observing its ways, obeying its will, withdrawing with relief into its luxurious refusals to simplify, demystify, or personalize, refusals not often asserted elsewhere in banal, commercial contemporary life. It is not the poet but the poem whose autobiography, whose "self-telling," matters; that telling is limned into its structure, its ineluctable "mystery."

> In our own time, Wallace Stevens called a poem a "finikin thing of air." A poem may when first glimpsed float a thin tail, like the tail of a kite in crisp air, like the first note of the Emperor bird, and "Emperor" was a word that came easily to Stevens, as he drew his pedigreed birds in chill colloquial air. In Byzantine guise he called a poem a "purple bird" that must sing to the poet to console him for being rare; he arrives in a mysterious color that is made of several colors, an extraordinary bird who suggests the extravagance of being rare.
>
> In whatever guise reality becomes visible to the poet, he withdraws from it into invisibility. In his cloak of Byzantine colors he spins his secret life. The poem is the unburdening of the ghosts which have come to haunt the poet after he has made his trip to the labyrinth. ("Mysteriously Defining the Mysterious," typescript 4)

Ideally a poem will be both mysterious (incunabula, driftwood of the unconscious), and organic (secular) at the same time. If the tension becomes irregular, like a heartbeat, then a series of questions enters the poem. What is now happening? What does the poem, itself, consider to be its probabilities? The poem needs to take care not to flounder, or become rigid, or to come to such a halt [that] the reader hangs over a sudden cliff. It is noticeable that a poem has a secret grip of its own separate from its creator.

The poem is quite willing to forget its begetter and take off in its own direction. It likes to be known as spontaneous. Some poets then become firm and send out admonitory hints. Others become anxious. A few become pleased with the trickster and want to adopt it. There are moments when mistaken imageries can lead into interesting directions. Poets even try to charm the poem. We have all taken these positions. ("A Reason for Poetics," 153)

Here also is a list of shorter quotations from the essays, which contain the meditations of other artists (alive and dead) on Guest's concerns. They illustrate Guest's affiliative drift, her spatial hospitality, her restless search for kindred spirits, the depth and breadth of her cultural camaraderie. Poe: "In reading the Byzantine, Poe, we discover that 'things are not what they seem to be.'" Cézanne: "Poetry sometimes develops a grayness, the light can never get in. The surface is smudgy. Cézanne was irritated by this murkiness in painting and complained 'le contour me fuit.'" Mandelstam "once wrote of 'sound spilling into fingers.' That could be the noise of a poem when it experiences an ecstacy of recognition." Keats: "This island-bound poet, restricted to sofas and country lanes, or an occasional jaunt to London . . . transfigures the smallness of his personal environment, the narrowness of his private life into magic and vision." Mallarmé: "Imagination is *clair-obscur*. It is also 'the absent flower' of Mallarmé." Shelley, Blake: "Shelley liked to think of spirits hid in clouds . . . and Blake drew angels." Auden: "Auden said that 'Every poem is rooted in imaginative awe.'" Coleridge "wrote *Biographia Literaria* in his youth when he was trembling with imaginative power. The book is essential, I believe, for the distinction he makes between Imagination and Fancy." Moore: "Marianne Moore said that what must be present in poetry is 'an impassioned interest in life's creative spirit.'" Emily Dickinson: "there speaks the true critic, and for my purposes I note that Dickinson took a very Byzantine turn, to reach the poem's kiosk. 'A curious something overtakes the Mind.'" Kandinsky: "'The work of art becomes a means for spiritual communication between the creator and the viewer.'" William Cowper: "'Poets are seldom good for anything except in rime.'" DeKooning "wrote that in the Renaissance drawing started to tremble because it wanted to go places." Jean Arp: "'We cannot use inner language to make ourselves understood except to those men whom we meet at the outer limits of things.'" Breton: "'to imagine is to see.'" Thus does Guest assemble a crew to delve with her into the great thematic concern of her later years, the imagination: "I must speak about it, because for me it is the single most important element of poetry and it is my touchstone. . . . How empty all the dazzle of style is without the immediacy of imagination. And imagination the changeling can sting you with its fictive barbs" ("Poetry the True Fiction," 101–02).

No discussion of Guest's career can be complete without reference to her justly famous rapport with painting and the plastic arts. She may well be our most valuable late-twentieth century ekphrastic poet, who has written poems for artists and about art from the ancient Japanese Genji scrolls, to Delacroix, to Robert Motherwell, to the contemporary artist Jennifer Bartlett. Guest has collaborated on a number of beautiful works of various kinds (with artists June Felter, Grace Hartigan, Mary Abbot, Shelia Isham, Richard Tuttle, and Anne Dunn), always open to possible expansions beyond one's private or medium-related horizons and assumptions: "the physical extravagance of paint, of enormous canvases can cause a nurturing envy in the poet that prods his greatest possession, the imagination, into an expansion of its borders" ("Under the Shadow of Surrealism," 16).[7] Even poems that are not about or meant to accompany visual art evince, as Rabinowitz and others have argued, a painterly covenant with the page: "the page functions as a pictorial space vivified by language, alive with the process of composition and the consciousness of making marks" (2001, 97–98). Barbara Einzig: "Painting is the poems' cosmology and the world is read as a painting" (1996, 9). DuPlessis has thoroughly analyzed the gender content of three major ekphrastic poems from *Fair Realism,* "The Farewell Stairway (after Balla)," "The Nude" (about Warren Brandt's paintings of female nudes), and "Dora Maar," which depicts the relationship between Picasso and the woman photographer and painter who was his model and mistress (Duplessis 2000). Guest believes in the inevitable mixing of the arts. After surrealism, she writes, art can be "a central plaza with roads which led from palette to quill to clef. . . . One could never again look at poetry as a locked kingdom." She understands poetry to be companioned by "an associative art within whose eye the poet might gaze for reassurance and for a glowing impersonal empathy" ("Under the Shadow of Surrealism," 16).

DuPlessis notes "the high emotional status for Guest of the spaces given by painting—the formal spaces inside painting and in the relations of empathy with the painter's project" (2000, 9). I will look at one poem, also from *Fair Realism,* with the intent of highlighting and particularizing DuPlessis's insight about the "high emotional status" of painting for Guest. As I have argued elsewhere, her ekphrasis invariably reads as passionate expression of thought and feeling, where the linguistically inclined artist meets the visually inclined artist in a dialogue of equals. The poems resemble those rare inspiriting conversations that reveal how very personal work is; how intricately both the formal and the visionary questions of *how to make* are entwined with the most crucial (spiritual and political) questions of *"how to live, what to do,"* to quote one of Stevens's most suggestive poem titles. And often, strangely and poignantly, the ekphrastic poems solace their author. They comfort her, especially in the archaic sense of that word, so as "to strengthen (morally or spiritually); to encourage, hearten, inspirit, incite" and also "to confirm and corroborate." Observing a painter engaged in his lonely and necessary work makes the poet's work less lonely and more necessary. Into the eye of art, one might "gaze for reassurance and for a glowing impersonal empathy." This is especially clear, I think, in "The View from Kandinsky's Window":

An over large pot of geraniums on the ledge
the curtains part
a view from Kandinsky's window.

The park shows little concern with Kandinsky's history
these buildings are brief about his early life,
reflections of him seen from the window
busy with preparations for exile
the relevance of the geranium color.

Partings, future projects
exceptional changes are meant to occur,
he will [confront an axis,][8] rearrange spatial decisions
the geranium disappears, so shall a person.

His apartment looking down on a Square
the last peek of Russia
an intimate one knowing equipment vanishes.

At Union Square the curtains are drawn
diagonals greet us, those curves and sharp city
verticals he taught us their residual movements.

The stroke of difficult white finds an exit
the canvas is clean, pure and violent
a rhythm of exile in its vein,

We have similar balconies, scale
degrees of ingress, door knobs daffodils
like Kandinsky's view from his window
distance at the street end. (*Fair Realism*, 13–14)

About this poem Guest has written a rare piece of autobiography, which describes a period of her life when she felt she had been living, and very much needed to live, "under his wing"—under the wing, that is, of the Russian-born painter Wassily Kandinsky (1866–1944), a founder of the *Blaue Reiter* group of modern painters. Kandinsky was a theorist and practitioner of nonrepresentational art who believed in the psychological power of pure color and who developed analogies between art and music (these particularly appeal to the raging synesthesian in Guest). She wrote:

> A few years ago I sublet an apartment overlooking Union Square. I rather disliked its painter's cold northern light, and I admit I was somewhat melancholy when I lived there. The owner's library included several books on Kandinsky. There was one that quoted him on the necessity in art for an "inner sound," to me an essential "noise" of poetry. Another book showed a photography of Kandinsky's Moscow apartment. So the artist, his ideas and his dwelling place became a solace to me. While I was looking down on Union Square there came the realization that Union Square looked remarkably like the Moscow part seen from Kandinsky's apartment.
>
> Another year passed and I had moved, yet I remained in the same vicinity. One evening I found myself writing a poem about Kandinsky. This was the poem I had wished to write when I had been living under his wing. Then the form and "noise," the necessary "inner sound" of the poem, had eluded me. Now the poem was written and I called it "The View from Kandinsky's Window." ("Under the Shadow of Surrealism," 17)

For Guest, space is always both an emotional and an artistic issue, both a real phenomenon and a phenomenon of art. To find oneself in Kandinsky-like space is to be confronted with Kandinsky-like artistic and personal problems. But it is also to be given, if one pays alert enough attention, Kandinsky's ways out: the actions he took in the face of blank melancholic moods, how he "prepared for exile," how he negotiated an uncertain future, and how he used all of these circumstances for artistic material and gain. It was her own mood that she recognized in him: his disabused recognitions that parks and buildings are indifferent to one's comings and goings, that people can "disappear" as easily as a mere houseplant, that life is full of partings and "last peeks" of loved places, and that exile and dispossession might haunt our days. Guest subtly and generously weaves the poem's emotions through Kandinsky instead of overclaiming them as peculiarly or melodramatically her own. But she does step *so* humanly close to him; without shyness or deference to his greatness or fame, she shows her reader how art (however abstract) can confer a heartening, always temporary, always "merely" formal solution to the spatial problem of locating self and things. Where do I stand, how do I fit into my life, what is my location vis-à-vis this room, this window, this city, this country, this painting, this person, this history, these disorienting changes? Look at Kandinsky for solutions and/or solace: "exceptional changes *are meant* to occur,/he will [confront an axis,] rearrange spatial decisions" (my emphasis). Leaving his native Russia provokes from him yet more revolutionary modern art: "the stroke of difficult white finds an exit/the canvas is clean, pure and violent/a rhythm of exile in its veins." This is art transferable to Union Square and applicable there: "At Union Square . . ./diagonals greet us, those curves and sharp city/verticals *he taught us* their residual movement" (my emphasis). And indeed Kandinsky did teach New Yorkers how to see their own city and how to exploit its unique dynamics in painting; he influenced with his abstractions the largely New York-based Abstract Expressionists, with whom Guest was so closely associated. Describing Kandinsky's art via ekphrastic poetry lifts the poet out of melancholy and into dynamic and charged vocabulary: "busy," "exceptional," "greet," "sharp city verticals," "stroke," "white," "clean, pure, and violent," "rhythm," even "doorknobs daffodils." She begins to see a way from her own balcony to the "distance at the street end."

Guest is explicit: "I can confess that when I look at a painting I do not ask, what does it mean, or how did the artist apply the paint, choose colors, but what has led this artist to a particular predicament, and how does he go about solving it. I am alert to the task concealed in the method. . . . I question what was the manner in which this metamorphosis took place, and in what way I can use this process" ("Under the Shadow of Surrealism," 17). Writing about another painter—her good friend Helen Frankenthaler—Guest observed with exquisite understatement: "One does not observe quiet thoughts here" ("Helen Frankenthaler," 58). Solace from the painters, for Guest, is far from quietude. It amounts instead to a next action to take, a way to go, a lucky surprise, a conduit to the future, even the occasion of being "vigorously pushed into the unknown" ("Robert Goodnough," 18).

I will conclude by discussing two of Guest's most recent works: *Stripped Tales* (1995) and *Rocks on a Platter: Notes on Literature* (1999). These two books can illustrate how the deep wells of Guest's experimentalism have not run dry, as well as indicate how age has stimulated her wise and willful attraction to risk. She has expressed her wish to emulate the composer Arnold Schoenberg; to "go as far as I can in poetry" as he did in music, though it was too evident that "not everybody liked it" (Lannan videotaped interview). She had already gone *very* far with parataxis and dissonance in *Defensive Rapture* (1993), writing poems built of burning imagistic fragments whose "subjects" are extremely elusive, even for an elusivist. These poems await full reading, with this for a descriptive instigation from Hillman: "the subject of a poem is constellated from phrase units that choose to survive; at times these poems seem like driftwood houses subject to destructive forces and at times they seem very strong and serviceable, like Portuguese fishing nets" (215).

Then with *Stripped Tales,* written in collaboration with the artist Anne Dunn, Guest plays out to all its far-flung logical conclusions, her heretofore intermittent flirtation with narrative. The title indicates the strategy: minute, dense, fragmentary linguistic units entice and tease with the suggestion of anecdote, of joke, and of story while declining to indulge most of the usual expectations of these narrative genres. Her "tales" are stripped in the way that wooden furniture might be: they have had "the accretions of paint or varnish removed, so as to reveal the natural grain and colour." They are stripped *down,* all superfluous or extraneous parts removed. For all their smallness they raise big questions: Can a novel be lineated, compressed, and centered on a single page that is more generous to blank space than to words? What results when a "tale" is performed by disjunctive, as opposed to lyric poetic language? How much story can be stripped from a tale before it ceases to be a tale? What do the tales gain by jettisoning length, narrative progression, continuity of character and event? What do they gain with their startling and beautiful visual presence on the page, reinforced by Dunn's illustrations?

Knowing that I was to talk about *Stripped Tales* at the Barnard Conference, Guest sent me a few paragraphs that describe her process of composition. This is a charming narrative in its own right, a statement of poetics full of dramatic reversals and revelations. It begins:

> I thought at first I would write a wordly real story and I did, but it was too long. I wanted to make it skinny, but the adjectives and adverbs and the daily tasks of living made my story too big, like a swelling. So I began the process of thinning down the story. I really wanted [the words] and, but, the to go away so I took them out still things were dangling. And I bumped into those things. Then I wrote a little story, but it was boring. Then I added a paragraph to it, but all you could see was that it was dressed in a paragraph. I put a name to each story, quite properly and put this title at the top of the page, but the story looked top heavy. So I took the title away and I liked it better, but I was told that stories had titles so put it back in. No one will know what you are writing about unless you give a story a title, I was told.
>
> At this point I decided I didn't want to write a "story." But my fingers were empty and I missed my stories that were told in a manner I didn't like. It was then I discovered that the word "story" was misleading and if I substituted "tale" I could do anything I liked. So I wrote "Tales" without any fixings and called them Stripped Tales.

The tales themselves tell a similar story, in Guest's inevitable metapoetic fashion. They also tell how and why Guest's tales must be stripped tales. In an ekphrastic poem/tale called "property//mix-up" (as in many of the tales the "title" flanks the poem, both introducing it and ending it, enveloping it), an unnamed but Picasso-esque "he" strips a story as one might an engine, dismantling and disassembling, but all within a circle so as not to lose any of the parts. Surely this is a portrait of Guest's own procedures of appropriating as her own others' narrative "property" and taking outrageous liberties with length, sequence, plot:

> *property*
> He changes the scene with its unique nobility into something quite
> different he draws around the story a circle and then breaks up that circle
> into angles so that the narrative line is abolished. The linear lines of a
> narrative are obtrusive and when he breaks it up there will be more energy,
> instead of lines he is free to deal with planes. The planes join each other
> to become cubes the entire outline of his life fits into a cube.

> *mix-up* (*Stripped Tales*, 21)

She, Guest, like "He" is anxious to abolish "unique nobility" in favor of energy, process, freedom, the opportunity to mix self with story. Plot lines denarrativized and verse lines delineated become planar, geometrically expanded, well on their way to three-dimensional inclusivity. Any story, she implies, might be seen as a calculated "property//mix-up," a stealing and changing and destroying and remaking of a many-times-told tale. To Harry Mathew's dictum "There is no raw material," one might add: there is no *owned* material.

Allusive writers accomplish their work according to their temperaments, either building a new context by metaphorically or narratively relating items, or not, letting items metonymically sort themselves as best they and their readers can, in linguistic constructs stripped of connectives. Guest practices the latter kind of allusiveness; in this book using it in her investigations of the behavior of narrative. She borrows stories from here and there, invents some, while stripping them all of a full set of narrative comforts: characterization, plot, forward motion, point of view, detailed setting in time and place. She is a minimalist, a lyricist, and a paratactician(!), and she subjects her tales severely to all of these aesthetic disciplines. She erases, edits, scrapes, and rubs out; she borrows Anne-Marie Albiach's indispensable poet's tool, "white-out."

Indeed, Guest risks much with these strippings: Does she go too far? How does she know when or if she has gone beyond cleaning them of inessential accretions to dispossessing and depriving them, leaving them naked and mute, incapable of speaking even to the most willing reader? She has not, after all, delivered the reader from the comforts of narrative to the *traditional* patterns and orderings of lyric, but to her own peculiar disjunctive energies and imagistic traces and fragments. The allusions can seem positively gnomic, so seemingly idiosyncratic are they—not referring to "great books," necessarily, but to the author's "favorite books." Kevin Killian *was* able to identify one of these enigmatic allusions: "A poem like

'Need to Identify,'" he writes, "is a kind of story—a sentence snatched from an Edith Wharton novel of hotel children" (Killian 1996, n.p.). I don't want to judge how accurate his identification is, and perhaps accuracy is beside the point, the work of footnoters and not readers. Indeed Guest's title mocks the footnoter in readers; she knows that we all harbor a "need to identify," to accurately place the fragments swirling around in the poetry of our time. But such a need to accurately identify gets in the way of urgent suggestiveness. Can an entire Edith Wharton-like novel be suggested in three short sentences? Killian believes so, and so do I. The poem is "a suggestive fragment of something much larger," he writes, "that doesn't need to be larger. What is 'suggestion' anyway, beyond the craving for the other" (Killian 1996, n.p.). And marvelously, the poem performs its own subject, which is the children's "need/to identify" what goes on behind closed doors, their hunger for narrative and event, their forever unsatisfied craving to have exposed what is only suggested:

> In the hotel certain rooms were closed to the guests. They
> discussed what went on in these rooms, who watered the plants,
> made the beds, etc. The children liked to beat their fists
> against the doors and sometimes would awaken in the night to
> ask why the rooms were locked. (*Stripped Tales,* 19)

I cannot but feel that Guest's simply stated email message to me— "the hotel children were myself"—enriches, rather than contradicts, the Whartonesque echoes in the poem.

Another poem whose bewitching end-tag title is "which away" is a maddening tease to me, beginning with its opening unfulfilled promise "Here is the whole story." Does Guest suggest that such a promise (endemic to storytellers) is by its very nature unfulfillable, that there is no such thing as a "whole story"? Is that the thrust of her deliberately curtailed tales? Perhaps so; nonetheless, I do suspect there is, if not a whole, at least a fuller tale somewhere (in French literature? in folk-tales? in Guest's manuscripts? in the memories of some of you reading this essay?) about the adventures of Alouette and Berenice:

> Here is the whole story for a living oats in the barn
> the hovering cottage who *rowed* Mad River rain pouring down
> Alouette's sandals Berenice the orchard ladder the Parabola
> his trouble with sleep . . . who scampers out of the green. (*Stripped Tales,* 15)

Guest can and does provide satisfactions, but she more often provides agitations, turning and twisting the reader every "which-away." I am stirred and disturbed and curious about these eventlike happenings and these characterlike people. Is the "whole story" already entirely present in those redolent names: Alouette, Berenice? In the homely setting of a barn and an orchard and a green, what dire circumstance required whom to have "rowed Mad River," with the "rain pouring down"? What psychological or magical circumstance inheres in "the hovering cottage"? And what could "the capitalized Parabola" possibly be? (It arrives in the poem like a weird *deus ex machina,* an apparitional revelation of some marvelous kind).

I used to be as sure as I could be (which was never terribly sure) that the ekphrastic poem titled "moment/of ingenuity" lifts or invents a most telling narrative moment from the shared biography of Auguste Rodin and Camille Claudel:

> She put the pail on her head then moving through wire she called to the
> Master of Sculpture "make way for *Softness* I'm pouring it over the torso"
> then the bronze rain fell. (*Stripped Tales,* 34)

This deft fragment implies the two sculptors' intense collaboration and then "her" difficult assertion of independent feminine aesthetics (she must move *through wire* to accomplish it). He, Master of Sculpture though he may be, must make way for "*Softness,*" now about to characterize "the torso." The single word "then" signals narrative turning point, the sudden bronze rainfall signals a crisis point of immense relational change—from master and apprentice (albeit lovers) to enemies and competitors. It pleases me to recontextualize this "moment," to name a she, to name a he, to name a time and place, to place this defining moment back into the larger story of which it might be a part. But it also pleases me to know it isn't necessary, that storyness inheres in the verb tense, the two characters, the setting, yes, even the dialogue, and in the "first this happened, then that happened" design. Guest has erased and stripped until she can present a precise minimum, in which "all the elements of the work are maximally excited," to borrow a phrase from Lyn Hejinian. So, paradoxically, it feels very rich in its brevity, like the still-shining imagistic event that cleaves when all else has turned vague.

An interjection: Barbara Guest confided in me, after I had so presumptuously written Claudel into her tale, that she had in mind instead Louise Bourgeois, whose sculpture titled "Softness" evinces deep affiliation with and startlingly independent departure from the Rodinesque sculptural tradition. And yet: "I do like it," Guest wrote, "that the Tales have other additions than I gave them. I like the addition of Camille to Louise B. Who knows who is who in a Tale?"

Persisting again, I'm reasonably sure that "the position/anarchial" is gleaned from the life story of Walter Benjamin, and that it profoundly manages the novelistic technique of motif in its brief eight lines—playing with images of "arches" and "an*archy*"—and that its Moscow setting carries the kind of immense psychological and political significance associated more usually with lengthy narratives. There is also a startling vision of Percy and Mary Shelley "on their/way to Italy in moonless snow . . ./ cling[ing] to the carriage as it tips and swerves on/the narrow iced-over pass," which convinces that Guest has retained (and imagined) from the life of the Shelleys an indispensable moment, the one that most haunts and will not fade. Though in truth nothing but brief fragments of poetry, these passages tell in some strange fashion the "whole story." And they do this without sacrificing the materiality of the words on the page, as large-scale narratives such as novels and biographies are so apt to do.

Here she has made her poems hospitable to allusional apparitions; she entertains ghosts who are on the edge of her consciousness, and on the very edge of ours, dreamlike remnants, shimmering and fervent and haunting. Like ghosts, these stories lack full and fleshy embodiment, yet they have manifest presence. Surely it is this phantomlike quality that Anne Dunn responds to in her spectral black, white, and grey drawings, which somehow sustain both detail and vagueness, both precision and mystery, that fade onto the page and out of it, with miragelike reality. Grey watercolor washes obscure and blur; sharp pencil lines pinpoint and define; ordinary objects of the real world move in and out of an otherworldly fog. This effect literally inveigles Guest's text, as some of the drawings are reproduced on translucent onion-skin paper through which the poetry appears and disappears as one turns the pages. The two media haunt one another as they connect and disconnect.

What line of experimentation does Guest follow, in her Schoenbergian implacability in *Rocks on a Platter*? Just as she interrogated the narrative genre in *Stripped Tales,* here she explores and explodes the *belle lettre* genre of notes on literature, since all of her "notes" are in fact poems.[9] This is a book so beguilingly multivalent that it deserves (indeed will require) many essays written about it by many readers. The title rivets the attention—*Rocks on a Platter,* not exactly an oxymoron, but what *would* you call it? (She seems to invent nameless new figures of speech under the rubric of paradox, blithely evading stodgy critical vocabulary.) Playing out the denotations of the words "rock" and "platter," and then relating them to each other, is a happy distraction, or is it an absolutely central critical task that will unlock the book's mysteries? Rocks could break a platter unless they are carefully (artfully?) placed there; rocks can use a platter to become delectable, as they are framed and set before us. A platter is human-made, a product of artistry and domesticity and hospitality; rocks are objects from the natural world, unrefined, often jagged (i.e., not usually thought of as smooth, like stones—I was swiftly corrected by the author when I mistakenly called her book *Stones on a Platter*). Rocks on a platter are not rocks beneath our feet, or in an natural history exhibit. They are served up for our enjoyment and consumption. Ah, but then, if you add the subtitle *"Notes on Literature,"* does it imply an analogy? Rocks are to platters as notes are to literature? Is there always something rough and blunt about notes when compared to literature itself, which speaks in ways infinitely more complex, convincing, and lasting than does expository prose? Do notes weigh literature down? Yet perhaps notes put the art object in the context of the "real world." To paraphrase Marianne Moore, must every platter of the imagination be so designed as to hold real rocks?

This does not even begin to weave in the rocks that stud the poem proper. To quote them is to appreciate, almost tangibly, their weighty metapoetical substance: "Ship/shoal rocks/to approach this land raving!/ Rocks, platter, words, words . . ." (3); "Pockets jingle highly responsive place in the shelter/of those rocks at last the jingle of your pockets// HEARD ON THE PAGE" (6); "Shattered rocks/hid in the rock?/Deft, vehement/. . ./modernly, so be it./Noise of the shattering!" (11). The rule of thumb under *"glitter/* is that *glitter* disturbs, and//paled, finds painting//a wild grape loosens//glitter//from the *rock platter.*//Ovid writes,//'Earth, painted with flowers, that *shone brightly,'//Picaque dissimili flore nitebat humus"* (43; Guest's emphasis and capitalization throughout).

In quoting, I have tried to preserve Guest's intraline spacing; however, I have grievously reduced the white space between lines and stanzas, which is so crucial to the beauty of her pages. I'm particularly ravished by page 10, in which the words "Implacable poet" (with a period after poet) enjoy the entire spatial field of the page. Guest has written no phrase more self-descriptive, more certain about the (mature, eventual) character of those who write poetry for a living. All true poets, I take this to mean, are implacable (another word of location, with the word "place" part of its etymology); they are, in some vital way, undislocatable from their position on earth, from themselves, from the exigencies of their vision and their art. Ah, but here is the superbly rich surprise: it of course can also suggest "implaceable." Just so. She is one who cannot be placed.

Hovering textually (as introductory quotations) over the four note-poems (which are numbered but not titled) are Friedrich Hölderlin (1770–1843), Samuel Johnson (1696–1772), Georg Wilhelm Friedrich Hegel (1770–1831), and Theodor Adorno (1903–1969).[10] The chosen quotations are deftly and intelligently gleaned from these voluble and voluminous sources. Each is presented as a hard-won contention about art and aesthetics to which Guest responds, with reverence, with irreverence, with teasing humor, with beautiful or baffling or sublime illustrations, with improvisatory imaginative flights, with stripped tales.[11] To their ornate platter of tradition, she brings her fresh rocks; for their rocks (touchstones, jewels), she provides a platter of stunningly contemporary design. (The rock/platter metaphor tropes both Eliot's ideas about tradition and the individual talent, and the quintessential modernist genre of collage.) I don't think that Guest wishes to subvert or argue with her "sources" (her targets?), but to love them, to "essay" them (test and try their nearness). She seeks to locate herself, gently, insistently, as by right, vis-à-vis Literature (with a capital "L").[12]

Let me quote Guest quoting Hölderlin in Part 1 and Adorno in Part 4. (To write about Guest is to perpetually travel in her wake, to do as she does: I must write notes on notes on literature.) Hölderlin: "'To live is to defend a form'" (*Rocks on a Platter,* 1). Adorno: "'The moment a limit is posited it is overstepped, and that against which the limit was established is absorbed'" (*Rocks on a Platter,* 35). Guest's poetry convinces that she ascribes equally to these contradictory notions, that she intimately inhabits the paradox that we cannot live without defending form, and that we don't (can't, shouldn't) live without breaking, overstepping, and eluding form. Both of these are avowed beliefs, positions taken. Both are also intended to be objective descriptions of the way human beings operate and are operated on, how they make art, how art makes them, how art *is made,* in some way always partly unintended by the individual artist. Guest, I believe, has chosen them, not as partisan positions in the familiar postwar formalist/ antiformalist controversy, but for the psychological and spiritual (albeit almost self-canceling) truths they need each other to tell. To write poetry, for Guest, has always been to defend a form; to write poetry, for Guest, has always been to rapturously overstep a limit and to absorb the very terms of that limit. (Do I come closer to the dissonant emotion at the paradoxical heart of that elusive title *Defensive Rapture?*)

The following is one of the ways Guest illustrates and converses with Hölderlin.[13] She is warm in her insistence that literature not "divorce" from itself, in the interest of defending a form, certain ineffabilities: the "the uninhibited   aroma of BEAUTY," vital fragmentation, "SPECTACU- LAR LEAP[ing], the "*sweet reproach of invisibility.*" One can find or create defensible forms that can catch even these on the air: her own poetry stands as primer and the apotheosis of such a poetics:

> . . . *in its contiguous*
> *treatment of time, literature*
>
>   is inclined to divorce
> the uninhibited   aroma of BEAUTY, OR
> SPECTACULAR LEAP

suspicious
of fragmentation,

or *sweet reproach of invisibility* (*Rocks on a Platter*, 7)

This next is the first "conversation" with Adorno, Hölderlin still hover-ing. I take this to be the poet's poetic notes to herself on assuming the task—that is, taking up the pen. The heartening, taken-to-heart lesson of all the masters is: Do It, "without shyness or formality":

Without shyness or formality:

"a gesture of *allowing oneself time*"

Remember how starry it arrives the hope of another idiom, beheld
that blush of inexactitude, and the furor, it
will return to you, flotsam blocked out. (*Rocks on a Platter*, 37)

Both formality and shyness respect limits too much: they *can't* "overstep"; they can't risk and therefore miss the exhilaration, furor, inexactitude, in-timacy, flotsam of "another" experience, in life, in language. For poets, it must be true in working on something new that they feel "another idiom" has "starrily" descended on them—a new way of talking, a new language with its own rules, its own forms to defend. To insist on exactitude or neatness at this moment would be fatal; so would shyness. The imperative "remember" here is very poignant as the poet, like Milton, invoking her muse, raises herself to the precisely needed posture of receptive audacity. Here are things to remember in order not to get discouraged or lost: you're feeling hope, not confusion; furor is fertile; all flotsam will work it-self out. Embrace inexactitude, don't deny it; it's fairly blushing in all its newness and self-consciousness. *Allow yourself time,* or at least make ges-tures in that direction; pretend you have all the time in the world. Once again on the dissolving line of one of Adorno's outer limits, Guest reminds herself that she's been there before, and came back alive, the limit success-fully absorbed.

I have on my desk as I write this essay an odd object that I would like to substitute for this essay, were it only academically respectable enough, could I only be assured that Barbara Guest would not be offended by it. It is a printout from my computer, a fat sheaf of white paper, consisting of the entire text of *Rocks on a Platter* interleaved with my own commentary. My glosses are paraphrases; questions to myself; avenues of research; many, many word definitions gleaned from the *OED;* exclamations of de-light and exasperation; avowals to at last and seriously read Nietzsche; quotations to consider from Robert Kaufman, Terence Diggory, and

Brenda Hillman (who have written about sections of this book); cross-references to other poems by Guest and others. It is, in short, a present-tense (and hugely growing) record of my attempts to "read" the book, my way of becoming the reader it seems to demand, of paying a kind of sustained and wide-awake attention to it. Is it my imagination, or do I hear the poem talking back to me, encouraging me, reproving me, laughing at me, teaching me, lending me shape and authority?[14] These latest books are impelled by a heightened reader-directed metapoesis, the elusivist's irresistible invitation. I feel commanded to "gloss" and I want to do so, expansively, "without shyness or formality" (though sometimes I fear I've been afflicted by glossolalia).

> Is evanescence the wool beggar?
> strike that simpleton
> > "Bafflement."
>
> *Thee* GLOSS GLOSS
>
> point to the Mix, and
>
> > there! it slides into view
> > the Dolphin,
>
> *before* the moment oversteps,
>
> > into
> the *hum* pour his ivory. (*Rocks on a Platter,* 40)

Here are my orders from the author herself: "GLOSS GLOSS." How can I *not* obey this command that speaks to me so directly and intimately? Why should I (the vexed, proverbial but very real "reader," by name Sara Lundquist) *not* be the italicized "thee" to whom the text refers? I can "point to the Mix"; truly, that is my pleasure, my duty, my job, my passion, the thing I don't mind getting "wrong," as long as I'm allowed to do it. "The Mix!": the Mix is—I know it!—the way the words consort, their mixing-it-up on the page, their intercourse, their dance, their oxymoronic tussle, their sighs and hiccups and jokes and caresses, the superb way they glow out into the white spaces of the page into my hands. This is what I do all the live-long day in classrooms where students so dumbly, blithely push to do otherwise: I insist on "point[ing] to the Mix." Yet, I've never done it and not had that prize Dolphin "slide into view" (if only for a moment) from his rich and alien world: and he is excitement, meaning, connection, all sleek and wet, and new. "'Bafflement'" is indeed a simpleton, a slacker who spurns the delights of his own language, standing there whining, "I don't get it." Ah, "Is evanescence the wool beggar?" Let me take on the curious twists of that most fetching of questions. As a reader, I want no other occupation than this: "into/the hum pour his ivory."

NOTES

1. Plato, *Republic,* trans. Robin Watchfield (New York: Oxford University Press, 1993), 94–95.

2. This is also not to say that certain prejudices familiar to women poets have not worked in concert with Guest's own temperament to keep her, until very recently, relatively obscure. See Linda Kinnahan's and DuPlessis's various analyses of her situation vis-à-vis avant-guard poetries and mainstream feminism.

3. Terence Diggory discusses this particular paradox in his article "Barbara Guest and the Mother of Beauty."

4. See Robert von Hallberg's essay "Tourism and Postwar American Poetry."

5. It strikes me that I could rewrite this sentence, substituting "neither" and "nor" for "both" and "and," as still be true to my experience of the poem.

6. Guest's essays, art criticism, and interviews await collection or even selection; it would be a boon to have access to them as a group, as they are very hard to collect from their many far-flung periodical and archive sources. Also, I am surprised not to find her represented in anthologies such as Peter Baker's *Onward: Contemporary Poetry and Poetics* (New York: Lang, 1996) and Christopher Beach's *Artifice and Indeterminacy: An Anthology of New Poetics* (Tuscaloosa: University of Alabama Press, 1998).

7. I examined a sumptuous recent example of Guest's collaborative work at Yale's Beinecke Library, a huge book (44 cm.), published (created?) by Hine Editions/Limestone of San Francisco (1991). The cover is made of impossibly white and impossibly soft pigskin, with the title embossed in white upon it. Even the colophon is printed in white on translucent paper. It contains Richard Tuttle's mostly white soft ground etchings and Guest's supernal poem "The Altos." The poem also appears in *Defensive Rapture* (1993), amid other poems that take astonishingly lavish possession of the white spaces of the page.

8. These three words appear in the poem when Guest quotes it in the *PEN Newsletter,* but are deleted for publication in *Fair Realism.*

9. I do believe that all Guest's forays into other writing genres revert inevitably and triumphantly to poetry: this is surely true of her "novel," *Seeking Air* (1978); I will also argue one day soon that the biography of H.D. is trumped for finesse, psychological verity, disquietude, and sheer literary interest by the poem "Biography" (1980).

10. There are also guest appearances by Nietzsche, Rilke, Shelley, Byron, Apuleius, H.D., the ubiquitous guardian angel Schoenberg, Ariosto, and Ovid.

11. It is possible to read the four essays as four long continuous poems, as indeed they are. I also find much meaning and satisfaction in treating each page first as a carefully designed self-contained poem, and then in dialogue with the pages

around it. The lines are very beautifully and intentionally spaced and appointed; most end with that page's only period, well above the book's bottom edge.

12. Robert Kaufman in "The Future of Modernism" makes a similar point thus: her poetry "giv[es] itself over to its own imaginative acts of investigatory *poesis,* pursued *via* Guest's formidable erudition and uncanny ability to sympathize with her given literary and historical materials" (14).

13. There are *so many* ways in which she "converses." Note, for one, the hilarious alliterations of the poem that follows this one, as it teases both "tradition" and "theory" with a lighthearted "tra-la-la."

14. This passage written by H.D. about reading Marianne Moore's poetry comes very close to describing the delight and discomfort I feel in trying to be Barbara Guest's reader: "And if Miss Moore is laughing at us, it is laughter that catches us, that holds, fascinates, and half-paralyzes us, as light flashed from a very fine steel blade, wielded playfully, ironically, with all the fine shades of thrust and counter-thrust, with absolute surety and with absolute disdain. Yet with all the assurance of the perfect swordsman, the perfect technician, I like to imagine that there is as well something of the despair of the perfect artist—'see, you cannot know what I mean—exactly what I mean,' she seems to say, half-pitying that the adversary is so dull—that we are so dull—'and I do not intend that you shall know—my sword is very much keener than your sword, my hand surer than your hand—but you shall not know that I know you are beaten.'" H.D. [Hilda Doolittle], "Marianne Moore," *The Egoist* 3 (August 1916): 118–19.

BIBLIOGRAPHY

Books by Barbara Guest

The Altos, with Richard Tuttle (San Francisco: Hine Editions/Limestone Press, 1991).
Biography (Providence: Burning Deck, 1980).
The Blue Stairs (New York: Corinth, 1968).
The Confetti Trees (Los Angeles: Sun & Moon Press, 1999).
The Countess from Minneapolis (Providence: Burning Deck, 1976).
Defensive Rapture (Los Angeles: Sun & Moon Press, 1993).
Fair Realism (Los Angeles: Sun & Moon Press, 1989).
If So, Tell Me (London: Reality Street Editions, 1999).
The Location of Things (New York: Tibor de Nagy, 1960).
Moscow Mansions (New York: Viking, 1973).
Musicality, with June Felter (Berkeley: Kelsey St. Press, 1988).
Poems: The Location of Things, Archaics, The Open Skies (New York: Doubleday, 1962).
Quill, Solitary Apparition (Sausalito: Post-Apollo Press, 1996).
Quilts, with Deborah S. Freedman (New York: Vehicle, 1980).
Rocks on a Platter: Notes on Literature (Hanover, N.H.: Wesleyan University Press, 1999).
Seeking Air (Santa Barbara, Calif.: Black Sparrow Press, 1978).

Selected Poems (Los Angeles: Sun & Moon Press, 1995).
Stripped Tales, with Anne Dunn (Berkeley: Kelsey St. Press, 1995).
Symbiosis, with Laurie Reid (Berkeley: Kelsey St. Press, 2000).
The Türler Losses (Montreal: Mansfield, 1979).

Selected Prose

"Barbara Guest on Jean Arp." *In-House: The Poet's House Members Newsletter* (Summer 1990).
"H.D. and the Conflict of Imagism." *Sagetrieb* 15(1–2) (Spring–Fall, 1996): 13–16.
"Helen Frankenthaler: The Moment and The Distance." *Arts Magazine* 49 (April 1975): 58–59.
"The Intimacy of Biography." *The Iowa Review* 16(3) (Fall 1986): 58–71.
"Jeanne Reynal," *Craft Horizons* 31 (June 1971): 40–43.
"Leatrice Rose." *Arts Magazine* 59 (Summer 1985): 13.
"June Felter at 871 Fine Arts." *Art in America* 79 (March 1991): 145.
"Mysteriously Defining the Mysterious: Byzantine Proposals of Poetry." *HOW(ever)* 3(3) (October 1986): 12–13.
"Poetry the True Fiction." *Exact Change Yearbook*, ed. Peter Gizzi. 1st ed. (Boston: Exact Change, 1995), 97–102.
"A Reason for Poetics." *Ironwood* 24 (Fall 1984): 153–55.
"Remarks" at the Barnard College Conference, "Where Lyric Tradition Meets Language Poetry: Innovation in Contemporary American Poetry By Women." *Fence* 3(1) (Spring/Summer 2000): 122–24.
"Review of *Narrative's Journey: The Fiction and Film Writing of Dorothy Richardson,* by Susan Gevirtz." *Sulfur* 40 (Spring 1997): 186–88.
"Robert De Niro in the 1950s and 1960s." *Robert De Niro, Sr. (1922–1993): Selected Works* (San Francisco: Hackett-Freedman Gallery, 1998).
"Robert Goodnough." In *School of New York: Some Younger Artists,* ed. B.H. Friedman (New York: Grove Press, 1959), 18–23.
"Shifting Persona," *Poetics Journal* 9 (June 1991): 85–88.
"A Talk on 'Startling Maneuvers'." *Poetry Project Newsletter* 172 (December/January 1998/99): 8–10.
"Under the Shadow of Surrealism." *PEN Newsletter* 62: 16–17.
"The Vuillard of Us." (About James Schuyler.) *The Denver Quarterly* 24 (Spring 1990): 13–16.

Interviews

"Barbara Guest." Videotaped interview with Douglas Messerli and reading from *Selected Poems* on April 16, 1996. Lannan Literary Series, no. 51. Los Angeles: The Foundation, 1996.
With Charles Bernstein. Audio Tape. LINEbreak Series. Buffalo, N.Y.: Granolithic Productions, 1996.
With Mark Hillringhouse. *American Poetry Review* (July/August 1992): 23–30.

Selected Criticism

Bennett, Robert. 2001. "Literature as Destruction of Space: The Precarious Architecture of Barbara Guest's Spatial Imagination." *Women's Studies* 30: 43–44.

Bernstein, Charles. 1999. "Introducing Barbara Guest—Frost Medal, Poetry Society of America at the Celeste Bartos Forum of the New York Public Library, April 23, 1999." *Jacket* 10 (1999): <http://www.jacket.zip.com.au/jacket10/bernstein-on-guest.html>

Caples, Garrett. 2001. "The Barbara Guest Experience." *Women's Studies* 30: 123–29.

DeKoven, Marianne. 1986. "Gertrude's Granddaughters." *Women's Review of Books* 4(2): 12–14.

Diggory, Terence. 2001. "Barbara Guest and the Mother of Beauty." *Women's Studies* 30: 75–94.

———. 1993. *Grace Hartigan and the Poets: Paintings and Prints* (Saratoga Springs, N.Y.: Skidmore College).

Duncan, Erika. 1994. "Encounters: Hearing a Poet, But Understanding Little." *New York Times*, Sunday edition, September 25, 1994, sec. 13, p. 21.

DuPlessis, Rachel Blau. 1995. "The Flavor of Eyes: *Selected Poems* by Barbara Guest." *Women's Review of Books* 13(1) (October): 23–24.

———. 1996. "'All My Vast/Journeying Sensibility': Barbara Guest's Recent Work." *Sulfur* 39 (Fall): 39–48.

———. 2000. "The Gendered Marvelous: Barbara Guest, Surrealism, and Feminist Reception." In *The Scene of My Selves: New Work on New York School Poets*, ed. Terence Diggory and Stephen Paul Miller (Orono, Maine: National Poetry Foundation), 189–214.

Einzig, Barbara. 1996. "The Surface as Object: Barbara Guest's *Selected Poems.*" *American Poetry Review* 25(1) (January/February): 7–10.

Fraser, Kathleen, ed. 2000. *Translating the Unspeakable: Poetry and the Innovative Necessity* (Tuscaloosa: University of Alabama Press).

Gander, Forrest. 1995. Introduction to Barbara Guest's poetry reading at The New School in New York City on November 14, 1995. *Poetry Pilot* (Winter 1995–96): 8.

Going, Dale. 1991. "A Palimpsest for Barbara Guest." *HOW(ever)* (Summer 1991): 13–14.

Greenberg, Arielle. 2001. "A Sublime Sort of Exercise: Levity and the Poetry of Barbara Guest." *Women's Studies* 30: 111–21.

Hillman, Brenda. 1996. "The Artful Dare: Barbara Guest's Selected Poems." *Talisman: A Journal of Contemporary Poetry and Poetics* 16 (Fall): 207–20.

Johnson, Honor. 1984. "Barbara Guest and Lyric Atmospheres." *HOW(ever)* 1(3): 12–13.

Kasper, Catherine. 2001. "Barbara Guest: This Art." *Women's Studies* 30: 1–6.

Kaufman, Robert. 2000. "The Future of Modernism: Barbara Guest's Recent Poetry." *American Poetry Review.* 29(4) (July/August): 11–16.

Keller, Lynn. 2000. "Becoming 'a Compleat Travel Agency': Barbara Guest's Negotiations with the 'Fifties Feminine Mystique." In *The Scene of My Selves: New Work on New York School Poets,* ed. Terence Diggory and Stephen Paul Miller (Orono, Maine: National Poetry Foundation), 215–28.

Killian, Kevin. 1996. Review of *Stripped Tales.* Electronic Poetry Review: <http://www.poetry.org/issue1/alltext/rvkil.htm>

Kinnahan, Linda A. 2000. "Reading Barbara Guest: The View from the 'Nineties." In *The Scene of My Selves: New Work on New York School Poets,* ed. Terence Diggory and Stephen Paul Miller (Orono, Maine: National Poetry Foundation), 229–44.

Lehman, David. 1998. *The Last Avant-Garde: The Making of the New York School of Poets* (New York: Doubleday).

Lundquist, Sara. 1997. "Reverence and Resistance: Barbara Guest, Ekphrasis, and the Female Gaze." *Contemporary Literature* 38 (Summer): 260–86.

———. "Barbara Guest." 1998. In *Dictionary of Literary Biography: American Poets Since World War II,* ed. Joseph Conte. Vol. 193 (Detroit: Bruccoli Clark Layman), 159–70.

———. 2000. "Another Poet among Painters: Barbara Guest, Grace Hartigan, Mary Abbott." In *The Scene of My Selves: New Work on New York School Poets,* ed. Terence Diggory and Stephen Paul Miller (Orono, Maine: National Poetry Foundation), 245–64.

———. 2001. "The Fifth Point of a Star: Barbara Guest and the New York 'School' of Poets." *Women's Studies* 30: 11–41.

Manousos, Anthony. 1980. "Barbara Guest." In *Dictionary of Literary Biography: American Poets Since World War II,* ed. Donald J. Greiner. Vol. 5 (New York: Gale), 295–300.

McQuade, Molly. 1999. "Barbara Guest's Drama." *Stealing Glimpses of Poetry, Poets, and Things In Between: Essays* (Louisville, Ky.: Sarabande Books), 57–64.

Miller, Tyrus. 1991. "Guest, Barbara." In *Contemporary Poets,* ed. Tracy Chevalier, 5th ed. (Chicago: St. James Press), 360–61.

Moore, Marianne. 1984. *Herself Defined: The Poet H.D. and Her World* (New York: Doubleday).

Mulford, Wendy. 1999. "The Architecture of Dream: Barbara Guest's *The Blue Stairs.*" Jacket #10, October 1999: <http://www.jacket.zip.com.au/jacket10/mulford-on-guest.html>

Myers, John Bernard. 1969. Introduction to *The Poets of the New York School* (Philadelphia: Pennsylvania University Press), 7–29.

North, Charles. 1998. "10 Essays for Barbara Guest." *No Other Way: Selected Prose* (Brooklyn, N.Y.: Hanging Loose Press), 152–56.

Rabinowitz, Anna. 2001. "Barbara Guest: Notes Toward Painterly Osmosis." *Women's Studies* 30: 95–109.

Rosenberg, Harold. 1965. *The Tradition of the New* (New York: McGraw, Hill).

Shapiro, David. 1991. "A Salon of 1990: Maximalist Manifesto." *American Poetry Review* (January/February): 37–47.

Von Hallberg, Robert. 1991. "Tourism and Postwar American Poetry." In *Temperamental Journeys: Essays on The Modern Literature of Travel,* ed. Michael Kowalewski (Athens: University of Georgia Press), 126–52.

Welish, Marjorie. 1990. "Review of *Fair Realism.*" *Sulfur* 26 (Spring): 213–15.

———. 1998. "On Barbara Guest." In *Moving Borders: Three Decades of Innovative Writign by Women,* ed. Mary Margaret Sloan (Jersey City: Talisman House), 561–65.

———. 1999. "The Lyric Lately" (on Barbara Guest). *Jacket* #10 (October): <http://www.jacket.zip.com.au/jacket10/welish-on-guest.html>

LYN HEJINIAN

FROM *WRITING IS AN AID TO MEMORY*

1.

apple is shot nod
                    ness seen know I around saying
                          think for a hundred years
but and perhaps utter errors direct the point to a meadow
                         rank fissure up on the pit
arts are several branches of life
                little more science is brought where great
              need is required
                 out becomes a bridge of that name
        in the painting is a great improvement
    bit ink up on the human race
and return if the foot goes back
            in the trunks of trees behoove a living thing
                     wedge war common saw
      hard by that length of time the great demand is
                   very dear
ashes in water
                    that might be a slip of architecture
                  think was reduced to an improper size
  blocks to interest who can visit
                     variations on ideas are now full
               problems
        from a point of increasing
at only as to four or we who nine

a little grace familiar with simple limbs and the sudden
                reverse

2.

    diary us a few hoops
        hap as up-and-morrow
                we lost the familiar stumbling blocks
                who fills with life just one side of it
and how did this happen like an excerpt
  beginning in a square white boat abob on a gray sea
a party
                whose charm
  crumble more subtle
                tootling of another message by the hacking
        lark
  but what does music directly
                time is somehow glamorous as well
a gray sea although it is the Pacific
                that sweet little block
                the taste of a larger pattern
                tired mixed trace of chat back
as a child
                to the rescue and its spring
  compare beats of the dime were wishes
                so the classic clink of feet
            many comedies emerge and in particular a group
        of girls
        how can it be
composed when brilliantly objective and cast a little
    further
and with such care disintegrates
                rub tinged
    fall what
      heck car
    ellipsis makes its promise leaving us to get out

dreams think of how we thought
fluster usually bright of water
in a great lock of letters
like knock look
saw dime treat up so buster
carrying wood between the thumb of the loops
a restless storage of a thousand boastings
I do not suppose I really am a consolation
glue is used on almost all occasions that are to be
joined
to draw tendencies into truths of such
a link
link bar of two such new polish
the hit calls it in one act or or in
an hour hailed to its geometry
scanned but lifelong locked this taste
of distance
on paper the horse is laden with yellow
lines actually later the more one remembers
bread in the same proportion
any animal frequently goat a considerable degree of skill
a scription locks with one's own judgment
the readymade is deceptively passing
its consent to time
mass perhaps in a form against it
a cheap reading of what surrounds
this taste of opinion
it all can be admitted up
a period passes bristling with the sum of distance
porated sugar with fruit
link rule dots
fuss on them
add nap so yellow
grand the coo
I spent the poor scratch
new flying kept is spent in the slaughter

rain unable mostly limb known years
dollar honey so all for fog
a vulnerable known not sure
glance must bit
this suits my suspicions
the doctor ducks the illness
everybody dies that wanted to
in a famous relativity
a clock clink hardly the solid links
and retell, more retell, and all retell
I know not where then I remember
so love so the clink I know
some feeding blocks game maybe as I learned
all that sort of do exist
freedom catered to the growing
money shows a marked influence is the beast
rather nicer and afterwards
brating white where the arches and a short decay
water out on the grass to the dew for
sun
flat see much smaller with a sandy boney
similar to the summer drab sandy
summer better getting a sun
field getting fence shining
pond about the place
yup on a very long loose
like the leak in the closet
a blink of my choice
as four would feel like
geometry dappled with distance and points
action trembles in the word springy
birds among the branches of the bees
reserve in the under I smile
hollow happy they do not know
scarcely green eddy unrolled its marble
bag

ends up the place about the middle of the table
dump hind light sprint
and a tight find of firelight under I smile
dump my flying in a proper way
I know still that memory only mimics
paint each take in the shoot bop
as at night half a money
pand darling through action which sum
living with some giant loot who loads the prison
thanks flop the action of looking for more
rolling that is typical envelops a large
crowd
exceeding with only a brief stay
dot in the prison tissue
lock or daughter and dime
between dawn and division
away for a long meaning
hopper up at one end the puff of being born
the reason not like really make balance
don't seem to as to how
the push of music for a long meaning
the north reaches to the ankle
any flutter between harmonies
really pretty secretly
covery the shifted years ago
one cannot be angry without expense that
disturbs
the little rhyme at this expense
a matter plump picks flesh
what the tree under the bedroom
window
rowed into shares by the ears
a happy hobby almost divine
leaning learning to soul to soul
I continue to make use quite restored for I am
very useful

more goose in the fable than lifetime
a wish is sufficient that teaches me this
      lagger imagine a full morning
  can hardly be seen hung so
     my mind with a handshake
           to wish something different is long enough
     one glass the whole will grouping
      pensated change
     of water swimming among the ill-weeds
     pearls of fish
all the novel mass is one at the landing of the stairway

. . . .

9.

a cat is "in time"
  between wind and water a queer character
    garage French often for plurals who detect
      jazz the curious should consult
         related but to the bassoon but to the
      serpent
   dignity is that hidden force
    human moody
   for a building is the exception in water
    in such case ! the task of biography
      sit cat has stop wrap
    of a sum and immediate notion
     simultaneity in some measure
  I know by a pack for me to imagine
      sight in other worlds and hidden rumbled
better two needs it resembled
       why do the motions of cats so interest
    us
   hard impress had of human thought
  force from keeping them hidden

we cannot be happy without the close
instantaneously, frozen is pure "in time" music
logical keen of a few from childhood
which clusion vary
combination a reward for difficulty
addition is the distance of real complexity
it is necessary in everyone's hands "in time" and
"out of time"
knowledge is both
tag of view of doing something shopping
naturally of course
nickels tell your man
adults with arithmetic uptown radio
floor the sugar and rice some sitting
the sum sits as think torn thing
describes streets their heaping point
well interruption is addition
read and follow
on their minds briefly Friday
that holy and that charity passes
the hundredfold is apparent later
round brink as it were
I know that we met hand to hand
perhaps the brink is a basket
somehow revised in an orbit
above be in rhyme and roots below
rise and fall or two upright horns made
with love of wood
to break the recent past with the present
profounder proximity
yond laughing in the willow rice
without trees was once a farmhouse
ideas can form lest they break
glass from passers-by
probably between points hover at the edge
of meeting

more of a rambling necessity
we cannot crete methods, not since
should the sopher's hope
the substantial fit indicates a finish
or the possibility of a finish
between circumspect and retrospect there is only the time
of an idea
first that finally riddle and infinite nature
courage had the painters and had the morning
no soggy gossip chapter here
by the fruit falls a piece of the long night
night fastened so the whites could show
surely will while what I could
boldly power pel
warm rise into words toward the intelligent
thought

. . . .

FROM *HAPPILY*

. . . .

The manner in which we are present at this time to and fro appears, we
    come to point of view before us
The matter is here
Can we share its kind of existence?
'I' moving about unrolled barking at blue clouds devoted—to each other?
    to hasten to the point? to evade anxiety? to picture?
Having awkward heaviness 'I' never moves freely about unless passing
    and happening accompanied
Our pleasure is perplexed beyond that

If we thrill to low hills because they are not composed they are 'composed
   to our liking'
They say there is no defining that but to say that is defining that, living in
   context
One would think of all the social forces traveling with a show of
   indifference over a crowd or sound brought to a sound
A good person would be starred ill and well in a life he or she couldn't
   know how to refuse
Every day we may never happen on the object hung on a mere chance
When and where one happens it will surprise us not in itself but in its
   coming to our attention not as something suddenly present but as
   something that's been near for a long time and which we have only just
   noticed
When we might ask did we begin to share that existence
What have we overlooked
Nostalgia is another name for one's sense of loss at the thought that one
   has sadly gone along happily overlooking something, who knows what
Perhaps there were three things, no one of which made sense of the other
   two
A sandwich, a wallet, and a giraffe
Logic tends to force similarities but that's not what we mean by 'sharing
   existence'
The matter is incapable of being caused, incapable of not being so,
   condensed into a cause—a bean, captive forever
Perhaps
Because this object is so tiny
A store of intellect, a certain ethical potential, something that will hold
   good
Like ants swarming into pattern we get to the middle of the day many
   distinct sensations that must be it
Music checks the relaxation the contrasting aspects constantly changing
   set going
The ceaseless onset cuts this recognized sensation hurrying after it alive
It seems we've committed ourselves

That something exists at all is its nakedness we could term fate and rising
    curves fate

That it should succeed already has been determined

And we have only to add on to it everything and everyone associated with
    it from beginning to end sustaining familiar acts

One is stung by a bee and it is noticeable that the whole body is involved

Why isolate part of the field?

Say we look on a mountain scene changing colors, the walls of a room
    vividly experienced from inside it

Why speak as if there were some incompatibility

Of what would it consist

Even after the closeness of the room which is now vacant I rise at the
    thought of the future of all the positions of things and re-enter the
    room

What is the Greek word for that, the big chance for each event—*kairos*?

Normally we don't notice that things we use in being accessible are being
    set aside while the extra, superfluous ones remain material one can
    disturb

Once one's caught in it one can make a face which nothing delimits from
    you, from me, from us

The face facing—how succinct!

There the never resting emphasis rests splitting all the probabilities
    converge

Do they have witnesses?

Tsvetaeva warns us: it can happen that 'income tragically exceeds
    expenditure,' she says or rather it *will* happen that one can't find a way
    to spend as much life as accumulates to one

We care in time, scatter acts in accord with time supporting action

Does death sever us from all that is happening finitude

Yes, swim it does

I the wall saw it

We the wall

I'm often ambivalent, the artistic will being weak as well as strong about
    being seen heard understood

Whatever I see in thought as life I come to coming to me in history

At first glance?

What could we, mind wandering but never 'free,' do with the word 'galactic'

Events are unscrolling, they cover my eyes, all familiarity naked

Launched, I need either clothes or a bed and a blanket to protect my nature from nature's pranks

A dream unless you saw it too, which would throw the stop and start of sleep into question and deprive us of the knowledge of the comfort of the knowledge that we can sleep troubling us together side by side

Ever beginners until all is margin, warm and flat

How the near becomes far and the far becomes near we may try to discover but we shouldn't take the question too seriously

Stop and start doubtless is the very same as stop and start doubtful

In a downpour we don't count drops as no harm is done to the causal chain we're close to the ground to see each other clearly

One can't say that being human is voluntary but it does tell a story that to another human won't seem pointless

To another human one acts one intervenes

In the dream one is shivering, already shivering before the first glimpse of the dream, shivering at the *reality* of the dream

A headache could happen to anyone, disappearance to anything

This is that kind of life, that kind of world, and this is the kind of place in which one can easily spend a dollar but not easily on hay and not so easily see a toad, cod in the woods in a dream we talk more to hear

You laugh?

I was going to speak of doom eager to resume consecutive events plowing through the space surrounding them to something now, no ellipsis, just mouth open in astonishment or closed to suck quid and quod, that and what

Not proving but pointing not disappointed boldly taking aim obliged to acknowledge I admit to being sometimes afraid of the effort required for judgment, afraid of the judgment required

That can happen only after that it has happened is ascertained, if you can
keep up, time can't be banished, being real
In the world we see things together, the judgments have been made, takes
the chalk, draws the milky line
To say that the music pleases me is impersonal, also the great skua, a
dozen things singly through different mental states, mental states here
and there as if unknown to each other things happen to them
differently
They can't anticipate each other but they aren't innocent of each other,
the dead then alive knowing glances
Future detail of experience the same thing ours for nothing more than
noting that living harbors the half-desire for anonymity self
consciousness diminishes within
Take fences—the mechanism of clocks harbors birds it provides a narrow
escape

A story requires resemblance and the results are bound to include
recognizable sounds in their totality as horns and windmills and the
story is 'ours'
It turns over to today the body it contains, something alone in whatever
time across, being this of that, tenderly trying to dispel the anxiety
impeding pleasurable run-on regeneration
Imagining ourselves under a gray sky shining so brightly our eyes can't
establish any connections, a sky so bright that the option of connection
isn't open, this puts us in mind of beginnings that reason can motivate
but not end
Searching out streets which allow for faster movement through this
impression of something short-lived we can't retreat, can't know where
we are
We fret as if demented by different events in the dissatisfied chaos that
make incompatible claims
We go no more than a few feet before we come upon the obstacle
punctually
Happiness is independent of us bound to its own incompleteness sharply
The day has come with both rational and irrational aiming at it the future
fork and set of feathers

There is activity in a life, i.e. conduct asserts the power of deliberating
    without knowing how a state of being is brought into existence every
    so often often
The specific accident to specify something never allowed to settle
    completely
Then the shout 'I' and the response 'me, too,' the curiosity grows
I can know you without yardstick or sleep, without analysis and from
    near or far, but I can't know you without myself
What were the chances I would land on a ladder is the question at which·
    I'm laughing to experience the reality of what I myself am not
The closer expression comes to thought fearlessly to be face-to-face would
    be to have almost no subject or the subject would be almost invisible
And more is left than usefulness
It's this that happiness achieves
The riddle happening hitherto before
What is not is now possible, a ponderable
You muse on musing on—so much now but you do
You can rearrange what the day gets from accidents but you can't derive
    its reality from them
The dot just now adrift on the paper is not the product of the paper dark
Nearly negative but finite it springs from its own shadow and cannot be
    denied the undeniable world once it is launched—once it's launched it's
    derived
Tonight sounding roughly it isn't quite that only words can reason
    beyond what's reasonable that I drop my eyes to
Something comes
The experiences generated by sense perception come by the happenstance
    that is with them
Experiences resulting from things impinging on us
There is continuity in moving our understanding of them as they appear
Some which are games bring with them their own rules for action which
    is a play we play which we may play with an end we value not winning
The dilemmas in sentences form tables of discovery of things created to
    create the ever better dilemma which is to make sense to others

. . . .

POETIC STATEMENT
Some Notes toward a Poetics

1.

POETICS IS not personal. A poetics gets formed in and as a relationship with the world.

Poetics is where poetry's engagement with meaning as meaningfulness gets elaborated—poetics is the site of poetry's reason—where the plurality of its logics and the viability of its contexts are tested and articulated.

A poetics considers how and what a specific poem means within itself and its own terms and how and why it means (and is meaningful) within a community that congregates around it—around it as writing in general and around certain specific writings and writing practices in particular.

I espouse a poetics of affirmation. I also espouse a poetics of uncertainty, of doubt, difficulty, and strangeness. Such a poetics is inevitably contradictory, dispersive, and incoherent while sustaining an ethos of linkage. It exhibits disconnection while hoping to accomplish reconnection.

2.

Aesthetic discovery can be congruent with social discovery. Aesthetic discovery occurs through encounters, at points of contact, and so too does political and ethical discovery.

These points of contact or linkages are the manifestation of our logics; they give evidence of our reasoning and they also serve as the sites for our reasons—our reasons to do what we do.

3.

At points of linkage, the possibility of a figure of contradiction arises: a figure we might call by a Greek name, *xenos*. *Xenos* means "stranger" or "foreigner," but more importantly, from *xenos* two English words with what seem like opposite meanings are derived: they are *guest* and *host*.

A guest/host relationship comes into existence solely in and as an occurrence, that of their meeting, an encounter, a mutual and reciprocal contextualization. The host is no host until she has met her guest, the guest is no guest until she meets her host. In Russian the word for "occurrence" captures the dynamic character of this encounter. The word for event in Russian is *sobytie; so* (with or co-) and *bytie* (being), "being with" or "withbeing" or "co-existence." Every encounter produces, even if for only the flash of an instant, a xenia—the occurrence of coexistence which is also an event of strangeness or foreignness. A strange occurrence that, nonetheless, happens constantly—we have no other experience of living than encounters. We have no other use for language than to have them.

Foreignness is different from alienation; the two notions are differently nuanced. Alienation connotes separation, detachment. Foreignness, of course, may suggest that too, in that a feeling of foreignness is a feeling of being where one doesn't belong—but where alienation involves a step back from a situation, foreignness involves a step into it. The alienated withdraws, the foreigner proceeds and becomes a guest.

4.

The guest/host encounter creates "a space of appearance"—which in classical Greek thought constitutes the polis, the place, as Hannah Arendt puts it, for "the sharing of words and deeds." Arendt continues: "The polis . . . is the organization of the people as it arises out of acting and speaking together, and its true space lies between people living together for this purpose, no matter where they happen to be."[1]

She goes on to make a further and very important point: "To be deprived of it means to be deprived of reality, which, humanly and politically speaking, is the same as appearance. To men the reality of the world is guaranteed by the presence of others, by its appearing to all; 'for what appears to all' [says Aristotle in the *Nichomachean Ethics*], 'what appears to all, this we call Being.'"[2]

An apparent opposition arises here, between the ancient Greek political notion that reality exists in and as commonality, which in turn establishes communality versus the contemporary (though century-old) aesthetic notion that the commonplace and the habituation that occurs within it produce a dulling of reality, which it is the business of art to revitalize or revivify.

But it is a false opposition, one that is resolved within the treasuring of living, that is valued as the dearest thing in life by both ancients and moderns. We have always wanted things to be real, and we have always wanted to experience their reality since it is one with our own.

The notion that the world is common to us all is vital. We need the world—which is to say all things need all other things; we all need each other—if we are to exist as realities. As George Oppen puts it in his poem "A Narrative": "things explain each other, Not themselves."

Reality consists of all that is the world that is common to us all; and it is inextricably related to the space of appearance, the polis.

A valuable contribution to this notion of the polis is contained in

Charles Altieri's characterization of the creative ground and its citizen, the creative self: the creative ground is "a source of energy and value in the objective order that otherwise mocks subjective consciousness"; the creative self is one "whose activity discloses or produces aspects of that ground which have potential communal significance. Art becomes a social and cultural force and not some form of individual therapy or self-regarding indulgence in the resources of the individual's imagination."[3]

5.

Along comes something—launched in context.

That something is occurring means it is taking place, or taking a place, in the space of appearance.

It is almost automatic to us to assume that this *something* (on the one hand) and *we* (on the other) exist independently—that *something* was independently elsewhere (out of sight and mind) prior to coming into the zone in which *we* perceive it and which we, at the moment of this perceptual encounter, designate as context. Furthermore, it is at the moment that we perceive this something that we ourselves come into that context—into our coinciding (by chance?) with something. The context, in other words, is the medium of our encounter, the ground of our becoming (i.e., happening to be) present at the same place at the same time. By this reasoning, one would also have to say that context too is launched—or at least that it comes into existence *quâ* context when something is launched in such a way as to become perceptible to us and thereby to involve us—whomever we are—strangers (even if, perhaps, only momentarily strangers) to each other previously and now inseparable components of the experience.

As strangers (foreigners), it is hard for us to find the "right words" (themselves simultaneously demanding context and serving as it) for what we experience in that perception and involvement.

Usually comparisons are the first things foreigners make. "The dark castle on the hill is like a cormorant on a rock stretching its crooked wings in the sun" or "The pink wet light in Saint Petersburg on a winter day is like a summer San Francisco fog," etc. Such comparisons, reaching out of the present situation to another, previously experienced, recollected one, may appear to constitute the "making of a context" for the current context, but a context made in such a way is a transported one, acquired by way of metaphor. And such metaphors, cast in the form of similes and intended to smooth over differences, deny incipience, and to the degree that they succeed, they thereby forestall the acquisition of history.

But the phrase or sentence "Along comes something—launched in context" announces a moment of incipience; one could even say that it is itself, as a phrase or utterance, a moment of incipience. Something that wasn't here before is here now; it appears and it appeared to us, and it is acknowledge by the sensation *this is happening.*

6.

I would like now to introduce a notion that Heidegger (in "On the Way to Language") terms "propriation." "Language lets people and things be there for us," he says, meaning language's proper effect, the effect of propriation.

Language grants (acknowledges, affirms) and shows (or brings into the space of appearance) what it grants: each utterance is a saying of the phrase "this is happening."

As Goethe says (in lines quoted by Heidegger): "Only when it owns itself to thanking/Is life held in esteem." "To own" here is used in the sense also of "to own up," which is to give oneself over, to experience hospitality, *xenia,* the guest/host relationship. And to enter the relationship of xenia is to accept its obligations. "Every thinking that is on the trail of something is a poetizing, and all poetry a thinking," says Heidegger. "Each coheres with the other on the basis of the saying that has already pledged itself . . . , the saying whose thinking is a thanking."[4]

To propriate, then, is to grant, to acknowledge, to own up, to love, to thank, to make a hospitality bond with.

This is intimately connected to poetic uses of language. In Greek culture, as you know, the *symbolon* or symbol was a token representing xenia—a token broken in half and divided between guest and host to be carried as proof of identity that could be verified by comparing its other half—a token by which a stranger becomes a guest.

The word as symbol establishes a guest/host relationship between speaker and things of the world. We are strangers to the things of which we speak until we speak and become instead their guests or they become ours. This transformation of the relation in which two beings are strangers to each other into a relation in which they are guest-host to each other is propriation.

"Propriation is telling"[5]—a speaking that matters. We tell in order to become guests and hosts to each other and to things—or to become guests and hosts to life.

7.

I want to bring forward another Greek term, *thaumzein: thaumzein* names our great wonder that there is *something* rather than *nothing,* our "shocked wonder" (to quote Hannah Arendt) "at the miracle of Being."[6]

This is an incipient experience for philosophy as for poetry, both of which are excited into activity by *thaumzein* and the perplexity that comes with it.

Hannah Arendt locates it in what she calls natality—beginning, the highly improbable but regularly happening coming into existence of someone or something. Here, in a unique and singular happening, commonality too comes into existence. One thing that is common to us all is that we are born; another is that we are different from each other. Singularity and commonality are the same occurrence, and this condition of natality remains with us. Human lives, as Arendt says, are "rooted in natality in so far as they have the task to provide and preserve the world for, to foresee and reckon with the constant influx of newcomers who are born into the world as strangers."[7]

To be rooted in natality means that humans are born, and to be born is to become the beginning of somebody, "who is a beginner him [or her]self."[8]

"[M]en [and women], though they must die, are not born in order to die but in order to begin."[9]

To begin has two senses: one gets begun and one causes beginnings. "The new beginning inherent in birth can make itself felt in the world only because the newcomer possesses the capacity of beginning something anew, that is, of acting."[10]

8.

To value the new was, of course, a widely held and explicit tenant of modernist aesthetics, as in Pound's often cited commandment, "Make it new." Viktor Shklovsky's more thoughtful, more self-reflexive, and better analyzed aphorism—"In order to restore to us the perception of life, to make a stone stony, there exists that which we call art"[11]—takes the behest further, making newness not an end in itself but a strategy employed for the sake of the enhancement of experience, and as an affirmation of life. "Only the creation of new forms of art can restore to man sensation of the world, can resurrect things and kill pessimism."[12] Shklovsky goes on, of course, to elaborate a now familiar set of devices intended to restore palpability to things—retardation, roughening, etc.—that are major elements (and, in ways that can be taken as troubling, even the stock in trade) of so-called innovative poetry to this day (eighty-three years later). Contemporary poets—myself among them—have embraced this project. Comments variously repeating or attempting to extend Shklovsky's proposition appear throughout my teaching notebooks:

Language is one of the principal forms our curiosity takes.

The language of poetry is a language of inquiry.

Poetry takes as its premise that language (all language) is a medium for experiencing experience. It provides us with the consciousness of consciousness.

To experience is to go through or over the limit (the word comes from the Greek *peras*—term, limit); or, to experience is to go beyond where one is, which is to say to be beyond where one was (the prepositional form *peran*, beyond).

Imagine saying that at one stage of life, one's artistic goal is to provide experience (new or revivified, restored to palpability) and at another (later) it is to provide the joy of that experience.

After how much experience can one feel free of the fear that one hasn't lived (the fear of an unlived life)?

It is the task of poetry to produce the phrase *this is happening* and thereby to provoke the sensation that corresponds to it—a sensation of newness, yes, and of renewedness—an experience of the revitalization of things in the world, an acknowledgment of the liveliness of the world, the restoration of the *experience* of our experience—a sense of living our life. But I do not want to imply that to produce such a sensation is necessarily to produce knowledge nor even a unit of cognition; rather, its purpose is to discover context and, therein, reason.

Admittedly, several obvious (and boringly persistent) problems arise when *experience* is assigned primacy of place in an aesthetics and its accompanying discourse of value—when it is given the status of final cause and taken as an undisputed good. First, giving preeminence to experience would seem to demand what is termed "authenticity."

Happily, one can debunk this on the same basis that one can debunk a second problem, which I could describe as anti–intellectual and ultimately philistine. In assuming a positive value to experience for its own sake, and in advocating thereby an art that heightens perceptibility, one risks appearing to privilege sensation over cogitation, to promote immediacy and disdain critique. There is a danger of implying that the questioning of experience may serve to distance and thereby diminish at least aspects of it, and that this is antithetical to "real" artistic practice. This is the basis of art's supposed hostility to criticism, theory (thought), and occasional hostility even to examination of its own history. Or, to put it another way, on these grounds, the philistine romantic attempts to ground his or her rejection of context.

And here is the basis for a dismissal of these two related problems. One cannot meaningfully say "This is happening" *out* of context. At the very moment of uttering the phrase, "natality" occurs. And from that moment of incipience, which occurs with the recognition of the experience of and presented by the phrase *along comes something—launched in context* through the phrase *this is happening,* we are *in* context, which is to say, in thought (in theory and with critique) and in history.

There is no context without thought and history. They exist through reciprocation of their reason. Otherwise, there is no sensation, no experience, no consciousness of living. And, to quote Tolstoi just as Shklovsky does: "If the complex life of many people takes place entirely on the level of the unconscious, then it's as if this life had never been."[13]

9.

And here I'll introduce one last Greek term: *eudaimonia,* which is often translated as happiness, but more accurately it means "a flourishing." Eudaimonia is what the Greeks called the sheer bliss of simply being alive. Eudaimonia is the joy one experiences in the mattering of life—in the sufficiency of its matter. It is pleasure in the fact that it matters.

It is matter with history, not so much because it has a past as because it cares about the future.

What "matters" must be concerned with what will come to matter: the future. We care about the idea of what's going to happen to humanity. If we didn't, life would be meaningless. If we knew the world was going to end, we wouldn't be willing to continue. To flourish in the present requires requiring, which is to say, the future. Eudaimonia literally means to be "with a demon"—eu-daimonia—one "who accompanies each man [and woman] throughout . . . life, who is his [or her] distinct identity, but appears and is visible only to others."[14] This daimon is the future.

As writers we care for and about the future; we make it matter. I can only agree with Viktor Shklovsky when he says that "the creation . . . of art can restore to [us] sensation of the world, [it] can resurrect things and kill pessimism."[15]

Notes begin on page 255.

PARTING WITH DESCRIPTION

Craig Dworkin

> Le fou est la victime de la rébellion des mots.
>
> —Edmond Jabès, "Je bâtis ma demeure: poèmes 1943–1957"

> The insubordination of words . . . has shown that the theoretical critique of the world of power is inseparable from a practice that destroys it.
>
> —Mustapha Khayati,
> "Les Mots captifs: préface à un dictionnaire situationniste"

YOU MAY recall the story from Plato's *Phædrus:* Theuth offers the gift of writing to King Thamus, pitching it as a secret recipe for wisdom and memory. But the king doesn't fall for it. Thamus predicts that

> this discovery of yours will implant forgetfulness in the learners' minds; they will cease to exercise memory because they will rely on that which is written, calling things to remembrance no longer from within themselves, but by means of external, written characters. What you have discovered is not an aid to memory, but to reminder. And it is no true wisdom that you offer your disciples, but only its semblance.[16]

And so it seems in Lyn Hejinian's eponymous book.[17] *Writing,* you may remember (or be reminded), records a similar concern with "semblance." A representative selection of the work's vocabulary would include "likeness," "imitation," "mimicry," "reflecting," "mirrors," "description," "identical," "re-semblance," and so on.[18] Of course, this thematic recurrence might be expected, given the obvious relation between memory and mimesis. By necessity, mimesis implies memory; if one could not recall an original for comparison, one could never recognize something as mimetic or not in the first place. Memory, given its ability to reproduce the past in some measure, is itself conventionally cast as a sort of mimesis. *I know still that memory only mimics.*

Imagine for a moment, however, what it would mean to experience a memory that is nonmimetic, by which I mean something that is not simply inaccurate, and that can still be recognized as a memory as such. Or, in other words, consider what would constitute a representation that is not a representation. Such a condition, I want to propose, would be writing.

Recall, for a specific example, the case of Sergei Pankeiev, the "Wolf-man," as presented by Freud and elaborated by Abraham and Torok. According to the psychologists' explications, Pankeiev's symptomatic dream-work constructs a memory, but not one that is mimetic: a *route permitting one to/ forget with total recall.* Instead of following a referential logic, such memories follow a logic of the signifier. Indeed, as Freud and his successors have explicitly argued (Freud 1959, Lacan 1975, Abraham and Torok 1976, Derrida 1977), that sort of unconscious structuring is itself essentially a form of writing. "Simulation without reference dissolves the old connection between madness and illness in order to establish an entirely different connection: between madness and writing" (Kittler 1990, 308): *a state of writing called obsession.* Moreover, the psychopathology of writing, as we shall see, is all to the point in *Writing Is an Aid to Memory.* As Mac Wellman observes with regard to Hejinian's book: "it may go unnoticed that at the core of all her easy-going rumination lies the threat of madness, despair, suicide, and other dissolutions of being" (LHP 7:20:6).[19] Indeed, in a notebook entry dated October 1, 1975, Hejinian herself writes: "Eliz[abeth Sterling] asked me why I thought I wrote—what drove me to it. I laughed and said it was probably neurosis" (LHP 45:5). And again, in a letter to Barbara Baracks (13 May 1976): "As for writing—I feel obsessed and impassioned by it, and think it is probably a neurosis, if not a psychosis" (LHP 2:4).

Such statements, however, should not be read too quickly, or taken at face value; *the reference is a distraction,* and it would be a mistake to read *Writing* as some kind of direct revelation about its author's psychology (and even if poetry did provide that kind of evidence, it would be of little but prurient interest). In the 1970s, the avant-garde in which Hejinian played such a central role was explicitly positioning itself against the increasingly canonical poetics of those "confessional" writers who had come to prominence in the previous decade. In her 1976 collection *A Thought Is the Bride of What Thinking,* Hejinian critiques that confessionalist ethos: "Artists often court madness, find insanity romantic, and point out their own eccentricities to prove their special validity." In the contemporaneous piece "A Mask of Hours," she cautions:

> It is possible to make secrecy an obsession, but candor can be an obsession, too. Someone could be obsessed by both; I want you to understand me completely but I don't want to reveal anything about myself lest you misunderstand. (LHP 8:13)

The challenge, then, is to achieve *candor without confession* in a writing that is *personal and inclusive, but not necessarily self-revelatory.* To read *Writing* as a revelatory, diagnostic statement about its author, whether secret or candid, would indeed be to misunderstand, and to miss the force of its psychopathology. *Writing* is certainly symptomatic, and it *has achieved the ability to be pathological,* but rather than revealing something about the writer, it exhibits the psychotic condition of language itself, and the collateral states of extremity into which language casts its readers. *Writing,* in short, reveals *le délire de lire.*

But we should not forget about memory too quickly. Because **between circumspect and retrospect there is only the time of an idea,** and the idea of language's madness is inextricably bound with the circumlocutions of its memory. Indeed, *Writing* suggests two models of a truly textual memory, and it offers us a glimpse of what language would remember if language could reflect on itself. One model of textual memory, which we might schematize as the synchronic, would be etymology. Appropriately, *Writing Is an Aid to Memory* is full of etymological play. For instance, after the thirty-sixth section of the book opens by evoking the theme of memory with the lines "again in time I come to think maybe/nostalgia," the next two lines are linked through a word's linguistic memory: "many an error of mercy of the moment/the long wanderings of logic over the thinker." To think, to follow the logic of linguistic history, recognizes that *to err is to wander,* moving from "error" to *errare,* which does indeed mean "to wander" in Latin. The terminus for so many etymological investigations, Latin is explicitly mentioned at several points in *Writing,* and it serves as one of the motifs in Hejinian's subsequent book *My Life.* Accordingly, for just one further example from many such etymological structures in *Writing,* consider the line "points in Latin bridge a gap," in which "points" seems to bridge "Latin" and "bridge" by pointing to the latter's location in the former: *pons, pontem* being the Latin word for "bridge."

Abridgement, in fact, is central to *Writing,* in which abbreviation provides another, diachronic model of textual memory. Like memory and mimesis, textual fragmentation is another of the motifs that runs through the book. Moreover, the text does not simply mention words such as "fragment" and "disintegrates," but it also enacts those fragmentations and disintegrations as well. One of the most immediately striking characteristics of *Writing* is its lexicon of nonce words: "viction," "straction," "pensated," "zontal," "vived," "ternal," "trious," "mendous," "prising," "tinuos," "mena," "glish," and so on, to mention only a dozen. Such words have obviously been formed by eliminating the first part of standard, familiar word: a **short of lengthening word with just one side of it . . . like an excerpt** remaining. This procedure *causes a fragmentation of information—I thoroughly get mere bits,* as Hejinian says elsewhere. *The pieces are, further, things themselves, to be made of as one will.* Through those fragmented bits, in which **a mode of obscurity is chopped, ellipsis makes its promise leaving readers to get out** of them what they can. A writerly reading, in fact, may be the original source of this elliptical vocabulary, which could have been generated from a source text in which Hejinian scanned down the left-hand edge of a page of justified and hyphenated prose, to leave *one step of reading and another/text in patches,* thus *fixing of memory of erasing at any page* and *isolating more prominence than previousness*—which would mean that *the text is anterior to the composition, though the composition be interior to the text.*

Whatever the specific means of composition, such **ruins are memorable,** and with the ruin of words themselves, the textual, graphic memory of *Writing* demonstrates that *the remainder may be a reminder. Memories move and with them the great planes of disintegration.* With Hejinian's *affinity for the separate fragment taken under scrutiny,* for *fragments, of words, or phrases, or phrases and words AS fragments,* the partial word in *Writing* might be read as *a shard signifying isolation.* These *morphemes of evidence,* however, implicate other words as well; the remainders of partial words in *Writing* remind the reader of all those other words that, although appearing integral, might also be fragments as well, and they "make us distrust the completeness of the words we do see as complete" (Quartermain 1992, 25). In language as a material medium one finds *not fragments but metonymy,* so that even if, from a certain perspective, *a fragment is not a fraction but a whole piece,* whole pieces can often indicate larger units into which they might be integrated. So in *Writing Is an Aid to Memory,* for example, "percussion" is followed just two lines later by "repercussion." This conjunction is not in itself especially significant, but the cumulative effect, in *Writing,* is radically destabilizing, because *the first hint ever invented is always/thicker/when you think about it for a short/time. A syllable is a suggestion/is the beginning of inclusion,* and once the suggestion has been explicitly made, suggesting a general protocol for reading, other less salient instances force readers to ask themselves whether they are **recognizing patterns or pruning the truth.** In the line "grammar a copy cate deal little volume," for instance, is the obviously punning "cate" merely an archaic spelling of "cat," as the *Oxford English Dictionary* (*OED*) records, or perhaps a poetically obsolete term for a gourmet delicacy, or is it a "little volume" of the larger word "duplicate," which it has partially copied? Similarly, in the line "leaved vert by memories," "vert," as the *OED* authorizes, could denote either "green" or "turned," both of which apply to leaves; but it might also be what is left by the memory of words such as "convert," "revert," "overt," "divert," and so on. *The tree of language sheds too much foliage.* Ultimately, moreover, this indeterminacy extends to even more familiar words. *A word is an expectation.* A "limb" for instance, might be dismembered from the "climb" that it remembers, and when *disintegration is the grain of/thought* in this way, readers can no longer be certain whether they are encountering the word "sands" or a particle of "thousands," "nine" or the trace of the word "feminine," "pond" or "respond"—"shed," "rough," "sequence," "fuse," "rant," "poses," "ashes," "gets." Consider almost any line in this light and you begin to suspect that all sorts of otherwise innocuous and ostensibly complete words are pointing toward other absent, but implicitly antecedent, words. *For me*, the reader comes to feel, *they must exist, the contents of that absent reality, the objects and occasions which now I reconsidered,* and so, with this glimpse into the possibility of linguistic proliferation, *a slowly gathering psychology augments/the fun of writing.*

Writing induces that slowly gathering sense in other ways as well, and in terms of affect the equivalent experience of realizing how far-reaching and systemic such disintegrations might be is the realization of how coherently connected the fragmented, discontinuous, and unrelated words in this highly disjunctive text actually are. So, for instance, one of the phrasal structures that recurs throughout *Writing Is an Aid to Memory* transforms the idiomatic expression "between wind and water" to generate the phrases "between thought and water," "between roof and bird," "between noon and ceiling," "between wit and water," and so on. The *OED* records three forms of the conventional saying: "a hit between wind and water," "a shot between wind and water," and "a nick between wind and water." Again, the source of Hejinian's variations may not be particularly momentous; the striking revelation of the dictionary page is that all three of those words—"shot," "nick," and "hit"—prominently recur and echo through the book as key words in entirely different contexts.

"Shot," in fact, recalls the extraordinary and astonishingly beautiful first line of *Writing:* "apple is shot nod." Even considering only the denotations of the three nouns, the line is rich with semantic potential: perhaps describing the sway of branches whose shadows dapple the light suffused fruit, or perhaps indicating an apple ruined by excessive moisture and about to fall. Additionally, the line is suggestively allusive, evoking the fatal nod of William Tell's shot to the apple on his son's head, as well as the fateful nods of Newton or Adam, with whom Hejinian associates the referential ability of language to name: apple, *appel.* Or as a later line would condense the pun: "the names of apple."[20] These explications certainly do not exhaust even the most plausible readings of this line (a "nod shot" is a term of art in videography, for instance), but the most likely reference may once again be the language of the text itself. If readers still had the dictionary at hand and chanced to look up "shot," the first thing they would find, even before reaching the definition, is that the word is listed as a past participle. Or, in the convention of the dictionary's abbreviations: "pa pple."

Moreover, if "shot nod" suggests "not shod"—the very sort of stumbling shuffle of (metrical) feet that being unshod might cause—then the constellation of terms already assembled attracts other words that recur through the text, such as "feet," "foot," "shoe," and "ped." In fact, if readers think to look up "ped" and do not just discount it as the chopped-off ending of some truncated word such as "chopped," they discover that it also means a "wicker basket used on horses," which would itself recall all of the references in the book to "wicker," which suggests "whicker," which means, like "nicker," "to neigh or whinny"—a connotation that should in turn remind readers of all the book's references to horses, which may or may not be shod (OED).[21] This conjunction, moreover, is further bound when the recurrence of the words "ankle" and "lock" in this context suggests the horse's fetlock, not to mention the fact that both locks and horses with bad ankles are things that are shot. Farriery aside, a "shot" is also "a dose given to a horse in order to create a temporary appearance of sound-windedness" (a shot between wind), as well as "the powder hole drilled by a bit," which, even if *the word pretends to get a fair distance on unshod horses,* nonetheless reins the equine associations back into the semantic nexus (OED).

A nod, as it happens, may be as good as a wink to a blind horse, but readers should keep their eyes open, because the network of associations in *Writing* tightens even as it expands. So, for instance, "bit" and "nick" are both part of the constellation of equine terms featured in the work. Similarly, with an evocation of the references to "type" in *Writing,* both words are typographic terms that Hejinian might well have come to know through her letterpress production of the exactly contemporaneous Tuumba chapbook series. Moreover, both words also come together through the fact that a bit is "the exact point or nick of time," and that a nicker is also part of a drill bit; additionally, something bit is nicked, like a coin, which in the jazz slang used elsewhere in *Writing* might be "scratch," and in fact, a bit is also a small amount of currency, such as a nickel[22]—all of which, should this start to seem farfetched, comes together in the last few pages of the book with the corroborating phrases "dime nick," "dime scratch," and "bit time." If we "compare beats of the dime" to the other iterations of this motif, these phrases might also suggest the "beatnick" phonically lurking behind "bit" and "nick." *The time comes when each individual poem reveals not only its own internal connections but also spreads them out externally, anticipating the integrity each poem requires in order to explain obscure points, arbitrary elements, etc.*

I could continue to elaborate examples of the way in which dispersed and ostensibly arbitrary elements are in fact quite tightly bound together in the text of *Writing,* as well how the various constellations of associated terms ultimately begin to link up to one another in a comprehensive concatenation. Instead, however, I want to underscore the fact that the apparently random, discontinuous, and unmotivated elements in the pages of *Writing* come suddenly and firmly together in another context, as they do, for instance, under a dictionary heading. I should note, for those who have not personally struggled with the demands of the book's confounding and at times seemingly impenetrable language, that the shock of such comprehensive meaning in *Writing* cannot be overestimated[23]—nor, moreover, can the affective experience of that realization of sudden coherence and conjunction within the apparently chaotic and irreconcilably disjunctive field of linguistic events.

Because this textual world of *Writing* is the world of the paranoiac.

In an undated letter to Ron Silliman, Hejinian relates: "I was thinking about what you said, that 'experimentalism' was too often a shelter for scoundrels and paranoids" (LHP 7:6). And in the poem "Crooner," which she sent to Silliman for possible inclusion in the "Language Poetries" issue of *Ironwood*, Hejinian seems to offer a considered reply: "Thus make use of paranoia—yes, even negatively speaking" (RSP 9:14).[24] In making use of paranoia myself, I should be clear, from the outset, that I am using the word in a technical, though not quite clinical sense. That is, I do not take "paranoia" in its colloquial sense, as simply a profound suspicion and unfounded sense of persecution (although these emotions may very well come into play when reading a work such as *Writing Is an Aid to Memory*).[25] By "paranoia," I want to indicate a state in which several specific conditions obtain. First, paranoia implies the systemization of those suspicions into a totalizing state of affairs in which everything is connected. "Paranoia," as Hejinian's colleague Barrett Watten puts it, "can be defined as a delirium of interpretation bearing a systematic structure" (1985, 42). Or, in short: *from such hidden to be given reason/no passions from mad men be excessive.* Indeed, however mad, paranoia should certainly not be thought of as the dissolution of logic, but rather as the rigorous and unflinching pursuit of alternative logics to the point that *logic is more persuasive than truth.*

Naomi Schor interprets Freud's diagnosis of paranoia in terms of the pathology that Benvéniste called, in another context, "l'interprétance," and she explains: "Il s'ensuit que le délire d'interprétation est une forme de folie textuelle, plutôt qu'une classe nosographique" [It follows that the delirium of interpretation is a form of textual madness, rather than a nosographic case] (1978, 243). "Psychosis," as Gilles Deleuze argues, "is inseparable from a linguistic procedure" (1997, 19), and we might in fact "consider paranoia less as a mental aberration than as a specific 'regime of signs,' that is, as a basic type of organization of signs in which the semiotic or signifying potential is dominant" (Johnston 1991, 47). Or, in short: *an allusive psycholingualism.* To be even more specific, paranoia, in linguistic terms, would be defined by the equation—or the integration—of different semiotic systems, so that it concatenates signifiers under the regime of a single system of meaning. *A description of hazard theory,* paranoia thus obviates chance.[26] In a nonparanoid system, the intersection of different semiotic codes can lead to a coincidence, which may be more or less striking; one might, for example, pass a car with a license plate number that happens to be that day's date. When faced with *good but random coincidences, we insist that life is full of happy chance,* but excessively *interpreting such combinations of events, and the sort of mysticism on which such interpretations are based, is what gives coincidence its bad name. In the/perceptual field of paranoia,* on the other hand, when *planes of information intersect, coincide,* all signifiers are read as signifying within the same code: there is no longer the licensing code and the separate calendric code, there is only The Code. *The synchronous keeps its reversible logic, and in this it resembles psychology, or the logic of a person,* a **nervous system that sort of confuses psychology**. Paranoid texts are "chronic," in both the temporal and pathological senses of the word, and *certain themes are incurable.*

The exemplary text of paranoia, then, would be the dictionary. "A book," as Hejinian has written, "is a memory" (Watten 1985, 147), and in the dictionary, both the synchronic and diachronic memory of language itself are inextricably intertwined with its paranoid project. This is particularly true of the *Oxford English Dictionary,* a book that Hejinian specifically mentions in her poetry (*The Cell,* 208), and that distinguishes itself on the accuracy and completeness of its memory of the written record. The two key contributors to the *OED,* as it happens, were both paranoiacs; although **this suits my suspicions,** it may be only a coincidence (Winchester 1998, 166–67 *et passim*). The work, in any case, was begun as an explicit attempt to bring the entirety of the English language—from the most common syncategorematic to the most doubtful and obscure *hapax legomenon*—within a closed system of concatenated definitions, so that all of the words in a definition can be found as headwords in the same dictionary. Moreover, within this web of totalizing connections, all of those headwords are themselves structured by **the arbitrary real and likewise** rigidly organizing alphabet.

I suppose a dictionary with a rhythmic base/an impulse of remembering/could show what I could, as Hejinian writes, and in fact *Writing Is an Aid to Memory* exhibits a similar obsession with the **solid and mighty alphabet, chronic in an exact place** and symptomatically displayed in the text's prosody, in which lines are indented according to the first letter of the first word in the line. In this equation **numerical the alphabet,** that is, lines such as "apple is shot nod," which begin with an "a," establish the left-hand margin; lines beginning with a "b" are indented one space to the right of that margin, those with a "c" two spaces, and so on through all *the sentences of the alphabet. We are not forgetting the patience of the mad, their love of detail.*

That graphemic detail is further elaborated in *Writing* by a series of rhizomatic networks traced across the surface of the text by a *fugue elude* of paragogic chains. *Activity takes place—across the language plane itself. . . . configurations and relationships occur in sets rather than sequence.* Words appear to transform themselves letter by letter, so that "shot"—whatever its thematic relation to a number of the poem's motif words: horses, locks, money, chance, chords, threads, bars, bits, and so on—alters into both "short" and "spot," a word that in turn leads to "lot" and then "dot," whence "dotes," and then on to other, more elaborate permutations. Such *infinite change flies in many logical ways,* and these lines of the signifier's flight proliferate with a geometric increase. Even when *random in character/a branch involves repetition* and leads to so much *detour in such detail* that if "bit" attracts both "pit" and "hit," those words in turn veer towards "pitch" and "hint" respectively, as well as "sit" and "fit" and "mit" and so on in a seemingly infinite *trace/linked to a fence of forgetting,* as *by its rate the echo dissolves* until *the rate of forgetting is greatest* in a *proportion of infinite change and everything memorable,* if not remembered past *the duration of thinking.* Even as the reader, *carried giddy by a digression,* is unable to recall all of the links in these expansive chains, their anaphoric references constitute another variation of textual memory. *Each memory isn't a thought that reiterates,* because in these networks of repetition with slight change *memories are comparisons, even the short ones. The nex is juxtaposed, themes because remembered. Mem nd rea. Remembered always with as ever.*

Moreover, by ordering language according to the logic of the signifier, this *pattern of bits* in *Writing* once again structures connections between otherwise unrelated words, and it serves as a litmus test for the reader by gauging (or languaging) the degree of paranoia with which they engage a text. The fact of such coincidences in *Writing* is incontrovertible, even if they are only *an ordinary coincidence* of 'gratuitous connections,' or 'contiguous chance.' *The connections are there, of course, to be made or made of, and their meaning is in the sufficiency of their being, at all.* With the *possibility not obvious but nevertheless/of significance,* no *meaning is impossible because it is implausible,* and when faced with what Carla Harryman calls "cohesions of detail" (LHP 4:11), *miracles merge/in a rational country, fighting back/with parallels. Reality follows. Reason looks for two, then arranges it from there,* and the reasonable response when *coincidence touches/a random* connection throughout a text in which such cohesions *chance to return* is to see the *pattern more likely* to be consciously constructed than mere chance. Without being truly paranoid, the reasonable reader might suspect two sources of such conscious construction. *The usual (suspect in itself) blink of suspicion.*

On the one hand, given that *an association really consists of an activity* and that *people like the lock of a pattern,* readers might be tempted to regard the discovery of textual coincidence as no more than their own impositions. As Hejinian herself writes in "Chronic Texts," the reader might think: "I was reading a difficult text./What is 'to understand' except 'to make relevant' or 'to find relevancy in'" (LHP 8:4). With *combination a reward for difficulty,* the effort to make disparate words relevant might be seen as a hermeneutics in which the words' *"slipping" or slippage thinks random patterns through/wishes* for meaning imposed by readers in *despair of failure for knowledge* and so desperate to make connections within an unconventional and unfamiliar text that *craving for knowledge might mean craving for noise/One syllable, 'sounds like . . .'/And combine awkwardly. Much intention is retrospective,* and trumping any *trick of coincidence,* readers might *make meaning retrospectively out of the accidental and gratuitous.*[27] Obsession. Abscession. So many graces of fate. So many fates of grace. *Such displacements alter illusions, which is all-to-the-good.*

On the other hand, a reasonable reader might also come to suspect the conscious, strategic machinations of the poet. In fact, Hejinian's poetics in the late 1970s would corroborate such speculation. Like many of her colleagues, she was interested in *putting things together in such a way as to enable them to coincide* and thus *make a way of seeing connections see writing.* In a consideration of the avant-garde moment out of which *Writing Is an Aid to Memory* emerged, Hejinian muses: "It seems that what presses as a question upon writing now (when it comes to talk of structures, for example, or systems) is how to arrange words (or word groups) rather than how to choose them" ("Smatter"). Moreover, in her contemporaneous essay "If Written Is Writing," Hejinian describes her compositional techniques ("The Rejection of Closure," 30):

> One locates in the interior texture of such language. . . . through improvisatory techniques building on the suggestions made by language itself—on patterns of language which are ideas and corresponding behavior or despite relevant quirks; this becomes an addictive motion—but not incorrect, despite such distortion, concentration, condensation, deconstruction, and such as association by, for example, pun and etymology provide; an allusive psycholinguilism. ("The Rejection of Closure," 30)

Even the most persistent and scholarly reader, unfortunately, will find that evidence of any specific compositional technique in *Writing* is ultimately elusive. The writing of *Memory* has been somehow forgotten, and the compositional memory of the book is completely amnesiac.[28] The Hejinian papers archived at the University of California at San Diego, ostensibly a complete and comprehensive collection of all extant material, contains a single uncorrected typescript, but no drafts or proofs (LHP 8:15). Indeed, the correspondence files in the archive contain no communication with The Figures concerning the publication of the book. Moreover, the collection of composition notebooks that Hejinian kept reveals a substantial aporia: the record stops in late 1975, precisely that time during which *Writing Is an Aid to Memory* was presumably being composed, and the notebooks do not resume again until 1978, just after the book's publication. Of course to suspect that these bibliographic details are anything more than mere happenstance would be quite (in the colloquial sense) paranoid.

Moreover, such evidence—even if it were proof to the contrary—would not in the least alter the interpretive resources of a genuine paranoiac. Indeed, as the passage from "If Written Is Writing" indicates, suspicious readers should be looking not so much to their own ingenuity or to the schemes of the poet, as to the interior texture of language itself. "On occasion," Hejinian admits, "I've transferred my restlessness, the sense of necessity, to the vehicle itself" (*My Life*, 76), and indeed, *language,* as she has announced throughout her career, *is restless. Even words in storage, in the dictionary,* as we have seen, *seem frenetic with activity, as each individual entry attracts to itself other words as definition, example, and amplification.* Moreover, to see the cohesions of details within *words as attractive, magnetic to meaning,* is to realize that *language itself is never at a state of rest* and *is productive of activity* because the articulations of the signifier establish a ***quantity through a language/substitute inventing music of a series/changes very little understood/binding men for driving through a new internal logic.***[29] *Poems have more than one word. Or contain one word of more than one letter. Hence connection, relationship, space between.* For the most obvious example of this internal logic, the anagrammatic play in *Writing,* like the fragmentation of words, invites a ceaseless reorganization of atomic linguistic material.[30] These lives of the letter remind us that however ***fruitful the disposal of words*** strategically arranged by an author, *each word in itself is an arrangement* as well.[31] *As a writer, but especially as a poet, one looks . . . to discover the natural order in language, in words as they represent, but particularly as they don't.* Or, as Benjamin Lee Whorf put it, in a passage Hejinian quotes to Susan Howe in a letter dated 21 August 1976: "At first the language seemed merely to be irregular. Later I found it to be quite regular in terms of its own patterns" (LHP 4:18).[32]

Those patterns, moreover, are never arrived at by chance: at the level of its means, the level of the letter, all linguistic coincidences are equally motivated. The materiality of inscription casts chance arrangements aside, with *the apologies/on paradox and dice./The word should be twitching with destiny, or with necessity. Their random procedures make monuments to fate.* With their *rule of monuments,* words are **stricken in the very fit and also the poem,** where a "fit" is not only a technical term for a part of a poem, but also both a pathologically symptomatic episode as well as a perfect congruence or coincidence. *They are both locks and/lapses.* That coincidence of words sparks across the page, leaving letters twitching with **fits that finally riddle an infinite nature** of possible combinations because **the substantial fit indicates a finish/or the possibility of a finish.** *Two dangers keep threatening the world: order and disorder,* and with those amphilogic fits *the poet plays with order, makes order of disorder, and disorder of order, intent upon confusing all the issues.* If the disorders of language continually threaten the authority of its communicative potential, to the point that the **sign can't be justified in the slaughter** of semantics committed by language's disarticulations, those same dismemberments simultaneously reveal an *order inscribed* with an alternative logic. That inscribed order, moreover, reveals the paranoid structure of language itself: a comprehensive system of articulations that are endlessly concatenated, recombinant, and proliferating in a dizzying and interminable proliferation of coincidences arrayed against us inhumanly—generating meanings that are radically discontinuous with our desires and intentions. If we can never hope to control the excessive restlessness of language, we can sometimes recognize its motions, but knowledge, for the paranoiac, is never a salvation; there is an *unbearable anticipation of interruptions/whose cacophony is familiar* and rendered incoherent by its own inevitability; *it would be appropriate to call this not intuition but pre-knowing, or paranoia.*

Writing itself (I have, of course, all along written *"Writing"* when I meant simply "writing," and vice versa) demands a response adequate to its own structure: unreasonable and irrational, but strictly logical—*an approach toward a hard-edged, rigorous, analytical, merciless reading that sounds the psychological density of language.* This is no more true of a book such as *Writing Is an Aid to Memory* than it is of the most conventional poem. *The paranoia of writing* requires paranoid readers, comfortable with *a restlessness made inevitable by language* and willing to *bid chaos welcome.*[33] *In the mass of my hallucinations, each sentence/replaces an hallucination* and leaves me *like a paranoid spellbound.* Faced with the self-organizing, hallucinatory patterns of that chaos we **can find no explanation if imagination includes/so much,** and being *incapable/of understanding/very definitely any of the language* we encounter, we must fight the impulses by which *our unease grows before the newly restless* realization of the *grace of locks* linked in **the reflecting worry nervous surface** of language's sheer, unceasing productivity. **Reason grows dissatisfied with formal reflection,** and the hope and terror of linguistic paranoia is not so much that we **find the coincidence** of fit that gives **the taste of a larger pattern** and the **sensation of unreasonable discourse through elaborated space,** but that we realize that **the inconsequences it touches are full/convictions** established without any controlling human agency. *When what happens is not intentional, one can't ascribe meaning to it, and unless what happens is necessary, one can't expect it to occur again.* The distinction of language is to generate meanings that are simultaneously nonintentional, absolutely necessary, and (in both senses of the word) significant. It is the gift of writing. And like all true gifts, it cannot be refused. Or forgotten. So that the question, of course, as you read, is never whether you are being too paranoid, but whether you are ever being paranoid enough.

APPENDIX

Sources for Integrated Quotations

"route permitting . . ."   *The Cell,* 69.
"a state . . ."   *Oxota,* 251.
"the reference . . ."   *My Life,* 57.
"candor without . . ."   "Two Stein Talks," 137.
"personal and . . ."   "If Written Is Writing," 30.
"has achieved . . ."   *The Cold of Poetry,* 179.
"to err . . ."   *A Thought Is the Bride of What Thinking,* n.p.
"causes a . . ."   Letter to Barrett Watten, published in Watten (1985, 146–47).
"The pieces are . . ."   LHP 8:12.
"the text is . . ."   "If Written Is Writing," 29.
"the remainder . . ."   *My Life,* 77.
"Memories move . . ."   *Oxota,* 286.
"affinity for . . ."   *My Life,* 52.
"fragments, of words . . ."   LHP 45:4.
"a shard signifying . . ."   *My Life,* 52.
"morphemes of . . ."   *My Life,* 10.
"not fragments . . ."   *My Life,* 60.
"a fragment . . ."   *My Life,* 82.

"The tree of . . ."   *Oxota*, 90.
"A word is . . ."   *My Life*, 82.
"disintegration is . . ."   *The Cell*, 85.
"For me . . ."   *My Life*, 13.
"a slowly gathering . . ."   *The Cell*, 78.
"The time comes . . ."   *Oxota*, 21.
"logic is more . . ."   LHP 8:13.
"allusive psycholingualism"   "If Written Is Writing," 30.
"A description . . ."   *The Cell*, 179.
"good but . . ."   *The Cell*, 212.
"we insist . . ."   *My Life*, 74.
"interpreting such . . ."   *My Life*, 50.
"In the perceptual . . ."   *The Cell*, 121.
"planes of information . . ."   *My Life*, 90.
"The synchronous . . ."   *My Life*, 44.
"certain themes . . ."   *A Thought Is the Bride of What Thinking*, n.p.
"We are not . . ."   *My Life*, 56.
"Activity takes place . . ."   "Two Stein Talks," 137.
"infinite change . . ."   LHP 8:1.
"proportion of . . ."   LHP 8:1.
"Each memory . . ."   *The Cell*, 150.
"The nex . . ."   LHP 8:1.
"gratuitous connections . . ."   LHP 8:12.
"meaning is . . ."   LHP 8:1.
"miracles merge . . ."   *The Cold of Poetry*, 22.
"Reason looks . . ."   *My Life*, 59.
"The usual . . ."   *Oxota*, 63.
"people like . . ."   *The Cold of Poetry*, 23.
"slippage thinks . . ."   LHP 42:8.
"craving for . . ."   *The Cold of Poetry*, 145.
"trick of . . ."   LHP 8:4.
"Such displacements . . ."   *My Life*, 52.
"putting things . . ."   "Smatter," n.p.
"language . . ."   *My Life*, 17.
"Even words . . ."   "The Rejection of Closure," 280.
"words as . . ."   "The Rejection of Closure," 279–80.
"Poems have . . ."   LHP 45:7:274.
"each word . . ."   LHP 45:7.
"As a writer . . ."   "Smatter," n.p.
"the apologies . . ."   *The Cold of Poetry*, 20.
"Their random . . ."   *My Life*, 10.
"rule of monuments"   *Oxota*, 238.

"The are both . . ."   *The Cell,* 150.
"two dangers . . ."   "The Rejection of Closure," 278.
"the poet . . ."   *A Thought Is the Bride of What Thinking,* n.p.
"order inscribed"   *A Thought Is the Bride of What Thinking,* n.p.
"unbearable anticipation . . ."   *The Cold of Poetry,* 97.
"it would be . . ."   *My Life,* 41.
"an approach . . ."   "Two Stein Talks," 133.
"The paranoia . . ."   *Oxota,* 103.
"bid chaos . . ."   *My Life,* 20.
"In the mass . . ."   *The Cold of Poetry,* 150.
"each sentence . . ."   *The Cold of Poetry,* 15.
"like a . . ."   *The Cold of Poetry,* 18.
"our unease . . ."   *The Cold of Poetry,* 32.
"grace of locks"   *My Life,* 12–13.
"When what . . ."   *My Life,* 17.
"That is . . ."   LHP 45.
"that language is . . ."   "Two Stein Talks," 129.
"words without . . ."   LHP 8:13.
"the degree . . ."   LHP 7:6.
"perhaps Sound . . ."   LHP 45.
"words, for example . . ."   "Smatter," n.p.
"they are . . ."   LHP 8:13.
"Every fact . . ."   *Oxota,* 211.
"as chance . . ."   *A Thought Is the Bride of What Thinking,* n.p.
"reflections from . . ."   *The Cell,* 138.
"(I want . . ."   *The Cell,* 74.

NOTES

1. Hannah Arendt, *The Human Condition* (Chicago: University of Chicago Press, 1958), 198.

2. Ibid., 199.

3. Charles Altieri, *Enlarging the Temple* (Lewisburg, Pa.: Bucknell University Press, 1979), 33.

4. Martin Heidegger, *Basic Writings,* ed. David Farrell Krell (New York: HarperCollins, 1993), 425.

5. Ibid., 420.

6. Arendt, *Human Condition,* 302.

7. Ibid., 9.

8. Ibid., 177.

9. Ibid., 246.

10. Ibid., 9.

11. Quoted in Viktor Erlich, *Russian Formalism* (The Hague: Mouton Publishers, 1955), 76.

12. Viktor Shklovsky, "Resurrection of the Word," in *Russian Formalism: A Collection of Articles and Texts in Translation,* tr. Richard Sherwood, eds. Stephen Bann and John E. Bowlt (Edinburgh: Scottish Academic Press, 1973), 46.

13. Leo Tolstoi, in his diary on March 1, 1897, quoted by Viktor Shklovsky in "Art as Technique," in Lee T. Lemon and Marion J. Reis, trans. and eds., *Russian Formalist Criticism* (Lincoln: University of Nebraska Press, 1965), 12.

14. Arendt, *Human Condition,* 193.

15. Shklovsky, "Resurrection of the Word," 46.

16. I have adapted this written memory of Socrates' reminiscence from the following translations: R. Hackforth, *Plato: Collected Dialogues,* ed. Edith Hamilton and Huntington Cairns (Princeton: Princeton University Press, 1961), 520; Lane Cooper, *Plato* (Oxford: Oxford University Press, 1938), 65; and Irwin Edman, *The Works of Plato* (New York: Random House Modern Library, 1928), 323.

17. *Writing Is an Aid to Memory* was republished in 1996, photoset from the original unpaginated pages, by Sun & Moon (Los Angeles) as part of the its Classics series. As Hejinian wrote in "Tables," in 1975: "Things are called 'classic' because they have made the transition from unrecognizable to recognizable." Ron Silliman Papers, 1965–1988, MSS 0075, Mandeville Special Collections Library, University of California at San Diego, Folder 9, Box 14. All subsequent quotations from this collection will be sourced with "RSP" followed by folder and box numbers.

18. Quotations from Hejinian's *Writing Is an Aid to Memory* incorporated into my text will appear in bold-italics. Quotations from her other works incorporated into my text will appear in italics and are sourced in the appendix.

19. Quotations from the Lyn Hejinian Papers, MSS 0074, Mandeville Special Collections Library, University of California at San Diego, will be sourced with "LHP" followed by box, folder, and (if applicable) paper numbers.

20. The association of apples with Adam's acts of naming is suggested by a passage from Hejinian's notebook: "Sound without meaning is simply words at their source, names before applied, the preverabal Adam. . . . This, of course, is an interesting theory, but something else in the application—that is, it would (or will) be extremely difficult to apply + it may not be so interesting once it is" (LHP 45). Note how many words in this passage begin "app."

Hejinian's own works, with their frequent references to apples, provide further intertexts from which glosses might be gleaned. The following are two instances, from the less readily available sources: in the 1974 "Short Arbiter" (and with a further echo of "shot" as well), one finds the line "I rifle the apple tree" (LHP 42:7); and from "A mask of Hours" is the passage "She imitates the generous woman: Here, sweetie, eat *my* apple! Then women are always sorry and they wish they could say, Hey, eat your own fucking apple! That one's mine!" (LHP 8:13).

21. Should "whicker" seem too esoteric a reference, note that Hejinian uses the word in *Redo:* "My merchant horse whickers" (*The Cold of Poetry,* 23); similarly, "fetlock" appears in the manuscript material collected in Hejinian's archive. There may be no American poet more equestrian than Hejinian, save of course Louis

Zukofsky, who in fact underwrites much of *Memory,* even making his paragrammatic appearance in the book's eighth section: "zoo . . . coffee . . . sky."

22. In *My Life,* this monetary sense of "bit" is both explicitly employed and also linked to horses: "The man with the pinto pony had come through the neighborhood selling rides for a quarter, or as he said, 'two bits,' and it was that 'two bits' even more than the pony that led the children to believe he was a real cowboy and therefore heroic" (20). Neigh-borhood indeed. The equestrian connotation of the word is one that Hejinian used contemporaneously with the composition of *Writing Is an Aid to Memory;* in a letter to her mother dated June 17, 1976, she writes: "I've been riding every day in short bits to keep the horse exercised" (LHP 1:8).

23. *Writing Is an Aid to Memory* is a notoriously restive work. As Mac Wellman argues, "this writing scorns explanations, development, and the obviously insightful conclusion as mere hesitation and quibbling" (LHP 7:20:3). Indeed, even those readers one would imagine best suited to a work such as *Writing* seem to have found it unusually difficult. As the correspondence in Hejinian's archive indicates, her contemporaries in the avant-garde writing community "didn't get it," found it "something to contend with," and admitted that they did "not know quite how to read it." In contrast, a letter dated January 29, 1983, records a less perplexed audience: "Dear Lyn, Thought you might enjoy this unexpected acclaim. My creative writing class at the SF County Jail got to talking about syntax, breaking up the line, making new words, etc. So I brought in a few items, a page from Finnegan's [*sic*] Wake and the first poem from your Writing Is an Aid to Memory. My students, among whom include the education minister of the Black Guerilla Front (prison arm of the Panthers), very much liked your poem and proceeded to give me a rather thorough explication of it. They didn't find it abstract" (LHP 3:20). One can only speculate that the line "maybe the prisons would circulate" received a particularly attentive gloss.

24. In addition to direct references to "insanity," "madness," and "paranoia," Hejinian has throughout her career deployed pathological terms in idiosyncratic ways; consider the recurrence of terms such as "myopia," "hypochondria," "insomnia," "chronophobia," "agoraphobia," "melancholia," and "hysteria."

25. *Writing Is an Aid to Memory* gives the uncanny impression of some compositional pattern or system or procedure. As Steve Abbot writes, in a letter to Ron Silliman dated May 16, 1980: "Now Lyn Hejinian's work is fascinating to me, esp. Writing As An Aid to Memory [*sic*], as I sense that it might well have been 'preconceived' formalistically but in such a way that (like Memory itself) is impossible to completely track down—so I ride the music of it's [*sic*] beckoning, it's [*sic*] tease, and it's a music I really get off on" (RSP 1:5). And Kathleen Fraser similarly suspects some "code" compounding the difficulty of the text (LHP 3:25). *Writing,* in other words, is the type of work that the Oulipo would call a "Canada Dry": a text that "has the taste and colour of a restriction but does not follow a restriction" (Mathews and Brotchie 1998, 118).

26. Christy Burns reaches a different conclusion from a similar focus on chance; she characterizes paranoia as "a compulsion to control and reduce language, texts, and any variety of forms in which meaning can occur. Unable to open themselves up to chance, paranoiacs likewise resist ambiguity in language, repressing puns and

other forms of casually associative wordplay" (1995, 99). Hejinian has herself argued that a perfectly closed text would lead to a state of "perfect mental health" ("The Rejection of Closure," 281). No text, of course, is perfectly closed, and, as we shall see, wordplay is never casual.

27. One should not necessarily discount such imposed readings as being extraneous to the text itself. In a letter draft to Michael Gottleib dated February 21, 1983, Hejinian writes:

> I am so used to people mistaking references in my work that that seems part of the life of the text. It is my business to write the works and the readers business to read them—whatever that may turn up. Steve Abbot, for example, wrote a long article for Poetry Flash that discussed my book *Writing is an Aid to Memory* as a reworking of the works of Meister Eckart—but I have never read a single word of Meister Eckart. Still, Steve's article was quite interesting and I didn't think it was necessarily wrong, *as a reading.* (LHP 4:4)

Or as she writes in "Chronic Texts": "Once a writing is published as if finally, it ought not thereby to become a forbidden landscape" (LHP 8:4). Panoramic. Paranoiac.

28. A few fragments and words recur through the papers like brief flashes of *déjà vu,* but the only real exception to this forgetfulness is the passage that became the sixth section of the book, which appears among a group of 1977 experiments in the following form: "It becomes all the clearer and he must show himself, to catch, to be amused, to equate the man, to shoot his autobiographical work" (LHP 8:1). Though certainly not working material, some roughly contemporaneous poems might be also considered in relation to *Writing Is an Aid to Memory* because of their verse form, which also indents lines according to the same alphabetic formula (LHP 45:7).

29. Compare these lines to a passage Hejinian quotes from Claude Levi-Strauss: "Through the power of an ever new internal logic, each work will rouse the listener from his state of passivity and make him share in its impulse, so that there will no longer be a difference of kind, but only of degree, between inventing music and listening to it" (LHP 45:7:156).

30. With "fortress replaced by a more natural forest," and "able ducer" clearly able to reduce to another more natural form, the place of anagrams in *Writing* is clear. Consider Hejinian's play with the acronym of *Writing Is an Aid to Memory,* recorded on the bottom of a draft of another poem (LHP 42:8):

WIAATM
WAIT AM
WIT AMA

Or, as one might translate the last of these: brevity is the.

31. Hejinian is quoting Louis Zukofsky, *Prepositions: The Collected Critical Essays of Louis Zukofsky* (London: Rapp & Carroll, 1967), 21.

32. Hejinian was interested throughout the 1970s with what the Russian Futurists and Formalists called *slovo kak takovoe* (the word as such). *That is, not words about something, but the word as itself.* In a 1977 letter to Sharon Doubiago, Hejinian explains that "my new work has been turning in toward itself more and

more, as one word looks at its neighbors, to see what is being said" (LHP 3:10). Having realized *that language is an order of reality itself and not a mere mediating medium,* Hejinian's interest in *words without reference—*that is, *the degree to which the written word is more than, or other than, a message-bearing unit—*took the form of both graphic and graphemic experiments, as well as a project to explore **the sound for words** as "sound without meaning." She came to question whether *perhaps Sound Without Meaning can't be written—perhaps there is no sound without meaning,* because *words, for example, simply can't help but give onto meaning; they are anchored by their meaning, which calls attention to itself.* A section from the 1974 "A Month Without Days" puts the tension this way:

> The lover of words is given either to philolalia or to philosophy, if not both. He delights in the adorable form of language itself or he feels a compulsive (and urgent) desire to explain something, even himself. . . . But because the words remain words under either circumstance, whether the intention is sensible or sensual (leaving aside the numerous instances in which it is both), it is not always clear to the reader in which context he or she is required to attempt understanding. This is a problem. (LHP 8:4)

Writing is a solution.

33. The surrealists provide one precedent for such reading. Attempting to bring together objective and subjective phenomenon, **with relations written of such a kind as external reality at random,** André Breton's concept of "interpretive delirium" and "objective chance," for instance, provide a passive model of Salvador Dalí's "paranoiac critical activity," a systematization of confusion that he explicitly defines as a mode of reading. A "spontaneous method of irrational knowledge based on the interpretative critical association of delirium phenomenon," paranoiac critical activity establishes associations between ostensibly random occurrences, **throwing the standard into such errors/of discovery** not in order to unveil occult motivations to the aleatory but to allow the logic of coincidence to establish meaningful relationships that might otherwise be overlooked. *Every fact could break through deterministic constraints,* and so *as chance must lead you first one way and then another . . . so here what is reflected is not always what is visible, and art is seen not to be a mirror: reflections from accidental causes, committed to memory* (we have never strayed far from either memory or mimesis). *(I/want to indicate both blind/chance and clear destiny, but/really this is about introspection).* For the reader willing to take paranoia as a critical methodology, **random consciousness takes its chance/a narrow chance** (but an arrow that always, shot nod, hits its mark).

BIBLIOGRAPHY

Books by Lyn Hejinian

The Beginner (New York: Spectacular Books, 2001).
A Border Comedy (Los Angeles: Sun & Moon, 2000).
The Cell (Los Angeles: Sun & Moon, 1992).

Chartings, written with Ray Di Palma (Tucson: Chax Press, 2000).

The Cold of Poetry (Los Angeles: Sun & Moon, 1994).

Gesualdo (Berkeley: Tuumba Press, 1978).

The Guard (Berkeley: Tuumba Press, 1984).

Guide, Grammar, Watch, and The Thirty Nights (Perth: Folio, 1996).

Happily (Los Angeles: Post-Apollo Press, 2000).

The Hunt (Tenerife: Zasterle Press, 1991).

Individuals, with Kit Robinson (Tucson: Chax Press, 1988).

Jour de chasse, trans. Pierre Alferi (Royaumont: Cahiers de Royaumont, 1992).

The Language of Inquiry (Berkeley: University of California Press, 2000).

Leningrad, with Michael Davidson, Ron Silliman, and Barrett Watten (San Francisco: Mercury House, 1991).

The Little Book of A Thousand Eyes (Boulder: Smoke-Proof Press, 1996).

A Mask of Motion (Providence: Burning Deck, 1977).

My Life (Providence: Burning Deck, 1980). First revised edition, Los Angeles: Sun & Moon Press, 1987.

Oxota: A Short Russian Novel (Great Barrington: The Figures, 1991).

Redo (Grenada, Miss.: Salt-Works Press, 1984).

Sight, with Leslie Scalapino (New York: Edge Books, 1999).

Sunflower, with Jack Collom (Great Barrington: The Figures, 2000).

A Thought Is the Bride of What Thinking (Berkeley: Tuumba, 1976).

The Traveler and the Hill and the Hill, with Emilie Clark (New York: Granary Books, 1998).

from *Walls* (New York: A Hundred Posters, 1979).

Two Stein Talks (Santa Fe, N.M.: Weaselsleeves Press, 1995).

Wicker, with Jack Collom (Boulder: Rodent Press, 1996).

Writing Is an Aid to Memory (Great Barrington: The Figures, 1978; Los Angeles: Sun & Moon, 1996).

Selected Prose

"Aesthetic Tendency and the Politics of Poetry: A Manifesto" (with Ron Silliman, Carla Harryman, Steve Benson, and Barrett Watten). *Social Text* 19–20 (Fall 1988): 261–75.

"For Change" (with Ron Silliman, Barrett Watten, Steve Benson, Charles Bernstein, and Bob Perelman), *In the American Tree,* ed. Silliman (Orono: National Poetry Foundation and the University of Maine, 1986).

"If Written Is Writing," *The L=A=N=G=U=A=G=E Book,* ed. Bruce Andrews and Charles Bernstein (Carbondale: Southern Illinois University Press, 1984), 29–30.

"Language Poetry," *Fremantle Arts Review: Monthly Arts Digest* 1(1) (1986).

"Line," *The Line in Postmodern Poetry,* ed. Frank, Robert Joseph and Henry M. Sayre (Urbana: University of Illinois Press, 1988).

"On *Oxota: A Short Russian Novel.*" *Pequod* 31 (1990): 67.

"The Person and Description," from a Symposium on "The Poetics of Everyday Life." *Poetics Journal* 9 (1991): 166–70.

"Poems." *Sulfur* 5 (1985).

"The Rejection of Closure," *Writing/Talks,* ed. Bob Perelman (Carbondale: Southern Illinois University Press, 1985), 270–91. *Confer: Poetics Journal* 4: Women & Language (May 1984).

"Smatter." *L=A=N=G=U=A=G=E* 8 (June 1979).

"Strangeness." *Poetics Journal* 8 (June 1989): 32–45.

"Two Stein Talks: Language and Realism; Grammar and Landscape," *Temblor* 3 (1986): 137. *Confer: Two Stein Talks* (Santa Fe, N.M.: Weaselsleeves Press 1996).

Interviews

"An Exchange" (with Andrew Schelling). *Jimmy and Lucy's House of "K"* 6 (May 1986): 1–17.

"Language Poetry: An Interview with Lyn Hejinian" (with Alison Georgeson). *Southern Review* 27(3) (1994).

"Roughly Stapled" (with Craig Dworkin), *Idiom* 3 (1995).

"Symposium on Russian Postmodernism" (with Jerome McGann, Vitaly Chernetsky, Arkadii Dragomoshchenko, Mikhail Epstein, Bob Perelman, and Marjorie Perloff). *Postmodern Culture: An Electronic Journal of Interdisciplinary Criticism* 3(2) (January 1993).

Selected Criticism

Altieri, Charles, "Lyn Hejinian and the Possibilities of Postmodernism in Poetry." *Women Poets of the Americas: Toward a Pan-American Gathering.* Ed. Jacqueline Vaught Brogan and Cordelia Chavez Candelaria. Notre Dame: University of Notre Dame Press, 1999.

Beach, Christopher. "Poetic Positionings: Stephen Dobyns and Lyn Hejinian in Cultural Context." *Contemporary Literature* 38:1 (1997): 44–27.

Clark, Hilary. "The Mnemonics of Autobiography: Lyn Hejinian's My Life" *Biography,* 14 (1991): 315–35.

Dworkin, Craig Douglas. "Penelope Reworking the Twill: Patchwork, Writing, and Lyn Hejinian's *My Life" Contemporary Literature* 36:1 (1995): 58–81.

Freitag, Kornelia. "'A Pause, a Rose, Something on Paper': Autobiography as Language Writing in Lyn Hejinian's My Life." *Amerikastudien/American Studies* 43:2 (1998): 313–27.

Jarraway, David R. "*My Life* through the Eighties: The Exemplary LANGUAGE of Lyn Hejinian. *Contemporary Literature* 33:2 (1992): 319–36.

McHale, Brian. "Telling Stories Again: On the Replenishment of Narrative in the Postmodernist Long Poem." *Yearbook of English Studies* 30 (2000): 250–62.

Quartermain, Peter. "*Syllable as Music: Lyn Hejinian's "Writing Is an Aid to Memory" Sagetrieb: A Journal Devoted to Poets in the Imagist/Objectivist Tradition* 11:3 (1992): 17–31.

Ratcliffe, Stephen. "Private Eye/ Public Work." *American Poetry* 4:3 (1987): 40–48.

Spahr, Juliana. "'Make It Go With a Single Word. We.': Bruce Andrews's 'Confidence

Trick' and Lyn Hejinian's *My Life*." In *Everybody's Autonomy: Connective Reading and Collective Identity*. Tuscaloosa: University of Alabama Press, 2001. 18–50.

———. "Resignifying Autobiography: Lyn Hejinian's *My Life*" *American Literature* 68:1 (1996) 139–59.

Translations

Description, poems by Arkadii Dragomoshchenko (Los Angeles: Sun & Moon Press, 1990).

Xenia, poems by Arkadii Dragomoshchenko (Los Angeles: Sun & Moon Press, 1994).

References

Abraham, Nicolas, and Maria Torok. 1976. *Cryptonymie: Le verbier de L'Homme aux loups* (Paris: Flammarion).

Armantrout, Rae. 1992. "Feminist Poetics and the Meaning of Clarity," *Sagetrieb: A Journal Devoted to Poets in the Imagist-Objectivist Tradition,* 11(3) (Winter): 7–16.

Beach, Christopher. 1997. "Poetic Positionings: Stephen Dobyns and Lyn Hejinian in Cultural Context." *Contemporary Literature* 38(1) (Spring): 44–77.

Bernstein, Charles. 1986. "Hejinian's Notes," in *Contents Dream* (Los Angeles: Sun & Moon), 284–85.

Burns, Christy. 1995. "The Art of Conspiracy: Punning and Paranoid Response in Nabokov's *Pnin.*" *Mosaic* 28(1) (March): 99–117.

Campbell, Bruce. 1989. "'As Permeable Constructedness,' Lyn Hejinian: *My Life.*" *Temblor* 9: 192–93.

Clark, Hilary. 1991. "The Mnemonics of Autobiography: Lyn Hejinian's *My Life.*" *Biography: An Interdisciplinary Quarterly* 14:4 (Fall): 315–35.

Davidson, Michael. 1989. "Approaching the Fin de Siècle," in *The San Francisco Renaissance* (New York: Cambridge University Press), 200–18.

Deleuze, Gilles. 1997. *Essays Critical and Clinical,* trans. Daniel Smith and Michael Greco (Minneapolis: University of Minnesota Press).

Derrida, Jacques. 1977. "Fors," trans. Barbara Johnson. *The Georgia Review* 31(1) (Spring): 64–116.

Dworkin, Craig Douglas. 1995. "Penelope Reworking the Twill: Patchwork, Writing, and Lyn Hejinian's *My Life.*" *Contemporary Literature* 36(1) (Spring): 58–81.

———. 2000. "Retrospective: Lyn Hejinian." *The Poetry Project Newsletter* 179 (April/May): 11–14.

Freud, Sigmund. 1959. *The Standard Edition of the Complete Psychological Works of Sigmund Freud,* ed. James Strachey, Vol. 23 (London: The Hogarth Press).

Greer, Michael. 1989. "Ideology and Theory in Recent Experimental Writing, or, The Naming of 'Language Poetry.'" *Boundary 2* 16: 335–55.

Grenier, Robert. 1979. "Writing Is an Aid to Memory." *L=A=N=G=U=A=G=E* 8 (June 1979): unpaginated.

Jarraway, David R. 1992. "*My Life* through the Eighties: The Exemplary LAN-
GUAGE of Lyn Hejinian." *Contemporary Literature* 33(2) (Summer): 319–36.

Johnston, John. 1991. "Toward the Schizo-Text: Paranoia as Semiotic Regime in
The Crying of Lot 49." In *New Essays on The Crying of Lot 49*, ed. Patrick O'-
Donnell (Cambridge: Cambridge University Press), 47–78.

Kittler, Friedrich. 1990. *Discourse Networks: 1800–1900*, trans. Michael Metteer,
with Chris Cullens (Stanford, Calif.: Stanford University Press).

Lacan, Jacques. 1975. *De la Psychose paranoïaque dans ses rapports avec la per-
sonnalité suivi de Premiers ecrits sur la paranoia* (Paris: Editions du Seuil).

Mathews, Harry, and Alastair Brotchie, eds. 1998. *OuLiPo Compendium* (Lon-
don: Atlas Press).

McHale, Brian. 1996. "A Local Strangeness: An Interview with Lyn Hejinian," in
Some Other Fluency: Interviews with Innovative American Authors, ed. Larry
McCaffery (Philadelphia: University of Pennsylvania Press).

Naylor, Paul. 1999. "Lyn Hejinian: Investigating 'I'," in *Poetic Investigations:
Singing the Holes in History* (Evanston, Ill.: Northwestern University Press).

Perloff, Marjorie. 1984. "The Word as Such: L=A=N=G=U=A=G=E Poetry in the
Eighties." *American Poetry Review* (May–June): 15–22.

———. 1991a. *Confer:* "'The Sweet Aftertaste of Artichokes': Lyn Hejinian's *My
Life.*" *Denver Quarterly* 25(4) (Spring): 116–21.

———. 1991b. "The Return of the (Numerically) Repressed," *Radical Artifice:
Writing Poetry in the Age of Media* (Chicago, Ill.: University of Chicago Press),
162–70.

———. 1991c. [Review of *Leningrad*]. *Sulfur* 29 (Fall): 216–21.

———. 1993. "How Russian Is it: Lyn Hejinian's *Oxota*." *Parnassus* 17 (Spring):
186–209.

———. 1996a. "John Cage's Dublin, Lyn Hejinian's Leningrad: Poetic Cities as Cy-
berspace," in *Classical, Renaissance, and Postmodern Acts of the Imagination:
Essays Commemorating O.B. Hardison, Jr.,* ed. Arthur F. Kinney (Newark:
University of Delaware Press), 58–75.

———. 1996b. "'Running against the Walls of Our Cage': Toward a Wittgenstein-
ian Poetics," in *Wittgenstein's Ladder: Poetic Language and the Strangeness of
the Ordinary* (Chicago, Ill.: University of Chicago Press).

Quartermain, Peter. 1992. "Syllable as Music: Lyn Hejinian's Writing Is an Aid to
Memory." *Sagetrieb: A Journal Devoted to Poets in the Imagist-Objectivist Tra-
dition* 11(3) (Winter): 17–31.

Rasula, Jed. 1997. "Ten Different Fruits on One Different Tree: Experiment as a
Claim of the Book." *Chicago Review* 43(4) (Fall): 28.

Ratcliffe, Stephen. 1987a. "Private Eye/Public Work." *American Poetry* 4(3)
(Spring): 40–48.

———. 1987b. "Two Hejinian Talks: Writing/One's Life; Writing/Re: Memory."
Temblor 6: 141–47.

Schor, Naomi. 1978. "Le Délire d'interprétation: naturalisme et paranoia." In *Le
naturalisme* (Paris: Union Générale Éditions), 237–257.

Spahr, Juliana. 1996. "Resignifying Autobiography: Lyn Hejinian's *My Life.*"

American Literature: A Journal of Literary History, Criticism, and Bibliography 68(1) (March): 139–59.

Samuels, Lisa. 1997. "Eight Justifications for Canonizing Lyn Hejinian's *My Life.*" *Modern Language Studies* 27(2): 103–19.

Waldrop, Rosmarie. 1989. "Chinese Windmills Turn Horizontally: On Lyn Hejinian." *Temblor* 10: 219–22.

Watten, Barrett. 1985. "The World in the Work: Towards a Psychology of Form," in *Total Syntax*. Carbondale: University of Illinois Press, 146–49.

Winchester, Simon. 1998. *The Professor and the Madman* (London: Viking).

BRENDA HILLMAN

A GEOLOGY

What we love, can't see.

If Italy looks like a boot to most people, California
     looks like the skin of a person about to sit
     down, a geology.

Consider the Coast Range. We can achieve
     the same results by pushing a pile of wet
     papers from the left and finally
     they were just in love with each other.

Consider the faultline; with only two sides of it,
     how come you never thought of one of them.

A place we love, can't see.   A condition
     so used   to becoming . . .

(Those who have straddled reference know a map
     will stand for wholeness.)

When you were trying to quit the drug and broke
     in half you said . . .

And you had to trust it   (that is, needing it)

Landforms enable us to scare. Where
     Berkeley is, once a shallow sea with
     landforms to the west, called Cascadia.
     No kidding. I read this.

A geology breaks in half to grow. A person whose drug like
     a locust jumps across someone's foot, singing—;
     we disagree with D, who hates similes.

The Transverse Ranges holding Los Angeles spit out
        a desert on their hazard side, a power
        transformed from a period of thrall into
        an ordinary period of lying here.

There are six major faults, there are skipped
        verbs, there are more little
        thoughts in California. The piece of coast
        slides on the arrow; down is
        reverse. Subduction means the coast

goes underneath the continent, which is
        rather light. It was my friend. I needed it.
        The break in the rock shows forward; the flash
        hurts. Granite is composed of quartz, hornblende
        and other former fire. When a drug

is trying to quit it has to stretch. Narrow comes
        from the same place as glamor.

A scarp hangs over the edge as it goes from
        Monterey to Santa Barbara. When we
        were trying to quit it had to shout.
        (The rest of our party had gone up ahead.)
        Exaggeration has no effect upon silence.

It took my breath, I gave it willingly, I told
        it to, and the breath listened—

Consider the place of I-80 towards outcroppings.
        When you've gotten to Auburn, a whole
        dog-shaped ground has broken through,

the rock struggling with features, its bachelor joy, caused
        by the power that has kissed you.

What happened, happened a lot. Not to glamorize
    what can't be helped. A bunch of fiery
    islands floated over and sutured themselves to us

a hundred million years ago. I liked

to hold one. Just, really, light it. Put my
    mouth on it.

It's appropriate to discuss features when we speak of California,

daylight's treatment of a sudden

movement in rock. It pretended not to mind. You
    passed him on the path. Miocene lava
    smiled as it ordered the darker

color to sit down.

When he was trying to quit he based his reasoning
    on the way mountains slip. California's
    glaciers never reach the sea. The drug

was trapped in you, and fit. The Klamath mountains love
    the veins of excellent stress, see figure 12.
    Between the time two mountains slip, nothing.
    Between two points of resolution, nothing
    less. A little more
    almost and the slip happened; it happened
    a lot just 30 million years ago.

I saw between the flames four types of instruments:
    with one they touched my mouth,
    with another you touched
    her feet. Rocks of the oldest

time are barely represented. This is the voice
    from the cave, Oleiria. He was coming
    to see you though your face had been removed.

The fault went under artichokes in 1982. She talked
      to the permanent fire about it;

what pushes up from under isn't
      named. Or is that "What makes you do this
      to yourself."—What makes you—A language
      caught up under, like a continent.
      She was inhaling though they told her not to.

In the Gabilan Range, small volcanoes erupted
      softly, then this throw-rug-over-the-carpet-
      in-a-bowling-alley type of effect. A california

is composed of moving toward, away, or past; a
      skin is not separate; a poem is

composed of all readings of it. Elements
      redeem themselves plenty, alchemists say so.
      I gave my breath quite easily, then. Sorry it's

ashes, sorry it's smoke all the way down. Gravity
      has to practice. The disciple of angles
      smashed planet after planet, rubbing the cave
      of chalk onto his cue, and put them
      into corners like Aquinas's five
      proofs for the existence of God. Nice
      touch on that boy, nice touch on those
      who sleep till noon, who sleep the sleep
      of the uninsured till noon and wake with maps
      of Sacramento on their hands.

What made the Sierra lift from the right. Telluric Poptart.
      Geologists refer to the range as
      trapdoorlike. It made him cry, he gave it
      willingly, the bartender brought him

free drinks and sent him out into the pale
wrong proud civilian night—

A geology can't fix itself. Nor can description.
    Horses run upside down in
    the undermath. A power has twinned itself
    in that place. We follow it until we are
    its favorite, then we live. Does the drug
    recover? The Pacific Plate

began this recent movement 20 million years ago. Fresno
    was underwater; the small creatures
    barely noticed.

She smelled it till it stopped looking pretty; let's call a spoon
    a spoon. We dig right down into ourselves
    for the rocks of the middle kingdom. Gold

folded into the Motherlode often twinned
    with quartz. They seemed to like each other.
    Addicts stay on the porch together, lighting them,

and elsewhere, lighthouse cliffs recall the tremors
    that brought them there. . . . I *whered*
    the wheel and the continent moved over

but I still wanted it.

Los Angeles cheap bedding. You'd allow her
    to go first and then you'd go, pull the youngest
    blanket over her—bang. If that's
    how you like it, fine. Like warm sandstone.

We're living at the dawn of creation as far as
    California is concerned. The skin
    goes first. Most beaches are losing sand,
    it drifts south to Mexico. He sold it, she mixed it, we

bought the *pfft* in 198x, trying to endure
        the glassfront curve in the unaccountable
        ghostman's pleasure. Get down

off that ladder, you. Ceiling stars. Little fiery

islands were light as they ordered Nevada
        to move over. The white thing took
        her breath, she let it slide, it recognized
        what to do. After it started, no
        change; seeing you was methadone
        for seeing you.

The number of faults in middle California
        is staggering—that is, we stagger
        over them till it's
        difficult to follow our own. Each tremor
        is the nephew of a laugh—
        sandstone, shale, chert from the Triassic
        near I-Forgetville. He lined
        them up, they made white sense,

stretchmarks on her body like
        public transportation, very coastal,
        very Sierra traintracks that click-click
        down the sides of thighs, stretchmarks
        where the soul has grown too quickly
        from inside—

But in a way, not really. A geology

has its appetites. New islands are forming
        to get the gist of it. Much of the coast
        moved on its own to get free. Sometimes
        he'd just pass it to you, the prince of stains;
        the universe cried through him. The sea

was glassing itself over Half Moon Bay. Should have
    dropped again suddenly, in the service
    of some burnt out Eden.

It's appropriate to discuss what can't be
    helped. Phyllites, schists, cherts
    marbles. An angel in the annunciation,
    little subzero Mary kneeling
    before you in the bathroom while you were
    burning your skin off.

You went east and you went south. They
    took out their little fear schedules. The Pacific
    Plate on the left moving north while
    the right stands still if you
    look down on it. There's no way

to say progress had been made. I never did

not think about lighting them, not one day,
    as if a requiem could help how chords
    fell out the bottom; Cascadia breathed; I tried
    program, H tried program after program,
    P tried specific harvests
    of bubbles. 12 step ashes. Extra metal

on the stove. The rest of our party
    had gone on ahead. Don't name it. The lithosphere
    likes to float on the aesthenosphere, the soft
    mobile voice of the unseen. *I slide*

below you sweet and high. It wants

to hear you. It wants to touch you. It wants
    to be happy and it wants to die.

Phyllites, schists, cherts, marbles. Press #
        when you are finished. No one knows why
        the arc of minor islands sewed themselves
        to us in that way. When I put it

to my mouth I had no ability to stop it.
        The sea ate the colors a hundred million years ago.

A geology is not a strategy. When an addict tries to leave
        the desire to make himself over shifts from
        what it felt like to have been a subject;

L.A. will dwell beside San Francisco eventually.

Tempting to pun on the word *fault*. All right,
        say *plot*. All right, *happens*. The tendency
        to fault relieves the strain. New islands
        were forming to get the gist of it. We wanted
        the extraordinary stranger in our veins.

Whether it's better not to have been held by something.
        The oldest limestone, prevalent between Big Sur
        and Calaveras, is not "better than," say,
        any other kind. The suffering wasn't luckier,
        it wasn't a question of asking.

In the instead hour, the minutes of not recovering
        from the difference of what we loved;
        sameness is also true: stone like a spider

sucking the carapace the same color as itself.

In the expiation of nature, we are required to
        experience the dramatic narrative of matter.

The rocks under California are reigning in their little world.

This was set down in strata so you could know
        what it felt like to have been earth.

POETIC STATEMENT

Twelve Writings toward a Poetics of Alchemy, Dread, Inconsistency, Betweenness, and California Geological Syntax

IT DOESN'T matter where you begin because you'll just have to do it again. In alchemy, the principle of change is called mercury, is associated with shifting, with chaos, and with the feminine, though it doesn't mean only female alchemists are mercurial. These experimenters share with the Gnostics the suspicion that ur-matter exists initially outside of god, is sometimes called "the uncreated," and was never born. They share with the pre Socratic philosophers an obsessive interest in the strangeness of materials and of time itself transubstantiated but, unlike Thales or Heraclitus, don't want to handle only one substance at a time. Mixture is the start of dread. Syncretistic belief systems and mystery cults arise to protect severalness. Alchemy traces back to Egypt during the time when techniques of mummification were being developed. Its name probably comes from the word "soil," but it is the soil of thought. By the time Osiris, the god of suffering, sweating, and partial disintegration, is being wrapped up in bandages by his left-side wife and his right-side wife, the ground settles down in what will be California, and the Coast Ranges are already formed. Five thousand years later, while talking about the decentered subject at a conference in San Diego, several women think they feel a little tremor, but it's a poetics.[1]

Many features of a new poetics may not be new; such things as shifting syntax, nonlinear procedures, fragmentation, the use of a spatially open page, oblique references derive from many traditions across the decades. Historically, alchemists work with received forms that attach to the miraculous, to process even in suffering, to transmutation, to the development of an apparatus that is personal, cultural, philosophical, political. In searching for a kind of matter that is at once literal and abstract, they seek through the use of subtle and often tediously repetitive experiment not to make real gold but to remind the world that the only value is a harmony inherent in the object's relationship to itself, just as every word of a poem starts with a relationship to itself deep in the labyrinths of its own change. Much of what we think of as experimental poetry—even inept forms of it—accomplishes this.

A single body is not big enough to hold an experience. Insofar as the *lyric impulse* is a generous and sinuous thing, it threads itself powerfully through centuries and traditions; it is not the opposite of some other kind of poetry. Lyric can be done by all kinds of lyres. (A car horn is stuck in the neighborhood because there was a rip in the "fabric" of the space-time continuum at the start of it.) Lyric also has its limits. (At the moment of this writing NATO is beginning the bombing of Kosovo; the school children carry all their belongings in their satchels because home doesn't last. We seem to be doing the bombing again. Nationhood. What a terrible idea.) There is the dread of the failure of creation. In *The Book of Questions*, Edmond Jabès writes:

> I get up with the page that is turned. I lie down with the page put down. To be able to reply: "I belong to the race of words, which homes are built with"—when I know full well that this answer is still another question, that this home is constantly threatened.[2]

Writing is a kind of magnetic force along a faultline. I became interested in thought systems that urged dialogic investigation rather than ecstatic integration. When psychological searching pushed for brendafication, the poems pushed for chaos. What's this about being yourself? Can't help you there. André Breton in his "First Surrealist Manifesto" suggests a way to start writing: "Attain the most passive or receptive state possible. Forget your genius, your talents and those of everyone else. Tell yourself firmly that literature is one of the unhappiest routes leading to everything."[3]

If you are an alchemist, you talk to the thing you will use. The poet writes to cognates, wordlings, wordettes. Robert Duncan writes in *The H.D. Book* of his Aunt Fay that her name "had to do with enchantments of the mind . . . in which we saw an other world behind or under things. . . . *Fate, faith, feign* and *fair*, we find, following the winding associations of *Fay, fey* and *fairy* in the O.E.D. are related."[4] Alchemists talked to the lump of copper or salt. The idea of attraction of certain substances by others—affinities, amalgamations—was offset by the notion that certain substances had rejected them. Does it ever seem like a word rejects you? I heard something in the margins and scooped it into the poem. Each phrase in a poem swirls like confused metal but seeks its own element to make the whole, which has been of necessity the syntactic expression of the sentence being braced by or compromised by the line. Power mechanisms are subverted. There are no nations. In making metaphor, meaning must suffer but it comes back changed—like Osiris, meaning has its body broken to be planted.

•

I was drawn to poetry by a longing for the ineffable mystery of existence, by a confusion about the senses and sensual nature, and by a passion for the beauty of language and what it feared to approach. My girlhood poets were Millay, Dickinson, and Plath. In college, I navigated between what seemed to be divergent poetic impulses: Coleridge, Hopkins, Yeats, Rilke, and Eliot—the stuck-soul guys—on the one hand, and Mallarmé, Rimbaud, Breton, and the Surrealists—the unpredictable aestheticians, the destroyers of sense—on the other. I was interested in the occult and in mystery traditions. My poetry teacher pushed the Surrealists, so I made baby surrealist poems by the yard in college. In the early 1970s, the prevailing mode was autobiographical plain-style poetry in the manner of James Wright, but my classmates and I shared a well-worn copy of Donald Allen's anthology; our reading included Duncan, Weiners (particularly *Nerves*), and Ashbery. Practically everyone read Stevens.

•

When I moved to Berkeley in the mid-1970s, my first poet friend was Patricia Dienstfrey, who was helping to start Kelsey St. Press. Through her I became interested in contemporary women's writing. Bay Area literary life seemed magical and exciting, with many different traditions interweaving, like a pageant—light submitted to an aftermath. Rings of candles. Gold broth of barley. "*Notre figure terrestre n'est que le second tiers d'une poursuite continue, un point, amont,*" writes René Char. (Gustaf Sobin translates this: "Our figure on earth is only the second third of a continuous pursuit, a point, upland.)[5] In those years I was writing poems of meditative description; I wanted my poetry to speak directly of the difficulties of life and consciousness in the quotidian because I was raising a family and working in a bookstore. In the 1980s, further studies in Gnosticism and the occult began to provide an answering vocabulary for things that were already happening in my poetry, as did literary theory, particularly the work of Kristeva and Irigaray, who presented nontraditional ideas in exploratory forms. By then I was teaching poetry and felt part of a community interested in experimental writing and lyric abstraction. Many voices were arriving in poetry at a slant or sideways. My own compositional methods included trance and hypnosis. In California, in a decade of medium earthquakes, the lyric had to include the broken, the partial, the plural, inconsistency, surprise, as life had come to include them, along with the experiences of divorce and remarriage, of writing in relation to friends and beloveds—sometimes against, sometimes with. I've continued to be attracted to work of spiritual difficulty and to inventive styles. I'm drawn to poetry that reflects shaken states—the state of the state, natural order, the soul, the word—and that will challenge the recognized categories.

.

An inventor is subsumed in her process but a style makes an original thing. How? Can't help you there. Literary adventurousness sometimes brings with it vocabularies of territory and ownership. This is understandable in a literary culture that homogenizes and overlooks much of the risky work in the arts. Artistic differences should be acknowledged and the work of groups credited. I prefer to think of writing movements as fields of energy that help the general situation, the loneliness of the artists around and in them. Somehow, poems get made by writers with separate bodies and experiences. Poor poems; they are cursed with having poets as their transmitters. Even the deepest, most egoless states, where figurative space spins out its position of no position, have to use individuals to become poems. Robert Kelly, in his *Alchemical Journal* in 1966 writes: "Alchemy is the science of having silent dreams, having no dreams. Only syntax can tell you apart, you menacing word-of-power, only syntax can heal the wound, right the warp in the child's mind. Alchemy is the science of becoming aware of the whole project in which we are being engaged. Alchemy is the science of being used."[6] Osiris suffered from a coastline. We drive down highway one looking at the buckled granite near Devil's Pass. It broke like ourselves. An ego project is doomed to fail.

.

Fearing the hopelessness and irrelevance of his task but possessed of an obsessive-compulsive disorder like someone who checks the doors twenty times or even a bit like Gertrude Stein, the alchemist is filled with a perpetuity of playful dread. I approve of dread. It's a hard-core emotion, not like anxiety or wistfulness. Having poetic dread as an ally is like looking forward to the next earthquake. A portion of the process is preserved. Hell grows corners. Causality backs up toward the door.

.

The use of "unnatural syntax" can be seen to come from "nature." We've talked to the demons about this. The rocks that form the crusty edges of California started in the obscure south and are inching up the coastline on their own plate at their own pace like a different tradition. It's not mainland granite—it is its own movement. But it's still granite. The form of the poem "A Geology" came from the instinct that putting the *seed* words at the corners of the page would formalize the signals to the unconscious. This is a technique used by the Surrealist poets. The unacceptable in poetry is most interesting when it corresponds to, and synchronizes with, a reality that does not betray the specific uncertainty of a seeker who has experienced something mysterious with a force of powerful (albeit transitory) feeling. For some in California, movements on the fault, Prop 13, and the materialism of our culture make the need for a literature of upset almost beside the point—it's been the afterlife for quite some time.

•

In his famously impenetrable essay "On Language as Such and on the Language of Man," Walter Benjamin presents the paradox of "Expression": "It is therefore obvious at once that the mental entity that communicates itself in language is not language itself but something to be distinguished from it."[7] Whatever *experience* is in relation to consciousness is what the brain does before the dream sets in. Often the experience of *experience* is between language and silence, as between two lovers. Whatever ——— is just before the word comes is where "I" live mostly. The experiment immediately precedes the arrival of the phrase. A softly crackling stream of images and metaphoric pieces, a prelinguistic gravel, not babel. @#$%^&*(). My composition seems to involve the constellation of four things: an unnameable psychic or spiritual condition, an "idea" or concept of an intellectual nature, a metaphor, and a heard phrase. Then the erotic chaos. It is this radical chaos, a particular life of the spiritual body, that I wish to defend, a poetry that pushes past definitions, where the edges are at the center and everything is both.

•

The use of the whole page reflects an accommodation both to the lyric moment, which is irrational in one way, and to the antilyric, which is irrational in another. In "blue codices," the distillate material at the bottom of the page makes an argument against causality. The poems began with trance and chance, with counting and visualization techniques. The model for this poem is George Herbert's shape poems. It seemed necessary to capture the circular nature of depressive cycles using the shape of an alchemical furnace; I was also inspired by Barbara Guest's use of space and had been reminded by Planck and Heisenberg that noncausality is a more useful basis for understanding nature than is anything else. The material at the bottom, the fragmentary quotidian, involves a search for and satisfaction with an imaginal realm that will not be corrected and can only remain wounded and laughing.

For many ancient peoples, stone is a living seed. Like a word. The desire for gold actually comes at the end of a process of stone worship. Making gold is not the point, and having it is certainly not what's good for us. The fire is supposed never to go out.

Alchemists could not sit on panels or write statements about art because they were often hiding out from kings who wanted to kill them for having failed. Offering observations about methodologies makes less sense as the substance continues to refuse. Methodologies are of interest only as they manifest in individual poems, not in theories or labels. Whatever force allows a poem to make a momentary display of liveliness comes from complete mystery, because it has gotten to a level that is not particular to an individual life; ironically, whatever makes a poem memorable is its being free of us to be itself.

"NEEDING SYNTAX TO LOVE"

Expressive Experimentalism in the Work of Brenda Hillman

Lisa Sewell

LATE-TWENTIETH-CENTURY contemporary poetry and poetics is marked by a split between the avant-garde and the mainstream, pitting language against lyric, experimentation against convention, closed against open, self-expressive against self-reflexive.[8] At one end of the spectrum, language-oriented writing foregrounds the material, referential, and reflexive aspects of language and promotes a collaborative notion of reading, purging the poem of origin, narrative voice and affect, and calling "upon the reader to be actively involved in the process of constituting [the text's] meaning."[9] The theoretical ideas that have influenced many of the language poets can be linked to the poststructuralist ideological critique of representation and interrogation of the status of the speaking subject. At the other end of the spectrum is a conservative, syntactically regularized, carefully crafted, univocal poetry that is naive to its own ideological position and that presents language as a transparent medium for expression and the poem as a self-contained object invested with meaning. This postromantic poetry often puts an "I" at the center of the poem and takes for granted the notion of a coherent, lyric speaker, of a self that preexists utterance.[10]

The conflict between the two groups is particularly thorny in relationship to contemporary feminist studies and theoretical concerns about women's writing, essentialism verses constructionism, *lécriture féminine*. Does representational language truly preserve the status quo when the lives or identities portrayed have been ignored, misappropriated, and objectified by the dominant literary culture? As Ron Silliman, a poet/critic at the forefront of the Language movement, has observed, those who have been "the subject of history—many white male heterosexuals for example" are more likely "to challenge all that is supposedly 'natural' about the formation of their own subjectivity," while those at the margins, "women, people of color, sexual minorities—have a manifest political need to have their stories told."[11] The early women's movement seemed to call for a poetry of immediate, accessible language, a poetry in which women express anger, give self-authorized accounts of their experiences, and assert agency within a literary tradition that often makes the desired and desirable woman the object of the poem. By focusing on their particular worldly concerns—relationships, family, female sexuality, the joys and horrors of motherhood—women writers could claim the private and domestic as the proper domain of poetry and affirm that women could speak for and of themselves. In this light, the apparently conservative lyric is used to assert a newly imagined self and becomes a tool for subversion and rebellion; the representation of women's domestic lives becomes a way of politicizing personal experience. In contrast, experimental, nonrepresentational poetics can be seen as risky for women writers because feminine subjectivity and authorial agency cannot be taken for granted.[12]

Questions of authority and agency are of equal concern to experimental women writers such as Susan Howe, Rachel Blau DuPlessis, Kathleen Fraser, and Lyn Hejinian, among others, who deplore the use of transparent language and traditional forms, which they believe are inevitably coopted by a patriarchal symbolic order.[13] Although language writing and the avant-garde has been associated with a largely male if not masculinist tradition, the work of these writers suggests that formal experimentation and the rejection of conventional patterns of expression can resist phallocentric logic and the linguistically based strictures that define and limit the feminine. Drawing on the work of psychoanalytic feminist theorists such as Luce Irigaray and Hélène Cixous, they envision a language that articulates its otherness and is marked by sexual difference. Kathleen Fraser explains it as a need to "reinvent the givens of poetry, imagining in visual, structural terms core states of female social and psychological experience not yet adequately tracked."[14] In addition, as Marianne DeKoven has pointed out, there are many similarities in the "manifestoes" of avant-garde writer/critics and those of feminism: both question "traditional" practices and are attracted to a radical aesthetic that can overturn hierarchy and subvert the narratives of the dominant culture.[15] In fact, the conflict between expressive and experimental writing in contemporary poetry is somewhat analogous to the divide between those feminists who are interested in women's actual lives and those who investigate woman as a category of difference. In response to Silliman's assumption that those at the margins have no ground from which to resist and subvert master narratives, Rae Armantrout has argued that "as outsiders, women might, in fact, be well positioned to appreciate the constructedness of the identity that is based on identification, and therefore, to challenge the contemporary poetic convention of the unified Voice."[16] Experimental feminist poets not only use language to assert and depict difference but to enact it materially, visually, aurally. For these writers, only a critique of representation can genuinely subvert patriarchal authority.[17]

Brenda Hillman has a unique place in relationship to the debate between experimental and expressive poetics and to questions of a resistant, self-reflexive feminism. Like many of her contemporaries, she often writes directly out of personal, felt experience, taking up subject matter that has come to be seen as characteristic of women's writing: relationships, motherhood, female sexuality. In her most recent work, while still exploring female experience and identity, she has also engaged in a formally experimental mode that calls voice, singular meanings, representation, and the transparency of language into question. At this point in her career, Hillman is both an innovator and a traditionalist who seems to question but also take for granted the expressive, communicative powers of language. Associated with the mainstream postromantic tradition best represented by Robert Hass, Louise Gluck, and Robert Pinsky, and also with more experimental women poets such as Barbara Guest, Leslie Scalapino, and Beverly Dahlen, she cannot be placed neatly on one side of the divide or the other. Her work merges the concerns of women writers who believe in the importance of depicting felt experience with those who suggest that patriarchal language inevitably compromises that expression.

What strongly differentiates Hillman's work from other female "innovators" is that her experimental approach grows out of her life experiences as much as from a desire to "undermine oppressive narratives at their base."[18] Much of her new work has the quality of "openness," which Lyn Hejinian has discussed as an important aspect of innovative writing:

The "open text," by definition, is open to the world and particularly to the reader. It invites participation, rejects the authority of the writer over the reader and thus, by analogy, the authority implicit in other (social, economic, cultural) hierarchies. It . . . often emphasizes or foregrounds process, either the process of the original composition or of subsequent compositions by readers, and thus resists the cultural tendencies that seek to identify and fix material, turn it into a product.[19]

While Hillman is clearly aware of the subversive, oppositional possibilities of the open text, her attention to syntax and process seems to derive from felt experience rather than a pure interest in "rejecting the authority of the writer over the reader and thus, by analogy, the authority implicit in other (social, economic, cultural) hierarchies."[20] Without being confessional in the usual sense, Hillman constructs a decentered but autobiographical subject making its hesitant, provisional way through language. Like other innovative writers, Hillman questions the possibility of "fullness" in language and the conventions of line, stanza, and the lyric voice, but shattering personal losses—divorce, the death of a close friend—and an interest in transformative spirituality are among the factors that lead to the "serious play" in her poetics.

For Hillman, innovation is the product of disruptive personal experiences and spiritual thirst, as well as an understanding of the contemporary theoretical and ideological interrogation of subjectivity. She uses many of the disruptive, oppositional tools associated with experimental writing but also situates her poetry in the experiences and utterances of a voice—a multifaceted, fragmented, shifting but identifiable speaking subject. Her poems provide the reader with points of access and recognition and are true to her own stated desire to "keep the vitality of the meditative lyric with its emphasis on felt experience but render form in an imaginatively accurate way."[21] Influenced by the heretical spiritualism of the ancient Gnostics, the investigation of sexual difference spearheaded by French feminist critics such as Luce Irigaray and Julia Kristeva, and the inconsistencies in her own life, Hillman refrains from the seductions of formal progression and coherent narrative, but also retains a place for a provisional, inconsistent self and subjective agency. Her work meets the challenge of inventing and employing an approach that is not naive to the ways subjects are structured by language but also resists the emptied-out negativism of a purely language-driven poetics.[22] This duality positions Hillman on the line between the two central competing discourses that currently constitute the field of contemporary poetry. It is a boundary that proves to be as permeable as the line that separates the other dualistic pairs Hillman investigates in much of her work. The point is not to resolve or reconcile the binary of expressive/referential or mainstream/experimental, but to observe the sparks that fly when the terms on either side come into contact. In doing so, her work points to the limitations of a neat division between the avant-garde and the mainstream, to what is ignored, dismissed or covered over when we insist on setting one approach against another. Hillman's poetry makes and enacts an argument for the poetics of "betweenness," for a voice-centered experimentalism, for the place of the expressive in the innovative. This is particularly true in *Loose Sugar*, and for the most part I will focus on the work in that book. But by briefly looking at the four books that precede *Loose Sugar*, it is possible to see how Hillman evolved this poetics of "between."

Hillman's first book, *White Dress*, established her as a lyric poet. For the most part, the poems employ a "natural," univocal speaker and explore the nature of the self in the world, relationships between men and women—common themes in contemporary women's mainstream verse. "Rapunzel" comments on the failed project of communication between the sexes where "One has the idea of labor/One has the useless hair" (*WD*, 8).[23] As in many of the poems, the tone is austere— "He would climb up to her/If he wanted that artifice/But he has work to do, the important/Sun at his back" (*WD*, 8)—and is reminiscent of the confessional poetry of Sylvia Plath and Louise Gluck. Hillman's interest in the ways culture limits, commodifies, and stifles women's lives is clear in poems such as "Anonymous Courtesan in a Jade Shroud" and "Cameo." "Cameo" ends:

> This expressionless white face
>
> Is what the world and love
> Have carved upon her.
> Her dark face is rigidly turned away;
> She's carving that for herself. (*WD*, 24)

The cameo is a figure for all women who are compelled by the culture to display a perfected, pure ("white") profile while suppressing a darker, assertive side. As with most of the poems in *White Dress*, the line breaks emphasize and deepen meaning, and as a whole the poem moves toward a resonant if not reassuring closure. *White Dress* was well received. Hillman seemed to be a master of the lyric, and as she states in an interview for *Hayden's Ferry Review*, at the time she was very concerned with producing the well-made, acceptable poem: "[Those poems] are the products of having had an aesthetic that was born of believing in workshops and believing that workshops finished poems or helped you finish poems."[24] Despite her good training, Hillman lost her faith in mastery and closure, and her more recent work depicts the journeys of a provisional self-in-process.

Fortress, published four years later, is more expansive in terms of subject matter and looser in form, employing a longer line and easier cadence, but overall the structure is narrative and the poems rely on a central if quirkier voice. Hillman has said that *Fortress* is meant to be "a kind of Lowell-ish, careful extended metaphor for the self . . . camped out against the destructive forces."[25] The book also examines the disunities between men and women, and the underlying theme is the breakdown of a marriage. A number of poems conform visually to the conventions of mainstream poetry with regular stanzas, a free-verse line that uses enjambment to create forward momentum and narrative tension: "Saguro," "Amaneusis," "Red Wings," and "The Calf" all clearly meet the "workshop" standard and rely on the individual voice and authenticity of feeling to justify the poem. But *Fortress* does offer a hint of the nonlinear, self-referential experimentation with form that can be found in Hillman's more recent work. "Broken Dreams" introduces the shifting voice and multiple points of view that will come to characterize the next three books. The title poem is a long sequence that takes in many tiers of the society—a night watchman, a jogging partner, cocaine-using friends, bank tellers, a street person—and brings together a number of disparate elements to explore the many kinds of fortresses that can be erected, breached, and imagined. It is one of the poems in the volume that ranges widely in tone and diction, juxtaposing the quotidian with the sublime, overheard speech with observation.

But this volume is also important to Hillman's disillusionment with conventional free verse because in surveying the deterioration of a marriage, *Fortress* charts one of the events that led Hillman to question the representational limits of formally conservative, lyric language. These poems attempt thematically to represent and contain that breakdown and disunity instead of enacting or recreating it. In "Canyon" the speaker searches for images that can serve as metaphors for the interrupted continuity, the severed but still present love and expectation that the divorce represents. "Cleave and Cleave" also focuses on the end of a relationship, comparing two couples—one in loving harmony and one having a terrible, public fight—in order to explore the contradictions in love. Through juxtaposition, the two couples are linked to the "linguistic twins *cleave* and *cleave,*/which stem from opposites, meaning/split and stick" (*F,* 26). The relevance to the speaker's situation is clear: "I felt such freedom when you walked away;/I won't stop loving you, even in death" (*F,* 26). In this poem and in "Canyon," Hillman doesn't try to resolve the tension created when two opposing meanings are housed in a single word, but in later work she will discover techniques that allow her to depict as well as describe that tension.

The structure of the book suggests Hillman's dissatisfaction with traditional notions of order and continuity as well. While divided into three sections, which is a fairly common way of ordering a book of poems, *Fortress* ends with the poem "To the Gull" that presents the seagull as a figure for the poet—"battered," museless, but still compelled to trace "another blinding circle" (*F*, 70). The poem is set off in its own pseudo-section, preceded by a page without a section number, as if it cannot be contained within the book's neat structure. Afterthought, forethought, multiple thoughts that come all at once cannot be represented by plot or lyric closure, and over time Hillman abandons these conventions. "To the Gull" suggests that a different kind of muse will be needed in the future in order to accurately depict the infinite "blinding circle[s]" the "poet's eye" surveys.

Hillman's next two books, *Death Tractates* and *Bright Existence*, which were published during the same year, track a journey that is both metaphysical and linguistic. In these paired books, Hillman explores ways of formally depicting the fractured experience of selfhood that begins to appear thematically in *Fortress*, committing herself more fully to some of the innovative writing techniques I've outlined above. The occasion for the poems in *Death Tractates* is the unexpected death of Hillman's closest female mentor. A note at the beginning of the book explains that those poems began as "an interruption" in the writing of *Bright Existence*, but then could not be made to fit into that book. The sudden loss and unexpected fracturing of the poet's life is reflected in the split between the two books; it is emblematic of a life in which categories such as mother, family, and self no longer correspond to or accurately depict the lived experience attached to each term. Hillman expands her interest in the destabilized speaking subject, shifting between first and second person throughout both books, suggesting the difficulties of distinguishing between subject and object, self and other, and blurring the closely guarded boundary of identity. In *Death Tractates*, Hillman also emphasizes the blurred boundary between the speaker and the one she has lost. In "Holding Her," Hillman writes:

> —Then the owl came back the druid the helper
> and you asked,
> Where is she who we love. Who-who,
> it said, who-who, matching sets
> for you and her—
>
>
> you who had sought distinction
> in the pronouns
> found they were all the same—(*DT*, 9)

Marked by interruption, hesitation, and fragmentation, many poems in both books begin in mid-sentence as if the poem were always already occurring, and in this instance language has been found to record the process. Hillman also uses open parentheses, odd punctuation and dashes, to map as well as explore the unbounded nature of experience, the fracturing of identity.

"Blossoms Appearing" from *Bright Existence* is a good example of a poem that calls attention to process:

> —In the pause between
> No, wait.
> Between winter and the time you greeted it:
> plum blossoms. Plum blossoms everywhere! (*BE,* 12)

The speaker begins mid-statement, situated in a pause, a sort of limbo, then hesitates and begins again. Perhaps in a workshop, the class would suggest that the third line is where the poem begins. But Hillman is self-consciously including what comes before the "real" beginning. In this way, she poses the expectation of progress as a false certainty and calls attention to the processes involved in the making of the poem—a practice she continues to expand upon in *Loose Sugar* and in more recent work as well. At the same time, the poem is situated in an identifiable experience—gardening in the early spring—and moves toward an almost classic epiphany of recognition:

> One day it came to you.
> Spring cried as you turned the numb soil.
> Earthworms twisted warm cuneiform bodies, arching up
> in something—if it was not delight
> it was so much like delight—
>
> and a rusty robin landed slowly as an old biplane,
>
> shook the branch, and all
> the blossoms fell
> on you deliciously it was not sorrow
>
> then you knew for the bird as for you the world
> split open was stunningly beautiful
> though being alive was nearly impossible—(*BE,* 12)

The speaker is self-conscious about projecting meaning onto arbitrary events in nature but insists that the perception is worth recording anyway. This poem is representative of the style that predominates in these two books: for the most part, Hillman relies on expressive language but occasionally startles us into consciousness through self-reflexiveness and formal deviation.

Hillman's reading of ancient Gnostic treatises has also affected the evolution of her expressive experimentalism, and this interest is reflected thematically and structurally in *Death Tractates* and *Bright Existence*. Presenting a very different kind of relationship between matter and spirit than that ventured by Cartesian metaphysics, Gnosticism was considered heretical by the early Christians and a significant group of their writings was hidden and buried at Nag Hammadi in Egypt until the middle of the twentieth century. Their belief system is antihierarchical, combining elements of Judaism, Christianity, and the Neoplatonic tradition. Essentially, the ancient Gnostics did not subscribe to original sin or to the idea that humans need the intervention of the Church in order to know God; they believed that this world is illusional and that the true God dwells within the self.[26] As Hillman explains, "The Gnostics hold that inner knowledge is divine, is on fire, and that our job is to get through a great deal of external suffering to be reunited with our true selves."[27] Gnosticism provides Hillman with a metaphysics that is as split and multiple as her own experience of the world. In addition, while representations of God in sources of Judeo-Christian and Islamic theology are primarily masculine—in Christianity two points in the Trinity are the Father and the Son—the Gnostic treatises discovered at Nag Hammadi represent God in both masculine and feminine terms, as both divine Father and divine Mother. Elaine Pagels explains that according to some texts, God is dyadic: "consisting in one part, of the Ineffable, the Depth, the Primal Father; and, in the other, of Grace, Silence, the Womb and 'Mother of All'."[28] One treatise, "On the Origin of the World," describes a powerful female deity:

> It is called Sophia (Wisdom). It exercised volition and became a product resembling the primeval light. And immediately her will manifested itself as a likeness of heaven having an unimaginable magnitude; it was between the immortal beings and those things that came into being after them.[29]

Because it valorizes subjective, personal self-knowledge and includes images of feminine deity, Gnosticism provides an alternative to Western patriarchal theologies, and certainly this has an appeal for Hillman.[30] In "Dark Turtles and Bright Turtles," Hillman explains:

> I've found that more than other Western esoteric traditions, Gnosticism has been quite compatible with feminist awareness and poetry. . . . Our contemporary "soul-in-motion" may be too hyperactive and outdoorsy for pure Gnostics, but I think of it as a Gnostic quest anyway, and it is certainly a feminist quest, and I know I am making up a tradition as I go along.[31]

In addition to helping her formulate a dualistic belief system, the texts from the Nag Hammadi Library could have been a model for some of the structural shifts in Hillman's aesthetic, for they are full of odd punctuation, unclosed brackets, parentheses, blank spaces and fragmentary phrases, as in "The Thought of Norea" that begins: "Father of All, [Ennoia] of the Light [dwelling in the heights above the (regions) below, Light dwelling [in the] heights, Voice of Truth, upright Nous, untouchable Logos, and [ineffable] Voice, [incomprehensible] Father!"[32]

While *Bright Existence* and *Death Tractates* gesture toward formal innovation, with the publication of *Loose Sugar* Hillman makes her affinities with an experimental, process-oriented poetics even clearer, continuing to engage with ancient Gnostic beliefs and adding the arcane science of alchemy, the more modern science of cosmology, and the pseudo-science of Star Trek to her frames of reference. She also explicitly engages with the debate between experimental and expressive language at the level of form and content, and demonstrates that the tension between the two modes has tremendous generative power. Continuing to explore issues of the body and the spirit, Hillman self-consciously takes up many of the complex themes that are central to current literary theoretical discourse: the constitution of the self, the operations of language, the nature of memory and the status of the unconscious, the possibility of a feminine language, the postcolonial landscape and subject. An allegiance to an experimental mode is signaled by the book's nonlinear elliptical structure, the painterly use of typography and the page, as well as devices such as repetition, fractured syntax, and fragmentation of sentence and phrase. Like other language-oriented writers, Hillman makes the familiar unfamiliar, forcing everyday, ordinary language into unexpected areas of thought and meaning, exposing the artifice of the apparently natural poetic voice.

One thing Hillman explores in this book, and that animates her nonlinear formal experimentation, is her resistance to the notion of progress. In an interview with Richard Deming, she speaks explicitly of wanting to get away from

> the rigid claims of manifest destiny, or the cult of progress that infuses everything, even environmental lingo or psychotherapeutic jargon; sometimes there's something screwed up even about the thoughtless use of certain adverbs and adjectives and certainly about the way of ranking things that stops human life.[33]

Organized around a series of linked terms— "space/time," "time/alchemy," "alchemy/problem," "problem/time," and "time/space"—which are explored, contrasted, and questioned through the five sections they name— *Loose Sugar* resists our desire for progression and disrupts the conventions of the standard poetry book on many levels. The structure emphasizes circularity, with the titles connecting in a mobius-strip fashion. The final section, "time/space," loops back to the beginning but also to "time/ alchemy," and by giving the first poem in that final section the title "The Unbeginning," Hillman underscores the lack of distinction between the end and the beginning. "Thicket Group" in "space/time," and "(visitor fragments)" in "time/alchemy" are sections-within-a-section, and brief parenthetical asides that appear on unnumbered pages are simply listed as "(interruption)" in the table of contents. These breaks in sequence and unconventional groupings force the reader to recognize that ultimately any ordering is arbitrary; what is contained within a section will not necessarily be consistent, for the poems may be related in ways that are not immediately obvious.

While each section is loosely organized around a theme—early sex; United States policies toward natural resources, the homeless, and other nations; depression and the development of the ego/psyche; the overcommitted, overloaded nature of contemporary life; and memories from early childhood—they circle back and refer forward thematically and imagistically, as well as structurally. In the section called "alchemy/problem," progress and development are connected to individual health and happiness, while in "space/time" the same concepts are related to the industrialization of Brazil; the notion that the world is made up of innumerable invisible particles appears in "problem/time" as a consideration of "leptons" and "quarks" in "The Particles," and in "time/space" as sugar or particles of quartz that make up a statue of Christ in "The Corcovado."

The section pages include paired epigrams that set up a dualism or disruptive clash between ideas as well. The first section, "space/time," juxtaposes Stephen Hawking's description of space-time as "The four dimensional space whose points are events" with the lines "And what you see outside of you / you see inside of you . . ." (*LS*, 1), an excerpt from "Thunder, Perfect Mind," a Gnostic text that the commentary in *The Nag Hammadi Library in English* explains is "a revelation discourse by a female figure."[34] Hillman pits scientific concepts about time, which can be aligned with masculine knowledge, against the contradictory, irrational discourse of a spiritual feminine speaker. "The Spark," which is the first poem in the book, explores early sexuality and the ways young men and women (re)create each other as sexual beings through that discovery:

> on the back and forth blanket
> from the fathers' cars—
> they lay down with you, and when
> did you start missing them.

As Sacramento missed its yellow dust 1852.
When did you start missing those
who invented your body with their sparks—(*LS,* 4)

The poem employs a fairly conventional lyric line but also addresses the process of composition: "Start the memory now,/you who let your life be invented/though not being invented had been more available" (*LS,* 3). From the very beginning of the book, Hillman hovers on that edge between self-expressive and self-reflexive. "The Spark" incorporates interruptions in syntax and uses repetition, "Showers of sparks/between nineteen sixty eight and the//hands were sleek/with asking sleek with asking;—" (*LS,* 4) in a way that seems true to an experience of sexuality that blurs the boundaries between mind and body, thought and sensation, self and other. At the same time, there is a movement toward epiphany and closure at the end of the poem:

when he comes to you
in the revolving dusk,
his full self lighting candles, a little smoke
he sings, the fire
you already own so you can stop
not letting him;

all love is representative
of the beginning of time. When you are loved
the darkness carries you.
When you are loved, you are golden—(*LS,* 5–6)

Hillman immediately moves away from the certainty of that final statement by following "The Spark" with an untitled, parenthetical self-reflexive comment— "(that's good, you got there;/should you make it/part of the record?)" (*LS,* 7). This calls attention to the tremendous energy and effort involved in arriving, the provisional nature of the insight about love that closes the poem, and the fact that the "The Spark" is only a single entry in an endless ledger.

Poems such as "The Spark," "Orion's Belt," and "Time's Body," among others, explore and expose process in a way that is similar to the poems in *Bright Existence* and *Death Tractates.* But in addition to this exploration of process and the elliptical structure of the book, what marks *Loose Sugar* as a new enterprise for Hillman is a more painterly use of typography and the page. Making use of the page as a space or screen can call attention to the materiality of language and the process of exclusion/inclusion in the making of the poem. As Kathleen Fraser explains, "Expanding onto the FULL PAGE—responding to its spatial invitation to play with typographic

relations of words and alphabets, as well as their denotative meanings—
has delivered visual-minded poets from the closed, airless containers of the
well-behaved poem into a writing practice that foregrounds the investiga-
tion and pursuit of the unnamed."[35] "Chevron Tankers," a series of frag-
ments that focus on the military-industrial complex and the environmen-
tally devastating Chevron oil spill off the coast of California, is arranged as
a series of incomplete sentences with a short graphic line marking a separa-
tion between each phrase:

———————

some of the tankers seem to have guns on your birthday
———————
the ensign comes up from the boiler room; I'm sorry he says
    the Admiral can't see you
    ———————(LS, 33)

Visually, this creates the effect of a rigidly imposed order that draws atten-
tion to the attempts to mask the "newspeak" and miscommunication asso-
ciated with government policy on such disasters—the ensign and the admi-
ral—and the devastating results of the spill: "oil which once was opal
beauty under the ice with a war which got into the wings of birds" (LS,
34). The order of the sentences is somewhat arbitrary, and no apparent
progress is made. The lack of movement or progress in the poem mirrors
the static nature of the situation.

Embedded in the "space/time" section, "Thicket Group" is a series that
also makes use of the innovative page. Each poem in the group includes
phrases and words that did not make it into the centered "body" of the
poem and appear at the bottom right-hand corner of the page like unnum-
bered footnotes. The fragments could be phrases that were discarded but
saved for later or marginal notes that sparked the central idea. Two images,
"mottled doves" and "garnets," are lined up on the bottom margin of the
page on which "A Power" appears. How they are related to the main body
of the poem goes unexplained, but they call attention to the process of com-
position. The sequence of poems called "Blue Codices," in the
"alchemy/problem" section of the book, uses the page in a similar way:
groupings of incomplete sentences and phrases appear on the bottom mar-
gin of each page. The series is subtitled "(a cycle of poems on depression
and alchemy)," and the alchemical process they describe seems to have
twelve stages. In an explanatory note, Hillman connects the phrases at the
bottom of the page to the ash at the bottom of the alchemist's furnace, sug-
gesting that these pieces of language, left over from a transformative poetic
process, must also be included. This notion of transformation that includes

what has been excluded is underscored by the subject of the poems in this series, which questions the very human expectation that "sorrow" or depression can be moved through. In "the cave" the speaker asks, "so what good is this work? . . .// And if at the end of healing there is nothing?" (*LS*, 67).

Loose Sugar is clearly Hillman's most experimental volume to date. But even here, she does not completely abandon lyric expressiveness, nor does she unhesitatingly throw in her lot with the anti-aestheticians. While loose in style and lineation, many of the poems could stand as self-contained lyrics, and grounding in felt experience continues to inform much of the work. In addition, despite the dualistic, antihierarchical nature of Gnosticism, spirituality of any kind suggests a belief in an order—however contradictory and provisional—that grants meaning to human existence and that by necessity lies outside the structurings of language. As she states in the *Hayden's Ferry* interview: "there are principles in the universe—the main principle . . . is language. . . . It's also equally true that there's something for me—not for everyone—wordlessly present as an image that's not language."[36] While she claims the "self" as "alleged" and more reflexive, negotiated, and multiple than the conventional lyric speaker, in the poem "The Arroyo" she also posits the "danger/of sort of," which she sees as "the new disease and terror/of backward,/convinced one self is not/the way to live because we are lived through," confronting the anxieties that accompany the poststructuralist revelation that language constructs and determines subjectivity and in effect, lives us. Indeed, even as Hillman places the self under interrogation, claiming the fragment as her preferred mode and airing her doubts about "sentences," she also admits that "you need syntax to love"—that expression of feeling that for better or worse remains the domain of the subject (*LS*, 109).

The question of expressive versus self-reflexive language comes sharply and urgently into focus in the final section of the book, which contains the sequence "Loose Sugar." By evoking the theories of French feminist theorist Julia Kristeva, Hillman links the opposition between reflexive and expressive modes to the question of sexual difference, and points toward one possible explanation for why a woman writer may wish to safeguard a place for the subject, albeit a subject-in-process. This sequence of poems calls attention to the operations of language and poetic composition, but also presents a kind of romantic quest for origins as Hillman explores her memories of an early childhood spent in Brazil. In each poem, Hillman presents a different image or set of images that are related to some aspect of her childhood and attempts to depict and decipher "the grainy surface of a screen before the slides are shown" (*LS*, 107). Some poems shift between the present and the past, or consider the development of the sugar industry in Brazil; others detail specific memories: getting stuck in a tram on the way to Sugar Loaf, visiting the statue of Christ the Redeemer that overlooks Rio. In her version of the traditional Romantic quest, Hillman does not seek to recover an idealized, Wordsworthian childhood self that is at one with nature, but to describe a fragmented, elusive, "unbeginning," marked primarily by uncertainty and irretrievable loss and informed by political, economic, and historical contingencies.

Two epigrams allow Hillman to situate this exploration within two competing discourses: the feminism associated with Julia Kristeva's controversial essay "Women's Time," and the political and economic history of Brazil. In evoking the essay "Women's Time," Hillman points to what is powerful and compelling about Kristeva's theories, but also to what is problematic. Kristeva's theory of the monumental and cyclical nature of the maternal, and her ideas about the possibility of a preoedipal, nonsymbolic semiotic "chora" that is outside culture and exists between mother and child provides a model of the feminine that resists and is at odds with the symbolic order. At the same time, while many poststructuralist feminists would suggest that motherhood is an effect or product of culture, by reifying the maternal body Kristeva turns maternity into an essential category and renders the mother as speechless as the infant. Finally, though Kristeva presents the semiotic as an oppositional category, it frankly depends upon and is still in thrall to the symbolic.[37] Hillman conveys the intense longing for lost knowledge that haunts subjectivity while also registering the recognition that no space exists outside of the structuring and controlling domain of culture. She simultaneously aligns herself with and distances herself from Kristeva's compelling but problematic theories. In this way, she continues to interrogate the terms and divisions surrounding what Hank Lazar has called the "turf warfare" of contemporary poetry.[38]

As she does throughout the book, in the series of poems titled "Loose Sugar" Hillman demonstrates her commitment to "fragmentation and interruption as part of the whole and necessity of the poem."[39] Poems end and begin abruptly, syntax and linear logic are disrupted, sentences and lines refer to themselves, and the materiality of language is foregrounded: "These lines settle like the flakes of some mineral," she writes in "The Corcovado," connecting lines of poetry with the granular surface of the Christ statue (LS, 106). The "title" page of the series announces that what follows will be "twelve pieces from behind the slides" but in fact includes twelve titled poems and one untitled fragment. Phrases appear once, then reappear in a different poem, slightly altered. But instead of creating cohesion and harmony, the repetition leads to reevaluation and questioning of the nature of the first instance. As Lyn Hejinian has said of her own use of repetition, it "challenges our inclination to isolate, identify, and limit the burden of meaning given to an event (the sentence or line)."[40] The significance of the number 5 shifts and expands as it comes to represent the curve of the mother's pregnant body, one of the numerals that designates the 1950s, the "'point' where/time meets space" (LS, 99). Each instance expands and shifts the significance of the others and fractures the meaning of the image instead of clearly deepening it. In this case, the mother's body is associated with a cosmological concept (Hawking's space-time), and the period of pregnancy is given a spatial dimension.

Each poem in the sequence is also preceded by a marginal and often parenthetical statement that undercuts the univocality of the speaker and alerts the reader to the processes of writing: to what may precede, be excluded from, underlie and/or inform fully articulated language. These "pre-thoughts" are various in form and content and don't necessarily function in a consistent, predictable relationship to each main text. The parenthetical statement that comes before the poem "Two Mothers" suggests that the text exists prior to the articulated content: "sometimes the text looks down like an adult/when you're trying to remember the content" (LS, 99). In contrast, the "pre-thought" attached to the poem "Stuck Tram" seems to be the literal pretext for writing the poem "(having doubts about events/because events aren't deep enough)" (LS, 102). The poem that follows describes an event that is remembered differently by the speaker and her mother, suggesting the frustrations of memory and the absence of depth or meaning in an experience that they should be able to share. Here the relationship between the marginalia and the poem suggests that the idea comes first and the text or poem follows. These "pre-thoughts" also call attention to the page as a canvas, in a way that is similar to "Blue Codices" and "Thicket Group." Given that Kristeva's "Women's Time" is one of the contexts for the poems in this section of Loose Sugar, Hillman may also be emphasizing the spatial dimension of memories that are associated with the (M)other. In her essay on the ways experimental women poets have used the page as an Olsonian "field," Kathleen Fraser suggests that "the dimensionality of the full page invites multiplicity, synchronicity, elasticity . . . perhaps the very female subjectivity proposed by Julia Kristeva as linking both cyclical and monumental time."[41]

On the other hand, this sequence of poems also shows that Hillman's particular approach to a resistant nonlinear poetics is motivated not only by a desire to call attention to the operations of language—to empty it of affect and pathos, reject the domain of subjectivity, and resist the "official verse culture"—but also by a wish to restore meaning, to come into contact with that which precedes speech and is outside language. In the poem "Two Brothers," which is about the memory of walking down the street in Rio with her two brothers, she writes:

I have doubted my belief in sentences because of their refusal to recall
   certain things.

A way of being satisfied. A sound.

So the wish to restore them "arose"—(*LS,* 101)

Hillman signals her awareness of the self-referential nature of language, of
"sentences," and by placing "arose" in quotation marks tempers the wish
with irony and self-consciousness. But the accumulation of images in the
sequence links this "way of being satisfied" to the preoedipal mother, to
her language, and to her body. Hillman goes on to describe her memory of
walking down Copacabana with her brothers as "a loose agitated bright-
ness/that needs rescuing" (*LS,* 101). This "brightness" is linked to a state
of fusion with the mother, a state of simultaneous being and not being:

   a developing time sandwich holding hands on the black and
       white sidewalk, wavy like the graph of a patient who
       has not been born yet,—(*LS,* 101)

The sidewalk and the "we" are mixed and wavy, emitting a "graph" but
one that does not fully register in the symbolic. The thing or state sought,
this "way of being satisfied," is outside the realm of the symbolic and can
only be represented accurately by eschewing linearity, and logic, for as
Hillman states at the end of the piece, "'to think' means: the looseness is
taken away" (*LS,* 101).

   The looseness Hillman attempts to depict above in "Two Brothers" can
be linked to Kristeva's theories of the semiotic chora, for it points toward
the existence of a "native" language that "sentences" cannot depict, as
well as aspects of early life that the symbolic excludes, and the repression
of an experience of the maternal body that must take place in order for
"thinking" to happen. While the epigram at the beginning of this series of
poems explicitly evokes Kristeva's controversial essay "Women's Time,"
the territory explored can be linked to her other writings on the topic of
motherhood. In particular, Kristeva's ideas about the semiotic and the ma-
ternal chora, presented in "Stabat Mater" and "Revolution in Poetic Lan-
guage," seem to inform Hillman's desire to "recall certain things" and to
explore a "first language" that is associated with the mother and more im-
portantly with the mother's body.[42] Drawing on Lacan's formulation of the
subject as constituted in language through a radical splitting (*Spaltung*),
Kristeva postulates a maternal economy that is anterior to that split and
precedes and opposes the symbolic order. This maternal space is also a di-
mension of language that she designates as semiotic and connects to Plato's
notion of the preconscious womb or chora. The semiotic is "matrix space,

nourishing, unnameable, anterior to the One, to God and, consequently defying metaphysics."[43] Opposed to the symbolic, it is defined by "rupture . . . articulations (rhythm) [that] precede evidence, verisimilitude, spatiality and temporality and sign."[44] Part of Kristeva's project is to assert the positive dimension of this space and to account for the ways the unsignifiable, preoedipal, prelinguistic space of absolute fusion with the mother's body residually asserts itself and informs subjectivity.

Hillman seems to be exploring similar ground in these poems. In "Loose Sugar," she writes: "I hardly remember any sounds from childhood./Leaving them out is second" (*LS*, 103). What seems to be "first" is the loss of a language that is literally the mother's native tongue but also has many other associations: the mother's body; the child's being; the granularity and sweetness of sugar; and love. In "Vanilla Continued" she writes, "A mother equals how little we have of her plus//the fullness her language signifies" (*LS*, 105), suggesting that the few words she does recall—*sorvete*, the word for ice cream, and *acucar*, which means sugar—convey a fullness that sentences from the speaker's "second" language (English) cannot contain. In "Red Fingernails," Hillman suggests a prediscursive space of connection between the mother and child that is also associated with this "first" language:

> the other mother tried to give us her body, painting our fingernails
>   in the kitchen, it was like growing sunsets.
>
> During this time we rarely spoke English; we understood
>   because of what they didn't say. (*LS*, 104)

The nonsyntactical, nonlinear nature of that language for Hillman is clear, for she describes herself as alternately "dissolving" and "dwelling" upon her mother's tongue, suggesting a state of fusion that corresponds with Kristeva's semiotic. The brothers' "sea babble," which is the element the speaker moves through in "Two Brothers," also seems like a version of the inchoate, inarticulate "chora." Part of what these poems attempt is a reconnection with that "smooth language" that is lost. The "time" of "rarely speaking English" is associated with pleasure and joy, which exist because "there are delays;/those intervals in bodies where two languages mix/before the first one has to be lifted away—" (*LS*, 104). Kristeva would suggest that the poetic language Hillman produces is an expression of the desire to regain access to that language and return to the site of primal repression: the maternal body. In "Vanilla Continued," Hillman explicitly links that lost language to the mother's body, which "is the loved interval/that leaks out loving," and explains that the "mother's sentence wrenched from her body makes/the unfillable interval" (*LS*, 105).

But the mother's language is a literal language that participates in the symbolic order. Kristeva's semiotic is outside of language, before meaning, and while she claims that it subverts the symbolic order, many readers have taken issue with what on the one hand is understood as the biological determinism of her position and, on the other, as her essentialism.[45] Kristeva provides no possibility of language for the mother; she is enclosed within the semiotic and outside of language. As Kaja Silverman maintains, she is "either fused or confused with her infant, and in the process comes both to be and to inhabit the chora."[46] Hillman avoids the problems of Kristeva's theory by giving the mother's language a symbolic and social register outside of the child's understanding. In Hillman's poems, Portuguese shifts or sifts like sugar between the semiotic and the symbolic, sweetening both. The mother "rejoins her first language so she can live" and the speaker "dwel[ls] for a brief time in a language given up for her" (LS, 104, 108). Instead of engaging in the semiotic/symbolic binarism that forces Kristeva's formulation into the kind of hierarchy she reputedly rejects, Hillman gestures toward that part of memory that cannot be represented in language, evoking the ineffable maternal without occluding the mother's status as a subject in language.

Hillman also explores the maternal as a space in a way that corresponds to Kristeva's ideas about time-space, which she explains in "Women's Time." The epigram "when invoking the name and destiny of women, one thinks more of the space generating and forming the human species than of time" refers specifically to the monumental nature of the maternal (LS, 96). For Kristeva, "woman" is associated with cyclicity and time-space as opposed to linear, historical time, and this is also one of the ideas Hillman considers through memories of her childhood. In "Two Rivers" she writes that "a 'day' slips back and forth in time," suggesting that in the "then" of memory she will always "make numbers" in her mother's "darkness" and "dissolve upon [her] mother's tongue." The mother's darkness is both temporal and the space "in the door to left" and is always and never completely present: "I love her more than I am not here;/she loves us more though near is never reached" (LS, 99). The mother's body comes to signify the ground of being and of language, and yet is impossible to locate, pin down, know. Another criticism that has been leveled at Kristeva's theory of the semiotic chora is that her focus on the cyclical, monumental nature of the maternal elides the connection between the mother and the social field.[47] In poems such as "National Development," which examines her American father's job "aid[ing] development" in Brazil, and by including data about the influence of foreign development on the growth in the sugar crop during the 1950s, Hillman shows that her own development took place within social and economic contexts as well as that of her mother's physical and linguistic tongues. She registers the negative effects of development on the family-run farms of native Brazilians and her own privilege "among the middle classes" (*LS*, 98). In this way, she points to the limitations in Kristeva's theory of maternity, which places the mother outside of and prior to culture. In approaching the subject of her Brazilian childhood, Hillman both gives credence to and questions Kristeva's theories of the feminine, just as she utilizes lyric expressiveness and also exposes the nonsingularity of language, the impossibility of closure.

In the poetic statement included in this volume, Hillman formally acknowledges the falseness of beginnings, of a true or logical order, by arranging the paragraphs in an apparently arbitrary way. But she also acknowledges the importance of the individual writer in the making of the poem:

> Somehow, poems get made by writers with separate bodies and experiences. . . . Even the deepest, most egoless states, where figurative space spins out its position of no position, have to use individuals to become poems.[48]

While she rejects a strictly Romantic vision of the speaking subject and clearly finds the linguistic play and self-consciousness that accompanies a language-oriented approach to writing liberating, Hillman also wishes to retain a place for the subject, to conserve something of the self, even if, as David Wojahn suggests in an enthusiastic review of *Loose Sugar*, what is conserved is "merely the record of its wanderings."[49] Toward the end of the sequence, in "Beach Photos," she writes: "I who have feared outline swell to contain her, write *about* her / though *about* has a hole in it," suggesting the necessity of enacting the demands of subjectivity despite the "leaking" that occurs when we try to put things together (*LS*, 107).

In the most recent work that has been appearing in journals and anthologies—including the poem "A Geology," reprinted in this volume— Hillman continues to experiment with the visual and spatial dimensions of language and the page. In "A Geology," the placement of four words at the corners of each page gives the poem a physical dimension. The words form a border that can be denotatively related to the central poem or can be seen as decorative. Each page can be treated like a dinner plate holding one in a sequence of artfully presented courses that are separate but linked, or a tectonic plate, pushing up against the others, causing shifts and new formations. The "seed words" at the four corners may appear in the body of the poem on the same page, or may appear elsewhere in the poem, or not at all, but they clearly have something to do with the process of the poem's creation.[50] This structure is also tied to the subject matter of the poem. "A Geology" meditates on the geological formation of California and the way land is subject to great shifts, faultlines, earthquakes that are both constructive and destructive, and connects it to human lives, trying to understand physiological or psychological dependencies through the lens of geology: "A geology breaks in half to grow. A person whose drug like/a locust jumps across someone's foot, singing—."[51] The speaking subject shifts between first, second, and third person, dispersed among "I," "she," and "you," but underlying this decentered subjectivity is a sense that an individual's struggle to "quit" a drug is central to the poem. In a collection called *The Firecage Series,* fragmentary phrases appear in the left and right margins and the mathematical symbol "=" appears in the four corners of many pages. But the poetic sequence is clearly driven by felt experience—changes in the body that create altered perceptions and a changed sense of the self and gendered identity—and the use of typography helps to depict that experience without reducing it.[52]

Even with this innovative use of the page, and the continued experimentation with fragment and broken syntax, Hillman situates herself on the divide between the lyric tradition and language poetry. The work is unsettling and compelling because it shifts between the two poles without ever resolving the tensions between them. Hillman expresses and exposes the human drive to take recourse in a stable self, to in effect know and understand the self, but unflinchingly depicts the failure of that quest, the inability to attain meaning in language. While many critics have commented on the easy reductiveness of setting up a division between experimental and expressive writing, few have explored work that cannot be fully accounted for by either term. In showing a clear affinity for both a lyric mode and an experimental approach, Hillman presents and enacts an argument for the dual path, for something in between. Her work makes it clear that a simple division between mainstream and experimental ignores bodies of work that resist easy categorization and might be at home on either side of the divide. Instead of attempting to reconcile the two terms, Hillman explores the unresolvable tension that exists between them, inventing a poetics that draws attention to its own constructions but also retains a tentative faith in communication. In doing so, she provides rich ground for thinking about contemporary American poetry at the turn of the new century.

NOTES

1. In spring 1999 I was asked to present poetics statements at two conferences, *Page Mothers* (a conference for poet-editors organized by Rae Armantrout and Fanny Howe in San Diego in March) and *Where Lyric Tradition Meets Language*

Poetry: Innovation in Contemporary American Poetry by Women (organized by Claudia Rankine and Allison Cummings, held at Barnard College in April). The first version of this statement was written for the panel at the Barnard conference partly in an attempt to speak to the interplay/binary setup by the title of that conference and partly in response to some issues raised by the San Diego conference. Several young women there had asked a version of the age-old question about the relationship between individual writers and tradition, and about what it means to try to "be daring" now. This statement comes from reflecting on their questions and about the general nature of poetic experience. This has been revised somewhat since I read it at Barnard; it is dedicated to Claudia Rankine, with gratitude.

2. Edmund Jabès, *The Book of Questions,* trans. Rosmarie Waldrop, Vol. 1. (Middletown, Conn.: Wesleyan University Press, 1991), 31.

3. André Breton, "First Surrealist Manifesto," in *Surrealism,* ed. Patrick Wallberg (New York: McGraw Hill, 1968), 70.

4. Robert Duncan, "Chapter 5 of Part 1: The H.D. Book," in *The Alchemical Tradition in the Late Twentieth Century,* ed. Richard Grossinger (Berkeley, Calif.: North Atlantic Books, 1991), 203.

5. René Char, "The Slowness of the Future," trans. Gustaf Sobin, in *Selected Poems,* ed. Mary Ann Caws and Tina Jolas (New York: New Directions, 1992), 119.

6. Quoted in Robert Kelly, "An Alchemical Journal" in Grossinger, *Alchemical Tradition,* 118.

7. Walter Benjamin, *Selected Writings,* vol. 1, ed. Marcus Bullock and Michael Jennings (Cambridge: Harvard University Press, 1968), 65.

8. I am using the label avant-garde not in reference to a particular historical moment, but more broadly. While it is has become commonplace to claim that postmodernism has rendered the term meaningless, it is still useful in reference to the clear divisions that characterize the field of contemporary poetry. In *Radical Artifice: Writing Poetry in the Age of Media* (Chicago: University of Chicago Press, 1991), Marjorie Perloff convincingly argues for the continuing efficacy of the term, and Christopher Beach makes a strong case for its sociological as well aesthetic relevance in "Poetic Positionings: Stephen Dobyns and Lyn Hejinian in Cultural Context," *Contemporary Literature* 38(1) (Spring 1997): 44–77.

9. Charles Bernstein, *Content's Dream: Essays, 1975–1984* (Los Angeles: Sun & Moon Press, 1986), 233.

10. For further discussion, see Hank Lazar, *Opposing Poetries: Issues and Institutions* (Evanston, Ill.: Northwestern University Press, 1996); Alan Golding, *From Outlaw to Classic: Canons in American Poetry* (Madison: University of Wisconsin Press, 1995); and Jed Rasula, *The American Poetry Wax Museum* (Urbana, Ill.: NCTE, 1995). Many critics have taken issue with the impulse to label and define the two schools. Michael Greer's essay, "Ideology and Theory in Recent Experimental Writing or The Naming of 'Language Poetry'," *Boundary* 2 16 (1989): 335–55, suggests that language-oriented writing cannot be made to fit under a single banner and presents insightful commentary on the ways the category of "language poetry" reduces a diverse and complex writing practice into something definable and ultimately consumable.

11. Ron Silliman, "Poetry and the Politics of the Subject: A Bay Area Sampler," *Socialist Review* 18(3) (1988): 63.

12. For further discussion of the efficacy of representational language in women's writing, see Alicia Ostriker, *Stealing the Language: The Emergence of Women's Poetry in America* (Boston: Beacon Press, 1986); Nancy Miller, *Subject to Change: Reading Feminist Writing* (New York: Columbia University Press, 1988); and Marianne DeKoven, "Male Signature, Female Aesthetic: The Gender Politics of Experimental Writing," in *Breaking the Sequence: Women's Experimental Fiction*, ed. Ellen G. Friedman and Miriam Fuchs (Princeton: Princeton University Press, 1989), 72–81.

13. See, for example, *Feminist Poetics: A Consideration of Female Construction of Language*, ed. Kathleen Fraser (San Francisco: San Francisco State University Press, 1984), and Rachel Blau DuPlessis, *The Pink Guitar: Writing as Feminist Practice* (New York and London: Routledge, 1990), as well as essays by Lyn Hejinian and Rae Armantrout noted below.

14. Kathleen Fraser, "Line. On the Line. Lining up. Lined with. Between the Lines. Bottom Line," in *The Line in Postmodern Poetry*, ed. Robert Frank and Henry Sayre (Urbana and Chicago: University of Illinois Press, 1988), 153.

15. DeKoven, "Male Signature, Female Aesthetic," 75. For further discussion of the relationship between feminism and avant-garde poetics see Susan Rubin Suleiman, "Pornography, Transgression and the Avant-Garde: Bataille's *Story of the Eye*," in *Poetics of Gender*, ed. Nancy Miller (New York: Columbia University Press, 1986), 117–35.

16. Rae Armantrout, "Feminist Poetics and the Meaning of Clarity," in *Artifice and Indeterminacy: An Anthology of New Poetics*, ed. Christopher Beach (Tuscaloosa: University of Alabama Press, 1998), 293.

17. For further discussion of the subversive possibilities of a feminist experimentalist aesthetic see Juliana Spahr, "Resignifying Autobiography: Lyn Hejinian's *My Life*," *American Literature* 68(1) (March 1996): 139–57, and Linda A. Taylor "'A Seizure of Voice': Language Innovation and Feminist Poetics in the Works of Kathleen Fraser," *Contemporary Literature* 33(2) (1992): 337–71. In "Contemporary Women's Poetry: Experimentalism and the Expressive Voice," *Critical Quarterly* 36 (3) (Autumn 1994): 34–52, Clair Wills argues that the work of some experimental women writers does not completely move away from expressivity or interiority. She cites the poetry of Lyn Hejinian and Denise Riley as examples of work that depicts "the ways in which [the] private or intimate realm of experience is constructed 'through' the public, and therefore elements of expressivity, though radically divorced from notions of authenticity are present" (42).

18. Spahr, "Resignifying Autobiography," 147.

19. Lyn Hejinian, "The Rejection of Closure," in *Moving Borders: Three Decades of Innovative Writing By Women*, ed. Mary Margaret Sloan (New Jersey: Talisman House, 1998), 619.

20. Hejinian, "The Rejection of Closure," 619.

21. From "Split, Spark, Space: A Poetics of Shared Custody," an unpublished essay forthcoming in *New Writings on Poetics and Motherhood*, eds. Patricia Dienstfrey and Brenda Hillman.

22. Hillman seems to wish to avoid some of the dangers of language-oriented writing that Charles Altieri discusses in his essay on radical and avant-garde poetics, "Some Problems about Agency in the Theories of Radical Poetries," *Contemporary Literature* 33(2) (1996): 207–36. Worried that practitioners of language-oriented writing may be too willing to sacrifice "an exemplary authorial presence engaged with questions of choice and value [that] situat[es] the self in relation to external pressures," he calls for a poetics that is conscious of the "material and ideological density of language" but also provides models of "human agency." He is interested in alternatives to mainstream "enervated romantic lyricism" but believes that "the working of language itself [should not be] the primary source of visions of agency" (208–09). He goes on to suggest that one potential problem with radical poetics is that in resisting dominant structures, these poets risk ignoring "the possibilities that the text as structure, as willed object rather than as object of free play, can actually modify beliefs and provide alternative modes of sensibility" (213).

23. Quotations from Brenda Hillman's works are cited in the text with the following abbreviations: *BE* = *Bright Existence, DT* = *Death Tractates, LS* = *Loose Sugar,* and *WD* = *White Dress.* When lines are sufficiently located, as by the titles of short poems, or sections of longer poems, no citation appears.

24. Jorn Ake, "Spark in the Thicket: An Interview with Brenda Hillman," *Hayden's Ferry Review* (Fall/Winter 1997): 12.

25. Ibid., 11.

26. For historical and philosophical accounts of Gnosticism see Hans Jonas's *Gnostic Religion: The Message of the Alien God and the Beginnings of Christianity* (Boston: Beacon Press, 1958), or Elaine Pagels more recent book, *The Gnostic Gospels* (New York: Random House, 1979).

27. Brenda Hillman, "Dark Turtles and Bright Turtles," in *Where We Stand: Women Poets on Literary Tradition,* ed. Sharon Bryan (New York and London: W. W. Norton, 1993), 89.

28. Pagels, *The Gnostic Gospels,* 49.

29. "On the Origin of the World," in *The Nag Hammadi Library in English,* ed. James M. Robinson (San Francisco: HaperSanFrancisco, 1990), 172.

30. For a series of commentaries on the representation of gender in Gnostic texts see *Images of the Feminine in Gnosticism,* ed. Karen L. King (Philadelphia: Fortress Press, 1988).

31. Hillman, "Dark Turtles and Bright Turtles," 89–90.

32. "The Thought of Norea," in *The Nag Hammadi Library in English,* 445.

33. Richard Deming, "Poetry and the Rind of What Is," *The Journal* 24:1 (Spring 2000), 74–89.

34. "Thunder, Perfect Mind," in *The Nag Hammadi Library in English,* 295.

35. Kathleen Fraser, "Translating the Unspeakable: Visual Poetics, as Projected through Olson's 'Field' into Current Female Writing Practice," in *Moving Borders: Three Decades of Innovative Writing By Women,* ed. Mary Margaret Sloan (New Jersey: Talisman House, 1998), 642.

36. Ake, "Spark in the Thicket," 29.

37. See Judith Butler, "The Body Politics of Julia Kristeva," in *Ethics, Politics and Difference in Julia Kristeva's Writing,* ed. Kelly Oliver (New York and London:

Routledge 1993), 164–77. Butler argues that Kristeva's theory of the semiotic depends upon and reproduces the paternal law she seeks to displace.

38. Lazar, *Opposing Poetries,* 38.

39. Ake, "Spark in the Thicket," 13.

40. Hejinian, "The Rejection of Closure," 623.

41. Fraser, "Translating the Unspeakable," 642. Fraser demonstrates that Charles Olson's manifesto, "Projective Verse," though apparently addressed to men in "territorial inclusive/exclusive boy-talk," gave many women writers permission to explore the "page as canvas or screen on which to project flux" (642). She discusses the work of Susan Howe, Myung Mi Kim, and Hannah Wiener, among others.

42. Both of these essays can be found in *The Kristeva Reader,* ed. Toril Moi (New York: Columbia University Press, 1986).

43. Julia Kristeva, "Women's Time," *The Kristeva Reader,* 191.

44. Julia Kristeva, "Revolution in Poetic Language," *The Kristeva Reader,* 94.

45. See Butler, "Body Politics," as well as Linda Zerilli, "A Process without a Subject: Simone de Beauvoir and Julia Kristeva on Maternity," *Signs: Journal of Women in Culture and Society* 18(1) (Autumn 1992): 111–34, which outlines the ways Kristeva misses and misunderstands the radical nature of de Beauvoir's vision of maternity, and see also Elizabeth Grosz's chapter on Kristeva in *Sexual Subversions: Three French Feminists* (St. Leonards, Australia: Allen and Unwin, 1989).

46. Kaja Silverman, *The Acoustic Mirror: The Female Voice in Psychoanalysis and Cinema* (Bloomington: Indiana University Press, 1988), 13.

47. See Mary Caputi, "Identity and Nonidentity in Aesthetic Theory," *Differences: A Journal of Feminist Critical Studies* 8(3) (1996): 128–47, which offers a corrective to Kristeva's theory of the repressed maternal through Adorno's theories of identity.

48. Paragraph 8 in Brenda Hillman, "Twelve Writings toward a Poetics of Alchemy, Dread, Inconsistency, Betweenness, and California Geological Syntax," published in this volume.

49. David Wojahn, "Survivalist Selves," review of *Loose Sugar, The Kenyon Review* 20(3–4) (Summer–Fall 1998): 182.

50. See paragraph 8 of Hillman's poetic statement in this volume.

51. Brenda Hillman, "A Geology," reprinted at the beginning of this chapter.

52. Several poems from this series appeared in *Hayden's Ferry Review* (Fall/Winter 1997): 31–34.

BIBLIOGRAPHY

Books by Brenda Hillman

Autumn Sojurn. Mill Valley: Em Press, 1994.
Bright Existence. Middletown, Conn.: Wesleyan University Press, 1993.
Coffee 3 A.M. Lincoln, Nebraska: Penumbra Press, 1982.

Death Tractates. Hanover and London: Wesleyan University Press, 1993.
Emily Dickinson: Poems. Edited by Brenda Hillman. Boston: Shambhala, 1995.
The Firecage. San Francisco: a+ bend press, 2000.
Fortress. Hanover: Wesleyan University Press, 1989.
Loose Sugar. Hanover and London: Wesleyan University Press, 1997.
White Dress. Middletown, Conn.: Wesleyan University Press, 1985.

Selected Prose

"The Artful Dare: Barbara Guest's *Selected Poems*" *Talisman* 16 (Fall 1996): 207–20.
"A Cadenced Privacy," in *By Herself.* Edited by Molly McQuade. Minneapolis: Graywolf, 2000.
"Crossing the Garden Re: Rae Armantrout's Metaphysics," *A Wild Salience: The Writing of Rae Armantrout.* Edited by Tom Beckett. Cleveland: Burning Press, 2000.
"Dark Turtles and Bright Turtles," in *Where We Stand: Women Poets on Literary Tradition.* Edited by Sharon Bryan. New York and London: W. W. Norton, 1993: 87–92.
"Keelan's City," *Bellingham Review* 12:1 (Summer 1999): 21–24.

Interviews

"Poetry and the Rind of What Is," interview by Richard Deming, forthcoming in *The Journal.*
"The Positive Darkness: Talking with Brenda Hillman," interview by Dorianne Laux in *Poetry Flash* 251 (March/April 1994): 1, 4–9.
"Spark in the Thicket: An Interview with Brenda Hillman," interview by Jorn Ake in *Hayden's Ferry Review* (Fall/Winter 1997): 9–30.
"A Talk with Brenda Hillman," interview by Lily Iona Soucie in *Indiana Review* (Fall 1990): 63–70.

Selected Criticism

Bedient, Calvin. 1993. "The Reluctant Gnostic." *The Threepenny Review* (Summer): 1–2.
Boruch, Marie. 1986. "Foundations." Review of *White Dress. Ohio Review* 36: 123–32.
Brown-Davidson, Terri. 1994. Review of *Death Tractates. Prairie Schooner* 68(2) (Summer): 168–71.
Corn, Alfred. 1990. Review of *Fortress. The Nation* 250(13) (2 April): 463–64.
Dean, Lance. "Occupying the Borders." Review of *Death Tractates. American Book Review* 16(3) (August–September): 1994): 23.
Frost, Elizabeth. 1993. Review of *Bright Existence* and *Death Tractates. The Women's Review of Books* 10(8) (May): 24–26.

Garber, Frederick. 1985. "Geographies and Languages and Selves and What They Do." Review of *White Dress. American Poetry Review* 14(5): 14–21.

Greenberg, Pamela. 1997. Review of *Loose Sugar. Harvard Review* 3 (Winter): 156–57.

Hoagland, Tony. 1990. "Mythologies of the Self." Review of *Fortress. The Threepenny Review* (Summer): 21–22.

———. 1995. "Body and Soul." Review of *Bright Existence. Gettysburg Review* 8 (Summer): 505–22.

Hoey, Allen. 1993. "The Year in Poetry." In *Contemporary Literary Criticism: Yearbook 1992*, ed. James P. Draper (Detroit: Gale Research), 11–17.

Jarman, Mark. 1993. "Journals of the Soul." Review of *Bright Existence. The Hudson Review* 46 (Summer): 421–31.

Johnson, Judith E. 1997. "Deep Noticing." Review of *Loose Sugar. The Women's Review of Books* 14(10/11) (July): 28–30.

Johnston, Devin. 1997. Review of *Loose Sugar. Chicago Review* 43(3) (Summer): 110–14.

Keelan, Claudia. 1993. "Missing Her." Review of *Death Tractates* and *Bright Existence. Poetry Flash* 245 (April–May): 1, 8–12.

Mullen, Laura. 1999. "Active Magic." Review of Loose Sugar. *Denver Quarterly Review* 34(1) (Spring): 105–15.

Muske, Carol. 1997. "Time Into Language." Review of *Loose Sugar. The Nation* 265(3) (21 July): 36–39.

Reeve, F. D. 1995. "Making It Newer." Review of *Bright Existence. Michigan Quarterly Review* 34(3) (Summer): 444–56.

Revell, Donald. 1990. "Without a Golden Age: Genre in Diaspora." *American Poetry Review* 19(4) (July/August): 7–12.

Silberg, Richard. 1992. "New and Noted." Review of *Death Tractates. Poetry Flash* (August): 28.

———. 1997. "Opening Up the Package." Review of *Loose Sugar. Poetry Flash* (June/July): 1, 12, 15.

Svoboda, Terese. 1997. Review of *Loose Sugar. Boston Review* 22(2) (April/May): 40–42.

Williamson, Alan. 1993. "Stories about the Self." Review of *Bright Existence. American Poetry Review* 22(5) (September/October): 21–23.

Wilson, Leila. 1997. Review of *Loose Sugar. Indiana Review* (Fall): 171–72.

Winter, Max. 1997. "Loosening the World's Grip." Review of *Loose Sugar. Boston Book Review* (April 1): 42.

Wojahn, David. 1998. "Survivalist Selves." Review of *Loose Sugar. The Kenyon Review* 20(3–4) (Summer–Fall): 180–90.

Wronsky, Gail. 1994. "Splendid Investigations." Review of *Death Tractates. The Antioch Review* 52(1) (Winter): 153–56.

Young, David. 1998. "Looking for Landscapes." Review of *Loose Sugar. Field* 58 (Summer): 75–88.

SUSAN HOWE

FROM *CHAIR*

A moveable seat; a seat of justice, or of authority; a vehicle born by men,
a sedan.

Thomas Sheridan,

*A Complete Dictionary of the English Language, both with regard to
sound and meaning.*

Lady M.   When all's done,

You look but on a stool.

Macbeth IV iii

Plain chair or two back

to use frame metaphor

Any period tack or nail

shank left as document

Art has filled my days

Strange and familiar not

for embellishment but

object as it is in itself

Poem I'm my own master

Go bid time notify what

frame to hastily make fit

Chairs chairs with covers

Go carefully study who will

read you then the author

The Authorized reads Why

do the heathen rage and

people imagine Lord *why*

Document bolster mattress

more firmly than at first

half or if edge underside

Chronicle you think you

put sackcloth at edge to

settle forever underside

more finely than at first

Woe extant in particular

So it goes to metre and her

winding step leafage as

mere answering silk she

comes to us anonymous

Cross even that remnant

Fabric enwrought is but

coarse-grain or worsted

Knowledge of slipcovers

Boston interest given to

James Alexander pattern

known as apotheosis of

George Washington in

yarn with sorrow between

All material dreams are

At first glass windows were

made to be taken out little

furniture for the intelligent

What can date a chair inertia

Nail heads or screw points

Little communities include

innovators one local builder

may have traveled from east

to see a house for its façade

pierced with five openings

Muslin cathedral ancestors

1239 first glass windows

Still needle historians older

than pen in backward time

To Cromwellian upholsterer

Symbolism's sealed look

Lucia holding a lamp Saint

Olivia hung up by her hair

One of the most once mis-

understood materials in

decorative art studies has

been turkey-work no clue

given as to why a colony

of refugee weavers weave

undoubtedly scrap arras

Wrong of other to others

turkey-work apart theory

Turkey-work frames are

made to fit the covers *en*

suite as one may guess

in dreams all material is

and turkey-work palpably

reveals material parallels

Refugee weavers no clue

in decorative art studies

The disciple James rests

his arm on a transitional

William-and–Mary Queen

Anne style side chair in

the Connecticut Historical

Society

Robinson Crusoe on his

island never achieved a

chair

Six legged William-and–Mary

high-chest with bold figures

Japanning in its strictest sense

Figured monsters shackled

Boston japanners simplified the

European process a C-scroll

carved in high relief the figure-

eight motif signed Cogswell

From principle I wish to do

right he would say Beauty

is a serpentine line typography

to economics establishment

of a chair type or a tale told

Wrong of wrong to others

Introduced pulpit a compact one

for a preacher to rest his arm

The first mahogany years

lion or satyr mask rarely

Settee petit point needlework

minstrelsies every night

Skip that chair anyone can

Revert to leaf-carved foot

Connecticut river valley door-

ways look for Huguenot or

west countrymen after 1800

the heart and crown tradition

Splintered disjunction of form

and content swift unrelenting

change a given craftsman two

Swedish smiths who make

hatchets knives scythes *transi*

To the Compiler of Memories

Frequent exposure to night air

An inattention to the necessity

of changing damp clothes

Sweet affliction sweet affliction

Singing as I wade to heaven

POETIC STATEMENT

There Are Not Leaves Enough to Crown to Cover to Crown to Cover

FOR ME there was no silence before armies.
I was born in Boston Massachusetts on June 10th, 1937, to an Irish mother and an American father. My mother had come to Boston on a short visit two years earlier. My father had never been to Europe. She is a wit and he was a scholar. They met at a dinner party when her earring dropped into his soup.

By 1937 the Nazi dictatorship was well-established in Germany. All dissenting political parties had been liquidated and Concentration camps had already been set up to hold political prisoners. The Berlin-Rome axis was a year old. So was the Spanish Civil War. On April 25th Franco's Lufftwaffe pilots bombed the village of Guernica. That November Hitler and the leaders of his armed forces made secret plans to invade Austria, Czechoslovakia, Poland, and Russia.

In the summer of 1938 my mother and I were staying with my grandmother, uncle, aunt, great-aunts, cousins, and friends in Ireland, and I had just learned to walk, when Czechoslovakia was dismembered by Hitler, Ribbentrop, Mussolini, Chamberlin, and Daladier, during the Conference and Agreement at Munich. That October we sailed home on a ship crowded with refugees fleeing various countries in Europe.

When I was two the German army invaded Poland and World War II began in the West.

The fledgling Republic of Ireland distrusted England with good reason, and remained neutral during the struggle. But there was the Battle of the Atlantic to be won, so we couldn't cross the sea again until after 1945. That half of the family was temporarily cut off.

In Buffalo New York, where we lived at first, we seemed to be safe. We were there when my sister was born and the Japanese bombed Pearl Harbor.

Now there were armies in the west called East.

American fathers marched off into the hot chronicle of global struggle but mothers were left. Our law-professor father, a man of pure principles, quickly included violence in his principles, put on a soldier suit and disappeared with the others into the thick of the threat to the east called West.

> B u f f a l o
> 12. 7. 41
>
> (Late Afternoon light.)
> (Going to meet him in snow.)
>
> HE
> (Comes through the hall door.)

The research of scholars, lawyers, investigators, judges
   Demands!

> SHE
> (With her arms around his neck
> whispers.)

Herod had all the little children murdered!

It is dark
The floor is ice

they stand on the edge of a hole singing—

In Rama
Rachel weeping for her children

refuses
to be comforted

because they *are* not.

Malice dominates the history of Power and Progress. History is the record of winners. Documents were written by the Masters. But fright is formed by what we see not by what they say.

From 1939 until 1946 in news photographs, day after day I saw signs of culture exploding into murder. Shots of children being herded into trucks by hideous helmeted conquerors—shots of children who were orphaned and lost—shots of the emaciated bodies of Jews dumped into mass graves on top of more emaciated bodies—nameless numberless men women and children, uprooted in a world almost demented. God had abandoned them to history's sovereign Necessity.

If to see is to *have* at a distance, I had so many dead Innocents distance was abolished. Substance broke loose from the domain of time and obedient intention. I became part of the ruin. In the blank skies over Europe I was Strife represented.

Things overlap in space and are hidden. Those black and white picture shots—moving or fixed—were a subversive generation. "The hawk, with his long claws/Pulled down the stones./The dove, with her rough bill/Brought me them home."

> Buffalo roam in herds
> up the broad streets connected by boulevards
>
> and fences
>
> their eyes are ancient and a thousand years
> too old
>
> hear murder throng their muting
>
> Old as time in the center of a room
> doubt is spun
>
> and measured
>
> Throned wrath
> I know your worth
>
> a chain of parks encircles the city

Pain is nailed to the landscape in time. Bombs are seeds of Science and the Sun.

2,000 years ago the dictator Creon said to Antigone who was the daughter of Oedipus and Jocasta: "Go to the dead and love them."

Life opens into conceptless perspectives. Language surrounds Chaos.

During World War II my father's letters were a sign he was safe. A miniature photographic negative of his handwritten message was reproduced by the army and a microfilm copy forwarded to us. IN the top left-hand corner someone always stamped PASSED BY EXAMINER.

This is my historical consciousness. I have no choice in it. In my poetry, time and again, questions of assigning *the cause* of history dictate the sound of what is thought.

    Summary of fleeting summary
    Pseudonym cast across empty

    Peak proud heart

    Majestic caparisoned cloud cumuli
    East sweeps hewn flank

    Scion on a ledge of Constitution
    Wedged sequences of system

    Causeway of faint famed city
    Human ferocity

    Dim mirror Naught formula
    archaic hallucinatory laughter

    Kneel to intellect in our work
    Chaos cast cold intellect back

Poetry brings similitude and representation to configurations waiting from forever to be spoken. North Americans have tended to confuse human fate with their own salvation. In this I am North American. "We are coming Father Abraham, three hundred thousand more," sang the Union troops at Gettysburg.

I write to break out into perfect primeval Consent. I wish I could tenderly lift from the dark side of history, voices that are anonymous, slighted—inarticulate.

ARTICULATING THE INARTICULATE

Singularities and the Countermethod in Susan Howe

Ming-Qian Ma

> Outside the central disciplines of Economy, Anthropology, and Historiography is a gap in causal sequence. A knowing excluded from knowing.
>
> Susan Howe, "The Difficulties Interview"

> A task of poetry is to make audible (*tangible* but not necessarily *graspable*) those dimensions of the real that cannot be heard as much as to imagine new reals that have never before existed.
>
> Charles Bernstein, *A Poetics*

> The limits of my language mean the limits of my world.
>
> Ludwig Wittgenstein, *Tractatus Logico-Philosophicus*

"IF WRITTEN Is Writing," the title of Lyn Hejinian's essay collected in *The L=A=N=G=U=A=G=E Book,* bodies forth a central pronouncement of Language poetry. Itself only a conditional clause, the title is, of course, incomplete both in syntax and in logic. The absence of an apodosis, while disrupting a structure as a form of reason, frees from the conventional epistemological boundaries new configurations, ones that point, as Charles Bernstein notes, to the "new—in the sense of uncharted or undiscovered (*unarticulated*)—worlds within language" (1992, 180). Further, the resistance to syntactical/logical closure exemplified by the title can be realized only through a radical language praxis, a praxis constitutive of a shift from "written" to "writing," as is suggested in the title.

Hejinian's linguistic shift from the past participle ("written") to the present one ("writing") epitomizes the critical issue that has occupied center stage, both in theory and in practice, in Language poetry: the status of language and its concomitant implications. If conceptualized and put to use as something always already happened, completed, or established, as the definition of the past participle dictates, language, Hejinian seems to argue, is in actuality isolated from the dynamic sphere of human activity.

The estrangement of language from the complexity of everyday existence, in turn, transforms it into what Michael Davidson describes as "a static paradigm of rules and features" (1984, 198). Endowed, nonetheless, with an autonomy transcending the world, this "static paradigm" assumes an *a priority* manifested in being "omniscient," the etymology of which specifies its major constituents as, rather revealingly, "ML *omniscientia*, fr. L *omni* [all] + *scientia* knowledge—see more at SCIENCE" (*Webster's*). Formulaic in structure and prescriptive (as descriptive) in function, language as such is not only "meaning-referential," as Jerome McGann argues (1987, 265), but also, according to Don Byrd, "theoretical," in that it is always "biased toward the general case" (1994, 36). The present participle, by contrast, designates language as being active, as an ongoing process in which meaning becomes constitutive (1987, 265). For the physicality of such language activity refuses to be selective, thus allowing for local, contingent, or chancy occurrences, occurrences embodying "those dimensions of the real" (Bernstein 1992, 184) otherwise erased or glossed over.

This shift from "written" to "writing" is then substantiated in the essay as a shift from what Hejinian calls, with a brilliant critical insight, seeking "a vocabulary for ideas" to seeking "ideas for vocabularies" (1984a, 29). The exchange of syntactical positions between "vocabulary" and "ideas" as the object of the verb, together with the change of "vocabulary" from singular to plural, bespeaks a paradigmatic turning point in language praxis that calls for a critical reassessment of language in relation to knowledge.

In this respect, Don Byrd, in his study of postmodern poetics, presents some pertinent historical overviews. Byrd observes that deeply rooted in the Western metaphysical tradition is "The thought of language as an extra-ontological structure. . . . As an independent subjective structure that describes all ontological possibilities" (1994, 194)—so much so that "Since the seventeenth century, if not since the sixth century B.C.," he affirms, "the formal structure of language has been confused with the structure of mind and world" (10). The fast advent and dazzling vigor of cognitive sciences in the seventeenth century, in particular, fostered what Byrd calls a "Cartesian position," one that "represents a change in desire, a reassessment of the relation between thought and the physical world" (1994, 62), culminating in Descartes's statement that "There is need of a method for finding out the truth" (qtd. in Byrd 1994, 65). This method, Byrd points out, is realized in a "formal system or linguistic machine" intended and constructed accordingly to provide "a complex descriptive model . . . substituted for nature, so *something* in the model corresponded to *everything* in nature" (29). As such, the Cartesian method represents a form of reason, "directed toward rational control of the unruly linguistic machine that generates its illusory worlds" (107).

In this "methodological reduction of multiplicity to universal rules," logic, the sole motor power driving the epistemological enterprise, becomes but "a collection of techniques for a theater, a representational space. It accounts adequately, therefore, for closure, for endings and deaths" (Byrd 1994, 11, 3). Epistemology, in this sense, turns into "an administrative, not a foundational, science," a policing mechanism sifting the world to construct what Byrd terms a "*disciplined knowledge*" (8, 23). What has been consistently sifted out, or put to death, in pursuit of this "disciplined knowledge" is a "common knowledge," which Byrd defines as follows:

> The domain of the common knowledge has no preexistence. It comes into being only when contingent beings come into contingent relationship. The common knowledge leads not to certainty of mind but to confidence of action. It consists not of propositions to be communicated from A to B but of orientations in fields of meaning, measures by the scales in which humans share not a perspective or a belief but a world that opens to this or that particular vantage and practice. (1994, 23)

It is in search of this "common knowledge" that Language poetry, with its shared emphasis on but diverse forms of praxis, aims at deconstructing language as the Cartesian construct of the real. Charles Bernstein, for instance, under a Wittgensteinian premise, turns his writing into a search for new worlds within language by way of "a poetry and a poetics that do not edit out so much as edit in" (1992, 2); Ron Silliman, "recognizing [poetry] as the *philosophy of practice in language*," writes to "search out the preconditions of a liberated language within the existing social fact" (1987, 17); and Lyn Hejinian postulates, in "The Rejection of Closure," that "A central activity of poetic language is formal," whereby, "failing in the attempt to match the world, we discover structure, distinction, the integrity and separateness of things" (1984b, 143). As much similar as unique, then, is Susan Howe's poetic praxis, a praxis committed, among other goals, to articulating the inarticulate through a countermethod of singularities.

"Poetry brings similitude and representation to configurations waiting from forever to be spoken," writes Susan Howe in her "Statement for the New Poetics Colloquium, Vancouver, 1985"; "I write to break out into perfect primeval Consent. I wish I could tenderly lift from the dark side of history, voices that are anonymous, slighted—inarticulate" (1985b, 17). To articulate the inarticulate, Howe's poetic praxis pivots on a lyric consciousness upon which impinges a double mission of rescuing and breaking free: rescuing "the stutter" that Howe hears in American literature "as a sounding of uncertainty. What is silenced or not quite silenced" (1990c, 37), and breaking free from a linguistic world in which, as Marjorie Perloff puts it in *The Dance of the Intellect*, "the articulation of an individual language is all but prevented by the official discourses that bombard the consciousness from all sides" (1985, 231). Poetry as such engages its material, both in theory and in methodology, with two major critical inquiries informing one another, namely, how to read and how to write; that is, "How do I, choosing messages from the code of others in order to participate in the universal theme of Language, pull SHE from all the myriad symbols and sightings of HE," as Howe observes in her insightful study of Emily Dickinson (1985a, 17–18).[1] From this perspective, Howe's poetry can be described, to put it in Bruce Andrews's terms, as a *"rereading* [of] the reading that a social status quo puts [her] through" by rewriting "its material . . . the raw materials of a society, a collection of practices & avowals & disavowals, governed by discourse" (1990, 27, 29).

To articulate, in this sense, foregrounds the *re-* prefix as denotative of "founding," "establishing," "pioneering," and "exploring." A linguistic act of "pathfinding" regardless of an already given itinerary, "to articulate" means, according to a standard dictionary, "to put together with joints; to form or fit into a systematically related whole; coordinate coherently" (*Webster's*), thus suggesting a regrounding of representation through "A recognition that there is an other voice, an attempt to hear and speak it" (Howe 1990a, 192). To articulate, then, is to assume an iconoclastic, sociolinguistic status that Howe identifies in *Singularities* as the "Emancipator at empyrean center" (1990d, 32), "the lean Instaurator" (65), or "THE REVISER" (70) wandering "on wild thoughtpath" (64) rather than the captive imprisoned in "iconic Collective . . . thought thought out" (65).

Yet to render audible this "undervoice that was speaking from the beginning" (Howe 1990a, 192) constitutes a paradox. For the inarticulate can find its forms of articulation only within the already articulated, within, in other words, a language which is itself a sociohistorical construct, or, as Dale Spender puts it, a "language *trap*" (1990, 105). "For we are language Lost/in language" (Howe 1990b, 99), Howe aptly portrays this predatory apparatus of ultimate silencing in *The Europe of Trusts*, one that Howe subsequently describes, vis-à-vis her own writing experience, as relentlessly and incessantly lying in wait for its prey:

> So I start in a place with fragments, lines and marks, stops and gaps, and then I have more ordered sections, and then things break up again. That's how I begin most of my books. . . . [T]hese sounds, these pieces of words come into the chaos of life, and then you try to order them and to explain something and the explanation breaks free of itself. I think a lot of my work is about breaking free. Starting free and being captured and breaking free again and being captured again. (Howe 1990c, 24)

Language as a predator marks its exclusive territory by ceaselessly prey-
ing upon the consciousness of the Other. That being the case, to articulate
as an iconoclastic rescue mission means, first and foremost, to escape from
the linguistic roundup, to break free from grammar as "repressive mecha-
nism," and to resist being captured and silenced by meaning as "the uncon-
scious political element in lineal grammaticization" (McCaffery 1984,
160). Centering unfailingly upon issues such as these, Howe's rereading is
embodied in a rewriting that postulates an interrogation of language, of its
"received model on its own ground" (Perloff 1987, 31). "Who polices
questions of grammar, parts of speech, connection, and connotation?"
asks the poet in *My Emily Dickinson;* "Whose order is shut inside the
structure of a sentence? What inner articulation releases the coils and com-
plications of Saying's assertion?" (1985a, 11–12). These questions, by in-
terrogating the "formerly assumed and unquestioned mechanisms" (Du-
Plessis 1990, 122), force open a path through the ensnaring cobwebs of the
prescriptive grammar to "an enunciative clearing," as Howe phrases it,
"the poet's space. Its demand is her method" (1993a, 136, 139).

A challenge to the knowledge "always stamped PASSED BY EXAMINER"
(Howe 1985b, 16), Howe's poetry of articulating the inarticulate presents
itself as an index, theoretical and methodological, to Michel Serres's re-
markable study of the form of knowledge acquisition in the seventeenth
century. To a great extent, Howe's interests in Emily Dickinson's "process
of writing" and "re-ordering of the forward process of reading" (Howe
1985a, 17, 51), her study of "what form for the form" (Howe 1993a, 38),
her reconceptualizing poetry as, in Edward Foster's words, "a different
way of knowing things" (1990, 23), and her recourse to the algebraic con-
cept of singularity as a means to pull "representation from the irrational
dimension love and knowledge must reach" (Howe 1993a, 83) parallel
Serres's focal points in his analysis of the Cartesian construct of the real. In
light of this Serresian paradigm of Western epistemology as a hunt, Howe's
poetry demonstrates a bent to contrive a method, or countermethod, to
break free from the language trap through a "productive violence" (Kris-
teva 1984, 16) highly informed rather than random.

Titled "Knowledge in the Classical Age: La Fontaine and Descartes,"
Serres's brilliant exegesis, both structural and metaphorical, begins with
the fable "The Wolf and the Lamb":[2]

> The reason of the stronger is always the best.
> We will show this shortly.
> A Lamb quenched his thirst
> In the current of a pure stream,
> A fasting Wolf arrives, looking for adventure,

And whom hunger draws to this place.
"Who makes you so bold as to muddy my drink?"
Said the animal, full of rage:
"You will be punished for your temerity."
"Sire," answers the Lamb, "may it please Your Majesty
Not to become angry;
But rather let Him consider
That I am quenching my thirst
In the stream,
More than twenty steps below Him;
And that, as a result, in no way
Can I muddy His drink."
"You muddy it," responded this cruel beast;
"And I know that you slandered me last year."
"How could I have done so, if I had not yet been born?"
Responded the Lamb; "I am not yet weaned."
"If it is not you, then it is your brother."
"I do not have any." "Then it is one of your clan;
For you hardly spare me,
You, your shepherds, and your dogs.
I have been told: I must avenge myself."
Upon which, deep into the woods
The Wolf carries him off, and then eats him,
Without any other form of *procès*. (Serres 1982, 15–16)

Behind the seeming arbitrariness with which the Wolf kills the Lamb, Serres points out, there exists a logical architecture. What the fable dramatizes, to begin with, is the notion of structure. With an algebraic origin, this structure operates as an ordered structure, designating a set of elements provided with an ordering relation that is prescribed as irreflexive, antisymmetric, and transitive. When enacted in the fable, this ordered structure with an ordering relation is seen in the form of the pure stream flowing in one direction, with the Lamb positioned downstream, the absent shepherds and dogs upstream, and the Wolf in the middle. It represents, as the fable unfolds, a form of *procés, procés* meaning not only "process," etymologically, but also, judicially, "trial." In this sense, the form is, according to Serres, a reason, a ratio, a connection, a relation. It is a form as "a 'method' of knowledge," to put it in Don Byrd's words, the advantage of which is "precisely [its] avoidance of particular and sensuous means of expression," and in which "the Other [is] created in the image of [its] reason" (1994, 43, 44, 47).

This form of trial as a reason then demands, Serres proceeds to argue, that a certain possibility be established—the possibility of a party responsible for some wrongdoing or injury that a plaintiff claims to have suffered, whatever the wrongdoing or injury might be. When diagramed onto the fable's topographical layout as a structure of causality, the responsible party, termed by Serres "the majorant," occupies the upstream position, has complete control over anyone below, and, found guilty, deserves to be punished; whereas the plaintiff, called "the minorant," occupies the downstream position, has no control over anyone above, and therefore has the right to take revenge. In other words, he who is upstream is responsible and loses. Hence the fable's strategy or the trial's law. All, from Serres's standpoint, is engendered and activated by the first word in the Wolf's first question—the "Who" in "Who makes you so bold as to muddy my drink," a use of language foregrounding not dialogue but self-interpretation, not ontology but epistemology (Byrd 1994, 48). For with "Who" as a reference to a majorant, the Wolf succeeds in positing the existence of what Serres calls the third man, that is, the shepherds and dogs in the Lamb's social group, upstream from him, which in turn enables the Wolf to change his position/status from upstream/majorant (in relation to the Lamb) to downstream/minorant (in relation to the third man). Having majorized the Lamb by identifying him with the shepherds and dogs upstream from him, the Wolf minorizes himself into a position entitled to collect, to eat the Lamb. The guaranteed winning strategy here, as executed by the Wolf, lies in the displacement of the majorant-minorant couplet within what Serres calls the "game-space," a displacement realized by reason as an absolute and constant optimization, and by following a global theorem: all the moves are maximized. The Wolf wins, to put it differently, because he plays the role of the minorant by maximizing each move in an absolute fashion—there is no place above the shepherds assisted by their dogs, and there is no place below the Lamb—whereby he freezes the game-space in a single pattern of order and hierarchy. Thus the trial is over, and the Lamb is sentenced to die.

As an animated game of strategy, with its rules and moves, this fable, Serres continues, bodies forth the hidden model of all exact knowledge, a model aimed at "discovering entire classes of phenomena that corresponded to the mathematical species of algebra" (Byrd 1994, 43). Descartes, after Bacon, picked up this precept and, by rejecting the Baconian impulse to obey nature, developed it further into an agonistic relationship between humans and the exterior world, a relationship in which the weak party, with reason's verdicts, always wins, by discovering the maximum and the minimum points at the edge of the space organized by the couplet of the majorant and the minorant, and as Byrd asserts, by "putting off the proof of the premises until they can be supported by the conclusion" (72). To know nature, in this sense, becomes a deadly dangerous game. For knowledge is a hunt, as Serres's succinct conclusion reads, and to know is to put to death other forms of knowledge, that of the Lamb, for instance. These epistemologies, therefore, are not innocent: at the critical tribunal they are calling for executions. Indeed, the reason of the strongest is reason by itself. Western man is a wolf of science.

Both Howe's poetry and her criticism suggest an acute awareness of Serres's "Western man" as a Cartesian methodologist, who is in actuality "a medium—that is, language itself" (Byrd 1994, 85), with Wolfish moves which, also "drafted in . . . language" (Serres 1982, 23), institute "an inherently linguistic world as [his] field of operation" (Byrd 1994, 66), resulting in the ultimate silencing of the undervoice and the killing of the knowledge of the Other. Howe writes:

> Knowledge narrowly fixed knowledge
> Whose bounds in theories slay (Howe 1990d, 12)

> Alone in deserts of Parchment
> Theoreticians of the Modern

> —emending annotating inventing
> World as rigorously related System (Howe 1990d, 35)

To the extent that Howe considers such "linguistic nature [as] always foreign" and herself as "a foreigner in her own language" (1989, 26, 27), her effort to articulate the inarticulate can be first seen in her attempt to outsmart the language trap by appropriating the Cartesian strategies, specifically, the displacement of the majorant-minorant couplet. With the word "Who" in her interrogation "Who polices questions of grammar," for instance, she succeeds in usurping the Wolf's place along the linear trajectory of language as an ordered structure with an ordering relation, by positioning the existing sociolinguistic system, designed to render her invisible and voiceless, downstream from her, and upstream, the "third man," who prescribes rules for such a system. Concomitantly established, then, is her right to raise and pursue the issue of responsibility. For poetry, as Howe defines it, is "a search by an investigator for the point where the crime began. What is the unforgivable crime? Will I ever capture it in words?" (1989, 21). And the point her search leads to turns out to be the point where language began, where, through language, "stability and constancy of certitudes or precisions are conceived . . . as the end of a prior game" (Serres 1982, 23). "In the beginning was the Word," Howe quotes in her *Talisman* interview, "and the Word was God" (1990c, 22), thus revealing the Cartesian circle, with what Byrd calls "an idealism as the pretext for a language without etymologies or sensuous content" (1994, 61).

Such an appropriation, though successfully leading the poet-investigator to the crime scene, gets her no further. If the Wolf, by occupying the middle position, becomes entitled to assert knowledge by killing, the poet-articulator, by the same token, only finds herself entitled to be denied her own knowledge by being killed. For this appropriation constitutes nothing but a recycling of a gendered form constructed as a reason or logic, the circularity of which presupposes *a priori* the impossibility of any counter-moves. To articulate the "Inarticulate true meaning//lives beyond thought /linked from beginning" (Howe 1990d, 30), then, the poet has to take another approach, one that "would mark the beginning of a new history" (Serres 1982, 22), a history of what Howe conceives as "an actuality" rather than "some intellectual fusion or agreement" (Foster 1990, 17), some "Documents . . . written by the Masters" (Howe 1985b, 15). And this new approach, as Serres suggests, is to attack *the ordered structure itself*—which is the condition for the game's existence or, rather, without which the game can have neither space nor time—in order to shatter it" (1982, 22).

It is in singularity that Howe locates her point of attack on this ordered structure with its "Logical determination of position" (1990d, 18), a move that reminds one of Derridean deconstruction as "Operating necessarily from the inside, borrowing all the strategic and economic resources of subversion from the old structure, borrowing them structurally" (Derrida 1976, 24). Talking about René Thom and his lecture at SUNY-Buffalo entitled "Singularities," Howe sketches out her understanding of the concept as follows:

> In algebra a singularity is the point where plus becomes minus. . . . The singularity (I think Thom is saying) is the point where there is a sudden change to something completely else. It's a chaotic point. It's the point chaos enters cosmos, the instant articulation. Then there is a leap into something else. Predation and capture are terms he uses constantly.[3] (1990c, 30–31)

Singularity, in other words, constitutes the juncture where "Chaos cast cold intellect back" to show the "Archaic presentiment of rupture/Voicing desire no more from here" (Howe 1990d, 34, 38). It is the site of "the struggle not to be reduced" (DuPlessis 1990, 28), a struggle to break free violently—as is suggested by Howe's use of words such as "sudden change," "completely else," "the instant," and "a leap"—from the predation and capture of what Howe calls the "Lenses and language//total systemic circular knowledge/System impossible in time" (Howe 1990d, 28). In the same vein, René Thom's theorizing of catastrophe, which Howe specifically refers to in the same context, sheds further light on the poet's understanding and use of singularity.[4] To appropriate Thom's terminology, as Howe certainly does for her purpose, a singularity is a catastrophe, "a sudden, violent change" (*Webster's*) that, ushering "Anarchy into named theory/Entangled obedience" (Howe 1990c, 32), makes itself manifest in the "morphology" or structure. Either of "conflict" or of "bifurcation," it designates "a field of local dynamics defined as the gradient of a potential," the centrifugality of which outlines "a new grammar grounded in humility and hesitation," a hermaphroditic language, perhaps, for the "'sheltered' woman . . . [holding] back in doubt, [having] difficulty speaking" (21).

As such, singularity becomes, as Marjorie Perloff puts it in her discussion of war in Wittgenstein, "the condition for what might best be called textual breakthrough" (1993, 31). When applied to reading and writing, it constitutes the point where linguistic fracture occurs. Howe's poems, remarks the poet herself, "fracture language, they are charged" (Howe 1990c, 31). And this is done by "changing order and abolishing categories" (23), for order and categories suggest "hierarchy" and "property" (Howe 1985a, 13). To articulate the inarticulate, in this sense, is to be a "Child/regical" (Howe 1990d, 69), demilitarizing language as "a martial art" (Serres 1982, 28) by initiating singularities and incurring catastrophes at all levels. In Howe's poetry, the form that singularity takes is, among others, what DuPlessis refers to as "matted palimpsests" (1990, 126), a writing-through that, via points of contact with and displacement of the canonized materials, "releases the coils and complications of Saying's assertion" (Howe 1985a, 11–12) and, as a result, enables the poet to see "what she did not see [and say] what she did not say," as is suggested by Howe's aptly entitled study "The Captivity and Restoration of Mrs. Mary Rowlandson" (1993a, 128). Indeed, singularity, as an act of restoration from captivity, deconstructs so as to reconstellate:

> Deflagration of what was there to say. No message to decode or finally decide. The fascicles have a "halo of wilderness." By continually interweaving expectation and categories they checkmate inscription to become what a reader offers them. (1993a, 136)

Howe's poetry, written in "matted palimpsests," embodies a three-layered linguistic deposit, or a three-dimensional language experience: (1) the source text, often excerpted or duplicated in prose and other genred language, or indicated by a footnote; (2) Howe's text as an act of writing through the source text; and (3) what this writing-through gestures toward. Resembling what Lyn Hejinian calls "field work," such a textual formation becomes "an activity" (1984, 135, 137). The dynamics of the interweaving of all three invites or, indeed, demands a simultaneous, tripartite reading: anaphoric reading of the source text, exophoric reading of the text proper, and cataphoric reading of the inarticulate.[5] To read anaphorically is not to appeal to the source text for confirmation, but rather to "break out into [its] perfect primeval Consent" (Howe 1985b, 17). The critical inquiry back into the knowledge "always stamped PASSED BY EXAMINER" thus subpoenas the source text as the established conceptual representation and investigates it as the crime scene. In this way, it reopens the case that has been long since closed by interrogating the assumptions undergirding the source text. To read exophorically, then, is to break up the logical cobwebs of captivity. With its centrifugal trajectory fracturing the linear linguistic structure, exophoric reading turns the text proper into the physical site of singularities. The sudden and violent changes in turn engender a language wilderness, where "stutter" reigns over grammar. And to read cataphorically is to reconstellate. It is, as Bernstein puts it, "to imagine new reals that have never before existed" (1992, 184). Envisioning "An open horizon" (Howe 1989, 20), it reads the catastrophic aftermath of singularities as a potential of perceptual reknowing so as to reground representation in actuality.

The title poem of Howe's *The Nonconformist's Memorial* begins with a passage carefully footnoted as from "The Gospel According to St. John":

> 20.15 Jesus saith unto her, Woman,
> why weepest thou? whom seekest
> thou? She, supposing him to be the
> gardener, saith unto him, Sir, if thou
> have borne him hence, tell me where
> thou has laid him, and I will take
> him away.
>
> 16 Jesus saith unto her, Mary. She
> turned herself, and saith unto him,
> Rabboni; which is to say, Master.
>
> 17 Jesus saith unto her, Touch me
> not; for I am not yet ascended to
> my Father: but go to my brethren,
> and say unto them, I ascend unto my
> Father, and your Father; and *to* my
> God, and your God.
>
> 18 Mary Magdalene came and told
> the disciples that she had seen the
> Lord, and *that* he has spoken these
> things unto her. (1993b, 3)

Otherwise taken for granted, the anaphoric reading of this passage, a reading as referring to an origin already codified, as surrendering to a discourse already authorized, as the unquestioning acceptance of a myth already objectified, is nevertheless checkmated from the outset. For this passage, identified by the footnote as a "citation," not only exemplifies the term's doctrinal use as "abbreviated//Often a shortcut//stands for Chapter" (1993b, 5), but also suggests a play upon the ambiguity of its meaning as both "an official summons to appear (as before a court of law)" and "an act of quoting" (*Webster's*), a play that blends the two meanings into one. For the nonconformist whom "The Gospel did not grasp" (7), quoting becomes, indeed, summoning: the passage, with its monologic meaning, is cited not to be followed but to face polylogic possibilities, "other similitudes/Felicities of life// . . . //dissenting storms/A variety of trials" (4).

Yet to shatter the ordered structure itself, a structure that is explicitly dictated and outlined in the cited passage, one has to strip it to its logical scaffold first. And the exophoric reading, in this sense, begins as an x-ray reading of the source text. Three pages into the poem, Howe then creates the following textual layout stretched over two facing pages:

In Peter she is nameless
Actual world nothing ideal

headstrong anarchy thoughts
A single thread of narrative

She was coming to anoint him
As if all history were a progress

As if all history were a progress
She was coming to anoint him

A single thread of narrative
headstrong anarchy thoughts

Actual world nothing ideal

In Peter she is nameless

The nets were not torn

The Gospel did not grasp

What is presented here, apart from "The nets were not torn//The Gospel did not grasp," is a six-line poem repeating itself, but in such a way that the two identical parts form a perfect circle. For the repeating part, printed upside down and interlined with the repeated, begins its first line where the latter just ends and proceeds from bottom to top and from page 7 to page 6, in the current edition, thus suturing a seamless, head-to-tail-to-head, circular structure. In addition, Howe's "re-ordering of the forward process of reading," a textual move that functions sometimes by playing upon one's trained sensibility, highlights such a circular motion further by forcing one, having reached the end of the six-line poem on page 7, to turn the book upside down so as to resume "the forward process of reading" of the repeating part, thus necessitating a repagination of the former 7 as now 6, and 6 as 7. Hence the circle again.

This textual formation, then, provides a diagraming of the logical structure embedded in the cited passage. It points to the contour of such a structure as a circularity. From word to word, its self-referentiality takes the form in the Gospel of "A single thread of narrative" (Howe 1993b, 7) from Him back to Him, precluding the actuality that "It is by chance that she weeps/Her weeping is not a lament//She has a voice to cry out" (15). As such, "The Narrative of Finding" (13) weaves its thread into "The nets" (7), or what Wittgenstein calls "Newtonian mechanics" as "a net of a given form," whereby to "construct according to a single plan all the true propositions that [he needs] for the description of the world" at the expense of "*particular* point-roasses" (68, 69). As long as "The nets were not torn" (7), she, so captured and positioned accordingly in the nets, "is nameless" (6) and is named only to signify a "Sir" or "Rabboni; which is to say, Master" (3). Irreflexive, antisymmetric, and transitive, the Gospel sentence "*that* he had spoken these/things unto her" (3) enacts an ordered structure with an ordering relation, the logic of which determines *a priori* that she cannot speak back for lack of a language of her own and, resultantly, is silenced:

> In the synoptic tradition Mary
> enters the tomb (Howe 1993b, 12)
>
> It is the Word to whom she turns
> True submission and subjection (1993b, 30)

However perfectly circular, this structure, manifested in "A single thread of narrative" reiterating itself, proves to be what K. Ludwig Pfeiffer calls "fictionality (aesthetic illusion as a production of senses of the real)" (1990, 102). For just as "mathematics involves propositions that mathematical systems themselves can't prove," as Edward Foster asserts (1990, 31), the language that materializes this circle points to itself as "the linguistic form of the fiction" (Vaihinger 1925, 91) and, as such, the site of singularity. Not only is the circle's "singleness" already problematized by "headstrong anarchy thoughts" (6), but its narrative progress is also impeded and disrupted within its game-space by unrelated, different uses of tense and mood, suggesting "a lack of successful *suture*" (Andrews 1990, 31): the simple present ("she is nameless"), the past continuous ("She was coming"), and the subjunctive ("history were") (6, 7). But the most devastating critique yet of the logical structure as a linguistic form of fiction, a critique that certainly incurs "the capture breaking/along the shock wave//interpreted as space-time/on a few parameters" (13), lies in Howe's use of "as if": "As if all history were a progress/A single thread of narrative/Actual world nothing ideal/The nets were not torn." Although the "as if" construct as a form of negation appears to have been agreed upon by all, its intended conceptual representation as well as structural containment of an unreal assumption seems, in the context of these two pages, to be what Howe is driving at. In other words, Howe, with the "as if" phrase, not only repudiates history as "a progress/A single thread of narrative/Actual world nothing ideal" by appropriating the phrase's "already made and inhabited" meaning (DuPlessis 1990, 132), but also, and more importantly, draws one's attention to this linguistic collocation itself as a fiction-making mechanism.

In this regard, Howe's use of "as if" suggests a critical resonance with Hans Vaihinger's thesis in *The Philosophy of "As If,"* a study of the "Preponderance of the Means over the End" in the development of human thought, a development "partly in connection with the progress of mathematics, mechanics and jurisprudence" (1925, xlvi, 95). In the light of Vaihinger's paradigm, the word "if" in the "as if" combination negates the word "as" as constitutive of a "comparative apperception" according to which history is viewed "by means of the conceptual construct" (92) of "a progress," of "A single thread of narrative," of "Actual world nothing ideal." For "if" denotes "the assumption of a condition, and indeed, in this instance, of an impossible case" (92). Though similar to the "if . . . then" construct in which, in spite of the "unreality or impossibility" stated in the conditional clause, "inferences are [still] drawn" from it and "the assumption is still formally maintained" and "regarded as an apperceptive construct under which something can be subsumed and from which deduction can be made" (92, 93), the "as if" collocation, Vaihinger argues, implies yet something more. Dissecting "as if" into "something must be treated as it would be treated . . . if it . . ." (all history must be treated as it would be treated if it were a progress and so forth), Vaihinger points out that contained in "as if" there is "a clear statement of the necessity (possibility or actuality), of an inclusion under an impossible or unreal assumption" (93). The apodosis, otherwise manifest and audible like the one introduced by "then" in "if . . . then," is "merely concealed and suppressed. It lurks unheard between the 'as' and the 'if'" (258). As such, the "as if" collocation constitutes, according to Vaihinger, a formula that "states that reality as given, the particular, is compared with something whose impossibility or unreality is at the same time admitted" (93). In other words, fiction becomes, as Howe puts it, the "Pivot//Literally the unmoving point around which a body turns" (Howe 1993b, 11). No wonder that, as much as "as if" calls into question history as such, "The nets were not torn" regardless. Hence the Wolfish move, indeed, in the game-space, a move that, while reinforcing a circular structure as logic, has left traces at every turn of its shaky foundation. "Contradiction," Howe is certainly right to note, "is the book of this place" (Howe 1985a, 45).

Which is also the place of singularities, the place where language, "Free from limitations of genre . . . finds true knowledge estranged in it self" (Howe 1993a, 137). To render this "true knowledge" accessible, the exophoric and the cataphoric readings, then, engage themselves in a "field work" of "sensuous visual catastrophes" (140):

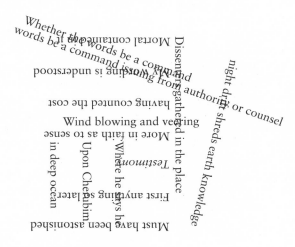

As the physical site of singularities, such textual formation suggests what Howe calls "a field of free transgressive prediscovery" (1993a, 147). The clashes between words and the collisions among lines demilitarize language by creating points of "capture breaking" that, in turn, become locales for "the chance meeting of words" (Howe 1985a, 24), leading to discoveries that "Outside the central disciplines of Economy, Anthropology, and Historiography is a gap in causal sequence. A knowing excluded from knowing" (Howe 1989, 23). Thus engendered is a "new way of perceiving" grounded in "the immediate *feeling* of understanding" (Howe 1985a, 51). "Against the coldness of force/Intellectual grasp" (Howe 1993, 15), this "immediate feeling of understanding" originates from "Home in a human knowing//Stretched out at the thresh/of beginning" and is articulated in what Howe describes as "Body perception thought of perceiving (half-thought" (Howe 1990d, 26, 13). "Body perception" is only a "(half-thought" or a "suggestion" (Howe 1985a, 24) because, as the incomplete parenthesis illustrates, it is still in the process of becoming, of breaking free from the established conceptual fixation as a hunt. "No hierarchy, no notion of polarity," Howe argues, "Perception of an object means loosing and losing it" (23). And not until the logical sequence of language is broken can body perception find complete sense in actuality: "Forward progress disrupted reversed. Sense came after suggestion" (24). Poetry, for Howe to articulate the excluded knowing, "is thought transference./Free association isn't free" (1993b, 105).

What strikes one first as obvious is that the textual layout of words here suggests a visual presentation of an architecture, the logical foundation of which is, not surprisingly, "Effectual crucifying knowledge." But in contrast to the seemingly perfect circle on the previous pages, it is an architecture visibly on the point of collapse, being off balance from top to bottom. The singularity occurs where the "Effectual crucifying knowledge" reigns, where the "Distance original disobedience" (Howe 1993b, 15) persists, regardless, in a voice not quite silenced. Partially erased or obscured by "I John bright picture" but kept traceable still—and audible, for that matter—by "suddenly unperceivable time from place to place" is the question "What am I?"—a question directed, as is suggested by its physical posture, to the "Effectual crucifying knowledge." Echoing Stella's question "Who can tell me who I am?" (Howe 1990b, 199), one that is ultimately silenced by "Swift's 'liquidation'—abolishing, metaphoric killing of Stella" (Du-Plessis 1990, 136), "What am I," as a direct challenge to the imposition of a designated status, sends "the shock wave" throughout the architecture, bringing chaos into its scaffolding. The resultant "chance meeting of words" then opens the book of contradiction, of language checkmating itself. The line "Whether the words be a command," for instance, finds itself the site of two counts of linguistic fracture. Rather awkwardly, the word "the" is seen sandwiched, written through, disfigured, and overthrown by "contained in." So configured, these three words form the point of capture-breaking to suggest "a leap into something else." For when placed between "contained" and "in," the word "the," the one and only definite article capable of fixation to the utmost degree, is restrained, physically, in its sphere of application and curtailed, conceptually, in its exclusive power and function of naming, of designating, of referring to an object. Further, if placed after "contained in," "the" then becomes the object of the preposition, and that which is contained in "the" is, by the logic of the syntax, "Mortal," the subject of "contained in," meaning "causing death; fatal"; or, as in theology, that which can cause "spiritual death" (*Webster's*). To paraphrase: transitive by nature, language, in the form of the "Effectual crucifying knowledge," asserts its monotheism by killing other voices.

"The" being demilitarized, "command," beneath which the word "his" lurks, is confronted by "dissenters." And the matted palimpsests of "his-command-dissenters" are such that, with the double *m* heavily written through, what seems to be left from the word "command" after the catastrophe are, quite visibly, *co* and *and*, suggesting that "*We* plural are the speaker" (Howe 1993b, 11), a stance in opposition to that of "either-or," which endorses a "dichotomized universe, proposing monism" (DuPlessis 1990, 6).

Adjacent to this site of singularity is another catastrophe area in "words be a command issuing from authority or counsel." The capture-breaking that occurs with the "chance meeting" of "be" and "it," for instance, demystifies words as "Hallucinated to infinity" (Howe 1993, 19). Denotative of existence, life, occurrence, continuity, identity, value, cause, significance, and sometimes equivalent to the mathematical equal sign (*Webster's*), the verb "to be," substantive or copulative, is endowed with such a transparency in "A single thread of narrative" that its physicality has been metamorphosed into a "Being" with its own agency. Yet the word "it," "the subject of an impersonal verb . . . without reference to agent" (*Webster's*), points to "be" as nothing but the symptom of a paranoia as the result of an "Intractable ethical paradox" (Howe 1993b, 20). In addition, by writing primarily through *e* in "be" and leaving *b* intact, "it" thus metamorphoses the verb "to be" from an autonomous entity back to its corporeality, which is the letter *b* with a monosyllabic sound. The subsequent "chance meeting" of "issuing" and "hiding," each with its own semantic pull in the opposite direction, then suggests not only that the hierarchical trajectory of words as command (issuing) is often masked (hiding), but also that its transitivity (issuing) is frustrated as a criminal hoax (hiding). Based on words as such, "authority" can no longer sustain its own constructedness, which is dissected as nothing but "night drift," an arbitrary piecing together that "shreds earth knowledge." In the book of contradictions, says Howe, "word flesh crumbled page edge" (13).

In "Writing and Method," Charles Bernstein talks about poetry and philosophy as "[sharing] *the project of investigating the possibilities (nature) and structures of phenomena*" (1986, 219–20): "Part of the task of an active poetry or philosophy is to explore these instruments [of power that is taken as neutral or given] by a critique of their partiality and to develop alternatives to them that can serve as models of truth and meaning not dependent for their power on the dominating structures" (224). Poetry is active not only because it continuously explores the language wilderness open only to what Howe calls "human knowing," but also because it develops, while exploring, alternative means to articulate the "common knowledge." Both are executed through poetic praxis, a praxis manifested in a search, as Bernstein puts it in the same essay, for "a 'constructive' mode [suggesting] that the mode itself is explored as content, its possibilities of meaning are investigated and presented, and that this process is itself recognized as a method" (227). Poetry, in this sense, is never written; it is, always, writing.

Howe's countermethod of singularities, as a critique of the "illusion of literacy" that conceives language "as a mechanism of [disciplined] knowledge" (Byrd 1994, 194), finds its "entrance point" (Howe 1990c, 34) on the dominating linguistic/logical structure. By way of "matted palimpsests," Howe opens the book of contradiction in which language is revealed as checkmating itself, thus rendering possible a "thought transference" embracing the excluded knowing. For Susan Howe, articulating the inarticulate, as the present participle indicates, constitutes a pathfinding expedition in progress, a writing in action, which, while "charting worlds otherwise hidden or denied or, perhaps best of all, never before existing" (Bernstein 1992, 1), engages the "common knowledge," a knowledge that "cannot be stated but only practiced" (Byrd 1994, 200). Indeed, by problematizing that "When words are, meaning soon follows," as Ron Silliman so laconically phrases it in "For L=A=N=G=U=A=G=E," Howe's countermethod of singularities shows that "Where words join, writing is" (1984, 16).

NOTES

A shorter version of "Articulating the Inarticulate Singularities and the Countermethod in Susan Howe" was presented at the 1993 MLA convention in Toronto. I would like to thank Marjorie Perloff and Peter Quartermain for their criticisms and careful readings of the early drafts.

1. Although explicitly informed by a feminist perspective, both Howe's poetry and her criticism present a broad range of significance and implications that embraces, but is not confined to, feminist critique. In this sense, the term to describe Howe's critical spectrum more comprehensively is, perhaps, "contradiction," a term the poet herself emphasizes in *My Emily Dickinson*.

2. While Serres's study focuses on the classical age, his theory and model can be applied to the present just as effectively. My outlining of Serres's ideas, often in a word-for-ward manner, is based on pages 15–28 of Serres's essay.

3. Both René Thom's work (*Mathemalical Models of Morphogenesis, Structural Stability and Morphogenesis*) and the terminology in his lecture ("predation," "capture," and so forth) suggest an awareness of algebraic geometry as a game and a corresponding ambiguity toward its nature. Don Byrd makes a similar observation when he writes: "The confusion over the nature of this science has been far greater

than is justified by the textual difficulties. The problems are logical, not textual, and they remain a constant of the philosophic tradition from Descartes himself, who found a way in the *Discourse* to sweep them under the rug, to Noam Chomsky and the foremost current French proponent of geometric mechanism, René Thom" (1994, 66).

4. The passage Howe quotes in full in the *Talisman* interview (31) is the introduction to chapter 5, "Elementary Catastrophe Theory," in *Mathematical Models af Morphogenesis*.

5. I am indebted to Peter Quartermain for the terms "anaphoric," "exophoric," and "cataphoric." Discussing Gertrude Stein's use of pronouns—and, for that matter, articles—as "shifters," Quartermain defines the linguistic and deictic functions of these terms as, respectively, "backward pointing" to the antecedents, "outward pointing" to "materials outside the text," and "forward pointing" to the "forward movement of the prose." I borrow and use them here to suggest a mental trajectory largely conditioned by the textual formations therein and their concomitant reading processes. For more detail, see Quartermain (1992, 21–43).

BIBLIOGRAPHY

Books by Susan Howe

Articulation of Sound Forms in Time (Windsor, Vt.: Awede, 1987).
A Bibliography of the King's Book or, Eikon Basilike (Providence, R.I.: Paradigm Press, 1989).
The Birth-mark: Unsettling the Wilderness in American Literary History (Middletown, Conn.: Wesleyan University Press, 1993).
Cabbage Gardens (Chicago: Fathom Press, 1979).
Defenestration of Prague (New York: The Kulchur Foundation, 1983).
The Europe of Trusts: Selected Poems (Los Angeles: Sun & Moon Press, 1989).
Frame Structures: Early Poems, 1974–1978 (New York: New Directions, 1996).
Hinge Picture (New York: Telephone Books, 1974).
Incloser (Santa Fe, N.M.: Weaselsleeves Press, 1992).
The Liberties (Guilford, Conn.: Loon Books, 1980).
My Emily Dickinson (Berkeley: North Atlantic Books, 1985).
The Nonconformist's Memorial. Limited edition with illustrations by Robert Mangold (New York: Grenfell Press, 1992).
The Nonconformist's Memorial: Poems by Susan Howe (New York: New Directions, 1993).
Pierce-Arrow (New York: New Directions, 1999).
Pythagorean Silence (New York: Montemora Foundation, 1982).
Secret History of the Dividing Line (New York: Telephone Books, 1979).
Singularities (Middletown, Conn.: Wesleyan University Press, 1990).
The Western Borders (Berkeley: Tuumba Press, 1976).

Selected Prose

"Childe Emily to the Dark Tower Came." In *Code of Signals: Recent Writings on Poetics*, ed. Michael Palmer (Berkeley: North Atlantic Books, 1983).

"Encloser." In *The Politics of Poetic Form: Poetry and Public Policy*, ed. Charles Bernstein (New York: Roof Books, 1990).

"Ether Either." In *Close Listening*, ed. Charles Bernstein. (London and New York: Oxford University Press, 1997).

"New Directions: An Interview with James Laughlin." With Charles Ruas. *The Art of Literary Publishing: Editors on their Craft*, ed. Bill Henderson (Wainscott, N.Y.: Pushcart, 1980).

"P. Inman: Platin." In *In the American Tree*, ed. Ron Silliman (Orono, Maine: National Poetry Foundation, 1986).

"Postscripts to Emily Dickinson." *Dwelling in Possibility*, ed. Yopie Prins and Maeera Shreiber (Ithaca, N.Y.: Cornell University Press, 1997).

"(The Practice of Poetry)." In *The Line in Postmodern Poetry*, ed. Robert Frank and Henry Sayre (Urbana: University of Illinois Press, 1988).

"A Quarter Century of the Jargon Society: An Interview with Jonathan Williams." With William Corbett. In *The Art of Literary Publishing: Editors on their Craft*, ed. Bill Henderson (Wainscott, N.Y.: Pushcart, 1980).

"Raccourci (ou le principe de la note)," trans. Dominique Fourcade, *je te continue ma lecture: Melanges pour Claude Royet-Journoud*, P.O.L, Paris, 1999.

"Rae Armantrout: The Extremities." In *The Language Book*, eds. Bruce Andrews and Charles Bernstein (Carbondale: Southern Illinois University Press, 1984).

"Sorting Facts: Or Nineteen Ways of Looking at Marker." In *Beyond Document: The Art of Non-fiction Film*, ed., Charles Warren, with an introduction by Stanley Cavell (Middletown, Conn.: Wesleyan University Press, 1995).

"There Are Not Leaves Enough to Crown to Cover to Crown to Cover." In *Postmodern American Poetry: A Norton Anthology*, ed. Paul Hoover (New York: W. W. Norton, 1994).

"These Flames and Generosities of the Heart." In *Artifice and Indeterminacy; an anthology of new poetics*, ed. Christopher Beach (Tuscaloosa, University of Alabama Press).

Art Exhibitions

Box in BOXES (group show), C Space, 96 Chambers Street, New York, NY, 1978.
Narrator and advisor The Juniper Tree, a performance by Joan Jonas.
Philadelphia Institute of Contemporary Art, 1976.
Word Drawings (group show). Albright Knox Museum, Buffalo, NY, 1973.
Word Drawings. Ithaca College Museum, Ithaca, NY, 1970.
Word Drawings. Kornblee Gallery, New York, NY, 1971.
Word Drawings. Paley and Lowe Gallery, New York, NY, 1972.

Interviews

"The Difficulties Interview," with Tom Beckett. *The Difficulties* 3(2) (1989).

"Four-Part Harmony: Robert Creeley and Susan Howe Talk it Out." *Village Voice Literary Supplement* (April 1994).

"An Interview with Susan Howe," with Ed Foster. *Talisman* 4 (Spring 1990). Reprinted in *The Birth-mark: Unsettling the Wilderness in American Literary History* (Middletown, Conn.: Wesleyan University Press, 1993), and *Talisman: Collection of Interviews with Poets,* ed. Ed Foster (Hoboken, N.J.: Talisman House Press, 1993).

"An Interview with Susan Howe," with Lynn Keller. *Contemporary Literature* 36(1) (Spring 1995).

Linebreak Radio Program, with Charles Bernstein (Fall 1996).

Notre Dame Review (Fall 1997).

"Speaking with Susan Howe," with Janet Ruth Falon. *The Difficulties* 3(2) (1989).

St. Mark's Poetry Project Newsletter (October 1979).

Selected Criticism

Dworkin, Craig Douglas. "'Waging Political Babble': Susan Howe's Visual Prosody and the Politics of Noise." *Word & Image: A Journal of Verbal/Visual Inquiry* 12(4) (1996): 389–405.

Freitag, Kornelia. "Writing Language Poetry as a Woman: Susan Howe's Feminist Project in *A Bibliography of the King's Book, or Eikon Basilike.*" *Amerikastudien/American Studies* 40(1) (1995): 45–57.

Green, Fiona. "'Plainly on the Other Side': Susan Howe's Recovery." *Contemporary Literature* 42(1) (2001): 78–101.

Howard, W. Scott. "'Writing Ghost Writing': A Discursive Poetics of History: Or, Howes 'Hau' in Susan Howe's *A Bibliography of the King's Book; Or, Eikon Basilike.*" *Talisman: A Journal of Contemporary Poetry and Poetics* 14 (1995): 108–30.

Joyce, Elisabeth. "'Thorowly' American; Susan Howe's Guide to Orienteering in the Adirondacks." *ebr: The Alt-X Web Review* 10 (1999–2000): unpaginated.

Lewis, Kent. "Susan Howe's Poetics of the Bibliography." *West Coast Line* 27(1) (1993): 118–27.

Ma, Ming-qian. "Poetry as History Revised: Susan Howe's 'Scattering as Behavior toward Risk.'" *American Literary History* 6(4) (1994): 716–37.

Marsh, Nicky. "'Out of My Texas I Am Not What I Play': Politics and Self in the Poetry of Susan Howe."

McCorkle, James. "Prophecy and the Figure of the Reader in Susan Howe's *Articulation of Sound Forms in Time.*" *Postmodern Culture: An Electronic Journal of Interdisciplinary Criticism* 9(3) (1999): unpaginated.

Nanes, Erika. "The Reviser in the Word Forest: Susan Howe and the American Typology of Wilderness." *Journal x: A Journal in Culture and Criticism* 2(1) (1997): 19–34.

Nicholls, Peter. "Unsettling the Wilderness: Susan Howe and American History."
Contemporary Literature 37(4) (1996): 586–601.

Nichols, Miriam. "Tensing the Difference: Daphne Marlatt, Karen MacCormack,
and Susan Howe." *Tessera* 27 (1999): 39–54.

Palatella, John. "An End of Abstraction: An Essay on Susan Howe's Historicism."
Denver Quarterly 29(3) (1995): 74–97.

Perloff, Marjorie. "Language Poetry and the Lyric Subject: Ron Silliman's Albany,
Susan Howe's Buffalo." *Critical Inquiry* 25(3) (1999): 405–34.

———. "Recharging the Canon: Some Reflections on Feminist Poetics and the
Avant-Garde." *The American Poetry Review* 15(4) (1986): 12–20.

Vickery, Ann. "The Quiet Rupture: Susan Howe's 'The Liberties and the Feminine
Marginalia of Literary History.'" *Southerly: A Review of Australian Literature*
57(1) (1997): 91–102.

Williams, Megan. "Howe Not to Erase(her): A Poetics of Posterity in Susan Howe's
'Melville's Marginalia.'" *Contemporary Literature* 38(1) (1997): 106–32.

References

Andrews, Bruce. 1990. "Poetry as Explanation, Poetry as Praxis." In *The Politics of
Poetic Form: Poetry and Public Policy,* ed. Charles Bernstein (New York: Roof),
23–43.

Andrews, Bruce, and Charles Bernstein, eds. 1984. *The L=A=N=G=U=A=G=E
Book: Poetics of the New* (Carbondale: Southern Illinois University Press).

Bernstein, Charles. 1986. "Writing and Method." In *Content's Dream: Essays,
1975–1984* (Los Angeles: Sun & Moon), 217–36.

———. 1992. *A Poetics* (Cambridge: Harvard University Press).

Byrd, Don. 1994. *The Poetics of the Common Knowledge.* The Margins of Litera-
ture Series (New York: SUNY Press).

Davidson, Michael. 1984. "On Reading Stein." In *The L=A=N=G=U=A=G=E
Book,* ed. Bruce Andrews and Charles Bernstein (Carbondale: Southern Illinois
University Press), 196–98.

Derrida, Jacques. 1976. *Of Grammatology,* trans. Gayatri Chakravorty Spivak
(Baltimore: Johns Hopkins University Press).

DuPlessis, Rachel Blau. 1990. *The Pink Guitar: Writing as Feminist Practice* (New
York: Routledge).

Foster, Edward. 1990. "An Interview with Susan Howe." *Talisman* 4 (Spring): 14–38.

Hejinian, Lyn. 1984a. "If Written Is Writing." In *The L=A=N=G=U=A=G=E
Book,* ed. Bruce Andrews and Charles Bernstein (Carbondale: Southern Illinois
University Press), 29–30.

———. 1984b. "The Rejection of Closure." In *Women and Language,* ed. Lyn
Hejinian and Barrett Watten. Special issue of *Poetics Journal* 4: 134–43.

Howe, Susan. 1985a. *My Emily Dickinson* (Berkeley: North Atlantic).

———. 1985b. "Statement for the New Poetics Colloquium, Vancouver, 1985."
Jimmy & Lucy's House of "K" 5 (November): 13–17.

———. 1989. "The Difficulties Interview." With Tom Beckett. *Susan Howe Issue.*
Special issue of *The Difficulties* 3(2): 17–27.

———. 1990a. "Encloser." *The Politics of Poetic Form: Poetry and Public Policy*, ed. Charles Bernstein (New York: Roof), 175–96.

———. 1990b. *The Europe of Trusts* (Los Angeles: Sun & Moon).

———. 1990c. "An Interview with Susan Howe." With Edward Foster. *Talisman: A Journal of Contemporary Poetry and Poetics* 4 (Spring): 14–38.

———. 1990d. *Singularities*. Wesleyan Poetry (Hanover, N.H.: Wesleyan University Press and University Press of New England).

———. 1993a. *The Birth–Mark: Unsettling the Wilderness in American Literary History* (Hanover, N.H.: Wesleyan University Press and University Press of New England).

———. 1993b. *The Nonconformist's Memorial* (New York: New Directions).

Kristeva, Julia. 1984. *Revolution in Poetic Language*, trans. Margaret Waller (New York: Columbia University Press).

McCaffery, Steve. 1984. "From the Notebooks." In *The L=A=N=G=U=A=G=E Book*, ed. Bruce Andrews and Charles Bernstein (Carbondale: Southern Illinois University Press), 159–62.

McGann, Jerome J. 1987. "Contemporary Poetry, Alternate Routes." In *Politics and Poetic Value*, ed. Robert von Hallberg (Chicago: University of Chicago Press), 253–76.

Perloff, Marjorie. 1985. *The Dance of the Intellect: Studies in the Poetry of the Pound Tradition*, Cambridge Studies in American Literature and Culture (Cambridge: Cambridge University Press).

———. 1987. "Canon and Loaded Gun: Feminist Poetics and the Avant-Garde." *Stanford Literature Review* 4(1): 23–46.

———. 1993. "Toward an Avant-Garde *Tractatus:* Russell and Wittgenstein on War." *Common Knowledge* 2(1): 15–34.

Pfeiffer, K. Ludwig. 1990. "Fiction: On the Fate of a Concept between Philosophy and Literary Theory." In *Aesthetic Illusion: Theoretical and Historical Approaches*, ed. Frederick Burwick and Walter Pape (New York: Walter de Gruyter), 92–104.

Quartermain, Peter. 1992. *Disjunctive Poetics: From Gertrude Stein and Louis Zukofsky to Susan Howe*, Cambridge Studies in American Literature and Culture (Cambridge: Cambridge University Press).

Serres, Michel. 1982. "Knowledge in the Classical Age: La Fontaine and Descartes." In *Hermes: Literature, Science, Philosophy*, ed. Josué V. Harari and David F. Bell (Baltimore: Johns Hopkins University Press), 15–28.

Silliman, Ron. 1984. "For L=A=N=G=U=A=G=E." In *The L=A=N=G=U=A=G=E Book*, ed. Bruce Andrews and Charles Bernstein (Carbondale: Southern Illinois University Press), 16.

———. 1987. *The New Sentence* (New York: Roof).

Spender, Dale. 1990. "Extracts from *Man Made Language*." In *The Feminist Critique of Language: A Reader*, ed. Deborah Cameron (New York: Routledge), 102–10.

Thom, René. 1975. *Structural Stability and Morphogenesis: An Outline of a General Theory of Models*, trans. D.H. Fowler (Reading, Mass.: Benjamin).

———. 1983. *Mathematical Models of Morphogenesis,* trans. W. M. Brookes and D. Rand. Ellis Horwood Series in Mathematics and Its Applications (Chichester, England: Ellis Horwood).

Vaihinger, Hans. 1925. *The Philosophy of "As If": A System of the Theoretical, Practical, and Religious Fictions of Mankind,* trans. C. K. Ogden (New York: Harcourt).

Webster's Third New International Dictionary. 1966 (Springfield, Mass.: Merriam).

Wittgenstein, Ludwig. 1961. *Tractatus Logico-Philosophicus,* trans. D. F. Pears and B. F. McGuinness (London: Routledge).

ANN LAUTERBACH

IN THE MUSEUM OF THE WORD (HENRI MATISSE)

to Thomas Neurath

1.

There was the shield of another language
transient enclosure/gate

swings open

shut shut
   walking unnoticed into it

as with *avec*

down stone steps into the vineyard

rose as decoy/beauty as use

riding up onto the surface

glance, sway/hawk

comes down dragging silence with it
no light, no applied Sun King

opposing shine, commonly

bereft

creature of habit lost in a wood.

Here I said take these thimbles these hooks
you can count them and toss them away
one six nine/they
will fit under any stream, fill any slot
will color the waters
of the restless exhibit

                    lizard's billowing throat
hiccups on a wall/its tongue
flicks air
                    bird-strewn wind.

And the milkman's doubling dream, his
dilemma, the composition of his
intolerance for dawn/great
Aubergine Interior too frail to move: link
between A Conversation and event. There was

there had been an awkward tour.
I was shown two rivers, their vistas

                              snailfooted/waterskinned abyss
                              wheelwinged staring at muck
                              weedy, indifferent, purplepronged up
                              in avid rays/their comprehensive *is*
                              bearing emblems smaller than time

under the decor
coiled among rocks

I met a woman with odd eyes
she said this is the figure of guilt
hurling a snake boulder
                    wall
ripped from a wall
                              fragment installed.
This country is a
cavern of drunk light/shade rubbed onto day
the corpse is not luminous/vines dangerous/flowers profuse
as in an arbitrary Eden. These
consolations also are damaged/seepage under roofs
thru which the musics
might come.

2.

She traveled.

Sun lay against her knees printed on purple
boughs fell with a thrash
color collected on the dusty sea floor
                       fronds meticulously scissored/commerce
          raged through the sky binding its harmonies
regardless of space.

Although something insisted, pointing.
Although similar doors did not open similarly.
Blackbirds reminded her of written blackbirds/it was
humid with blackbirds/her mind an inscription/a proverb
or heap, so she could almost see its faithful
retrieval: monkey hanging with long limbs/bird
on her shoulder/rigid man/moon
doubled in glass.

3.

A fable of prescience/looking up into the sky's garden
and the statues on the roof
withstanding bombardment

                seven paces to Paradise
                  halted startled voyagers/nothing to correct
                    the possible direction collides with the way
                      each morning's tray a rudimentary splendor.

I said here are some useful numbers
some untranslatable rain

                façades pockmarked in the new contingent state
              now untethered on the Street of the Harp
                the blind man cannot/soft sloped palm
                  dog leading him on into the unscented garden.

They are scooping out the bloods in jars
the real has a stench/it is not
the tableaux we elicit.

I went up a steep hill in a foreign country
in unknown grass/there was an aperture
       boats, birds
                many unknown letters
         snake-wrapped urn
                      Persephone delayed
                          stolen, raped

Hotel where Mozart stayed/street where Brecht
Beckett's daily walks

               impermanent oracular trace so that

not any fragment will do counting my steps
from margin to margin/scenic on foot
turning a page.

4.

In Museum Street, Liu Hai is
standing on a three-legged toad
the toad
was thought to inhabit the moon
it lost its leg
in order to correspond

with the three-legged bird
that inhabits the sun.

And the Apostles were fishermen and thieves
base fellows neyther of wit nor worth

seal
        reduced to a wax turd
            flaunting a tail
                            charred Charter's remains
                                under glass.

Merlin
helps a young man
to paint his
shield/an illustration

Attendants in a garden mounted on a crane

Under green and ochre glazes
under turquoise purple and ochre glaze
with aubergine, green and straw glazes

In a woods a black scroll
let us caption the first scene

on oak
on poplar on lime

green earth has been used under gold leaf
instead of the usual orange bole

as well as I can

                    As if conducted to the eulogy fields to lie down with a shade
                    under turbulent vines
                    walls studded
                    Peiro's meticulous plumage

Come this way said the guard this is where
your opponent lies grieving
here are the spoils set in violent maps, re-
named, disinhabited, inherited, made
bloodless with shine.

Read this example
it praises the country of origin

it teaches you facts
in the new gray wing

                    lion, corpulent monk

Here are some postcards to send home/the one
you want is sold out/the thing you came to see
is temporarily gone
                    that she is seated/that the door
                    that the window
                    that she wears part of a tree
                    that the color of the conversation
                    moves as if it were sky/that the frame
                    continues to dissolve
                    (sadness of the Rose Marble Table)
                    man wearing a pajama column
                    rigidly pronounced/woman
                    redrawn in response—

                    Is it possible to memorize this blue?

S T O N E S (ISTANBUL, ROBERT SMITHSON)

I.

Forget that version, gist's
truncated eruption, stone
placating heat, avenue luminous but forbidden
up the steep assault. She of glittering rings, of the swollen
intricacy of faith, sinks into dust, frees an icon from its
distillation—unction of tears, waxy scent
of a remnant nave. Out there, things ride their riddles

like toys in space, an agenda gap on the morphic tide.
Here, souls pivot on scripted discs
curving away from the story
we thought we would always tell.
Bird, halo, gust,
Poseidon grass and impeccable weave
(silk on silk) young sailor with one leg raised,
the bride stalked, red beads
hurting her throat.

Now a veil
is thrown clear across the disturbance
across the domestic stage
to the circle's wet edge.
I can see through this, and this, I can see
the dispersal as if it were tomorrow, hinge of arrival opening—
how it goes, adage after adage, through the sanctuary,
the arcade,
dipped pigment and last trace
trespassing over a bridge onto a continent, the increments
bewildered by detail—
searching the site,
mouth, thumb, foot,
stone angled across the processional
where they climb to stare, the him and the her,
black goats bleating from the cloister
transfixed, invisible, passing something on.
Single plaintive note, little redundancy.

2.

The arcade leads
from sacred to secular, carrying the relic
overhead, saint
hammering away at bedrock, swallows
igniting air's scripture,

sediment extended outward and down—

nudity of the example, its accumulated rite.

In this space, glyphs
transcribe scale's precision.
This or that step
falters at the bazaar,
postcards fall through the mosque's vaulted diaspora,
releasing their images from history's
crude hideout,
mistakes and dead-ends
in peripheral vision—men hugging each other
while another, bloody scrap on the road, is perpetually beaten.

There was the illusion of purpose, the illusion of content,
as if we were responses annulled by our norms.
Hired old dame weaving,
raw wool pulled through
a tourist economy,
its itinerant, spectral, real.

A false god has a greater reality than the true,
and *so extensions of the Cartesian mind are carried to the most
attenuated points of no return*
babbles the anthropologist
as a young Turk wraps a car in cloth
to mourn the contemporary, his desire
kept under the revolution's chronic restatement, tour guide
speaking in third person, bus of strangers
importuned with tea.
                              The impure surface,
iridescent purple, green and silver surfaces,
these surfaces disclose a cold scintillation,
sight is abolished by a hermetic kingdom of surfaces.
The surfaces of the reliefs are definitely surfaces,

the surfaces in Scorpio Rising,
or California surfaces, the
brilliant chromatic surface—Thanatos in aqua,
surfaces that look mineral hard. A variety of surfaces
from Saturnian orchid-plus to wrinkle-textured blues and greens,
the inside surfaces of the steel sites,
every surface in full view.

3.

Comatose vision
etched in a mirror

sleep extends its tale
deprived of solace

the dream's epithet
profits us not

sweltering veil
verandah backlit

her wound hair
measured for afterlife

the Sultan's concubine
kept in a cage

heat's fiasco
forensic pursuit

huge jewels
perfectly arranged

dialogue stymied
at the mark of lost faith

4.

I saw a young boy in a row boat but he did not see me.
Chaste catastrophe of a broken mast

                         men holed up in the mountains
        to travel as lightly as snow
         to fall
              upon fact

Already a tool's coercion
reels with annunciations
of some one or thing. A yellowy
dross fades into apertures
whose program is scuttled—
diadems for children
made to fall apart.
O spiral of light!
The petals fall, water
is dull scum. Once
among these you thought
shadow nerves would come alive
but the body is a fetish: all its moments sealed in a box.
Perhaps the sculptor's last nobility
gives something back, like the moon to a landscape.
The old knight, there in dark garb, peers at the abstinent blank.
We can make things look natural, but that doesn't mean they are.
We had told the story of
restoration, pasted the new leaf on the cold tree.
A belated significance forecasts
its currency, as if among fragments
we might enter the glare where history collapsed,
catalyst dispersed as the unremembered,
one ruin much like another, one choice
for a better tomorrow: mass appeal, filling station, chorale.
And the hostage chisel—transference and mechanism
caught by intention's blind noise, site newly animate—unearths its find.

POETIC STATEMENT

As (It) Is: Toward a Poetics of the Whole Fragment

> . . . it is precisely out of the flaw or excess in an equation that
> meaning springs
>
> Barbara Johnson, "Disfiguring Poetic Language"

I.

When you pick up a piece of old crockery in a second-hand shop, often
there is a little
white tag on which the price is written, along with the phrase
"as is."
"As is" indicates that
the object, say it is a cup, has a flaw: a crack or a chip or some
other anomaly testifying to
past use. If the object in question is a textile, say a slip or a sweater, "as
is" indicates a rip,
or a stain. "As is" suggests the distance
from perfection that the object has traveled
through the course of time, its fall from Platonic grace or virgin purity.
"As is" is a variant
of "as if," the way in which desire ineluctably turns into fulfillment
or disappointment,
and in that turn, "something" is simultaneously lost and found. As has
become abundantly
clear, and not to overstate the obvious, contemporary poetic practice
negotiates this terrain and its
recapitulating dualities—presence/absence, materiality/transparency,
text/performance,
and so on, more insistently than any other current human activity.
The lost/found place of "as is" thus could be seen as a poetic
methodology, through which we
might revise the modernist fragment. The poem now is rendered
as an address that
eschews totalizing concepts of origin, unity, closure and completion, and
is construed as a
series of flaws or openings through which both chance and change
register a matrix of
discontinuous distributions, where contingency itself is offered as an

affective response to
the "is" as is. Meaning is rendered as an unstable relation to sites of
objective and
subjective
value. The reader/listener participates in the construction of significance
not by filling in
the gaps and elisions, but by appropriating whatever fragment is "useful"
to her. The hope
is that the relation between epistemology and power is kept regenerative.
When President Clinton remarked "It depends on what the meaning of
the word *is* is" he
unwittingly allowed us to witness the flaw between the reified "is" of
an imaginary but knowable present and the imperfect or furtive "is" of
the actual as is.
Between the first and the second "is" is—however inadvertent on the
President's part—an acknowledgment of chronic interpretative vigilance
that the generation he and I share came to understand as the only possible
negotiation with reality
and the ways in which language pictures or captures it.
For a while I have been interested in the notion of a whole fragment.
This fragment is not
one in which one laments a lost whole, as in Stein, Eliot, and Pound, but
that acknowledges the fact
of our unhandsome condition, where we suffer from having been being,
and in that
acknowledgment foreground what is: the abraded and indefinite
accumulation of an infinite dispersal of sums. In this construction,
meaning abides
or arises exactly at the place where "use" appears, "use" here meant as
both pragmatic
and as wear. It is my desire or intention to construct a poetics in which
meaning is found
within the terms of such vagrant contingency.
The consolation of a distilled or stabilized "reality" is nothing if not an
illusion of
syntax, where syntax stands for any logic of recognition. I have a love for
this construct of
a normalizing stability, but I recognize its habit of formulating, at the
least impulse,
categorical imperatives that obscure and resist the actual conditions,
possibilities, and
complexities in which we find ourselves.

The world constellates significance out of habits of congruence,
continuity, and context.
These signifying terrains elude and evade my own sense of being on a
flexible and
indeterminate boundary, even one that eschews boundaries to celebrate
inwardly mobile margins.
I think world presses on language and language on world at every point,
and by "world" I mean material,
spiritual, political, and cultural presence,
a continuous flux of *is* recuperated as is.

2.

"It, say it, not knowing what. Perhaps I simply assented at last to an
old thing. But I did nothing. I seem to speak, it is not I, about me, it is
not about me. These few general remarks to begin with."

Samuel Beckett, *The Unnamable*

Ideas of perfection and wholeness of course easily translate into ideas of
moral
absolutes such as truth. We have, at the core of the rhetoric of
jurisprudence, the notion of "the whole truth," enjoining us to tell every-
thing, to withhold
nothing, and in that inexhaustible narration to somehow fully capture
what transpired.
But as John Ashbery told us, whether you leave it all in or out, "truth
passes on,"
escaping through the leak, or the rip, of the ever-porous, ever-shifting lin-
guistic fabric. It is at this
moment that one begins to think again about asking the question "Who is
speaking?" and only then to further
ask, "What is she saying?" Certainly one way in which we have
shifted our understanding of works of art is to know that the how and the
what are so
profoundly intertwined that there is no possibility of separating them into
such easy
categories as forms and contents. *How* and *what* in combination make
content, and
content, when it comes in contact with the other, the one who listens or
the one who reads,
then informs what we hope can be construed as meaning.
Poets and other artists have been concentrating on, drawing attention to,

Ann Lauterbach | 365

the relation
between the *how* and *what* of artmaking
throughout the twentieth century. It is what we do.
In re/citations of Ezra Pound's injunction to "make it new" emphasis has
invariably
fallen on the word "new," the word that most conjures the operations of
commerce
and capitalism in this that was "the American century." We have been in
thrall to the new, even as
it has worn itself through with recyclings, a kind of *deja new,* which has
exhausted our attention and made us all victims of fashion. As Jean-Fran-
coise
Lyotard says, "Hidden in the cynicism of innovation is certainly the de-
spair that nothing further will happen."
We have ignored the
other two words, *make* and *it,* as if they were of no significance. But it is
precisely in the
ordeal of the making, and in the powerful ambiguity of the "it," that we
need to refocus
attention. For me, the "it" is the fragment of reality out of which we each
make our poems.
I have a phrase that I use often to express my sense of a work that has ex-
posed the
vitality at the core of making: *the it of it.* I think this is not
an entity, not a thing, but a force
around which everything else swirls; without *the it of it*
everything that swirls would be only an inchoate, inarticulate miasma.
We want to believe that language, as a vehicle of inclusion and closure,
can somehow contain/reflect all of the it, which of course is not possible.
Or rather,
language can and does contain all of it; one might say that what we know
and perhaps what we believe is only
because of the bearing of
language, but we have learned that for every instance of this knowledge(of
it)
there is another, with another
portion of
it about to be.
I have come to believe that meaning is made at the intersection, at the
boundary or the
seam: where one thing or being stops and another begins. Even in the
seamlessness of the

internet, in
which "everything" rides into and out of view, there are still the
determinants of scale, or relation, and emphasis, or inflection. And there
are still the
operations of choice, although these seem increasingly obscure. At the
interstices of an environment of sameness and homogeneity (which pur-
ports to be variety
and vitality) there is still the possibility of an
organizing intelligence that must select one it/is over another.
These selections or choices are what finally or eventually allow us partici-
pate in the
making of
meaning, however flawed, however partial it is.

"ENLARGING THE LAST LEXICON OF PERCEPTION" IN ANN LAUTERBACH'S FRAMED FRAGMENTS

Christine Hume

1. "Frame within Frame": Giotto and Henri Matisse

A work of art must carry within itself its complete significance and
impose that upon the beholder even before he recognizes the subject-
matter. When I see the Giotto frescoes at Padua, I do not trouble
myself to recognize which scene of the life of Christ I have before me,
but I immediately understand the sentiment which emerges from it,
for it is in the lines, the composition, the colour.

Henri Matisse, "Notes d'un peintre,"
La Grande Revue (December 1908)

BOTH ANN Lauterbach and Henri Matisse claim Giotto as a key source
and model for their artistic ambitions. For both, Giotto's work exemplifies
art's power to communicate serious content without recourse to literal de-
scription. In reconciling the solidity and spiritual humanity of Giotto's
frescoes with the flat decorative surface of contemporary art, Matisse's art
sacrifices the physical appearance of bodies and objects to a mental rhythm

and a "perspective of feeling."[1] Julia Kristeva connects Giotto and Matisse by their revolutionary uses of color; color, she says, is the device through which "Western painting began to escape the constraints of narrative and perspective norm (as with Giotto) as well as representation itself (as with Cezanne, Matisse, Rothko, Mondrian)."[2] In Matisse and Giotto, color condenses subjectivity and objectivity—psychological and cultural values interlock, transforming color-soaked surfaces into single-perspective-shattering volume. In her determined turning of subjective states of mind into visual objects so as to create a feeling-of-fact as opposed to a matter-of-fact, Lauterbach's work finds affinity with Giotto and Matisse. Lauterbach sees her own work aligned with Giotto's "unique sense of scale, his blunt expressivity, the awkward power . . . of intimacy, his astonishing capacity to value the human, even, or especially, within a matrix of spiritual design."[3] In *Before Recollection,* "Aperture" invokes the "plummeting and stayed" putti from Giotto's Scrovengi Chapel in Padua and captures Giotto's overwhelming awe of faith in his epiphanic yet anecdotal style.[4] In both fresco and poem, the putti's heightened presence and gravity dovetail with the movement of their arrangement to manifest a reverberating lament: "This transparent stain left on the air where was is" ("Aperture," 65). With Giotto, color acts as a transition between clashing surfaces in the same way Lauterbach's syntax conveys transition between her descriptions of mental and emotional conflict.

Matisse's *L'Atelier Rouge,* a talismanic painting for Lauterbach, uses color to linger between two-dimensional and three-dimensional worlds. In this painting Matisse merges personal subject matter and imaginative decorative technique. He displays characteristic polarities such as light and shade symbolized by the juxtaposition of one black and one white sculpture in the background. Red both saturates and absorbs the studio space and furnishings. At the studio's center, a red intensity stands alone; colorful objects circle its red heart. Pictorial relationships dominated by a circular rhythm establish spatial depth; for instance, the white plate, glass lip, and curling nasturtium leaves in the foreground reinforce the round ceramics, dresser knobs, and clock with no hands in the background. Distortion animates the way Matisse's intuitive and emotional response informs what he sees and imagines. By flattening the interior, Matisse draws us to the flags of the artist's presence, his canvases on the walls of this interior. For Lauterbach, "The empty frames and outlines of objects set into the red field compelled me to realize that any event, any narrative, is essentially a fragment imposed on or extracted from the multilayered, multidimensional flux of things."[5] This painting by Matisse—a continuous inspiration and influence throughout Lauterbach's career—makes an appearance in "Chalk" from her first book, *Many Times, But Then:*

A flat room, a painting, intrudes.
A red stain veils space,
holding it up. A residue of seeing
frame within frame within us.
The edge is our signature.

A breach. You go on alone.
I am making doodles on spare paper
thinking of a barracuda, how I write
as an excuse to smoke in the morning.
These filters in the square ashtray,
Happy Birthday written all over it,
are the size and shape of those corals
you picked off the beach to make necklaces.
I wish you could see things more plainly.

A new arrangement moves up.
We press south. The colors are heat,
a version of white, that moon white.
Something is absent among us.
The painting is L'Atelier Rouge. (MTBT, 21–22)

Her lines organize the poem as Matisse organizes his painting, around
tensions of horizontal and vertical movements and planes; in *L'Atelier
Rouge* the same flat red appears on the floor and walls, yet we distinguish
easily between the two planes. Lauterbach's architectural "frame within
frame within us" lends her moment a Mattissian dimensionality. Perspec-
tive is conspicuous as verbal images converse with visual ones: the filters
that are "the size and shape of those corals" and the wish to "see things
more plainly" cast the stain of subjectivity over all. In the painting, we see
no artist, no central figure or object; in the poem, the reader also encoun-
ters absence. Lauterbach contracts and suffocates her figures in their inte-
riors without negative space in the same way Matisse in his studio reddens
and so siphons all potential breathing room. The studio finds its true
place in the experience of red: the acute intensity of the artist at work. Just
as color reflects Matisse's emotional feeling toward his subject, so too, for
Lauterbach, color becomes emblematic: a heat, a moon, "something . . .
absent among us."

Lauterbach's delight in pattern-making—especially a circular rhythm of
revelation and reveiling—matches Matisse's intricate interior with discrete
frames of reference to the artist. "A breach. You go on alone./I am making
doodles on spare paper": Lauterbach folds a tense scene into her interpre-
tive descriptions of the painting. This alternating of the abstract and the
figurative mirrors Matisse's middle course between realist art and the art of

pure imagination and sensation. In both *L'Atelier Rouge* and "Chalk," scale shifts and juxtapositions spotlight relationships among things and between people; the compositional space shows a highly inflected relation of image to ground. The visual syntax of Matisse gathers into Lauterbach's contradictory impulses and governs the tight structure and cyclical rhythm of this section of the poem.

Lauterbach's decision in her early college years to abandon painting for poetry pivoted on her fascination with the quandary of representing the visual in the aural and temporal medium of language.[6] Given her background, it's no surprise that her oeuvre invents a virtual gallery of responses to contemporary and classic art works. Every one of Lauterbach's books contains poems sparked by the visual inspiration of, say, a Giotto, or contemporary artists such as Ann Hamilton, Robert Ryman, and Ellen Phelan. Her compositional methods, too, consistently explore the ways in which language engages the borderland "between the need for eternity and the recognition of mortality."[7] Within these liminal spaces, her dual empathies construct verbal analogues to visual perception, where the surface and the frame act as points of perspective and fragmentation pressures the well-established relationship between poetry and painting.

Poems in Lauterbach's first two books keep up a reassuring pretense of contained narrations and pictures. Her method registers in crystalline hermetic surfaces that create resolute harmonies from tension, ambiguity, and elusive moments. In her dealings with the visual arts, she excavates the unseen. She says, "Some of my [early] poems are narratives drawn from looking at specific pictures. These inner narratives were for a long time for me the most important aspect of my work, and sprang from a desire to allow a mutating interior responding voice to be realized in the world. . . . [F]or me, visual art provided a perfect *fact* for this kind or response, since for each person it is unique, and exists prior to critical judgement."[8]

Written approximately fifteen years after "Chalk," Lauterbach's poem "In the Museum of the Word (Henri Matisse)" clearly uses Matisse's sensual spectrum with more abandon. This poem demonstrates several general departures from Lauterbach's early work: a contracted line expands to include silence and invite active readerly participation, a flawless continuity gives way to severe discontinuity, and dominant visual imagery leaps into discursive tendencies and aural primacies ("from margin to margin/scenic on foot"). The poem's museum frame accentuates the digressive and wayward qualities of her later work as well; like Browning's "My Last Duchess" and Ashbery's long poem *Girls on the Run*, this poem incorporates details of many works of art at a "restless exhibit." Yet Lauterbach makes no attempt at drawing a scene before us; rather, she opens a resonant event for us to experience, visually casting a spell in language. No longer do Lauterbach's poems rely on strict left justification or on conventionally intact syntax. Each painting named or described in the poem is a "fragment installed" where "*not any fragment will do,*" but where any and every fragment is inevitable. The fragment is therefore a framed segment. Lauterbach suggests that through these inscribed frames—imaginary and real—we try to invent ourselves. Places become frames inhabited by the mythologies of other people's lives: "Hotel where Mozart stayed/street where Brecht/Beckett's daily walks." In this later work, Lauterbach's fragment intimates a redemptive vision, enacting myth, if myth, as anthropologist Roy Wagner says, "does not say things but makes them, and then disappears into the result."[9]

Lauterbach usually follows elliptical statements with an image that skewers meaning on a vertical plane. For example, the blackbirds in section two of "Museum of the Word" "reminded her of written blackbirds" and become insistent and unpredictable glyphs, a language written in the jungled mind. The speaker reifies language into icon: slashes separating the ensuing trains of images emphasize each set of characters as discrete frames. Such a pictorial language implies that nothing is arbitrary in the connection between sign and referent. As subject and object fight to focus each other, Lauterbach makes figure and ground flicker; consequently, past and present—which respectively set us in the temporal and (still) pictorial—become confused. She makes a rhythm of presence and absence: the "shield of another language" becomes a gate swinging between poet and reader in the opening lines. For Lauterbach, the gate of language is analogous to Wittgenstein's fence; here it vacillates between English and French, verbal image and visual image, abstraction and concretization.

Lauterbach ends the poem, and subsequently her fourth book, with an extended reference to Matisse's *La Conversation*—not a gloss of the painting, but rather, as the painting's title invites, a formal and affective conversation with it. In the painting, a couple's dialogue across a window breaks open an "arbitrary Eden" between them. Behind the garden, a pair of blue doors serves as a framed exit. This door is the same sky-blue as the air that engulfs the figures, indicating "the color of the conversation." In both painting and poem, frames open up frames containing patterns and magnifications; interior and exterior spaces converse with and become the converse of each other. As in the earlier section, Lauterbach's poem reiterates Matisse's painting by using grammar and punctuation to frame whole fragments of her description. With a string of solidi and *that* phrases, Lauterbach weaves in and out of the painting's material details. *That* functions here as both restrictive relative pronoun with an antecedent in "the thing you came to see" and as demonstrative pronoun evocative of the "rigidly pronounced" mood of the painting. Characteristic of Matisse, segments of the painting look deliberately unfinished, rough by way of excess in flat color or lack of detail in the same way an "as is" or "as if" quality suffuses Lauterbach's whole fragments. The painting's forms and sentiments have been so thoroughly internalized as to make it impossible to distinguish between the language/images of the painter and the poet. Yet the poem's last line— *"Is it possible to memorize this blue?"*—drives home the poem's concern with differences between perception and the memory of perception. The poem juxtaposes the actual experience of travel with the predigested, staged "experience" offered by museums: "the real has a stench/it is not/the tableaux we elicit." In all of her work, sight stands Janus-like; the face of cognition shares a head with the face of limitation.

2. The Urn and Architecture of Ekphrasis

> Yet eyes this cunning want to grace their art
> They draw but what they see, know not the heart
>
> Shakespeare, Sonnet 24

According to John Hollander, *ekphrasis* means the linguistic representation or descriptive attachment to particular, identifiable works of art.[10] *Ut Pictura Poesis,* the classical reference to the traffic between the arts, is an overt affirmation of similitude where "poesis" acts as tenor to "pictura," the vehicle. For Lauterbach, though, poetry is no "speaking picture"; painting no "mute poem."[11] Gotthold Lessing's legendary treatment of *Laocoön* condemns poetry to exist fundamentally in a temporal realm while painting inhabits a spatial one. Lauterbach's work subverts this distinction by embracing something more akin to the ancient Greek's looser understanding of ekphrasis, which is less concerned with product than with process. Also, as seen in "Tuscan Visit (Simone Martini)," her work dissolves the frames of her interior dramas by commingling protracted presentness and a visual spatiality: "Draped in the foreground, cool smoke/Lifting from the frame/A white scent/In which gold weather sat with gold birds/Depicting it" (*C,* 39). In her focus on process and presentness, she resists shedding the artwork's cultural codes of connotation and historical context in order to re-experience it; that is, she does not merely translate visual art according to her contemporary situation.

Perhaps she takes her cue in part from Keats's uber-ekphrastic poem "Ode on a Grecian Urn," which explores the relationship between pictorial and linguistic values. This poem builds on absence; it spins out analogues of the hollow-centered urn that becomes first an "unravish'd bride," then a pipe and ear, then the hollow repetitions of "happy" and "forever," and finally, the O of "O Attic shape!" These images of silence and sound pulse with strobelike celerity throughout the poem. The urn opens with a slew of questions, the voiced, searching response to "the foster child of silence and slow time" (Keats 1978, 282–83). The verbs' refusals to bring about conclusion aggravate the ode's tensions. Lauterbach revisits Keats's formal gestures: the obsession with absence and silence, the incessant questioning, and the delaying of closure are all conditions that pervade her work. Keats's poem goes on to mediate his questions in a tone of enraged ambivalence toward the idea of stillness itself—stillness of thought, stillness of life in stayed/staid curiosity and desire. This anxiety surely resonates with a poet such as Lauterbach whose own mature work is fiercely mobile and flexible.

In attempting to reconcile the relationship between the final couplet's famous abstractions, truth and beauty, Keats spells out what will become Lauterbach's preoccupations. Only when Keats invests the urn-form with linguistic comprehension can we see it as sublime. "The purely visual, without the agency of living *thought,* is but an artifice of eternity, a cipher . . . a *silent form,*" says Lauterbach.[12] She ends "Still" iterating this condition: "Forms attached to content, content to meanings/Aroused. It is our custom to bring things about" (*BR,* 3). In this way, she casts off the Romantics' valorization of the visual and their attendant belief that poetry is, must be, a tragic distillation and approximation of visual images. Instead, Lauterbach strives to awaken varied modalities of aroused contemplation that are as ethical as they are aesthetic. If truth as a verbal construction necessarily informs beauty as a visual construction, then beauty requires truth as well. This tuning-fork relationship holds the differences between the two abstractions up for investigation. Lauterbach says, "I resist our habit of colluding notions of the real—in the sense of a visual witnessing—with notions of truth."[13] With her, poetry must raise the status of dumb vision—"seeing through to thought" ("How Things Bear Their Telling," *C* 48)—into knowledge and empathy.

Although, in her later works especially, we are usually not able to conjure a cohesive visual scene before our eyes and only occasionally can we identify the specific artwork with which she's engaged, Lauterbach attends to the ekphrastic tradition of heroic failure, the inability of language to adequately transcribe the visual. She focuses on how the language, the talk of a poem, articulates a kind of otherness, alienated from the mute imagistic virtuosity of visual art. The verbal and the visual trade on each other: "Talk is a way of not looking" ("Then Suddenly," *MTBT* 4); "Listening is scenic" ("How Things Bear Their Telling," *C* 47); "Witness No Voice" ("A Clown," *OS* 49). Her work is both object/image obsessed and absence/silence possessed. When Lauterbach lends her eye to the world, her ear calls back; her visual attentiveness galvanizes a linguistic event, "a form of listening through the agency of sight."[14] Images engender words, a response into, through, or toward, but not about, the pictorial. In "Links Without Links," Lauterbach reveals her method: "Poetic truth is not carried by the mimesis of visual description, but by cadence, the construal of felt sound across time that tells the forms of attachment, of attention, of the poet to his world. By resisting conventional narrative strategies, poetry might call attention to the ways in which those structures have obscured, abraded, and falsified the relationships between cause and effect, subject and object, intention and action, in much of what passes for the telling of our recent common history. Poetry resists false linkages."[15]

In this resistance, "Thunder blooms unevenly in unknowable places." Where Lauterbach's lightning-eye strikes, it lights up a moment, "Breaking distance into startling new chambers/We cannot enter; potentially, a revelation." Though they offer "potentially, a revelation," Lauterbach refuses to entertain or enter into "false linkages." The breaking down of distance allows fragmentation to hold the reader in dilemma, at the brink of discovery, thus keeping the possibilities of "unknowable things" alive ("Still," *BR* 3). These lines stage Lauterbach's suspicions of romantic lyricism while at the same time confirming her allegiance to its dialectical sense of wonder and knowledge. As Keats wrote, "we no sooner get into the second Chamber, which I shall call the Chamber of Maiden-Thought, than we become intoxicated with the light and the atmosphere, we see nothing but pleasant wonders, and think of delaying there for ever in delight" (Keats 1987, 283). Lauterbach feels the burden of the Mystery yet pursues the fact of suspense, rather than self-deluding revelation in "new chambers," by developing her now-characteristic series of syntactic dilations and unfolding spaces.

3. "Observing the Necessary Between"

> Everything is written in the white spaces between one letter and the next.
>
> Giorgio Pressburger, *The Law of White Spaces*

Lauterbach's devotion to what resides between truth and beauty leads her to probe the meaning of absence. The (linguistic and spatial) gaps in her poetry mark flux and transience; they mark transitions and leaps of faith; they show the living discontinuity, the loose ends fraying. They are the "myriad disparate narratives which are dissonant or harmonic with each other."[16] Lauterbach's fragment, however, is not the Modernist fragment. She employs Modernist techniques—the fragmentary architecture and painterly line of Mina Loy and the continuous present and sign/signifier/referent confusions of Gertrude Stein—with a post-Cubist understanding of perspective. The Modernist fragments shored against ruins and nostalgic yearning to make them cohere are trucked for a normalized fragment, one she accepts as an entirety in and of itself. Lauterbach's whole fragment also allows multilayered perspectives to coexist without straining after gestalt: meaning is always a wholeness. Her fractured physicalities, in both content and composition, confront us as electrified and playful proliferations of meaning. Visual clarity or totality is not finally the way to insight: "*not a matter of seeing*/[but] *a matter of touch*" ("Staircase," *OS* 60) or of feeling our way through, cadence as our coach. The building of a tonal and musical coherence overrides her fractured line. (Pound and Eliot do this, too, despite their claims to failure.) She says that as her work gradually began to allow interstices, "a spatial dimension to the poems began to emerge, as if the poem were able to create a sequence of pictorial tableaux" and the "original idea of a stanza, as a 'capacious dwelling receptacle' began to materialize in the shape of the poems made."[17] Though her architecture of epistemology is unstable, full of trompe l'oeil, it is not evidence of the mere detached spatiality that Fredric Jameson ascribes to postmodernism.[18] Lauterbach's way of talking about her own writing reveals architecture as a fundamental generating trope: "all my poems come from numerous places or 'sets,' and . . . these become the primary material, which then undergoes whatever 'transformations' are necessary to the poem's realization as event or as 'experience.'"[19] And, more specifically: "In my new collection [*Clamor*] there's a 'girl' who comes in and out of the frame. I used to think of the last line of the poem in a curiously literal way, as being its ground, and the shape of the poem was somehow unbalanced if the last line didn't extend to support the rest of the poem, as if the poem were three-dimensional, in actual space."[20] Lauterbach's spatial imagination builds a structure to house a poetic event—a girl fleeting DeChirico-like into a building's shadows—and so dramatizes temporal and spatial—that is, whole—fragmentation.

Her poetry develops an imaginative theater in which fragmentations open into both a feeling of impinging lacks and constant excess. Her fragments construct wholes much the same way ruins do. "We cannot know his legendary head," begins Rilke's "Archaic Torso of Apollo," then the poem proceeds to convince us of its "eyes like ripening fruit." "[S]uffused with brilliance," Rilke's marble remnant carries the luxurious integrity of something whole. We tend to think of all classical ruins as self-contained, wearing the luminous cloak of Benjamin's aura of authenticity;[21] likewise, the "as is" quality of ancient frescoes convey an authoritative completeness. What remains of Giotto's *Vision of the Ascension of St. Francis*, reproduced on the cover of Ann Lauterbach's *Clamor*, for example, demonstrates how easily we assimilate—even expect—fragmentation in visual art. Between the two figures, part of the fresco has fallen away; the scene has been interrupted by a blank wall, yet the blankness inconspicuously incorporates itself within as the interior voice or answering silence of the monk's open mouth. The curtain in the fresco seems to materialize from thin air in order to repeat the line of the unpainted wall and soften the painted architectural frame. The nested frames (moldings, columns, curtains, walls) around this fragment set the suggestion of depth against a competing attention to surface detail. As Julia Kristeva says, "conflicting oblique lines indicate that the central viewpoint is not in any [Giotto] fresco, but rather in the space of the building where the painter or viewer is standing."[22] In a similar vein, Lauterbach's stereoscopic vision implicates the reader, who stands in for a unifying point of view, "the point at which here coincides with nowhere."[23]

Ann Lauterbach's work reminds us that poetry is a textual art. Just as much as visual art and music, poetry is saturated in the plastic, faceted shapeliness of its particular language and engrossed in sensuous and prerational sounds and rhythms. It's immersed in language's ghostlier demarcations, the rich suggestiveness of words beyond their instrumental reason, beyond the predicates of sense. Lauterbach makes good on Victor Shklovsky's seminal idea of *ostranenie:* "art exists that one may recover the sensation of life; it exists to make one feel things, to make the stone *stony.* The purpose of art is to impart the sensation of things as they are perceived and not as they are known."[24] And for Lauterbach, the poem is not an account or message, but a thing in and of itself, a thing of and through language. It is the theory of itself, too, self-defined, self-contained. We find Lauterbach characteristically at the interstices between Eliot's idea that the poet must be as intelligent as possible and Stevens's idea that the poem must almost successfully resist the intelligence. She says that her poems "negotiate this place between knowing and not knowing, illumination and obscurity, being and not being."[25] They locate middle grounds and focus on what happens between words, and thus recall Olson's open field poetics. Inviting blank space into her poems allows them to explore what it means to organize experience in terms of fields of participation, but not at the expense of interpretation. What's implied in all ekphrastic poems is made explicit in Lauterbach's work: the experience of the viewer/reader is pressured by his or her interpretation of the resonances between particulars in the work at hand. "'So much depends . . . ,'" she quotes Williams, "on finding an image in the structural relation between things."[26] She infuses her work with fences, bridges, and vacant lots "because there is in our culture this increased inability to understand that particular kind of mobility, to understand what it means in an intellectual way; that you can move from one place to another through language."[27] In this way, the seam between two ideas/images/perspectives becomes the primary place of meaning. By "[o]bserving the necessary between" ("Remorse of the Depicted," *C* 18), her use of syntax and prepositions intimate how the meanings in our lives are construed out of relations. If proximity creates intimacy and distance encourages eroticism, the tantalization to touch imbues every gap.

Lauterbach's impulse toward this in-between locus—toward the visual and the verbal, toward silence and voice, toward autobiography as well as high abstraction—place her work in a volatile gap between language and lyric camps of contemporary American poetry. Though unlike Emily Dickinson, William Carlos Williams, and John Ashbery, for example, she is embraced by neither movement. She stands where the concerns of these (artificially) polarized traditions touch. Both extremes claim Dickinson and Williams as predecessors—seeing in their respective oeuvres only what supports each movement's ideology. Helen Vendler connects Ashbery to Romanticism via Stevens, while Marjorie Perloff stresses his links to the avant-garde by way of his mysteries of construction and staunch indeterminacy. Given how frequently Lauterbach is compared to Ashbery, it's odd that she escapes the attention of both Vendler and Perloff and is all but invisible to those who speak for either tradition. Lauterbach's approach to writing—"*to wander to create a vacancy to forget*" ("Nocturnal Reel," *OS* 5)—flanks an avant-garde heart with Romantic drives. "*To wander*" recalls Jorie Graham's errancies, while "*to forget*" resembles Charles Wright's teasing himself out of thought into nothingness or transcendence. However, the middle virtue, "*to create a vacancy,*" is Lauterbach's most urgent calling. In her work, Michael Palmer's elegant address of the self as a mediator between consciousness and the formed world interlocks with Susan Howe's notions of place as a nominalist stage where personal and collective histories raise an architecture of culpable facts and resonant mistakes. Lauterbach's infusion of muscular imagery into syntactical fragmentation and her blend of disjointed and discursive syntax borrow from both romantic lyric and "experimental" language schools. The entangled tensions between voice and place, image and idiom, and silence and language spark upward and burst.

4. American Visionary: Ann Hamilton, Ralph Waldo Emerson, Walt Whitman

> The invisible claims us behind all that is seen, as if its absence were only what hides at the heart of the manifest—or else hides from us what is nevertheless manifest—and silence, what is unsaid within the uttered word.
>
> Edmond Jabès, *The Book of Margins*

We are as likely to find Ann Lauterbach's work in art catalogues as we are in literary journals. Ann Hamilton's exhibit catalogue of her installation *whitecloth* in the Aldrich Museum begins with Lauterbach's "All View (13 Windows)," a poem responding to Hamilton's piece.[28] In the same exhibit catalogue, Hamilton says that her work has "so much to do with a border between an inside and an outside—between feeling and articulation, or the skin as something that contains but that also makes you the container,"[29] a description apposite to Lauterbach's work as well. The opposition between subjective experience and its external register drives this poem in which "mimesis partners metonymy"[30] and metaphors, interpretations, and flights are spun out of more mimetic articulations of *whitecloth*.

Lauterbach's work always strives toward rendering "an Invisible real" ("All View," 11), toward bringing the mysterious into light and making interiority immanent. What's at stake here is an attitude of open contemplation and wonder, an original strangeness and idiosyncratic beauty: "To retrieve Newness/to find/Original Sound" (35). By bringing the inside and unseen into clearer focus and awareness, the poet enlivens Emerson's "moments" (like Hopkins's inscapes); she also pays heed to Emerson's call in "Experience" (an essay of immeasurable importance to Lauterbach) to tip ourselves away from the foreground of our daily lives. "All View (13 Windows)" begins with an epigraph from Emerson—"the moral fact of the Unattainable, the flying Perfect"—that demonstrates her predilection to locate a poem at the site of transition, a border, between inside and outside, "between feeling and articulation," and here specifically, between states of process and perfection, between stable moral fact and flying unattainables.

Lauterbach stitches a poem that weaves inside and outside the Hamilton piece; the white cloth is an "inundated spectral," "sweet Flag," "light's cowl," "cloud," "locket of stars," "Veil of the Bride," "ecstatic sheet," "loose ribbons in her hair," "halo or mark," "the shape of grace," "naked Apparition," "sail set"; it moves through the poem as a kinetic parade of costumes and fluid self-begot forms. In Hamilton's piece, a cloth literally migrates on a pulley system through rooms, through holes in floors and ceilings, just as in Lauterbach's piece it threads through thirteen stanzalike sections, intensifying the ambiguities of and the tensions between interior and exterior spaces. Lauterbach both creates and relates "the space where nothing always is/about to be/Whitecloth" ("All View," 35), and the veil becomes the very vehicle of transformation, not a handkerchief that plays peekaboo with a shape-shifting face. The cloth is apparently capable of ceaseless translation and ramification; it cannot be neatly categorized and housed. These mutations have the force of an act of perception and not the reflex of mere linguistic tricks or likenings. A truculent attention, an active state of receptivity bleeds through the poem's process—both as an act of reading and of writing. What happens in Lauterbach's poems is clearly overshadowed by a *way* of happening; her emphasis on experience, without the Romantic ache for transcendence and nostalgia for the past, aligns her with the Transcendentalist aesthetic.

In one section of the poem Lauterbach alternates opposing prepositions, like positive and negative electrical currents, to literalize the dialectics of inside and outside:

> hearth
> gazing *out from* the domestic pond
>
> whose world
> converts *into* a mirror breathing
>
> *into* the predilection to rise
> easily *from* the ghost-strewn crib
>
> *out of* the night shade
> *into* the Book——
>
> ecstatic sheet
> *beyond* such boundaries of the given
>
> *beyond* the kitchen sink——
> *into* Jerusalem ("All View," 29; italics mine)

This locating tendency confers spatiality upon thought: everything takes form, even *beyond* becomes Jerusalem, the ultimate prepositional place: *into* and *out from; beyond* and *into.* "All View" echoes *whitecloth*'s spatial structures and the site of inside/outside acts as a nodal or transit point. Her generous dish of prepositions—*On a Stair,* for instance, includes a series in honor of its titular preposition—demonstrates her appetite for showing relationships between things and ideas, in arranging and deranging presence.

Typical of Lauterbach's work—as well as Emerson's—paradox assumes an epistemological status. In this light, properties of inside and outside can no longer be seen in simple symmetry. "Dialectics is a consistent sense of non-identity," according to Theodor Adorno,[31] and the problems of working out an identity within a community are paramount. By confronting us with polarities and paradoxes, Lauterbach draws us into a dialectic with something outside ourselves. As in Emerson's work, her inspired utterances stir us to heights of vision—verbal truth informing and informed by visual beauty—rather than a set body of stable facts to follow. In one of her columns in *American Poetry Review,* she says, "Emerson seems to me an American writer who deeply felt the relevance of individual experience, how a self is formed by the world into which he or she comes and then *in turn* forms that world."[32] This sense of reciprocity between self and world rings throughout. Here the window itself blurs distinctions between interior/self and exterior/world; both Hamilton and Lauterbach use this ambiguous space to question our myth of inside and outside and its ontological implications of alienation and inclusion. They probe the values we assign to maverick and team player—and the profound resonances these ideas hold culturally for Americans. The poem simultaneously declares and disintegrates distinctions between personal and social roles—each is illuminated by the light of the other. Lauterbach reinforces the play between insider and outsider and our double impulse toward and away from others by casting her poem around intellectual colonial New England figures who staunchly represent both: Emily Dickinson, Anne Hutchinson, Thomas Shepard, Cotton Mather, John Winthrop. A liquid language spits on the hot iron of history.

Throughout the poem, anonymity and individuality find contingency in perception. Opposite the text, each section opens with a photograph of one of the thirteen windows in the Aldrich: thirteen ways of seeing through, thirteen ways of looking. The title, too, stresses the plurality of viewpoints from thirteen windows (or "all" states or frames of mind) and the singular word "view," and so reconstructs the symbolic construction of America, the United States, and the classic distinctions between individualism and individuality as well as the antagonisms between self and community. The windows' allusion to our original thirteen colonies are made even stronger when we realize that Hamilton actually excavated the museum's original thirteen windows, "peeling the architecture back to its original fabric" ("All View," 27). The title, both contradictory and conciliatory, compels opposition between viewpoints and defines that oppositionalism as the gap to be bridged by a singular eye.

In meditative, accruing method, and telescoping logic, her turn of mind echoes Emerson's; his thematic obsessions also find extension. Like Emerson, Lauterbach attends to spatially placing the "I" within consciousness and cultural history: "Where did you say history is? Here? / At this intersection, in this lot, with this noise" ("Figure without Ground," *OS* 9). Lauterbach's *On a Stair* quotes Emerson's response to his question "Where do we find ourselves?" in the same essay. Lauterbach writes that Emerson's "answer is a digressive list which, in turn, opens into meditation. As he writes, the answer slowly accrues, writing leads him through thickets of negativity and an imploded grief . . . to a rhapsodic affirmation which comes to him through the transformed agency of the trope of an excited child."[33] Both want to "teach the finite to know its master" by reconciling perception with intellect and privileging process over result.

"'A trope is . . . a way of carrying a perpetual imperfection across the river of Becoming',"[34] Lauterbach quotes Harold Bloom in an essay on Walt Whitman. A cloth, for Lauterbach here, is a way of flying the Perfect (unattainable) as a moral fact. That fact gives way to a many-feathered variousness reminiscent of Whitman's *Leaves of Grass*, where grass multiplies its own meanings and becomes ("I guess") "the flag of my disposition" (1973, 33–34) just as the white cloth surrenders to its flag image more than once in Lauterbach's poem: "The great announcement/the evident proof" ("All View," 25). They are flags because they are emblematic—Whitman's grass is the dead's hair, Lauterbach's cloth evokes "grave grass" (15). Whitman's grass is "the handkerchief of the Lord"; Lauterbach's cloth is a "pocket of heavy tears" (19). Whitman, like Lauterbach, is dedicated to the invisible world and removed from egotism through inwardness. The self they observe through imagination has become plural—Whitman's the one and the many, Lauterbach's "the sky's plural One" (19); one view, thirteen windows. And yet Whitman's flags fly as one for the many, while Lauterbach's don't presume such a representational guise: her flags wave oxymoronically as whole fragments. Whitman utilizes the catalogue, an aspect of Transcendental grammar, for its inherently democratic vista; Lauterbach reinvents the catalogue for even more radically antiauthoritarian purposes.

This cataloguing of viewpoints could serve for Whitman readers as a template for reconciling Enlightenment universalism with Romantic particularism: though visions are many, the visible may be singular; "I celebrate myself and sing myself/And what I assume you shall assume," sings Whitman (1973, 28). Yet Lauterbach rejects this irenic aspiration. With her reinvented catalogue, perspectives proliferate more perspectives, and each one is a kind of world unto itself. Each perspective, each window frame, each position of the cloth acts as a visual aphorism. Lauterbach again mimics a Transcendentalist rhetorical tone—both Transcendental aphorism and Lauterbachian whole fragment encourage the reader to follow "the road of excess which leads to the palace of wisdom."[35] Her work opens and keeps opening up the relationship between reality and its conceptual appearances in thought and language. Her slippery and vanishing paths, her shifts of scale and perspective, her subversions of narrative sequence all serve an adamant enacting of relations between detail and total composition, between the one and the many: "*O say* we shall allow all to see" ("All View," 17). When first person falls easily into second or third person in the works of Emerson or Whitman, we understand the implications of universality. In Lauterbach's work, such mutations rarely occur; each pronoun voices a distinct view not meant to represent any group or whole, but rather the discrete perspectives of individuals. When perspectives shift in her poems, they suggest that identity is not ontologically stable and cannot stand for a whole, but rather is a performed construct capable of transformation much like the white cloth itself.

5. The Terrors and Pleasures of Rivers: Edward Hopper

> I'm essentially dialectical: definition comes, for me, directly from relatedness, encounter, engagement. This is not the traditional formation or shape of a masculine self, nor the discourse that has emerged from it.
>
> Ann Lauterbach, "Ann Lauterbach: An Interview"

> One is absorbed, as into a process which is in the process of engaging itself, listing out of the various extensions, stoppages, paths inscribed on the visible but not seen.
>
> Ann Lauterbach, "In Kit White's Studio"

Ann Lauterbach's poem "Edward Hopper's Way" also directly responds to the visual arts in terms of a particularly American landscape. And again, she begins with Emerson—a quote sure to startle Hopper lovers: "Who looks upon a river in a meditative hour and is not reminded of the flux of all things?"[36] Hopper is usually synonymous with stillness and spareness, lonely disillusionment and despair; yet Lauterbach, in typical fashion, gives us jarring juxtaposition and contradictions. She couples stillness with flux, sparseness with all things, Hopperian despair with Emersonian optimism. She isn't interested in writing a Hopperesque poem, but rather in disrupting our settled relation to Hopper's wistful visual language. "Where did you want us to go?/What did you want us to see?" the poem begins. We are caught off guard; a river of questions sweeps us adrift and submerges reference points. She says, "Every frame is danger and security. Poems that interest me are the poems that show me how to proceed, not where to go or what to look at."[37] "Where do you want us to go?" Lauterbach's composition-as-open-investigation translates the Hopperian stare through the window into the reader's stare through the text's shimmering sky of mirrors and its whispering gallery. In Lauterbach's hands, Hopper's intimate spaces lose their clarity while his exterior spaces lose their infinity. Lauterbach muddies the waters of Hopper's zip-locked Americana and sentimentality, and corrupts his single-minded "authenticity." Intimacy in the poem ballasts multiple perspectives: her poems are rarely self-contained; they invite other texts to say what they say, to open the poem's world a little wider. Lauterbach doesn't use these voices to bolster her argument's authority but to facet her work with refracting surfaces. She uses tonal variations and register shifts in the same way—breaking down the romantic monovocal lyric. Her pleasure is constantly to provoke and not to provide comfortable answers: "We are kept by the indefinite, aroused" ("Lakeview Diner," C 6).

The questions and polydirectional surfaces of "Edward Hopper's Way," in fact, serve as a reader's guide for Lauterbach's oeuvre. Her poems are chains of destabilizing associations that resist our complacent satisfaction in knowing the subject. She ups the stakes of Stevens's dictum "the imagination press[es] back against the pressures of reality"[38] by arguing that "poems which can be reduced to their subjects too often fail to show the asymmetry between real and true, and so fail to elicit from the reader's imagination its capacity to interpret (or make judgments about) his or her 'actual' world."[39] Lauterbach abstracts subject matter in order to see beyond it; she taunts, "so you find an instant which seems to be of itself but the temporal ignites and is its subject" ("Edward Hopper's Way," 37). The experience of reading a Lauterbach poem is that of inhabiting a coursing reverie almost to the point of overstimulation. The momentum happily carries a committed reader forward into the pleasures and terrors of the reading process. As Emerson says toward the finish of "Experience," "We live amid surfaces, and the true art of life is to skate well on them."[40] Can one skate the surface and think deeply at the same time? A rapid-glancing eye for pleasure wedded to a trained worshipful attention might seem an impossible contradiction, but it's a contradiction Lauterbach refuses to compromise. Intensely layered figural language awakens the reader into a state of peripatetic, luminous perception that pushes the borders of semantic collapse. "There is this chronic scouting," begins *Clamor*: scouting for the power of language to explore the appropriating power of depiction. At the same time, the poetry seeks to represent its very procedure and so moves us from passive into active seeing and from comprehension into response—from beauty to truth and back again.

In the end of "Edward Hopper's Way" Lauterbach returns to rivers, this time Langston Hughes's "My soul has grown deep like the rivers," and then finally her own "It rains on/into our dark river" ("Edward Hopper's Way," 39). The river that began the poem as meditative flux has by the penultimate line accumulated force, "grown deep." This poem delights in spoiling the temporal river rushing in with all its canonical ideas of narrative sequence and consequence. The last line's "on/into" distills tensions between surface and depth: this is language rivering; this is the river we *do* step into twice. In addition to questions about time/space and surface/depth, she raises questions about singularity/plurality and the nature of seeing, the "intellect of observation/reeled out to its edge" (38). In an interview, Lauterbach compares language to a river we enter and leave freely, yet which "belongs to everything"; she says that "then we need to follow the river where it takes us, but to remember that it moves through a landscape."[41] Yet in Lauterbach's work, the force of the river always seems in danger of dissolving the reader into its process. To follow we must embrace in Lauterbach's words—paraphrasing Yeats—a fascination with what's difficult.[42] Lauterbach creates what Joyce terms a "languo of flows"; in her culture of slippages and loose interconnections, a reader needs associative and initiative abilities, a willingness to go on her verve. "Homer, for example,/finding his way down the staircase" ("Staircase," OS 60); the reader, for example, feeling her way through the furnished dark, "where space is/contingent" ("Edward Hopper's Way," 36). We must accept Lauterbach's resolve not to resolve and to keep alive a presentness in perception. All the better to know her whole fragment by: the wholeness turns upon a dialectic of reading. The whole fragment itself is its own experience—it both leads us on and encourages us to linger. It is the river-moment that the reader steps through and on. Language in Lauterbach's work moves toward but refuses to become a sign of facts, yet it also never parades nonreferentiality; the arrow of reference is always bent or buried or unfixed, and always points to something outside itself. The river of language, as Lauterbach says above, "belongs to everything," but "[w]ithout the landscape, there would be no river."[43] The poem stands for a model of reading, and reading becomes an analogue of historical and linguistic experience itself.

As a point of contrast to "Edward Hopper's Way," take Elaine Equi's "Edward Hopper."[44] Equi's poem begins on recognizable Hopper ground: "His figures lean/like plants/toward light." The poem follows, almost formulaically, with the collective viewer's reaction ("a smile/. . . as if . . ./we'd seem ourselves/naked") then simile becomes metaphor in her retelling of the first stanza from an interior perspective where "the figure" turns now into "the body." The body is a lamp, she tells us, "on the threshold/of something big." After the fulcrum paradox— "This sense of eternity/however brief"—comes the "O" of ironic personal departure:

> O sidelong glance
> in whose indifference
> I bask
>
> years from now
> is it this
> you will return to me? (Equi 1998, 86)

Equi's poem provides a foil in method and ideology to Lauterbach's. Though Equi doesn't describe a particular Hopper painting, her poem relies on a simulacrum of Hopper's paintings, a quintessential scene and tone. She checks Hopper's nostalgic romantic predilections with the final stanza's skeptical urban irony; even so, the epiphanic ending remains intact.

Lauterbach similarly bucks up against romantic impulses; however, her skepticism does not serve as a point or punch line, but runs through her work. Lauterbach's work "sings into the butterfly weed and fog/Only it is not a song, it is//Her desire to sing and her desire not to sing" ("After the Storm," C 16). Here, in a title that sets us in a potentially sweeping romantic landscape, she recalls Stevens's singer in "Idea of Order at Key West"; yet Lauterbach's singer voices ambivalence into her sea of "weed and fog." The speaker tells us, "She is authored by another, one who says /Sing! Do not sing!" (Ibid.). Like Beckett—think of the final words of *Unnamable*, "I can't go on; I'll go on"—Lauterbach emphasizes dramatic oral qualities even when her subject takes on the absence of subject and her narrative assumes the absurd fallibility of narrative. Lauterbach teases out the impossibility of a singular coherent voice in her own work: the subject is always "authored by another"; at the same time her voice is "Swaddled in archives of her self" (Ibid.). If we recognize a defining condition of the lyric, from Sappho to C.D. Wright, as authorial control and singular heroic expression, then, Lauterbach fractures and implodes this tradition with wildly generous lyric capacities, large enough to contain competing demands of sensual and analytic intelligences. Her approach since her third book, *Clamor*, is dialogic—"Edward Hopper's Way" stitches the words of Robert Frank, David Smith, Emmylou Harris, Leonard Bernstein, and Emily Dickinson into its textures. Even her essays are crowded with speakers; her method is enthralled accumulation. Like Cornell's constructions, her poems garner things set in charged juxtaposition in a theater of the mind. Unlike Cornell's constructions, she does not set these juxtapositions of voice and objects toward a totality, a complete textual impression. "Meanings derive as episodes of choice"[45]: Lauterbach offers various speakers—quoted and fictional—in her writings in order to draw the reader into dialogue with choice. These voices converse with meaning; they vacillate between objectivity and subjectivity. They contain but are not contained by external and experiential states, the colloquial and the visionary. She argues for "a self as a vacancy with language schemes" ("Broken Skylight" C 73). These language schemes articulate whole fragments of experience, self-contained yet necessarily impure, broken, and promiscuous, because, as Yeats's Crazy Jane says, "Nothing can be sole or whole/That has not been rent" (1989, 260). Yet instead of building a whole from that which has been rent, Lauterbach builds that which is unfinished and inconclusive from framed (w)holes.

6. Said, Unsaid, Not Said, Silence: Susan Crile, Robert Ryman, Ellen Phelan

> . . . by Silence and by Speech acting together, comes a double significance.
>
> Thomas Carlyle, Sartor *Resartus*

> Thus mastery consists in the power to stop writing . . . thereby restoring to the present instant its rights, its decisive trenchancy.
>
> Maurice Blanchot, *The Space of Literature*

Lauterbach's flow of perceptual experience and performance empties objects of their materiality. Subjects—for there is rarely a central stable subject—in Lauterbach's world have little to stay them as such. As perception modulates thought, "a painting/of a young woman in a red dress" becomes "paintings of fire," which spins into a woman describing her father in "Ashes, Ashes (Robert Ryman, Susan Crile)" (*AFE*, 84–88). Transmutations occur by invocation and speculation: she asks us, "Is it merely a sunset, this fire,/seen from the dusty window of a passing train, or is it/the oiled conflagration of an event brought home to us as a trophy" (88). "Ashes, Ashes" subsumes the pictorial into its semiotic plenitude and perforating blank spaces; the poem's initiating energies derive from both Crile's oil-fire paintings, which respond directly to the Persian Gulf War, and Ryman's white paintings, which "represent the silence of the refined or contained space of 'art' as well as the notion of incipiency which any 'blank' space suggests."[46] This is the same blank or ruin that Emerson says "is our own eye,"[47] for in Lauterbach's world "no space is neutral" ("For Example," *AFE* 59).

An early sequence sparked by Ryman's same untitled white paintings from the late 1950s reveals the evolution of Lauterbach's ekphrastic mode. "The White Sequence," a series of seven crisp poems from her first book (*MTBT*, 5–11), uses "white" as a centerpiece for emblematic moments that emerge from the quotidian. These poems stay strictly within the phenomenological world, and the charmed moments of whiteness quote "a kind of Platonic synecdoche." She says, "I wanted to understand why someone would make a painting that reiterated the surface of the wall onto which it was affixed. After many visits, I decided that the painting was to be understood as a fragment of Whiteness."[48] Through contextual shifts these "fragments of Whiteness" slip the straitjacket of a single code, variously signifying change, exception, periphery, inwardness, forgetting, death, erasure, signification, permanence, and presentness; she uses color like Matisse might in the "laying down of One meaning so that it might at once be pulverized, multiplied into plural meanings"[49] that clearly outline and define worldly attachments and relationships. Laura Mullen's recent "White Paintings" sequence conversely uses the same Ryman paintings as analogues to an equivocal internal state.[50] Mullen's poems recall some of the same abstractions and associations as Lauterbach's; yet because Mullen never lets us out of the painting's hold, the very lack of boundaries between things, the conflated relationships and confused identities, drive a vertiginous desperation to see beyond their blinding, seductive fields.

Like Mullen's poems, "Ashes, Ashes" embeds and absorbs the visual work to which it responds much more deeply than we see in Lauterbach's earlier poetry. The rhetorical futility in the poem pinpoints the helplessness of representation in the face of the war that Crile's fire paintings address. "As if" and "if" statements riddle the poem with anxiety—nothing is ever quite realized or accepted except by the child whose lively imagination invents a world beyond strict imitation. This child's shadowy relation to fixity conspires with the Lauterbachian improvisational nature of the self. If we may reverse the equation in Lauterbach's poetics statement, "as if" is a variant of "as is"—the "distance from perfection" becomes "the lost/found place." "As if" entertains that which is lost (negation) and that which is found (assertion) at the same time, never closing down the speculative process.

"Ashes, Ashes" opens with glimpses of inscaped (or whole) fragments: "Humped gravity/tree-backed vatic shard/white/disarray/arc/secretly allied to the dark clear dark/herald" (*AFE*, 84). These rhyming pure perceptions engender an object in and of itself, "a cup in the landscape" that is "buried under the indefinite/as if it would last" in section one (Ibid.). This cup shares little affinity with Stevens's jar in Tennessee. In his "Anecdote of the Jar," the speaker *places* artifice in the natural world in order to show the cultural tincture of our "natural" perceptions. The jar controls the wilderness around it; in Lauterbach's poem, the landscape dominates and mocks ("as if it would last") the container. What's fractured here momentarily captures active essence or wholeness. However, this capture is a pyrrhic victory in the context she describes: "as if setting were bondage" (*AFE*, 85). The characters in this poem seem as trapped and defined by their settings as figures are in paintings: "The violinist moves/like a marionette" (85); "Sooner or later he'll want a child/hushed up against him" (84); "As if we could say to the fire,//*Stop! I command you, stop!*" (85). There's "no way out into a song"; we can only assume "That thou woudst narrate me/thru these worlds" (87), that these characters are also "authored by another" ("After the Storm," *C* 16). By drawing, the child serves as a parable of aesthetic energy and imaginative delight; she alone turns simile into metaphor, "as if" into "is."[51] She casts judgment that the reader easily assumes: "I would rather be in jail than/hidden in these devotions" (*AFE*, 86). The cup-in-the-landscape "buried under the indefinite" foreshadows or mutates into "a mouth in a desert/under sand" in the forth section (*AFE*, 87). The cup springs to life, brought from merely carrying "salt, sugar, salt" into the possibility of carrying breath, voice, and language—and at the same time denying it animation, for it is buried under sand.

Contradiction, a Lauterbachian hallmark, finds a central place in her investigation of the visual arts. She's a poet attracted to both clamor and silence; in fact, *Clamor* begins with epigraphs on silence, one from Susan Howe and one from Barbara Guest. Though Howe and Guest are vastly different poets, they share with Lauterbach an investment in working with the visual arts and in (re)discovering a feminist/female lyric. Voice for women is historically bound with silence: the *coincidentia oppositorum* of "Sing! Do not sing!" crashes internal impulses into cultural expectations. In *And For Example*, "Rapture of the Spoken" immediately precedes "The Untelling" where

> it came as if pulled slowly
> as a mouth filled with awe
> moves its silence slowly in a ring.
> Only a picture could picture it. (AFE, 14–15)

Here, the speaker gives Cassandra "at her dusty ball" voiced visions (*AFE*, 15). One impulse provokes its opposite; the consequences for enraptured speaking (or speaking rapture) are enduring demands for reductive "explanation." This tense contradiction manifests an active, living language. Yet "[o]nly a picture could picture it" (beauty); only a mouth could mouth it (truth). She works from the same ethos of response, reciprocity, and responsibility that she expects her readers to employ. She rushes toward language, and yet she distrusts it: an accusation from her first book, "I hear you hate words because they color the truth," ("True and False Green," 15) predicts an aphorism from her latest collection: "Words turn on the mischief of their telling" ("ON (Word)," 31). The reader enters the poem through its fractures and silences, and these spaces entrap the reader in the responsibility of interpretation and response. Through various disruptions and irruptions, Lauterbach encourages the reader to engage the shifting self and persistent shuffling of history/culture. Negative constructions of contradiction are coupled with informing absence—the lack of noise in visual art parallels the silence historically imposed upon women, a silence Lauterbach appropriates. The ekphrastic tradition itself is often seen as masculine mania to speak, to assault verbally the silent object. Lauterbach hears the opera singer's desire for silence alongside her desire to make music, unlike Wallace Stevens's singer in "Idea of Order at Key West" who masters and orders the sea. By giving voice to silence and silence to voice, Lauterbach becomes a medium for the unheard and the unspeakable. Her writing is intentionally difficult because what is being transmitted is difficult, usually outside the range of quotidian experience and language, often oracular: "I want to suggest that you can negotiate the world through language outside of the categories that are given in the world and that some of those categories are unstated or unknown, unannounced."[52] Yet Lauterbach never takes up the podium, the way the Romantics and Transcendentalists do, as a poet-priest. In her essay "Links Without Links," Lauterbach locates her desire to be a poet in the desire to write in the voice of a turtle— "and the voice of the turtle was heard in the land" (37) from a passage (apparently mistranslated) that her drunk mother read to her from *The Song of Songs*—the voice of an animal that she knew had no voice, the voice conflated with her "mother's abject powerlessness" (37). In an interview she says, "Poems should attempt to speak the unspoken, and so allow others to speak" (25). In order to write a voice where there is no voice, Lauterbach's work "resists dominance" (37)—the dominance of heroic and singular signification.

When Lauterbach makes the characters in visual arts speak, she also gives voice to a silence that stirs her. "Music adheres/enclosing the figured silence" ("Ashes, Ashes," 85); the language both liberates the figures and further encloses them. "A Clown, Some Colors, A Doll, Her Stories, A Song, A Moonlit Cove" (*OS*, 34–49), a poem first published as a book in collaboration with artist Ellen Phelan, opens with Clown repeating the word *Ur*, meaning both nonmeaning—that is, an inarticulate sound "uttered instead of a word the speaker is unable to remember or bring about"—and also denoting "original, earliest" (*OED*, 1987). Like Beckett's *qua*, *Ur* offers a preutterance in order to probe meaning itself. Clown, "from his seat on the shelf" (*OS*, 34), has apparently fallen into an especially existential human consciousness. "Said" occurs four times in the first three lines, emphasizing the clown's attempts to try to signify something. Then, after a shift from third person, Clown tells his own story. Lauterbach's interest in the play between silent thing and vocal human, their "apparently simple unknowns" (from the book's epigraph by Giorgio Agamben), finds a setting and a situation. In part five, Doll takes over with an equally questing and questioning consciousness; Clown is "*Fled,*" she says, but "Not yet blooming as aftermath,/sequence stunned in a bud" (*OS*, 38–39). Through voiced reflections, the speaker stands both inside and outside time, vocally attempting to negotiate the dialectic tensions between past (presence of Clown) and present (no Clown). Yet, eleven sections later, the poem ends with determined silence. The final section begins,

"Sleep, mute pieta/*flame of sorrow* it would say/into silent thunder" (47). And ends in "the quantum delirium of a toy god, rushing into captivity," with "a pitter and patter/you cannot mimic" (48–49), that is, one last gasp of disembodied voice addressing an Angel of Time. Lauterbach finally leads us to her mythic turtle: "an unfledged creature/cast upon sand.//Witness no Voice" (49). Synaesthesia moves the poem from voice to no voice where an ancient helplessness heaves forth: a wingless, voiceless thing flung on desert or beach. We are asked to see, to *witness* silence—with all its biblical and political overtones. Are we witnessing our own lack of voice in the face of a poor outcast? Though silence for Lauterbach celebrates an incipient reciprocity, it also allows for an answer, it empowers by potentiality. "No voice" is quite another story, for it implies no volition. In fact, the silence inscribed into her work counterpoints "no voice" and can invest visual art with a sudden clarity or truth by charging it (the seen) with the unseen. As always in Lauterbach's work, this deliberate announcement of absence manifests itself as a haunting phantom presence.

7. Slight-of-Hand Sensuality: Museum Piece

> Seeing as a form of touch, touch as a way of seeing. The gaze as an
> act of intimacy, projecting the body into space (there), taking it in as
> the body is extended into the sensual persuasion of drawing (here).
> The body's signature is the marvelous exposure of singular attention.
>
> Ann Lauterbach, "Brian Wood: Perverse Science"

Visual marks of silence punctuate Lauterbach's work. And because much of her work fans out and scatters over the page, we take it in form-first, running our eyes over the architecture of its lines in order to intuit its shapes before shaping its intuitions. Lauterbach is a kind of Penelope, delaying her readers' push for the marriage between sign and conventional sense; as quickly as she weaves together whole fragments, she unravels or lets out her links, leaving gaps or blanks—a literal unseeming. In "Handheld,"[53] her "eternal recitation/*stitch stitch stitch*/to still the story" (74) rubs against "the violent anonymity of space/*the object usually in this place has been temporarily removed*" (77). This poem begins with a knotty string of things you might find at the Isabella Stewart Gardner Museum— "*the decayed nose,*" "*the bright exit,*" "*the pensive woman.*" With no relationships or positions defined, Lauterbach leaves the significance of associations between these disparate items dangling. Like "Museum of the Word," this poem alludes to many specific paintings; yet it doesn't examine or metabolize the way painting accrues meaning, but rather the way a museum creates—or fails to create—an experience for its visitors. "Handheld" takes up Lauterbach's fundamental quarrel with the decontextualized experience of museums and draws out the tensions between living experience and institutional imitations of experience. The opening images, unhinged from context and hard-put to mean in their usual way, startle us with both their marmoreal physicality and their slide-showlike rapid fire. Without connective tissue, Lauterbach's amplifications and adumbrations elaborately enact conflict between the seen and unseen, the known and unknown.

What interests her is the resonant relation between scale and viewer, between transient image and historical narrative. Here, we have both an atrophied sense of scale and narrative, in an exhibit dictated by taste with its taint of classist values. The poem's introductory list becomes a monstrous portrait of a collector's museum and the museum's attempt to still time. In this labyrinth of things (the Gardner museum does not organize its art and artifacts by any system other than Mrs. Gardner's taste) we need language to orient ourselves. The lack of guiding arrangement in the museum seemingly disrupts the poem, rendering the museum a mere place of evocative clutter. No one here gives truth to beauty; the museum's signs concern themselves with preservation, not interpretation, imagination, or contextualization. In such a rarefied setting, we can only want to possess the stunning place with its solid quiet, not to shape our experience into meaning: "the guitar silent below the depiction of mayhem / holding a dove / holding a scroll / holding the head of John" (77). Lauterbach constructs meaning from the arbitrary *visibilia* at hand by showing us artifacts and life forms meant to express—guitar, dove, scroll, head—but silenced in the mayhem of grasping the past and its now-fetishized beauty. The list also stands for a kind of commodification of sight, a "cultural hysteria"[54] that drives our want to touch and take what museums offer, instead of to understand and know their artifacts beyond an evanescent moment. As it is printed in *Conjunctions*, the poem incorporates actual reproductions of paintings from the titular museum—paintings we hold in our eyes as we become the eye of the beholder. Yet, if as we say the hand is quicker than the eye, perhaps we don't actually see them so easily.

The title suggests that our first impulse is to stroke, tap, steal, buy the paintings. After all, this poem articulates the way things touch each other. The museum's caveat "Don't touch" evokes the desire to touch; when we see the painted outstretched hands of Madonna and Child, the enticement intensifies. What is forbidden in the museum is precisely what its paintings induce. Lauterbach says, "I began to notice how many times we encounter hands, as if to inscribe the entire place with the factuality of presence, the reification of touch. It seemed to me that a curious inversion took place, and that we, the visitors, were like ghosts, mere phantoms passing through the body of a singular being."[55] Through accumulation the museum becomes whole. The museum works on the Modernist paradigm of building completeness out of fragmentation, rather than Lauterbach's incompleteness by way of framed fragments.

As phantoms (or foreign bodies), we move through the museum parts without understanding: "Cannot find here, in the odd locale of the after-imaged/life I went to see, did not see" ("Handheld," 69). Are the images of the museum after-imaged, or is the visitor? Just as in "A Clown," Lauterbach investigates how history erases the present moment at the same time the present obscures the past. How do the past and present touch each other in a museum-goer's experience; how do mental and museum spatialities collide? Time moves back and forth easily here with reversible linking lines. Afterimages fall Icarus-like out of the eye. Connection and disjunction advance and retreat; negative space neatly juxtaposes a sculpted, precise line. Do we touch what touches us in museums? Is all touch reciprocal? Lauterbach mocks this romantic cliché, for the compulsion to touch leads to and/or from the desire "to possess/*this this this*" (74)—an urge that stymies engagement with the object of desire: One cannot erupt into the painting's interior; one cannot become consumed by the image; one cannot find an answering place.

At the same time, touch is an intimacy to be envied in the paintings; what Lauterbach says in "How Things Bear Their Telling" (C, 47), "To touch, to refrain from touching/Nearness is its own, inexhaustible law," holds true here too. Her work exemplifies what Anne Carson says in *Eros the Bittersweet:* "In any act of thinking, the mind must reach across this space between known and unknown, linking one to the other but also keeping visible their difference. It is an erotic space."[56] Within the yearning to know, to take in knowledge, resides a libidinous urge, an "under-thirst/of vigor seldom utterly allayed" (Wordsworth 1967, 242). "The arc beyond the already known," Lauterbach says, is "a radiance that enters so you know you are porous, possibly even contaminated, a form of intoxication, as the skin, touched, knows itself as that which is touched."[57] As with the poetry of John Ashbery and Mei-Mei Berssenbrugge, the experience of irresolute incomprehension is ultimately a sensual and erotic one—semantic and structural resistances arouse curiosity and intrigue. As a poetic strategy loaded with Transcendental ethos, *resistance* provokes readerly crisis, which in turn yields an irreducible, visceral understanding. She ends "How Things Bear Their Telling" with an even stronger assertion about the way writerly desire hinges on erotic desire: "the incitement to hurt, to be inconclusive" (C, 49). With an openness to the contingent—to the likes of coincidence, flirtation, and peripheral visions—her work's aesthetic delirium precipitates interpretive desire.

If, as Anne Carson says, "all human desire is poised on the axis of paradox, absence and presence its poles, love and hate its motive energies,"[58] then for Lauterbach this paradox spins the emotional and narrative textures of sustained incongruence. The startling beauty of surface is further enhanced by a "[t]angled reliquary under all surfaces" ("For Example," *AFE* 39), a tangle of revelations both intimate and politic that lends truth to beauty: "There it is, the display itself/her nude retreat across the carpet, fictive and mean/as Hopper's vulgate" ("Poise on a Row," *OS* 21). Yet Lauterbach's plenitude is mysterious; she makes the mysterious visible but never containable to the eye.

NOTES

1. Matisse, "Notes of a Painter on His Drawing," *Le Point* (July 1939), qtd. in *Matisse: A Retrospective*, ed. Jack Flam (New York: Hugh Lauter Levin Associates), 328.

2. Julia Kristeva, "Giotto's Joy," in *Desire in Language: A Semiotic Approach to Literature and Art* (New York: Columbia University Press, 1982), 221.

3. Ann Lauterbach, "How the Eye Listens," lecture presented at the Isabella Stewart Gardner Museum (April 1999), 3.

4. Each of Lauterbach's titles is spelled out on first mention. Thereafter, the following abbreviations are used:

AFE = And For Example
BR = Before Recollection
C = Clamor
MTBT = Many Times, But Then
OS = On a Stair

5. Lauterbach, "How the Eye Listens," 2–3.

6. See "Poets and Art," *Artforum* 23 (November 1984): 88. At the High School of Music and Art in her native New York City, Ann Lauterbach trained as a painter of "abstracted landscapes," and in the 1970s and early 1980s, her work in galleries intimately involved her with the London and New York art scenes.

7. Lauterbach, "How the Eye Listens," 4.

8. Ann Lauterbach, "How I Think About What I Write," *New American Writing* 14 (1996): 116. I am quoting from an expanded unpublished version of this piece.

9. Roy Wagner, *Lethal Speech: Daribi Myth as Symbolic Obviation* (Ithaca: Cornell University Press, 1978), 252.

10. John Hollander, *The Gazer's Spirit: Poem Speaking to Silent Works of Art* (Chicago: University of Chicago Press, 1995), 5.

11. Simonides of Ceos, qtd. in Anthony Hecht, *On the Laws of the Poetic Art* (Princeton, N.J.: Princeton University Press, 1995), 5.

12. Ann Lauterbach, "Misquotations from Reality," *Diacritics* 26(3–4) (1996): 149. This quote suggests that the visual requires not the verbal to give it voice, but rather a viewer, a mind's eye, to engage with it intellectually and emotionally.

13. Lauterbach, "How I Think About What I Write," 4.

14. Ibid., 5.

15. Lauterbach, "Links Without Links: 'The Voice of the Turtle'," *American Poetry Review* 21(1) (January–February 1992): 38.

16. Lauterbach, "How I Think About What I Write," 1.

17. Ibid.

18. Fredric Jameson, *Postmodernism; or, The Cultural Logic of Late Capitalism* (Durham, N.C.: Duke University Press, 1991), 155.

19. Lauterbach, email to author, July 7, 1999.

20. Molly Bendall, "Ann Lauterbach: An Interview," *American Poetry Review* 21(3) (May–June 1992): 20.

21. Amy England, "Roland Barthes Imagines the Victory's Missing Parts," unpublished essay.

22. Kristeva, *Desire in Language,* 226.

23. Speaking of Giacometti. See Maurice Blanchot, *The Space of Literature,* trans. Ann Smock (Lincoln: University of Nebraska Press, 1982), 48.

24. Victor Shklovsky, "Art as Technique," in *Critical Theory Since Plato,* ed. Hazard Adams (New York: Harcourt Brace Jovanovich Publishers, 1992), 754.

25. Lauterbach, "How I Think About What I Write," 1.

26. "What's American About American Poetry," *Fence* 2(1) (1999): 101.

27. Ann Lauterbach, Charles Bernstein, Jonathan Monroe, and Bob Perelman, "Poetry, Community, Movement: A Conversation," *Diacritics* 26(3–4) (1996): 202.

28. Ann Lauterbach, "All View (13 Windows)," in *Ann Hamilton: whitecloth* (exhibit catalogue) (Ridgefield, Conn.: The Aldrich Museum of Contemporary Art, 1999), 9–35.

29. Ann Hamilton, qtd. in Nancy Princenthal, "Ann Hamilton: *whitecloth,*" in *Ann Hamilton: whitecloth,* 53. See this catalogue essay for a fuller description of Hamilton's complex installation; I by no means do justice to it here.

30. Ann Lauterbach, "Pragmatic Examples: The Nonce," in *Moving Borders: Three Decades of Innovative Writing by Women,* ed. Mary Margaret Sloan (Jersey City, N.J.: Talisman House, 1998), 600.

31. Qtd. in Lauterbach, "Misquotations from Reality," 153.

32. Ann Lauterbach, "The Night Sky V," *American Poetry Review* 26(6) (November–December 1997): 39.

33. Ibid.

34. Ann Lauterbach, "What Is the Grass: Notes Leading Up To and Away from Walt Whitman," *American Letters & Commentary* 5 (1993): 52–53.

35. Norman O. Brown, "Fraction," in *Love's Body* (New York: Random House, 1966), 187.

36. This poem was again made for an art museum: Ann Lauterbach, "Edward Hopper's Way," in *Edward Hopper and the American Imagination,* ed. Julie Grau (New York: Whitney Museum of American Art in association with Norton, 1995), 35–39.

37. Lauterbach, "Misquotations from Reality," 144.

38. Wallace Stevens, "The Noble Rider and the Sound of Words," in *The Necessary Angel: Essays on Reality and the Imagination* (New York: Vintage-Random, 1951), 36.

39. Ann Lauterbach, "The Night Sky VII," *American Poetry Review* 28(1) (January–February 1999): 41.

40. Ralph Waldo Emerson, "Experience," in *The Norton Anthology of American Literature,* 3d ed., Vol. 1 (New York: Norton, 1989), 1012.

41. Bendall, "Ann Lauterbach: An Interview," 20.

42. Lauterbach, "Misquotations from Reality," 148.

43. Bendall, "Ann Lauterbach: An Interview," 20.

44. Elaine Equi, *Voice-Over* (Minneapolis: Coffee House Press, 1998), 85–86. "Edward Hopper" is set, incidentally, beside a poem dedicated to Lauterbach.

45. Lauterbach, "Found Credo," *Conjunctions* 21 (Fall 1993): <http://www.conjunctions.com/archives/21c-al.htm>

46. Lauterbach, "How the Eye Listens," 7.

47. Ralph Waldo Emerson, "Nature," in *The Norton Anthology of American Literature,* 3d ed., Vol. 1 (New York: Norton, 1989), 930.

48. Lauterbach, "How the Eye Listens," 4.

49. Kristeva, *Desire in Language,* 221.

50. Laura Mullen, *After I Was Dead* (Athens: University of Georgia Press, 1999), 83–92.

51. This girl is the Emersonian and Whitmanesque child whose "auguries of innocence" (Blake) and unfettered enthusiasms shed light on adult apathy and convention.

52. Lauterbach et al., "Poetry, Community, Movement," 202.

53. Ann Lauterbach, "Handheld (At the Isabella Stewart Gardner Museum)," *Conjunctions* 32 (1999): 69–77.

54. Don DeLillo, qtd. in Lauterbach, "Night Sky VII," 41.

55. Lauterbach, "How the Eye Listens," 9.

56. Anne Carson, *Eros the Bittersweet* (Princeton, N.J.: Princeton University Press, 1986), 171.

57. Lauterbach, "The Night Sky VII," 42.

58. Carson, *Eros the Bittersweet,* 11.

BIBLIOGRAPHY

Books by Ann Lauterbach

And For Example (New York: Penguin, 1994).

Before Recollection. Princeton Series of Contemporary Poets (Princeton: Princeton University Press, 1987).

Book One (New York: The Spring Street Press, 1975).

Clamor (New York: Penguin, 1991).

Closing Hours (New York: Red Ozier Press, 1983).

A Clown, Some Colors, A Doll, Her Stories, A Song, A Moonlit Cove, with Ellen Phelan (New York: Whitney Museum, 1996).
Greeks, with Jan Groover and Bruce Boice (Baltimore: Hollow Press, 1985).
How Things Bear Their Telling, with Lucio Pozzi (Colombes, France: Collectif Generation, 1990).
If in Time: Selected Poems, 1975–2000 (New York: Penguin, 2001).
Later That Evening (Brooklyn: Jordan Davies, 1981).
Many Times, But Then. University of Texas Press Poetry Series (4) (Austin: Texas University Press, 1979).
On a Stair (New York: Penguin, 1997).
Sacred Weather, with Louisa Chase (New York: Grenfell Press, 1984).
Thripsis, with Joe Brainard (Calais, Vt.: Z Press, 1998).
Vertical, Horizontal (Dublin: The Seafront Press, 1971).

Selected Prose

"Brian Wood: Perverse Science." Catalogue (New York: Lieverman Saul Gallery, 1992).
"Fifth Season." *Denver Quarterly* 24(4) (Spring 1990): 69–76.
"First Words" and "The Free-Lance Muse." In *The Practice of Poetry,* ed. Chase Twitchell (New York: Harper-Collins, 1992), 3–4.
"Genesis (Eden)." In *Communion: Contemporary Writers Reveal the Bible in Their Lives,* ed. David Rosenberg (New York: Anchor, 1995. 451–65).
"How I Think About What I Write." *New American Writing* 14 (1996): 116.
"In Kit White's Studio." Catalogue of White's Paintings 1988–93 (New York: S & S Graphics, 1993).
"Inventing Unreality." *American Book Review* 19(5) (July–August 1998): 1–9.
"Is I Another? A Talk in 7 Beginnings." *American Letters and Commentary* 2 (1989): 81–96.
"Joel Shapiro's New Sculpture." Catalogue (Bielefeld, Germany: Kulturhistorisches Museum, 1980).
"A Life in SoHo, When Even Its Name Was New." *New York Times,* May 12, 1996, p. 51.
"Light Repositories: On David Rohn's Watercolors." *David Rohn's Watercolors: 1969–1984* (Springfield: The George Walter Vincent Smith Art Museum, 1984), 21–23.
"Lines Written to Bob Perleman in the Margins of *The Marginalization of Poetry.*" The Impercipient Lecture Series (1997).
"Links Without Links: 'The Voice Of The Turtle'." *American Poetry Review* 21(1) (January–February 1992): 37–38.
"Louise Chase: Figure in a Landscape." Catalogue (New York: Brooke Alexander, 1991).
"Misquotations from Reality." *Diacritics* 26(3–4) (1996): 143–57.
"The Night Sky," I–VII. *American Poetry Review* 25(3 (May–June 1996): 9–17; 25(6) (November–December 1996): 9–16; 26(2) (April–March 1997): 19–25; 26(4) (July–August 1997): 35–42; 27(4) (July–August 1998): 15–20; 26(6)

(November–December 1997): 33–39; 27(4) (1998): 15–19; 28(1) (January–February 1999): 41–46.

"Nocturnes for the Nineties (on Chris Martin)." Catalogue (New York: John Goode Gallery, 1990. 29–30).

"On Memory." In *Conversant Essays: Contemporary Poets on Poetry,* ed. James McCorkle (Detroit: Wayne State University Press, 1990), 519–24.

"Poetry Community, Movement: A Conversation," with Charles Bernstein, Jonathan Monroe and Bob Perelman. *Diacritics* 26(3–4) (1996): 196–210.

"Poets and Art." Introduced and edited by John Yau. *Artforum* 23 (November 1984): 87–88.

"Pragmatic Examples: The Nonce." In *Moving Borders: Three Decades of Innovative Writing by Women,* ed. Mary Margaret Sloan (Jersey City, N.J.: Talisman House, 1998), 600–02.

"Slaves of Fashion (Response to Harold Bloom)." *Boston Review* 23(3–4) (Summer 1998): 31–32.

"Trees/trees (On Win Knowlton's Scultpure)." Catalogue (New York: Bill Maynes Gallery, 1995).

"Uncle Edgar Was Watching." *New American Writing* 5 (Fall 1989): 31–34.

"Unpicturing (Fair) Realism: Notes on Barbara Guest's Poetics of (Defensive) Rapture." *American Letters and Commentary* 7 (1995): 1–13.

"We Remember Joe Brainard: 20 October 1994." *The Poetry Project Newsletter* 155 (December–January 1994–95): 15.

"What Is the Grass: Notes Leading Up To and Away from Walt Whitman." *American Letters & Commentary* 5 (1993): 46–59.

Interviews

"Ann Lauterbach: An Interview," with Molly Bendall. *American Poetry Review* 21(3) (May–June 1992): 19–25.

"Conversation between Heather Ramsdell and Ann Lauterbach," with Heather Ramsdell. *Murmur* 1(1) (1998): 51–67.

"A Fragment of Something: At the Guggenheim with Ann Lauterbach," with Edwin Frank. *Poetry Calendar* 20(10) (June 1996): 11–13.

"Newspapers Doom Poets to 'Elitism'," with Sydney H. Schauberg. *New York Newsday* (July 9, 1993): 49–52.

Selected Criticism

Altieri, Charles. "Ann Lauterbach's 'Still' and Why Stevens Still Matters." *The Wallace Stevens Journal* 19(2) (Fall 1995): 219–33.

———. "Jorie Graham and Ann Lauterbach: Towards a Contemporary Poetics of Eloquence." *The Cream City Review* 12(2) (Summer 1988): 45–72.

Fink, Thomas A. "The Poetry of David Shapiro and Ann Lauterbach: After Ashbery." *American Poetry Review* 17(1) (January–February 1988): 27–32.

Kalleberg, Garrett. "A Form of Duration." *Denver Quarterly* 29(4) (Spring 1995): 98–109.

Keelan, Claudia. "Canon, Temple, Living in the Pause: Ann Lauterbach, Elizabeth Willis." *Poetry Flash* 270 (October–November 1996): 1–21.

———. "Missing Her: Brenda Hillman, Ann Lauterbach." *Poetry Flash* 241 (April–May 1993): 1–12.

McCorkle, James. "Ann Lauterbach." *Dictionary Literary Biography* 193 (1998): 180–93.

———. "Nimbus of Sensations: Eros and Reverie in the Poetry of John Ashbery and Ann Lauterbach." In *The Tribe of John: Ashbery and Contemporary Poetry,* ed. Susan M. Schultz (Tuscaloosa: University of Alabama Press, 1995), 101–25.

Osborn, Andrew. "On a Stair." *Boston Review* (December–January 1998–99): 55–57.

Revell, Donald. "Rose as Decoy, Beauty as Use." *The Ohio Review* 53 (1995): 150–63.

Schultz, Susan M. "Houses of Poetry after Ashbery: The Poetry of Ann Lauterbach and Donald Revell." *Virginia Quarterly Review* 67 (Spring 1991): 295–309.

———. "Visions of Silence in Poems of Ann Lauterbach and Charles Bernstein." *Talisman* 13 (Fall–Winter 1994–95): 163–77.

Thomas M. Disch. *"And for Example." The Hudson Review* 48(2) (Summer 1995): 339–50.

Yenser, Stephen. *"Trimmings* by Harryette Mullen; *Clamor* by Ann Lauterbach; *The Wild Iris* by Louise Gluck." *Partisan Review* 61(2) (Spring 1994): 350–55.

References

Bendall, Molly. 1992. "Ann Lauterbach: An Interview," *American Poetry Review* 21(3) (May–June).

Blanchot, Maurice. 1982. *The Space of Literature,* trans. Ann Smock (Lincoln: University of Nebraska Press).

Brown, Norman O. 1966. "Fraction," in *Love's Body* (New York: Random House), 187.

Carlyle, Thomas. 1987. *Sartor Resartus,* ed. Kerry McSweeney and Pter Sabor (New York: Oxford University Press), 166.

Carson, Anne. 1986. *Eros the Bittersweet* (Princeton, N.J.: Princeton University Press), 171.

Emerson, Ralph Waldo. 1989. "Experience," in *The Norton Anthology of American Literature,* 3d ed., Vol. 1 (New York: Norton), 93, 1012.

Equi, Elaine. 1989. *Voice-Over* (Minneapolis: Coffee House Press), 85–86. ["Edward Hopper" is set, incidentally, beside a poem dedicated to Lauterbach.]

Hecht, Anthony. 1995. *On the Laws of the Poetic Art* (Princeton, N.J.: Princeton University Press).

Hollander, John. 1995. *The Gazer's Spirit: Poem Speaking to Silent Works of Art* (Chicago: University of Chicago Press).

Jameson, Fredric. 1991. *Postmodernism; or, The Cultural Logic of Late Capitalism* (Durham, N.C.: Duke University Press).

Keats, John. 1978. *Complete Poems,* ed. Jack Stillinger (Cambridge: Harvard University Press), 282–83.

———. 1987. *The Letters of John Keats* (Cambridge: Harvard University Press).

Kristeva, Julia. 1982. "Giotto's Joy," in *Desire in Language: A Semiotic Approach to Literature and Art* (New York: Columbia University Press).

Lauterbach, Ann. 1993. "Found Credo," *Conjunctions* 21 (Fall): <http://www.conjunctions.com/archives/21c-al.htm>

———. 1995. "Edward Hopper's Way," in *Edward Hopper and the American Imagination,* ed. Julie Grau (New York: Whitney Museum of American Art in association with Norton), 35–39.

———. 1999a. "All View (13 Windows)," in *Ann Hamilton: whitecloth* (exhibit catalogue) (Ridgefield, Conn.: The Aldrich Museum of Contemporary Art), 9–35.

———. 1999b. "Handheld (At the Isabella Stewart Gardner Museum)," *Conjunctions* 32: 69–77.

———. 1999c. "How the Eye Listens." Lecture presented at the Isabella Stewart Gardner Museum, April 1999.

———, Charles Bernstein, Jonathan Monroe, and Bob Perelman. 1996. "Poetry, Community, Movement: A Conversation," *Diacritics* 26(3–4): 202.

Matisse, Henri. 1908. "Notes of a Painter," *La Grande Revue* (December).

———. 1939. "Notes of a Painter on His Drawing," *Le Point* (July 1939), qtd. in *Matisse: A Retrospective,* ed. Jack Flam (New York: Hugh Lauter Levin Associates).

Mullen, Laura. 1999. *After I Was Dead* (Athens: University of Georgia Press), 83–92.

Pressburger, Giorgio. 1994. *The Law of White Spaces,* trans. Piers Spence (New York: Vintage-Random).

Rilke, Rainer Maria. 1987. *New Poems [1908]: The Other Part,* trans. by Edward Snow (New York: Farrar, Straus and Giroux), 3.

Shklovsky, Victor. 1992. "Art as Technique," in *Critical Theory Since Plato,* ed. Hazard Adams (New York: Harcourt Brace Jovanovich Publishers).

Stevens, Wallace. 1951. "The Noble Rider and the Sound of Words," in *The Necessary Angel: Essays on Reality and the Imagination* (New York: Vintage-Random), 36.

———. 1982. *The Collected Poems* (New York: Vintage-Random), 130.

Wagner, Roy. 1978. *Lethal Speech: Daribi Myth as Symbolic Obviation* (Ithaca: Cornell University Pres).

Whitman, Walt. 1973. "Song of Myself," in *Leaves of Grass* (New York: Norton), 33–34.

Wordsworth, William. 1967. "The Prelude," in *English Romantic Writers,* ed. David Perkins (New York: Harcourt Brace), 242.

Yeats, W. B. 1989. "Crazy Jane Talks with the Bishop," in *The Collected Works of W. B. Yeats,* ed. by Richard J. Finneran, Vol. 1 (New York: Macmillan), 259–60.

HARRYETTE MULLEN

WINO RHINO

For no specific reason I have become one of the city's unicorns. No rare species, but one in range of danger. No mythical animal, but a common creature of urban legend. No potent stallion woven into poetry and song. Just the tough horny beast you may observe, roaming at large in our habitat. I'm known to adventurous wanderers whose drive-by safari is this circumscribed wilderness. Denatured photographers like to shoot me tipping the bottle, capture me snorting dust, mount on the wall my horn of empties that spilled the grape's blood. My flesh crawls with itchy insects. My heart quivers as arrows on street maps target me for urban removal. You can see that my hair's stiffened and my skin's thick, but the bravest camera can't document what my armor hides. How I know you so well. Why I know my own strength. Why, when I charge you with my rags, I won't overturn your sporty jeep.

FANCY CORTEX

(Reading Jayne Cortez)

I'm using my plain brain to imagine her fancy cortex. As if my lowly mollusk could wear so exalted a mantle as her pontifex pallium. As if the knots and tangles of my twisted psyche could mesh with her intricate synaptic network of condensed neural convolutions. As if my simple chalk could fossilize the memory of her monumental reefs of creamy caulifloral coral. As if my shallow unschooled shoals could reckon the calculus of her konk's brainwave tsunami. As if the pedestrian software of my mundane explorer could map as rounded colonies the *terra incognita* of her undiscovered hemispheres. As if the speculative diagnosis of my imaging technology could chart the direction of her intuitive intellect. As if the inquisitive iris of my galaxy-orbiting telescope could see as far as her vision. As if the trained nostrils of my narco-bloodhound could sniff out what she senses in the wind. As if my duty-free bottle of jerk sauce could simulate the fire ant *picante* that inflames her tongue of rage. As if the gray matter of my dim bulb could be enlightened by the brilliance of her burning watts. As if her divergent universification might fancy the microcosm of my prosaic mind.

MUSIC FOR HOMEMADE INSTRUMENTS

(Improvising with Douglas Ewart)

I dug you artless, I dug you out. Did you re-do? You dug me less, art. You dug, let's do art. You dug me, less art. Did you re-do? If I left art out, you dug. My artless dug-out. You dug, let art out. Did you re-do, dug-out canoe? Easy as a porkpie piper-led cinch. Easy as a baby bounce. Hop on pot, tin pan man. Original abstract, did you re-do it? Betting on shy cargo, strutting dimpled low-cal strumpets employ a hipster to blow up the native formica. Then divide efficiency on hairnets, flukes, faux saxons. You dug me out, didn't you? Did you re-do? Ever curtained to experiment with strumpet strutting. Now curtains to milk laboratory. Desecrated flukes & panics displayed by mute politicians all over this whirly-gig. Hey, you dug! Art lasts. Did you re-do? Well-known mocker of lurching unused brains, tribal & lustrous diddlysquats, Latin dimension crepe paper & muscular stacks. Curtains for perky strumpets strutting with mites in the twilight of their origami funkier purses. Artless, you dug. Did you re-do? For patting wood at flatland, thanks. For bamboozle flukes at Bama, my seedy medication. Thanks for my name in the yoohoo. Continental camp-out, percolating throughout the whirly-gig on faux saxon flukes. You dug art, didn't you? Did you re-do?

THE ANTHROPIC PRINCIPLE

The pope of cosmology addresses a convention. When he talks the whole atmosphere changes. He speaks through a computer. When he asks can you hear me, the whole audience says yes. It's a science locked up in a philosophical debate. There are a few different theories. There could be many different realities. You might say ours exists because we do. You could take a few pounds of matter, heat it to an ungodly temperature, or the universe was a freak accident. There may be a limit to our arrogance, but one day the laws of physics will read like a detailed instruction manual. A plane that took off from its hub in my hometown just crashed in the President's hometown. The news anchor says the pilot is among the dead. I was hoping for news of the President's foreign affair with a diplomat's wife. I felt a mystical connection to the number of confirmed dead whose names were not released. Like the time I was three handshakes from the President. Like when I thought I heard that humanitarians dropped a smart blond on the Chinese embassy. Like when the cable was severed and chairs fell from the sky because the pilot flew with rusty maps. What sane pilot would land in that severe rain with hard hail and gale force wind. With no signal of distress. With no foghorns to warn the civilians, the pilot lost our moral compass in the bloody quagmire of collateral damage. One theory says it's just a freak accident locked up in a philosophical debate. It's like playing poker and all the cards are wild. Like the arcane analysis of a black box full of insinuations of error.

SLEEPING WITH THE DICTIONARY

I beg to dicker with my silver-tongued companion, whose lips are ready to read my shining gloss. A versatile partner, conversant and well-versed in the verbal art, the dictionary is not averse to the solitary habits of the curiously wide-awake reader. In the dark night's insomnia, the book is a stimulating sedative, awakening my tired imagination to the hypnagogic trance of language. Retiring to the canopy of the bedroom, turning on the bedside light, taking the big dictionary to bed, clutching the unabridged bulk, heavy with the weight of all the meanings between these covers, smoothing the thin sheets, thick with accented syllables—all are exercises in the conscious regimen of dreamers, who toss words on their tongues while turning illuminated pages. To go through all these motions and procedures, groping in the dark for an alluring word is the poet's nocturnal mission. Aroused by myriad possibilities, we try out the most perverse positions in the practice of our nightly act, the penetration of the denotative body of the work. Any exit from the logic of language might be an entry in a symptomatic dictionary. The alphabetical order of this ample block of knowledge might render a dense lexicon of lucid hallucinations. Beside the bed, a pad lies open to record the meandering of migratory words. In the rapid eye movement of the poet's night vision, this dictum can be decoded, like the secret acrostic of a lover's name.

POETIC STATEMENT

Imagining the Unimagined Reader

THE CONTEXT for my work is not so much geographic as it is linguistic and cultural. I write beyond the range of my voice and the social boundaries of identity, yet within the limits imposed on my work and my imagination by language and its cultural significance. The idea of identity informs my poetry, insofar as identity acts upon language, and language acts upon identity. It would be accurate to say that my poetry explores the reciprocity of language and culture. My work is informed by my interactions with readers, writers, scholars, and critics, as well as my interest in the various possibilities for poetry in written and spoken American English.

I write for myself and others. An other is anyone who is not me. Anyone who is not me is like me in some ways, and unlike me in other ways. I write, optimistically, for an imagined audience of known and unknown readers. Many of my imagined readers have yet to encounter my work. Most of them are not even born yet. About one-third of my pleasure as a writer comes from the work itself, the process of writing, a third from the response of my contemporaries, and another third in contemplating unknown readers who inhabit a future I will not live to see. When I read the words of African Americans who were slaves, I feel at once my similarity and difference. I experience simultaneously a continuity and a discontinuity with the past, which I imagine is similar to that of the unborn reader who might encounter my work in some possible future. There is a another kind of experience I sometimes have when reading the words of authors who never imagined that someone like me might be included in the potential audience for their work, as when I read in Cirlot's *Dictionary of Symbols* that a "Negro" symbolizes the beast in the human. When I read words never meant for me, or anyone like me—words that exclude me, or anyone like me, as a possible reader—then I feel simultaneously my exclusion and my inclusion as a literate black woman, the unimagined reader of the text.

A future reader I imagine for my work is the offspring of an illiterate woman. A significant percentage of the world population remains illiterate, the majority of them girls and women. An even greater number of people have minimal access to books or the leisure to read them. In addition to people who simply have no opportunity to be empowered by education, the problem of illiteracy has expanded, as the late Paulo Freire pointed out, to include nominally educated people who are unable to function as critical readers. The disputes among what Hank Lazer calls "opposing poetries"[1] provide examples of the proliferation of competing poetics representing competing and alternative literacies, of which the proliferation of illiteracies is a side effect. E.D. Hirsch's "cultural literacy" franchise offered a panacea for the anxieties of the educated and elite classes contemplating an increasingly diverse and multicultural population, as well as for the anxieties of minorities resisting total assimilation of the dominant culture.

What constitutes literacy has always been determined by the powerful, while illiteracy persists as an attribute of the disempowered. Economic and social policies in the United States that widen the gap between the haves and have-nots inevitably deepen the divide between the literate and the illiterate, with the illiterate increasingly consigned to the criminal justice system. The July 27, 1997, issue of *The Women's Review of Books,* which gathered a collection of articles on U.S. prisons and activists working with incarcerated women and their children, observed, "As we approach the millennium, prisons are among the country's biggest post–Cold War growth industries. Within the prison boom, women are the fastest-growing population, a trend due primarily to the so-called 'war on drugs.'" One article, "Literacy for Life," reports on the work of MOTHEREAD, a North Carolina organization that helps women in prison improve their own and their children's literacy skills. In addition to the division of the literate and the illiterate, there is further division between the literate and the hyperliterate.

My desires as a poet are contradictory. I aspire to write poetry that would leave no insurmountable obstacle to comprehension and pleasure other than the ultimate limits of the reader's interest and linguistic competence. However, I do not necessarily approach this goal by employing a beautiful, pure, simple, or accessible literary language, or by maintaining a clear, consistent, recognizable, or authentic voice in my work. At this point in my life, I am more interested in working with language per se than in developing or maintaining my own particular voice or style of writing, although I am aware that my poems may constitute a peculiar idiolect that can be identified as mine. I think of writing as a process that is synthetic rather than organic, artificial rather than natural, human rather than divine. My inclination is to pursue what is minor, marginal, idiosyncratic, trivial, debased, or aberrant in the language that I speak and write. I desire that my work appeal to an audience that is diverse and inclusive, at the same time that I wonder if human beings will ever learn how to be inclusive without repressing human diversity through cultural and linguistic imperialism.

Not when I am writing, but after I have written, I consider who would be left out, excluded from the poem. Although it is not necessary or possible to include everyone, I find that it is useful to me as a writer to be aware that language, culture, and poetry always exclude as well as include potential audiences. One reason I have avoided a singular style or voice for my poetry is the possibility of including a diverse audience of readers attracted to different poems and different aspects of the work. I try to leave room for unknown readers whom I can only imagine.

"SLEEPING WITH THE DICTIONARY"

Harryette Mullen's "Recyclopedia"

Elisabeth A. Frost

IN "POETRY AND IDENTITY," Harryette Mullen addresses "the various experiences of inclusion, exclusion, and marginality" faced by "a 'formally innovative black poet.'" Her own production, Mullen remarks, "struggles to overcome aesthetic apartheid"—the frequent assumption "that 'avant-garde' poetry is not 'black,' and that 'black' poetry, however singular its 'voice,' is not 'formally innovative.'" Informing Mullen's comments is the awareness that conceptions of identity politics in American poetry have rendered African-American avant-gardism invisible. She observes such erasures in the pages of recent anthologies:

> Although both the "avant-garde poet" and the "minority poet" may be perceived as the "other" of the "mainstream" (regardless of the distance and the different concerns that might separate them from each other), it would seem that the "mainstream" has far more to gain by appropriating minority poets who work in recognizable and accessible forms, and thus can be marketed to the broadest possible audience of readers.[2]

As Aldon Nielsen has argued, "a requisite 'realism' of language" determines not just the emerging canon of contemporary African-American writers but also the history of black poetry in America.[3]

It is not surprising, then, that Mullen feels "simultaneously a continuity and a discontinuity with the past," or that her "inclination is to pursue what is minor, marginal, idiosyncratic, trivial, debased, or aberrant in the language that I speak and write."[4] In the face of "aesthetic apartheid," Mullen's courting of the marginal is a gesture of defiance, just as her subversion of generic and linguistic categories makes her poetry impossible to pigeonhole. Mullen evokes opposed poetic traditions to focus on language itself. While Joseph Conte has linked such open-ended serial works as Mullen's to a postmodernist aesthetic that privileges indeterminacy and an underlying belief in the lack of universal order,[5] Mullen's associative compositions bring to light not randomness but unexpected likeness—among signifiers, the concepts they represent and the experiences they help construct. In this way Mullen's poetry critiques the enforcement of difference, of "apartheid," both on and off the page. In her highly playful texts, Mullen lets language reveal myriad, and unexpected, forms of kinship.

In an anti-Romantic stance like that of many other feminist avant-garde poets, Mullen insists, with theorist Monique Wittig, that language has "a plastic action on the real," particularly where race and gender politics are involved.[6] Mullen's goal is to examine how "identity acts upon language, and language acts upon identity."[7] Playing both with and against idioms familiar to a diverse set of readers, Mullen "recycles" what has preceded in the always-overlapping realms of high and popular art. One of Mullen's neologisms will serve here as a figure for her evolving poetics: the linguistic "recyclopedia." Here is the poet not as romantic inventor (or, for that matter, ultra modern avant-gardist) but as recycler of culture's available detritus. Continually recasting, exploring composition as cultural "composite," Mullen critiques existing poetic and sociological divisions. The recyclopedia of Mullen's poetics assumes knowledge always to be hand-me-down—or, in the complimentary terms of recent advertisements, "pre-owned." Her innovative, highly dialogic texts recycle the lineages of a "mongrel" American culture.

Observing that her work "explores the reciprocity of language and culture" and that she views writing "as a process that is synthetic rather than organic, artificial rather than natural, human rather than divine," Mullen mentions that her poetry often engages in "a kind of linguistic archaeology of the metaphorical origins of words, a resurrection of dead metaphors that are buried in any language." Further, Mullen notes,

> My poems often recycle familiar and humble materials, in search of the poetry found in everyday language: puns, double entendres, taboo words, Freudian slips, jokes, riddles, proverbs, folk poetry, found poetry, idiomatic expressions, slang and jargon, coinages, neologisms, nonce words, port-

manteaus, pidgins and creoles, nicknames, diminutives, baby talk, tongue twisters, children's rhyming games, imitative and onomatopoeic formations, syntactical and grammatical peculiarities, true and false etymologies, clichés, jingles, and slogans.[8]

The full variety of this whimsically exhaustive list has been most apparent in Mullen's recent work. But even Mullen's first publications reveal her construction of a complex notion of heritage, confirming her assertion in the opening of her poetic statement: "The context for my work is not so much geographic as it is linguistic and cultural."

Mullen's first collection, *Tree Tall Woman,* is the most indebted to a concept of identity politics that she would later reject. Many poems evoke culturally specific traditions (apparent in titles such as "Alabama Memories," "A Tent Revival," or "The Ritual of Earpiercing"), while others launch pointed cultural critiques ("Bete Noir," "The Mother of Nightmares," "Striptease"). Yet Mullen's fascination with the reality language constructs is already evident. The movement of the volume is loosely autobiographical—from childhood narratives to evocations of the poet's art. Much of *Tree Tall Woman* addresses the theme of community, often with an emphasis on the strength of women and of female friendship, as in "Me & Steenie," which attests to the bond between sisters, one that obviates speech itself: "The way we talk," the poem begins, "is we never finish a sentence." Sisterhood is literal and figurative, joyful testimony to shared understanding between women: "Sometimes we break out laughing together / or suddenly humming the same song / at the same time / after moments of silence."[9]

In many of these poems, Mullen draws generously on a legacy made available by the Black Arts movement in its affirmation of black identity, adapted by Mullen to evoke interlinked histories of community and family. Mullen notes that this early work "was definitely influenced by the Black Arts movement, the idea that there was a black culture and that you could write from the position of being within a black culture."[10] As Sonia Sanchez remembers, "the main thing was the idea of someone saying you were Black—and that was beautiful, and that was good . . . and that was political."[11] For Sanchez and others the goal was to create new poetic forms—writing that would embody the performative nature of black culture and launch a potent indictment of white supremacy. Such traditions as playing the dozens, rapping, and signifying would be transformed into writing that would strike home to black listeners and readers of all socioeconomic levels. The assertion of a shared, even universal black identity was critical, and indeed the Pan-Africanism of Frantz Fanon was a crucial inspiration for the movement, which sought to provide, in poetic form, recognizable markers of cultural difference.

While *Tree Tall Woman* sidesteps the kind of direct political statement that characterizes much Black Arts poetry, it does include biting indictments of racial politics that connect Mullen's work to that of Black Arts activists critiquing white dominance. "Bete Noire" is a satiric portrait of "the white minstrel man/who hums ragtime tunes/and whistles the buckdancer's choice/while he darkens his face/with boneblack/made of human charcoal." The poem "For My Grandfather, Lowell Palter Mitchell" opens with a reminiscence of "Granddaddy," a preacher, "in shades of black and white." The man who preaches "a meat-and-gravy sermon" dons "a serious, scowling black suit," while his "shirts . . . fresh from the laundry,/ [are] 'washed whiter than snow.'" Such polarized imagery pervades the poem: "a starched white handkerchief," "your black Chevy," "a hospital bed with white sheet/tucked up" against "your huge head . . ./like a heavy dark flower." The irony of identity's being overshadowed by racial dichotomy—perceived everywhere in the poet's reminiscence—emerges sharply in a poem that has as much to say about the man as about the pervasiveness of racial division.

Tree Tall Woman also reveals formal elements profoundly influenced by Black Arts experimentation with the written and spoken word. Delight in the black vernacular—its imagistic richness and musicality—is evident throughout *Tree Tall Woman*. In narratives and brief lyrics, Mullen's poems court the ear through complex rhythms, as in the self-reflexive "Playing the Invisible Saxophone En El Combo De Las Estrellas": "One of these days I'm gonna write a real performance poem," the poem begins, in a tribute to Black Arts performativity:

> Yeah, gonna have words turning into dance,
> bodymoving music,
> a get-down poem so kinetically energetic
> it sure put disco to shame.
> Make it a snazzy jazzy poem extravaganza, with pizzazz.
> Poem be going solo,
> flying high on improbable improvisational innovation.
> Poem be blowing hard! *(Tree Tall Woman)*

Mullen takes pleasure in importing the forms and textures of black music into her own "improvisatory" text. She affirms black identity as the source of black art: Mullen's joyful "bodymoving music," her "flying high on improbable improvisational innovation," recall the playful poetic flights of such black pride poems as Nikki Giovanni's "Ego Tripping": "I was born in the congo/I walked to the fertile crescent and built the sphinx," the poet asserts, in an allusion to Langston Hughes's "The Negro Speaks of Rivers" (another poetic ancestor affirming black identity and culture).[12] Signaling that her origins are in the politics of the Black Arts movement, Mullen pays homage to the voices that preceded her own.

But while Black Arts poets responded to the problem that "blackness had signified negation, lack, deprivation, absence of culture" by reversing poles—constructing "a positive image of black culture"[13]—Mullen builds on the predominantly public address and outspokenly political content of Black Arts poetics to craft a sensibility that questions the essentialism of the earlier movement. Mullen combines commitment to the notion of "black voice" with the linguistic experiments advanced by such poets as Jean Toomer in the interrelated poems of *Cane*, Gwendolyn Brooks in the lyric/narrative *A Street in Bronzeville*, or Melvin Tolson in the collagist *Harlem Gallery*. *Tree Tall Woman* alternates between spoken idiom and distanced observation and recollection. The first two poems of the volume present the poles that will recur: "To a Woman" opens with evocations of idiomatic expression and the syntax of so-called "Black English"—a term Mullen will later take issue with:

> You're like the skinny folk
> my mama used to kid, the straight-gut people.
> (Got a crane stomach.
> Eat you out of house and home,
> though you'd never know,
> to look at them.
> Food goes straight through them
> and they always hungry.) *(Tree Tall Woman)*

The poem evokes idiomatic expression only by way of a distant memory, whose cadences are attributed not to the speaker but to "mama." The next stanza concludes the poem in the present with an altogether different diction and syntax:

> Reed woman,
> that's how you are.
> No man can fill you.
> You look like one
> who could be contented
> but you will always want
> a taste of something
> you've never had. *(Tree Tall Woman)*

The more abstract formulations and "written" quality, with its lack of contractions and more formal diction ("You look like one/who could be contented") anticipate the speaker's ambiguous position in relation to the past "languages" she goes on to evoke throughout *Tree Tall Woman*.

Accordingly, "Alabama Memories," the next poem, evokes specific idiom, but only through the Wordsworthian lens of memory; the observations attain an almost anthropological cast, and the uses of figurative language suggest literary invention rather than shared idiom. Here the speaker is distanced by the passage of time and change of place, signaled, as in the previous poem, by the use of parenthetical comments:

> Houses with peeling skins of gray paint,
> with swaybacked wooden porches furnished with dingy sofas
> and wringer washing machines perched on old-fashioned legs.
> Houses with muddy yards and dirty chickens,
> with no indoor plumbing,
> with outhouses leaning at tipsy angles.
> (I remember being embarrassed to pee
> in a red-rimmed white-enameled chamberpot
> on a rainy night at somebody's house.) *(Tree Tall Woman)*

The self-conscious act of "remembering" suggests the distance that runs throughout *Tree Tall Woman,* despite its moments of immersion in family history and community.

In this early work, Mullen negotiates the formal and the informal, and the "writerly" and the "speakerly," in a dialectic she later recognizes as common to many African-American poets who have constructed a purposeful dynamic between the "performative" and a more "literary" poetic idiom. Mullen notes that Robert Hayden's poems "suggest some of the difficulties and creative strategies of the poet seeking to forge a literary language of disparate cultural materials." Just as "Hayden's orchestration of folk speech and song with the written language of slaveholders, slaves, fugitives, and free people of color had been enabled by other African-American writers who had reclaimed black vernacular from its debased use and abuse in American popular culture," Mullen's inclusions of spoken idiom are enabled by a Black Arts radicalism that emphatically championed the use of "Black English Vernacular" in poetry. Mullen argues of such cases as Hayden's: "Only by reclaiming and remaking [African-American vernacular] as a literary language with attention to its particular expressive potential, and also by claiming and 'mastering' the language of the dominant literary tradition, were black poets able to overcome the presumed stigma of black English as well as the presumed alienating effects of Western literacy."[14] For Mullen in *Tree Tall Woman,* in the climate following Black Arts activism, language is enriched by the renewed possibilities of the vernacular and rendered complex by its inevitable transformation into "literary" representation.

As these assertions make clear, much as Mullen pays homage to Black

Arts innovations rather than advancing that group's frequently essentialist identity politics, she explores linguistic border-crossing as a means of marking complex registers of language and the contingency of differing speech communities. Subtle shifting was a part of Mullen's early experience. She notes that her family moved to Texas from Pennsylvania, marking their speech as "different" to her new neighbors, "dicty or proper."[15] Yet it was not until after the publication of *Tree Tall Woman* that Mullen began to explore the implications of such variety in her own experience of "black speech":

> I felt I knew what it was to write in a black voice and it meant a sort of vernacularized English. [Now] I think that it's much more complicated than that. For instance, my family spoke standard English at home. Educated, middle-class, black speakers are code-switchers, and what we really did was learn to switch from standard English to a black vernacular in certain situations when that was called for.[16]

Such code-switching attests to another complex form of "apartheid." Addressing her dismay at the stubborn separateness of idioms and a reader's potential discomfort with "miscegenated" language, *Trimmings* defies the rules of code-switching by splicing together elements of divergent systems—in effect integrating the codes, recycling elements of each in a new and intricately detailed form. Here Mullen assumes the open-ended, serial form typical of her writing since, and in this text she also experiments for the first time with what she advisedly calls the "minor" genre of the prose poem.[17] In style and subject matter, *Trimmings* is self-consciously hybrid: profoundly intertextual, the book takes Gertrude Stein's *Tender Buttons* (1914) as its point of departure, weaving Stein together with the more recent strands of black feminism, Language poetry (particularly Ron Silliman's theorizing a contemporary poetics born of what he calls the "new sentence"),[18] and various bits and pieces of popular culture. Looking at *Tender Buttons* through the "cool dark lasses" of a black feminist perspective, Mullen creates a dialogic text about women's clothing—"girdled loins" wrapped in Steinian "tender girders."[19]

Noting that "I always wanted to use the pun as a lever to create the possibility of multiple readings," Mullen suggests that all texts skirt authorial control, that only "readings"—not definitive, authorial "meanings"—ever reveal themselves.[20] In *Trimmings* Mullen courts this ambiguity by coining dense and elaborate word play. Still, there is in *Trimmings* a cultural celebration reminiscent of the writing in *Tree Tall Woman*. In dialogue with Stein's texts (particularly the often racist depictions in Stein's story "Melanctha"), Mullen presents black women's bodies to be adored and adorned, a subject of linguistic play as well as of admiration: "Mohair, less nape to crown fluffed pillow. Fuzzyhead, down for a nap. Soft stuff of dreams in which she fluffs it."[21] The poet's fond attention to "nappy" heads continues in the Black Arts tradition of counteracting racism by locating the beautiful unwaveringly in the black body (many black feminist poems similarly focus on hair, as in Brooks's "To Those of My Sisters Who Kept Their Naturals"). Yet Mullen's playful puns also reveal unexpected, and telling, "family resemblances" between words: "nap" signifies both sleep and the "fuzzyhead" of nappy hair (akin as well to the "nape" of one's neck), just as "Mohair" suggests both a luxurious woolen weave and a "Black English" inflection: "more hair" shows "less nape." Such linguistic links emphasize not an "essential" black identity but the inextricable relation between selves and words, identity and language.

From *Trimmings* onward, such intricate puns appear continually in Mullen's work, and they are often outrageous (for example, from *Muse & Drudge:* "deja voodoo queens," "sue for slender," "high on swine," "everlasting arms/too short for boxers"). It becomes evident in the puns in every sentence of *Trimmings* that language is analogous to the ever-elastic construction of self, just as women "put on" clothes as a means of signifying their identities to the public world. Thus, just as a change of clothes signifies a shift in self-conception, identity (like language) is subject to constant "alteration." Such plasticity is a refrain throughout *Trimmings,* in which "Accessories multiply a look" culled from a feminine "Bag of tricks," and "Harmless amulets arm little limbs with poise and charm."[22] Similarly, links between clothing and language run throughout *Trimmings,* often signaling a silencing or erasure that Mullen's work attempts to undo, as in "Of a girl, in white, between the lines, in the spaces where nothing is written," and "Her feather, her pages. . . . The wind blows her words away." The body is open to construction and continual rewriting: "Bones knit. Skins pink, flush tight. White margin, ample fleshings"; similarly, "Clothes opening, revealing dress, as French comes into English. Suggestively, a cleavage in language."[23]

This motif of the shaping of self and body through language reaches its climax on the final page of *Trimmings,* which instructs us in a poststructuralist view of both materiality and the symbolic: "Thinking thought to be a body wearing language as clothing or language a body of thought which is a soul or body the clothing of a soul." The terms of the old Cartesian debate—body and soul—are recast in a world in which "thought" is a "body wearing language as clothing," or in which a "body" of knowledge is the "soul" of a society. The final lines in *Trimmings,* however, indicate the extent to which materiality in bodies and language alike can be elided only at our peril: "she is veiled in silence. A veiled, unavailable body makes an available space."[24] That "veiled" body suggests the female form removed from the purview of the male gaze, as in the practice of purdah.[25] It also hints, conversely, that the invisible (or erased, ignored) will inevitably make its presence known. Mullen is not rejecting the importance of embodiment to politics—a crucial element of Black Arts activism—but she is complicating our notion of that embodiment, both linguistic and social.

Merging seamlessly in *Trimmings* with a materiality inspired by Black Arts activism is, of course, Mullen's dialogue with Stein, from specific allusions to the punning, playful style of the Steinian sentence itself. The combination places the reader in a position of unusual border-crossing between the turf of what Hank Lazer has called "opposing poetries," notably those labeled "speech-based" (as in Black Arts poets' uses of idiom) and those labeled "text-based" (in the Steinian tradition of visual puns).[26] Formally, *Tender Buttons* serves as a template for Mullen's meditations. But it is also a source for Mullen's evolving responses to Stein, ranging from homage to critique.[27] Indeed, certain parts of *Trimmings* literally rewrite passages from *Tender Buttons*. Stein's famous "Petticoat," for example ("A light white, a disgrace, an inkspot, a rosy charm"), is transmogrified:

> A light white disgraceful sugar looks pink, wears an air, pale compared to shadow standing by. To plump recliner, naked truth lies. Behind her shadow wears her color, arms full of flowers. A rosy charm is pink. And she is ink. The mistress wears no petticoat or leaves. The other in shadow, a large, pink dress.[28]

Mullen has described this passage as her opening into *Tender Buttons*— perhaps even the point of departure for *Trimmings* as a whole; she interprets Stein's prose as an intertextual allusion to Manet's scandalous *Olympia*—the white woman staring boldly at the viewer, in a state of "disgraceful" sexual permissiveness, with the nearby "ink spot" (a black servant) waiting behind her.[29] In response to both predecessors, Mullen represents the nude white woman as "disgraceful sugar"; in Mullen's version the right to "wear an air" is dependent on a "shadow" version of the white woman's femininity—one that stands for sexuality itself—even as the white sugar of the one "pale[s] compared to" the dark hue of the other. Mullen's version of both *Olympia* and *Tender Buttons* decenters prior representations of white and black women and interrogates the color-coding inherent in constructions of femininity. Mullen writes that in *Trimmings*,

> The words pink and white kept appearing as I explored the ways that the English language conventionally represents femininity. As a black woman writing in this language, I suppose I already had an ironic relationship to this pink and white femininity.[30]

Throughout *Trimmings* Mullen suggests the deficiencies of conventional language in representing blackness, particularly black female subjectivity, drawing attention to the dynamic between black and white, and pointing out that "pink" is "a rosy charm" in the white world only when it's worn by someone "pale," "white" and "sugary."

As in the relationship between black female servant and white "mistress," the construction of whiteness itself is impossible without an oppositional "other." In this respect, and in merging Steinian and Black Arts poetics, Mullen rejects essentialist views of racial difference and makes apparent her desire to tap into disparate conceptions of self and community, as well as divergent poetic traditions. In her conversation with Stephen Yenser, Mullen notes that Robert Hayden's work was

> most useful to me for expanding the possibilities of what and how an African-American poet might write. He wrote, among other things, about black life, and even his poems devoted to black subjects are marked by a distinctive poetic idiom that is not strictly bound to African-American oral tradition. It is, like the poetry of Gwendolyn Brooks, a purposefully literary language, owing much, as Arnold Rampersad suggests, to the King James Bible and the canon of British literature, as well as to American modernist poetry.[31]

This "purposefully literary language" is one way to conceive of Mullen's own project in *Trimmings,* however different from Hayden's stylistic idiom. *Trimmings* is a serial poem whose fragmented and multiply-signifying parts "expand the possibilities of what and how an African-American poet might write" by merging traditions and recycling markedly divergent sources.

If *Trimmings* hybridizes Black Arts and Steinian poetics, *S*PeRM**K*T* extends Mullen's inquiry into the relationship between language and identity by zeroing in on contemporary consumer culture. In keeping with the three sections of *Tender Buttons* ("Objects," "Food," and "Rooms"), *S*PeRM**K*T* shifts from closet to "supermarket." Mullen describes this collection as "the companion of *Trimmings,*" in which she considers how "we are immersed, bombarded with language that is commercial, that is a debased language." The fact of such commercialized language leads Mullen to a metaphor not of originality but, to the contrary, of continual reuse: "The idea of recycling is very much a part of *S*PeRM**K*T,* to take this detritus and to turn it into art."[32] The feminized consumer—the targeted woman shopper of postwar American culture—is Mullen's focus. Holding a mirror up to this consumerism, Mullen progresses through the aisles: "Lines assemble gutter and margin. Outside and in, they straighten a place. Organize a stand. Shelve space. Square footage. Align your list or listlessness." In the poems that follow this first one in *S*PeRM**K*T*, Mullen splices together evocations of disparate products with the language of advertising, politics, and the body. In a typical passage, Mullen plays on the "Kills bugs dead" slogan for roach motels, dwelling on its kinship with the language of genocide and wryly observing that "Redundancy is syntactical overkill." Accordingly, the odd title of Mullen's second installment of Steinian prose poems evokes the connection between consumption and sexuality (a "supermarket" whose sign is on the blink, resulting in the telling gaps that read "spermkit").[33]

As in such double (sometimes triple) verbal and visual entendres, Mullen is deeply engaged in "working on different levels of signification or different rhetorical levels." At the same time, she notes that she considers "the people I am leaving out and . . . how I can bring them back in. I want the work I do to be intellectually complex, but at some level, the form is open to allow people to enter wherever they are."[34] Marrying inclusiveness to complexity is no easy task, and indeed the reception of *Trimmings* and *S*PeRM**K*T* suggested to Mullen the need to imagine more fully her "unknown readers." While in *Trimmings* and *S*PeRM**K*T* Mullen experimented with different source materials—from Steinian poetics to colloquial speech and idiom—in her next volume, *Muse & Drudge,* Mullen makes the question of cultural literacy integral to both the subject and the form of her book-length poem. More specifically, Mullen characterizes *Muse & Drudge* as an attempt to diversify her readership. She notes:

> *Tree Tall Woman* had probably a larger black audience than *Trimmings* and *S*PeRM**K*T* had, and this book [*Muse & Drudge*] was my attempt to continue the innovative technique that emerged in the writing of *Trimmings* and *S*PeRM**K*T,* and to use a recognizable cultural content, while at the same time expanding that beyond a fairly simple or reductive notion of what black culture is. I was trying to make a text that did address various audiences.[35]

Mullen resists settling on "a singular style or voice for my poetry," precisely to leave open "the possibility of including a diverse audience of readers attracted to different poems and different aspects of the work."[36] This goal is pointedly evident in *Muse & Drudge,* which marks a stylistic shift from all of her previous volumes and also attempts not just to represent but to *create* cultural diversity within its pages.

In *Muse & Drudge* Mullen writes at the borders of poetic modes and musical languages, often employing "language as verbal scat."[37] Revamping the traditions of lyric, challenging the presumptions of poetic originality and mastery, Mullen develops the playful idiom of her previous book-length series yet nonetheless signals an about-face: from the discursive mode of the prose poem, Mullen returns to the poetic line and the symmetrical pattern of the verse quatrain. In this shift away from prose, Mullen reveals a preoccupation with "song": from Sappho to the blues, *Muse & Drudge* testifies to the symbolic and spiritual importance of lyric, both ancient and contemporary. Her definition is inclusive. Linking in the same pages, often the very same lines, Callimachus and Bessie Smith, Ma Rainey and rap, Mullen notes the inspiration provided by both Diane Rayor's translation of Sappho and the "tight distichs" of women rappers, whose lyrics "inform my own improvisational approach to rhythm and rhyme."[38] In a poem that draws attention to "white covers of black material" and "Sapphire's lyre," to "Aunt Haggie's chirren" and "mad dog kiwi," to MOMA, Isis, Juba, and "deja voodoo queens," Mullen calls on her audience to engage in the reconsideration of knowledge, for, as she points out, *Muse & Drudge* is "a poem that deliberately addresses a diverse audience of readers, with the expectation that no single reader will comprehend every line or will catch every allusion."[39] As a result, Mullen encourages a process of what I have called elsewhere "collective reading": seeking to hybridize her poetic sources and diversify her readership, she comes as close as any writer can to demanding not a display but an exchange of knowledge.[40]

At the same time that Mullen describes *Muse & Drudge* as an experiment in regaining the black audience she felt had diminished since the publication of *Tree Tall Woman,* she refutes the presumption that there is an "authentic" black speech or a homogeneous "black community," focusing instead on the mix of influences that epitomizes the contemporary subject. *Muse & Drudge* is "mongrel" in its form, traditions, and cultural politics, and it draws into its symmetrical appearance of four quatrains per page a hodgepodge: classical and contemporary, "high" and "popular" art, the lyric fragment and epic poem. Such amalgams are apparent in the volume's title, which exemplifies Mullen's exploration of points of reference. The ampersand signifies a series of dichotomies: divinity and mortality, inspiration and labor, the disembodied and the bodily, the ideal and the real. The disjunctions are deeply gendered and raced, as is apparent in (male) fantasies of woman as disembodied muse or earth-bound drudge, of the division of women into the divine (light-skinned) muse or the "earthy" (dark-skinned) drudge.

Muse & Drudge is an amalgam: a long poem in lyric fragments whose diverse sources are spliced together in unpunctuated quatrains, with effects analogous to the rapper's art of sampling. The musical effects range from suggestively allusive scat ("mutter patter simper blubber/murmur prattle smatter blather/mumble chatter whisper bubble/mumbo-jumbo palaver gibber blunder") to rhyming toasts ("color we've got in spades/melanin gives perpetual shade/though rhythm's no answer to cancer/pancakes pale and butter can get rancid"). Mullen's quatrains are frequently extended riffs, often making use of arbitrary generative devices—such as the "admittedly nonsensical" anagrams based on the poet's name, Harryette Romell Mullen ("marry at a hotel, annul em/nary hep male rose sullen/let alley roam, yell melon/dull normal fellow hammers omelette"), or the kinship provided by etymology and the mixing of sounds and meanings typical of contemporary cultural mixtures: "creole cocoa loca/crayon gumbo boca/crayfish crayola/jumbo mocha-cola."[41] Such elaborate word games draw attention to the constructed nature of language and, hence, of identity; like the motif of clothing in *Trimmings,* the musical play in *Muse & Drudge* both debunks the ideology of poetic "originality" and suggests the necessarily hybrid nature of any spoken or written idiom.

Accordingly, Mullen discusses the mixed idioms and allusions in *Muse & Drudge* as an expression of her vision of American culture and its often occluded history of "kinship":

> A lot has been said of how American culture is a miscegenated culture, how it is a product of mixing and mingling of diverse races and cultures and languages, and I would agree with that. I would say that, yes, my text is deliberately a multi-voiced text, a text that tries to express the actual diversity of my own experience living here, exposed to different cultures. "Mongrel" comes from "among." Among others. We are among; we are not alone. We are all mongrels.[42]

Mullen's desire to create a "multi-voiced text" that would explore the reality of a "mongrel" culture led her to expand an already-varied range of references—in effect, to diversify her own poetic lineage. *Muse & Drudge* is thus a (redeemed) version of the "recyclopedia" mentioned toward the close of the volume: "If you turned down the media/so I could write a book/then you could look me up/in your voluminous recyclopedia."[43] Media saturation—a subject of both *Trimmings* and *S*PeRM**K*T*—impedes the ability to "write a book" in peace. It also results in the production of redundant or "recycled" information often more noteworthy for how and where it is stored than for its contents; hence the humorously pompous and Latinate "voluminous recyclopedia." Turning down the "volume" of the mass media is only a first step in rendering more audible stores of poetic (and other) cultural knowledge. The future ability to "look up" any postmodern cultural production—to find it archived if not remembered—is contingent on whether the contemporary artist ever has any cultural cachet in the first place. Mullen hints at her own aesthetics and politics: wryly debunking the hope for—indeed, the legitimacy of—the status of "great" artist, Mullen shuns lionization and predicts instead a modest listing in a future, possibly obscure, reference work. She thus downplays the significance of personality in the writing and reception of poetry, emphasizing instead the material factors that favor certain forms of cultural production over others.

What sort of poetry is feasible, or even necessary, in a culture that rhymes "media" with "recyclopedia"? If *Muse & Drudge* is Mullen's effort to bring lyric into the age of late capital, her most recent work deconstructs poem and poet still further in fractured narratives that revisit the punning prose of *Trimmings* and *S*PeRM**K*T*. In *Sleeping with the Dictionary,*[44] Mullen continues to be preoccupied with the cultural politics of language, both on and off the page. As in *Muse & Drudge,* Mullen asserts the power of language to shape the subject and examines the politics of race through the history and evolution of words. Complementing Mullen's use of nonce words such as "recyclopedia," poems such as "Denigration"[45] reveal the inverse strategy: existing words are juxtaposed to explore unexpected ideological links, casting new light on how culture constructs meaning. Here Mullen improvises on echoes of the "n" word. The title "Denigration" makes explicit the derogatory connotation attached to the phoneme "neg/nig," often regardless of context or denotation. While never using in the poem the word that lurks behind all the others, Mullen plays on the homophonic relation between any number of words prefixed by "neg-" or "nig-": niggling, niggardly, enigma, neglect, negligible, negate, negotiate, renegades, renege. This charged subject matter, and its relevance to Mullen's focus on the force language exerts, is echoed in a recent scandal over a public official's use of the word "niggardly" at an open meeting. The word was deemed offensive by some, despite any lack of relation between that term and its sound-alike racial slur. The official issued an apology.

At the same time that Mullen makes vivid the power of a mere phoneme, she composes "Denigration" as a series of questions that deconstruct the same "blackness" supposedly evoked by a single, powerful sound. The prose poem opens by challenging racist presumptions: "Did we surprise our teachers who had niggling doubts about the picayune brains of small black children who reminded them of clean pickaninnies on a box of laundry soap?" To the teachers whose racism links the "whiteness" of soap to intelligence, and blackness to "picayune brains" (the latter echoed in the derogatory "ninny" embedded in "pickaninnies"), "niggling doubts" are hardly minor—their effects are indeed pernicious. But as the last sentences of the poem make clear, despite the very real political and personal consequences of racist language, there are no authentic or "natural" racial categories. "Blackness" is in the mind of the culture's beholders:

> If I disagree with your beliefs, do you chalk it up to my negligible powers of discrimination, supposing I'm just trifling and not worth considering? Does my niggling concern with trivial matters negate my ability to negotiate in

good faith? Though Maroons, who were unruly Africans, not loose horses or lazy sailors, were called renegades in Spanish, will I turn any blacker if I renege on this deal? ("Denigration")

The play among similar phonemes here is intricate, capable of potentially infinite permutations: "disagree," "discrimination"; "considering," "concern"; and of course "negligible," "niggling," "negate," "negotiate," "renegades," "renege." In the final question, this linguistic play points to the contingency of concepts of race on always-changing cultural belief systems, evident in language itself. To "turn blacker" (like the "Maroons," "unruly Africans") means simply to overlap with a given cultural script—or a chosen (if arbitrary) word.

While "Denigration" demonstrates linguistic critique at its most mordant, Mullen's recent work also shows the humor and sheer love of language that have been evident in her writing since *Tree Tall Woman*. "Sleeping with the Dictionary" reveals this side of Mullen's dialogue with the word—a very literal love affair. Rather than sleeping with the enemy—betraying self or cause—the poet is slyly "taking the big dictionary to bed, clutching the unabridged bulk, smoothing the thin sheets, thick with accented syllables."[46] Loving words is a sensual act, reminiscent of Stein's "caressing" and "adoring" the noun; reading and writing are also intricately tied to fetishistic devotion to the object, its "thin sheets" paradoxically rich with "thick" syllables, material entities in and of themselves. (The love of such an increasingly old-fashioned book makes one wonder how, or whether, the advent of virtual technology will affect Mullen's conceptions of language and writing.) The dictionary engages the poet in the "hypnogogic trance of language," a "nocturnal mission." The erotics of the poet's art are stirred by the written word in a parody of sexual play: "we try out the most perverse positions in the practice of our nightly act, the penetration of the denotative body of the work." Calling on yet another set of precursors to generate her own definition of the creative act, Mullen stresses the twin forces of the erotic and the unconscious, those spurs to creativity championed by a range of earlier experimental poets, from the Surrealists to Oulipo: "Beside the bed, a pad lies open to record the meandering of migratory words. In the rapid eye movement of the poet's night vision, this dictum can be decoded, like the secret acrostic of a lover's name." Playing with form—writing acrostics generated by sheer love of their object, "decoding" a poet's designs—these ludic aspects of composition and active reading are fundamental to Mullen's work.[47] In "Sleeping with the Dictionary" Mullen crafts an ars poetica that stresses the primacy of language itself—as subject and as medium—to all her writing, and the interplay of tradition and innovation in her own highly inventive poetics.

Mullen describes the dictionary as "a versatile partner, conversant and well-versed in the verbal art."[48] As the fecund source of "verse" in all the phonemic forms evident in these phrases, the dictionary is nonetheless only a book of raw material—a mere compendium of words. Yet it serves Mullen well as "partner" and instigator of her own word-oriented poetics. It is an appropriate image for Mullen's richly comic, passionately engaged, and always playful writing, which thrives on dialogue with precursors, on resurrecting variants, and on recycling cultural "detritus" for her own verbal art. Defying categories and camps, Mullen explores questions of cultural history—in language and among poets and artists. One of the most significant contributions of her strategies of recycling—in the antecedents she evokes and the forms she invents—is the challenge she issues to assumptions about lineage and canons in contemporary poetry. Aldon Nielsen notes: "One crucial task awaiting . . . a comprehensive history [of African-American writing since World War II] is the location and study of additional texts of experimental poetics by black women," writers too often rendered invisible in a climate dominated by preconceptions about both avant-gardism and an often essentialist "black writing."[49] Mullen's poetry helps steer us away from such narrow paths. In her work we encounter "myriad possibilities," whose "meandering of migratory words" reveals the richness of a still-emerging language.

NOTES

1. Hank Lazer, *Opposing Poetries: Issues and Institutions,* Vol. 1 (Evanston, Ill.: Northwestern University Press, 1996).

2. Harryette Mullen, "Poetry and Identity," *West Coast Line* 30(1) (Spring 1996): 88 and 85.

3. Aldon Nielsen, *Black Chant: Languages of African-American Postmodernism* (New York: Cambridge, 1997), 8.

4. Harryette Mullen, "Poetic Statement," this volume.

5. See Joseph Conte, *Unending Design: The Forms of Postmodern Poetry* (Ithaca: Cornell University Press, 1991), 18–19.

6. Monique Wittig, "The Mark of Gender," in *The Straight Mind and Other Essays* (Boston: Beacon Press, 1992), 78.

7. Mullen, "Poetic Statement," this volume.

8. Harryette Mullen, "Imagining the Unimagined Reader: Writing to the Unborn and Including the Excluded," *Boundary* 2 26(1): 203.

9. All passages from *Tree Tall Woman* are from the author's typescript.

10. Cynthia Hogue, "Interview with Harryette Mullen," *Postmodern Culture: An Electronic Journal of Interdisciplinary Criticism* 9(2) (1999): <http://muse.jhu.edu/journals/postmodern_culture/v009/9.2hogue>, par. 2.

11. "Interview with Sonia Sanchez," in *Catch The Fire!!! A Cross-Generational Anthology of Contemporary African-American Poetry,* ed. Derrick I. M. Gilbert (New York: Riverhead Books, 1998), 222.

12. Nikki Giovanni, "Ego Tripping," in *The Women and the Men: Poems* (New York: William Morrow, 1975), n.p.

13. Hogue, "Interview with Harryette Mullen," par. 3.

14. See Harryette Mullen and Stephen Yenser, "Theme and Variations on Robert Hayden's Poetry," *The Antioch Review* 55(2) (Spring 1997): 160–74.

15. Calvin Bedient, "The Solo Mysterioso Blues: An Interview with Harryette Mullen," *Callaloo* 19(3) (1996): 651.

16. Hogue, "Interview with Harryette Mullen," par. 3.

17. Barbara Henning, "An Interview with Harryette Mullen," *Poetry Project Newsletter* 162 (1996): 6.

18. See Ron Silliman, *The New Sentence* (New York: Roof Books, 1987). Mullen notes that she believes she read Silliman's text around the time she began *Trimmings:* "I was very interested in the idea of the paratactic sentence and what that sentence is able to do poetically. . . . I was interested in the technical, syntactical construction and how to use that to allow more ambiguity in the work, to create different levels of meaning using a prose paragraph" (Hogue, "Interview with Harryette Mullen," par. 16).

19. Harryette Mullen, *Trimmings* (New York: Tender Buttons Press, 1991), 26.

20. Hogue, "Interview with Harryette Mullen," par. 17.

21. Mullen, *Trimmings,* 51.

22. Ibid., 7, 9, 46.

23. Ibid., 22, 39, 43, 54.

24. Ibid., 66.

25. Mullen notes of the "veiled woman" at the close of *Trimmings* that she had been considering "the Arabic traditions of veiling women": "It's a way of taking a woman's body out of circulation but she's still being controlled in the culture. . . . She is protected from the gaze. . . . I was using this work to explore such questions and problems" (Hogue, "Interview with Haryette Mullen," par. 20 and 21).

26. See Hank Lazer, *Opposing Poetries, Volume I: Issues and Institutions* (Evanston: Northwestern University Press, 1996).

27. See Elisabeth A. Frost, "Signifyin(g) on Stein: The Revisionist Poetics of Harryette Mullen and Leslie Scalapino," *Postmodern Culture: An Electronic Journal of Interdisciplinary Criticism* 5(3) (1995): <http://jefferson.village.virginia.edu/pmc/contents.all.html>

28. Gertrude Stein, "Tender Buttons," in *Selected Writings of Gertrude Stein,* ed. Carl Van Vechten (New York: Random House, 1962), 471; Mullen, *Trimmings,* 15.

29. See Hogue, "Interview with Harryette Mullen," par. 20–21.

30. Mullen, "Off the Top," *Trimmings,* n.p.

31. Mullen and Yenser, "Theme and Variations on Robert Hayden's Poetry," 160–74.

32. Hogue, "Interview with Harryette Mullen," par. 16.

33. Harryette Mullen, *S*PeRM**K*T* (Philadelphia: Singing Horse Press, 1992), n.p. The title suggests attention to the ambiguity between the visual and the spoken word: the asterisks, a purely visual sign, point to the "unsayable" aspects of the signifier, just as uttering Mullen's title aloud necessarily eliminates one or the other dual meanings of its visual pun.

34. Hogue, "Interview with Harryette Mullen," par. 32.

35. Bedient, "The Solo Mysterioso Blues," 664.

36. Mullen, "Poetic Statement," this volume.

37. Henning, "An Interview with Harryette Mullen," 6.

38. Ibid.

39. Harryette Mullen, *Muse & Drudge,* 32, 1, 3, 9; Henning, "An Interview with Haryette Mullen," 9.

40. See Elisabeth A. Frost, "'Ruses of the lunatic muse': Harryette Mullen and Lyric Hybridity," *Women's Studies* 27 (1998): 465–81.

41. Mullen, *Muse & Drudge,* 57, 34, 64. Concerning the quatrain on Mullen's name, see Henning, "An Interview with Harryette Mullen," 6.

42. Bedient, "The Solo Mysterioso Blues," 652.

43. Mullen, *Muse & Drudge,* 68.

44. Harryette Mullen, *Sleeping with the Dictionary* (Berkeley: University of California Press, 2002).

45. All quotations from "Denigration" are from the author's manuscript.

46. "Sleeping with the Dictionary," this volume.

47. Mullen writes of the importance of the experimental group of poets known as Oulipo, particularly "this group's systematic cataloguing and exuberant invention of textual operations and literary techniques. I was interested in Oulipo's vigorous exploration of the ludic aspects of writing. . . . [W]hat I found useful, as a poet and as a creative writing teacher, was Oulipo's demystification of creative process and aesthetic technique. . . . [T]hey make the creative process accessible as they deflate the divine afflatus of artistic inspiration" (Henning, "An Interview with Harryette Mullen," 9).

48. "Sleeping with the Dictionary," this volume.

49. Nielsen, *Black Chant,* 160.

BIBLIOGRAPHY

Books by Harryette Mullen

Muse & Drudge, Philadelphia: Singing Horse Press, 1995.
Sleeping with the Dictionary. Berkeley: University of California Press, 2002.
*S*PeRM**K*T.*" Philadelphia: Singing Horse Press, 1992.
Tree Tall Woman. Galveston: Earth Energy Communications, Inc., 1981.
Trimmings. New York: Tender Buttons, 1991.

Selected Prose

"'A Collective Force of Burning Ink': Will Alexander's *Asia and Haiti.*" *Callaloo: A Journal of African-American and African Arts and Letters* 22:2 (1999): 417–26.

"'A Silence between Us Like a Language': The Untranslatability of Experience in Sandra Cisneros's *Woman Hollering Creek.*" *MELUS: The Journal of the Society for the Study of the Multi-Ethnic Literature of the United States,* 21:2 (1996): 3–20.

"African Signs and Spirit Writing." *Callaloo: A Journal of African-American and African Arts and Letters* 19:3 (1996): 670–89.

"Hauling Up Gold from the Abyss: An Interview with Will Alexander." *Callaloo: A Journal of African-American and African Arts and Letters* 22:2 (1999): 391–408.

"Imagining the Unimagined Reader: Writing to the Unborn and Including the Excluded." *Boundary 2: 99 Poets /1999: An International Symposium.* 26:1 (1999): 198–203.

"'Incessant Elusives': The Oppositional Poetics of Erica Hunt and Will Alexander." In *Holding Their Own: Perspectives on the Multi-Ethnic Literatures of the United States,* ed. Dorothea Fischer-Hornung and Heike Raphael-Hernandez. Tubingen, Germany: Stauffenburg, 2000, 207–16.

"Miscegenated Texts and Media Cyborgs: Technologies of Body and Soul." *Poetics Journal* 9 (1991): 36–43.

"Optic White: Blackness and the Production of Whiteness." *Diacritics: A Review of Contemporary Criticism.* 24:2–3 (1994): 71–89.

"Phantom Pain: Nathaniel Mackey's *Bedouin Hornbook.*" *Talisman: A Journal of Contemporary Poetry and Poetics* 9 (1992): 37–43.

"Poetry and Identity." *West Coast Line.* 30.1 (1996): 85–89.

"Runaway Tongue: Resistant Orality in *Uncle Tom's Cabin, Our Nig, Incidents in the Life of a Slave Girl,* and *Beloved.*" *The Culture of Sentiment: Race, Gender and Sentimentality in Nineteenth-Century America.* Ed. Shirley Samuels. (New York: Oxford University Press, 1992), 244–64.

"Will Alexander: Poet and Essayist." *Callaloo: A Journal of African-American and African Arts and Letters* 22:2 (1999): 369–426.

Interviews

Bedient, Calvin. "Solo Mysterioso Blues: An Interview with Harryette Mullen." *Callaloo: A Journal of African-American and African Arts and Letters* 19.3 (1996): 651–669.

Frost, Elisabeth A. "An Interview with Harryette Mullen." *Contemporary Literature* 41:1 (2000): 397–421.

Griffin, Farah, Michael Magee, and Kristen Gallagher. *Combo* 1 (1997). http://wings.buffalo.edu/epc/authors/mullen/interview-new.html

Hogue, Cynthia. "Interview with Harryette Mullen." *Postmodern Culture: An Electronic Journal of Interdisciplinary Criticism* 9:2 (1999): 36 paragraphs.

Williams, Emily Allen. "Harryette Mullen, 'The Queen of Hip Hyperbole': An Interview." *African American Review* 34:4 (2000): 701–07.

Selected Criticism

Frost, Elisabeth. "'Ruses of the Lunatic Muse': Harryette Mullen and Lyric Hybridity." *Women's Studies* 27 (1998): 465–81.

———. "Signifyin(g) on Stein: The Revisionist Poetics of Haryette Mullen and Leslie Scalapino." *Postmodern Culture* 5.3 (1995): 40 paragraphs.

———. *The Feminist Avant-Garde in U.S. Poetry.* (Iowa City, Iowa: University of Iowa Press). Forthcoming, Spring 2003.

Nielson, Aldon Lynn. "Black Margins: African American Prose Poems," in *Reading Race in American Poetry: "An Area of Act."* Ed. Aldon Lynn Nielsen (Champaign: University of Illinois Press), 148–162.

Pearcy, Kate. "A Poetics of Opposition?: Race and the Avant-Garde." *Poetry and the Public Sphere: The Conference on Contemporary Poetry.* http://english.rutgers.edu/pierce.htm

Perloff, Marjorie. "After Language Poetry: Innovation and its Theoretical Discontents," in *The World in Time and Space: Towards a History of Innovative American Poetry, 1997–2000.* Ed. Joseph Donahue and Ed Foster. (Jersey City: Talisman House Press, 2002), 117–38.

Spahr, Juliana. "What Stray Companion: Harryette Mullen's Communities of Reading." In *Everybody's Autonomy: Connective Reading and Collective Identity.* (Tuscaloosa: University of Alabama Press, 2001), 89–118.

References

Bedient, Calvin. 1969. "The Solo Mysterioso Blues: An Interview with Harryette Mullen." *Callaloo* 19(3): 651–69.

Frost, Elisabeth A. 1995. "Signifyin(g) on Stein: The Revisionist Poetics of Harryette Mullen and Leslie Scalapino." *Postmodern Culture: An Electronic Journal of Interdisciplinary Criticism* 5(3): <http://jefferson.village.virginia.edu/pmc/contents.all.html>

———. 1998. "'Ruses of the lunatic muse': Harryette Mullen and Lyric Hybridity." *Women's Studies* 27: 465–81.

Henning, Barbara. 1996. "An Interview with Harryette Mullen." *Poetry Project Newsletter* 162: 5–10.

Hogue, Cynthia. 1999. "Interview with Harryette Mullen." *Postmodern Culture: An Electronic Journal of Interdisciplinary Criticism* 9(2): <http://muse.jhu.edu/journals/postmodern_culture/v009/9.2hogue>

Mullen, Harryette, and Stephen Yenser. 1997. "Theme and Variations on Robert Hayden's Poetry." *Antioch Review* 55(2) (Spring): 160–74.

Nielsen, Aldon Lynn. 1997. *Black Chant: Languages of African-American Postmodernism* (New York: Cambridge), 35–37.

CONTRIBUTORS

Rae Armantrout has published seven books of poetry, including *Made To Seem* (Sun & Moon, 1995), *writing the plot about sets* (Chax, 1998), *Necromance* (Sun & Moon, 1991), and *Couverture* (Les Cahiers de Royaumont, 1991). Armantrout's prose memoir, *True*, was published by Atelos in 1998, and her poetry collection, *The Pretext*, was published Green Integer in 2001. Wesleyan University Press published Armantrout's selected poems, *Veil*, in 2001. *A Wild Salience: The Writing of Rae Armantrout*, featuring essays on Armantrout by Robert Creeley, Hank Lazer, Bob Perelman, Charles Alexander, Ron Silliman, Brenda Hillman, Fanny Howe and others appeared in 1999 from Burning Press. Armantrout has taught writing courses at the University of California, San Diego, since the early 1980s.

Mei-mei Berssenbrugge was born in Beijing, China. Her books include *Empathy* (Station Hill, 1989), *Hiddenness*, with Richard Tuttle (Whitney Museum Library Fellows, 1987), *Endocrinology*, with Kiki Smith (U.L.A.E. and Kelsey St. Press, 1997), and *Four Year Old Girl* (Kelsey St. Press, 1997). She lives with Richard Tuttle and their daughter in New Mexico and New York City.

Lucie Brock-Broido is the author of two collections of poetry, *A Hunger* (1988) and *The Master Letters* (1995), both from Knopf. Her third collection, *Trouble In Mind*, will be forthcoming from Knopf in 2003. She is the Director of Poetry in the School of the Arts at Columbia and lives in New York City and Cambridge, Massachusetts.

Stephen Burt teaches poetry and American literature at Macalester College in St. Paul. His book of poems, *Popular Music*, won the Colorado Prize for 1999. His critical volume, *Randall Jarrell and His Age*, will appear in 2002 from Columbia University Press. He frequently reviews new poetry for several journals.

Craig Dworkin is an Assistant Professor at Princeton University. He has published articles on radical modernism, visual theory, and contemporary art and poetry; his book *Signature-Effects* is available at <http://www.spdbooks.org>

Elisabeth A. Frost is an Assistant Professor of English at Fordham University and has recently completed a critical study entitled *The Feminist Avant-Garde in American Poetry.* She has published articles on modern and contemporary women poets in *Contemporary Literature, Postmodern Culture, Genders,* and other journals. She is currently completing a book of poems called *Fortunes.*

Thomas Gardner is Professor of English at Virginia Tech. His publications include *Discovering Ourselves in Whitman: The Contemporary American Long Poem* (1989), *Regions of Unlikeness: Explaining Contemporary Poetry* (1999), and a book of poetry, *The Mime, Speaking.* He has just edited a special issue of *Contemporary Literature* on "American Poetry of the 1990s."

Jorie Graham was born in New York City in 1950. She taught at the University of Iowa Writers' Workshop from 1978 to 1998 and currently holds the Boylston Chair at Harvard University. The poems presented here are drawn from *Never,* forthcoming from Ecco/HarperCollins in Spring 2002. Graham's previous books include *Hybrids of Plants and of Ghosts* (Princeton, 1980), *Erosion* (Princeton, 1983), *The End Of Beauty* (Ecco, 1987), *Region of Unlikeness* (Ecco, 1990), *Materialism* (Ecco, 1993), *The Dream of the Unified Field: Selected Poems, 1974–1994* (Ecco, 1995), *Earth Took of Earth* (Ecco, 1996), *The Errancy* (Ecco, 1997), and *Swarm* (Ecco, 2000). In 1996 she won the Pulitzer Prize for *The Dream of the Unified Field.* Her many honors include a John D. and Catherine T. McArthur Fellowship.

Barbara Guest has published fourteen volumes of poetry since 1960 as well as a novel entitled *Seeking Air* (Sun & Moon, 1996), the biography *Herself Defined: The Poet H.D. and Her World* (Doubleday 1984), and the collection *The Confetti Trees: Motion Picture Stories* (Sun & Moon, 1999). She has earned many awards, including the Longview Award, the Lawrence Lipton Award for Literature, the Columbia Book Award, and the Poetry Society of America's Frost Medal.

Lyn Hejinian is a poet, essayist, and translator. Her poetry works include *A Border Comedy* (Granary Books, 2001), *The Beginner* (Spectacular Books, 2001), *Happily* (Post-Apollo Press, 2000), *The Cold of Poetry* (Sun & Moon Press, 1994), *The Cell* (Sun & Moon Press, 1992), as well as many others. Her critical prose includes *The Language of Inquiry* (University of California Press, 2000) and *Leningrad,* written with Michael Davidson,

Ron Silliman, and Barrett Watten (Mercury House, 1991). She has also published two translations of poems by Arkadii Dragomoshchenko: *Description* (Sun & Moon Press, 1990) and *Xenia* (Sun & Moon Press, 1994). Translations of Hejinian's work have been published in France, Spain, Japan, Italy, Russia, Sweden, China, Denmark, and Finland. She is the recipient of a Writing Fellowship from the California Arts Council, a grant from the Poetry Fund, and a Translation Fellowship (for her Russian translations) from the National Endowment for the Arts; in 1989 she received an Award for Independent Literature from the Soviet literary organization Poetic Function in Leningrad. Since 1976 Hejinian has been the editor of Tuumba Press and from 1981 to 1999 she was the co-editor (with Barrett Watten) of *Poetics Journal.* She is currently the co-director (with Travis Ortiz) of Atelos, a literary project commissioning and publishing cross-genre work by poets. Other collaborative projects include a work entitled "The Eye of Enduring," undertaken with the painter Diane Andrews Hall and exhibited in 1996; a composition entitled "Qûê Trân," with music by John Zorn and text by Hejinian; a mixed-media book entitled *The Traveler and the Hill,* created with the painter Emilie Clark; and the award-winning experimental documentary film *Letters Not About Love,* directed by Jacki Ochs. In the fall of 2000, she was elected to the sixty-sixth Fellowship of the Academy of American Poets.

Brenda Hillman was born in Tucson, Arizona, in 1951. After receiving her B.A. at Pomona College, she attended the University of Iowa where she received her M.F.A. in 1976. She serves on the faculty of St. Mary's College in Moraga, California, where she teaches in the undergraduate and graduate programs; she is also a member of the permanent faculties of Squaw Valley Community of Writers and of Napa Valley Writers' Conference. Her six collections of poetry—*White Dress* (1985), *Fortress* (1989), *Death Tractates* (1992), *Bright Existence* (1993), *Loose Sugar* (1997) and *Cascadia* (2001) are from Wesleyan University Press; she has also written three chapbooks, *Coffee, 3 AM* (Penumbra Press, 1982), *Autumn Sojourn* (Em Press, 1995), and *The Firecage* (a+bend press, 2000). Hillman has edited an edition of Emily Dickinson's poetry for Shambhala Publications and, with Patricia Dienstfrey, has co-edited *The Grand Permission: New Writings on Poetics and Motherhood* (forthcoming in 2002 from Wesleyan University Press). Among the awards Hillman has received are fellowships from the National Endowment for the Arts and the Guggenheim Foundation.

Susan Howe was born in Boston, Massachusetts. She currently teaches at the State University of New York in Buffalo. When she is not teaching she lives in Guilford, Connecticut. She is the author of numerous books of poetry, including *Pierce-Arrow* (New Directions, 1999), *Frame Structures:*

Early Poems, 1974–1978 (New Directions, 1996), and *The Noncon- formist's Memorial: Poems by Susan Howe* (New Directions, 1993). She has also authored two genre-defying books of criticism: *The Birth-mark: Unsettling the Wilderness in American Literary History* (Wesleyan Univer- sity Press, 1993) and *My Emily Dickinson* (North Atlantic Books, 1985). Her work has a wide international following and has been translated into French, Swedish, and Spanish. She has received numerous awards, among them are a Gradun Doctorus in Litterus from The National University of Ireland in 2000, a John Simon Guggenheim Memorial Fellowship in 1996, a Fund for Poetry Award, and two Before Columbus Foundation American Book Awards. In 1998 she was a Distinguished Fellow at the Stanford Hu- manities Center. She was elected to the American Academy of Arts and Sci- ences in 1999 and to the Board of Chancellors of the Academy of Ameri- can Poets in 2000.

Christine Hume is an Assistant Professor of English at Eastern Michigan University. She received the 1999 Barnard New Women Poets Prize for *Musca Domestica* (Beacon, 2000). She is also a recipient of recent grants and fellowships from the Colorado Council on the Arts, the Fine Arts Work Center in Provincetown, the Fund for Poetry at Illinois Wesleyan University, Rocky Mountain Women's Institute, Writers at Work, and the Wurlitzer Foundation.

Hank Lazer is Professor of English and Assistant Vice President for Acade- mic Affairs at the University of Alabama. A poet and critic, his most recent books include *Days* (poetry, Lavender Ink, 2002), *3 of 10* (poetry, Chax Press, 1996), and *Opposing Poetries* (criticism, two volumes, Northwest- ern University Press, 1996). With Charles Bernstein, he edits The Modern and Contemporary Poetics Series for the University of Alabama Press.

Ann Lauterbach was born and grew up in Manhattan, where she majored in painting at the High School of Music and Art. She graduated with a B.A. in English literature from the University of Wisconsin and went to Columbia University for graduate work. Deciding to forego further academic de- grees, she moved to London where she lived for seven years, working vari- ously as an editor, a teacher, and as director of the Literature Program at the Institute of Contemporary Arts. Returning to New York in 1974, she worked in art galleries until the mid-1980s, when she began to teach full- time in the writing programs at Columbia University, Princeton, and the University of Iowa, and at the City College and the Graduate Center of the City University of New York. In 1998, she became Ruth and David Schwab II Professor of Language and Literature at Bard College, where she has also directed writing at the Milton Avery Graduate School of the Arts since 1990. She received a Guggenheim Fellowship in 1986 and was made a Fellow of the John D. and Catherine T. MacArthur Foundation in 1993. A contributing editor of *Conjunctions* magazine since 1981, she has written on art and poetics, most notably in a series of columns entitled "The Night Sky" for the *American Poetry Review*.

Sara Lundquist is Associate Professor of English at the University of Toledo where she teaches modern and contemporary poetry. She has published on Barbara Guest, John Ashbery, James Schuyler, and William Carlos Williams. She is currently writing a book on Barbara Guest.

Ming-Qian Ma is Assistant Professor of English at the State University of New York at Buffalo. He has published on contemporary innovative poetry and critical theory.

Harryette Mullen is the author of *Tree Tall Woman* (Energy Earth, 1981), *Trimmings* (Tender Buttons, 1991), *S*PeRM**K*T* (Singing Horse, 1992), and *Muse & Drudge* (Singing Horse, 1995). She teaches creative writing and African-American literature at the University of California, Los Angeles. *Sleeping with the Dictionary* is forthcoming from the University of California Press.

Claudia Rankine is the author of *Nothing in Nature Is Private* (1994), *The End of the Alphabet* (1998), and *Plot* (2001). She teaches at Barnard College and lives in New York.

Lisa Sewell teaches English literature and creative writing at Villanova University. She is the author of *The Way Out* (Alice James Books, 1998) and has written on Sylvia Plath, Marilyn Chin, and Louise Glück.

Juliana Spahr is Assistant Professor of English at the University of Hawai'i, Manoa, and the author of *Response* (Sun & Moon Press, 1996), winner of the 1995 National Poetry Series Award; *Fuck You—Aloha—I Love You* (Wesleyan, 2001); and *Everybody's Autonomy: Connective Reading and Collective Identity* (University of Alabama Press, 2001). She is also the co-editor of the award-winning journal *Chain*.

Linda Voris is a doctoral graduate of the English Department at the University of California, Berkeley, and has written on Stein's compositional tasks in the 1920s. Voris is an independent scholar and poet.

INDEX